HANDEL

By the same author:

Non-fiction

THE COMPANION GUIDE TO THE SHAKESPEARE COUNTRY

HANDEL
The Man and his Music

by

JONATHAN KEATES

St. Martin's Press
New York

Library of Congress Catalog Card Number: 85-40017

ISBN 0-312-35846-6

First U.S. Edition

10 9 8 7 6 5 4 3 2 1

To Gerard McBurney

A hitherto unknown portrait of Handel,
attributed to Joseph Highmore
(Collection of Nicholas Salaman Esq)

Contents

		page
1	The Liberal Arts	11
2	Caro Sassone	27
3	Popery in Wit	49
4	Noble Oratories	69
5	A Nest of Nightingales	86
6	Discords in the State	111
7	Airs of a Modern Cast	143
8	Music, Ladies and Learning	165
9	The Fate of Harmony	186
10	All for War and Admiral Haddock	207
11	A British Sixpence	230
12	Brave Hallelujahs	247
13	Next to the Hooting of Owls	264
14	Overplied in Music's Cause	280
15	Great and Good	297
	Notes	328
	Bibliography	339
	General Index	340
	Index of Handel's Works	345

List of Illustrations

Handel, attributed to Joseph Highmore *frontispiece*

Cardinal Pietro Ottoboni *c.* 1690 by
Francesco Trevisani *facing page* 30

Rome in Handel's day; the Piazza di Spagna 31

Handel painted by Balthazar Denner, 1721 66

The 1st Duke of Chandos, *c.* 1730–40. Attributed to
H. van der Myn 67

Frederick, Prince of Wales, and his sisters, 1733,
by P. Mercier 180

Vauxhall Gardens. The Grand Walk, with the orchestra
playing 180

Berenstadt, Cuzzoni and Senesino performing in *Flavio* 181

Green Park, April 1749. The 'magnificent structure'
erected for the fireworks 181

Mary Delany in 1782 by John Opie 304

Facsimile of the first page of the autograph score
of *Messiah* 305

Introduction

This book is an attempt to tie together the details of Handel's life and work by making use of the wealth of recent musicological research on the composer carried out during the last 30 years. Within this period almost twice as much as was ever known about him before appears to have been brought to light, and more material continues to appear.

The work is thus a compilation rather than an original contribution to Handel studies but one which, it is hoped, will make accessible to the general reader facts about the man and his music which are otherwise available only in specialized publications. Mine is not, however, that sort of vanity which assumes the last word has been said, and I offer no defence of those places where inaccuracy or vagueness may have betrayed me. There is always more work to be done in the cause of a master whose popularity stands in equal proportion to the amazing neglect of many of his greatest works.

This may explain my occasionally somewhat combative attitude in discussion of his music. Handelians have their favourites and their not-so-favourites (at least one of the major oratorios, admired by many, is uncongenial to me) but I hope I have managed to spread my partialities evenly. I shall be pleased if some of my enthusiasm rubs off on the reader.

I have enjoyed writing this book, and my enjoyment has been substantially assisted by the individuals and organizations referred to in the acknowledgments. No prizes, however, are offered to the first critic unoriginal enough to suggest that the author of *The Companion Guide to the Shakespeare Country* has no business to be writing a life of Handel, or to those who would wish to put a musicological 'Keep Out' notice on him. I commend this book to the reader in whom Handel's music can still induce awe and joy.

J.K.

Acknowledgments

My first acknowledgment must be to Hilary Davies, who originally commissioned the book and was unfailing in her encouragement. I am equally grateful to David Burnett for his adoption of the project and to Richard Wigmore, a more astute Handelian than I, for his patient and resolute editing.

Winton Dean read this book in its earliest stage and, in offering much useful criticism, showed a courtesy towards an upstart amateur which all scholars might study to emulate. I was also grateful for advice, in the actual process of writing, from Robin Lane Fox and Gerard McBurney.

At City of London School thanks are due to my colleagues Anthony Gould, Nicholas Byrne and Roy Reardon. Elsewhere to the following: Margaret Gardiner, Maria Maschietto, Mary Sandys, Mrs G. Fallows, John and Thekla Clark, Edoardo Betti, Mark Elder, James Fenton, John Fleming, Hugh Honour, Gianni Guidetti, George Gutwirth, James Loader, Patrick O'Connor, Michael Rose, Dr Richard Portes and Nicholas Salaman.

My thanks also to the staff of the British Library, the London Library, the Cambridge University Library, the Public Record Office, the public libraries of Oxford, Kensington and Islington, the Biblioteca Marciana and the Fondazione Giorgio Cini (Venice) the Conservatorio Luigi Cherubini (Florence) the Pierpont Morgan Library (New York) and the New York Public Library. My particular gratitude to the staff of the Music Reading Room in the Bodleian Library (Oxford) where most of my useful work was carried out amid an atmosphere of quiet attentiveness almost unimaginable elsewhere.

Finally my indebtedness is recorded to the subject of this book. His music offers a reason for existence.

J.K.

The Liberal Arts

On 2 May 1696, the Oberpräsident Eberhard von Danckelmann, treasurer to the Margrave of Brandenburg, was sent a request for the payment of an outstanding bill; the letter ran as follows:

> Most worthy sir, You have received from Herr Dr Wiesener a most humble request for payment of 100 thalers from the privy purse for the cure of Andreas Rudeluff, the knife swallower. Since I, as surgeon, have done my best in this two-year cure, and have brought out the swallowed knife from his stomach and body, with God's help and a careful hand, and thereby cured him completely, and have most humbly given His Highness the knife in its original form in a case, in your presence, I would therefore most humbly request His Highness to grant me the favour, as much as seems fit, to recompense me for my painstaking operation, in your position as highly esteemed patron. I shall thank you most humbly, and shall ask God, from the depths of my heart, to give you health and long life. I remain Your Excellency's most obedient servant, Georg Händel, medical practitioner.

The subject of the doctor's operation was a sixteen-year-old peasant boy from the village of Maschwitz, near the city of Halle in Upper Saxony. One day, while playing with his friends, he had swallowed a horn-handled knife, and his parents had taken him, after ineffectual doses of warm beer and cotton wool, to Wiesener and Händel, who then began their prolonged but ultimately successful treatment. The boy, who must have been remarkably tough, was slowly cured by the use of magnetic plasters which drew the instrument out of the oesophagus into the throat. Finally, with the release of much '*überaus stinckende Materie*' the knife was pulled out and young Andreas, we are told, rejoiced and praised God. A rather touching close to the whole episode is provided by the fact that he was impressed enough by his doctors to become a surgeon himself, and lived till a ripe old age.

Georg Händel was one of the most renowned doctors in the Germany of his day and a welcome attendant at the princely courts surrounding Halle. His father, a Silesian coppersmith, had moved westwards from Breslau during the early stages of the Thirty Years War, presumably in search of a climate more favourable to Protestantism. Georg, his third son, born in 1622, gained his first medical experience as a *feldscher*, or military sawbones, in one of the Saxon regiments then on campaign. Study at Hamburg and Lübeck under the famous physician Andreas Konigen was followed by a spell as a ship's barber on a merchant vessel trading to Portugal.

As the war continued its dreary and inconclusive course, Händel's skills were inevitably in demand among the Protestant armies. Thus he joined the Swedish service for another turn as a *feldscher*, but a more obvious guarantee of future success was his deftness in mending the Elector of Saxony's broken arm. The delighted Elector recommended him to the three princes of Anhalt and the neighbouring Count Stollberg, he was nominated to posts at the courts of Brandenburg and Weissenfels, and became official doctor to the village of Giebichenstein on the outskirts of Halle. In the city itself, at the '*Zum gelben Hirsch*' ('The Yellow Hart') next to his house in the Kleine Klausstrasse, he was granted a licence to sell local and foreign wines.

A prosperous and gifted young doctor could have had no trouble in looking for a wife. Händel, following the custom of the day, chose within his own profession and married the widow of the surgeon to whom he had been apprenticed, 'through priestly copulation', according to the quaint expression used by the preacher of his funeral sermon. Medicine remained a family business: of Georg and Anna Händel's six children, two of the daughters married doctors and the two sons who survived childhood followed their father's calling.

It would have surprised nobody in Halle that, on Anna's death in 1682, the elderly surgeon should forthwith have contemplated a second marriage. Disparity in age was unimportant in seventeenth-century wedlock, and in any case we have little record of the feelings of 31-year-old Dorothea Taust as she prepared for priestly coupling with a man of 60 and became stepmother to a grown-up family.

The Tausts, like the Händels, had been refugees from the Habsburg empire 'for love of the pure evangelical truth', and Dorothea's father was the pastor of Giebichenstein and Crollwitz. His daughter, pious, cultivated and intelligent, was the object of a good many proposals before the doctor's, but had rejected them all through an intense loyalty to her parents, which had kept her at the parsonage even when a fever epidemic carried off a brother and sister. Doubtless it was during this period that Händel met her. Some persuasion and a little private prayer seem to have brought her round to the idea of marrying him, and on St George's day, 1683, Pastor Taust conducted the ceremony himself, in the church of St Bartolomaeus at Giebichenstein.

Four children were born to the Händels (it was later calculated that the old man could lay claim to 30 grandchildren and great-grandchildren). Of the two daughters Johanna Christiana died in 1709 when barely 20, and the elder, Dorothea Sophia, later married a local lawyer Dietrich Michaelsen. A son born a year after the Giebichenstein wedding only lived for an hour. In 1685 Dorothea Händel gave birth to her second son, Georg Friederich.

The exact date of his birth is unknown, but since the register of the Liebfrauenkirche in Halle records his baptism on Tuesday 24 February, it is thought that he must have been born on the previous day. He was christened Georg after his father and maternal grandfather and Friederich probably in honour of his father's princely patron of Brandenburg. The godparents were his aunt Anna, Philipp Fehrsdorff, one of the Elector of Saxony's stewards, and Zacharias Kleinhampel, a medical colleague of Dr Händel's. The birth probably took place in his parents' house on the corner of the Kleine Ulrichstrasse, a tall, roomy building with one of those lofty attic storeys so typical of its period.

This attic, indeed, provides the scene for the first anecdote in a Handelian chronicle. Mainwaring, the composer's earliest biographer, tells us that the doctor hated music and that young Georg Friederich had to indulge his secret passion on a clavichord smuggled into the garret. Clavichords, however modestly proportioned, are not easily smuggled anywhere, and there is no evidence for the old surgeon's having had 'ears of an untoward make'. The fact that a more or less identical story is told of Handel's younger contemporary, Thomas Augustine Arne (in his case it was apparently a spinet), makes the tale, with its strong flavour of wisdom after the event, somewhat suspect.

In all probability it was a secure and happy childhood in a community which was far from being provincial or backward-looking. Halle lay on the right bank of the Saale, a tributary of the Elbe, in the rolling cornlands of the Saxon plain, girdled by ramparts and reached by paved causeways to avoid the frequent floods. Like other towns in central Germany, most notably nearby Magdeburg, it had taken its knocks in the Thirty Years War: there were two sieges, one by imperial troops, another by the Swedes. At the Peace of Westphalia the city, which till then had belonged to the Bishops of Magdeburg, was to pass to Saxon control until the reigning Elector's death, when it was to be handed over to Brandenburg.

The transfer of authority was a distinct benefit to Halle. What might otherwise have remained a backwater became a place of considerable cultural and strategic importance in the Prussian domains. The tolerant policy of Elector Frederick William re-established the Jews in the city and brought the rich technical skills of the Huguenots, expelled from France at the revocation of the Edict of Nantes. Huguenot expertise made Halle a centre for wig-making, glassblowing and carpet-making. It was already well known for the production of woollen and silk stockings, exported to England, Poland and Russia, and for a type of dark beer known as *Puff.*

As a focus of musical and literary activity it had become noted during the Renaissance and early Baroque periods. A troupe of English players visiting the town in 1611 had given performances of *The Merchant of Venice* and eleven years later *Don Quixote* received its first German translation here by Joachim Caesar. Musical life was always buoyant: there was a band of city waits and a tradition of fine organ building, embodied at its best in the great organ of the Domkirche, built at the end of the sixteenth century by Esaias and David Beck, and considered worthy of mention by Michael Praetorius in his 'Syntagma Musicum' (1619) where the specification is listed in detail. Among the city's outstanding composers had been the prolific Samuel Scheidt, notable for his loyalty to his birthplace, despite the plagues and warfare of the 1630s.

Halle was not all sophistication and prosperity. Travellers noted with displeasure its curiously gloomy air, created by the dingy-looking house fronts along the narrow, tortuous streets. Little of importance, however, marked the life of the city and its surrounding villages during Handel's early years. There was a plague of field mice in 1686 (it had been caterpillars five years previously), a miraculous hail formed of pine resin in 1690 'so great that it might be gathered up by handfuls', and a deformed child born to a woman whose husband was suspected of having committed sodomy with her. The severe weather conditions prevailing throughout Europe during the last decade of the century brought an especially hard winter in 1692, memorable for the news that the cold had killed 500 people in Moscow, and from time to time the unpredictable Saale overflowed its banks and flooded the fields between the raised roadways.

No record exists of Handel's schooling, though it is obvious that he was well taught. Protestant Germany provided some of the finest education in contemporary Europe, and Halle boasted two good schools. One had been founded as a private establishment by August Hermann Francke, a member of the Lutheran group known as the Pietists, the influence of whose humane, broadly sympathetic view of erring mankind can be found throughout Handel's work, colouring the mood of the late oratorios such as *Susanna* and *Theodora* and traceable even in *Messiah*. The other was the public *Stadtgymnasium*, which Handel probably attended.

So far from being the guzzling boor occasionally portrayed, he was undeniably gifted with a well-defined literary taste and an extraordinary knack of tongues. Friends in later life, treasuring his powers as a raconteur, found that they needed to know at least four or five languages in order to appreciate his stories. More than any other Baroque composer, he developed an acute sensitivity to the echo and association of words and images, and in studying his music we can begin also to gauge the powers of an amazingly complex memory. One of his chief London amusements was visiting picture auctions (he was the owner of two Rembrandts) and his work is suffused with an intense visual awareness.

If such traits as these were developed in the schoolroom, the young Handel is likely to have found out for himself the pleasures of the countryside which, as contemporary maps and prospects make clear, came right up to the foot of Halle's city walls. Like many other eighteenth-century musicians he responded passionately to nature, seizing avidly on opportunities for portraying the sights and sounds of country life. His rural muse is not that of the townsman viewing the peasantry with a patronizing smile or indulging pastoral nostalgia, but the product of a true feeling for the natural world.

His parents' choice of a career for him is likely to have been dictated by considerations of a secure profession. His two half-brothers were doctors and his maternal uncles were clergymen, so it is not surprising that his father apparently designed Georg Friederich to be 'bred to the law'. Several of his musical contemporaries and friends, such as Georg Philipp Telemann and Johann Mattheson, were law students, and some, such as Johann Kuhnau, Bach's predecessor as cantor of the Leipzig Thomaskirche, and Johann Gotthilf Krieger, whom Mattheson calls a '*braver jurist*', managed successfully to combine the two professions.

Any preconceptions of this kind on Dr Händel's part were to be altered by the outcome of a significant journey to the ducal court at Weissenfels, made when the boy was about ten years old. Mainwaring, whose circumstantial detail in this case makes the story credible, tells us that Georg Friederich, who wanted to see his half-brother Karl, the duke's valet, was refused a place in the coach as the doctor 'thought one of his age a very improper companion when he was going to the court of a Prince, and to attend the duties of his profession'. With characteristic tenacity young Handel waited until his father's carriage left the house in the Kleine Klausstrasse, and then followed it on foot. The roads out of Halle must have been unusually crowded or else very bad, as the boy was able to catch up with the coach a little way from the town. The old man, impressed, gave in and the two set off together.

Weissenfels lies a few miles east of Halle and is now a thriving industrial centre. For 60 years, from 1680 until the mid-eighteenth century, it provided a capital for the duchy originally created by the Elector of Saxony for his second son August in 1656. Under August's son Johann Adolf I the court was a rich and cultivated establishment, dignified in later years by such figures as the palace chaplain Erdmann Neumeister, celebrated as a religious poet whose works provided Bach with cantata texts, and Johann Philipp Krieger, court composer and pioneer of German opera (perforce, since Italian librettos were not countenanced at Weissenfels).

The duke apparently heard Handel playing the organ in the palace chapel and 'something there was in the manner of playing which drew his attention so strongly' that he asked who was at the instrument. Karl Händel replied that it was his little half-brother. We can rule out Mainwaring's tale that the duke lectured the old doctor on what a crime it was 'against the public and posterity, to rob the world of such a rising Genius' but his influence as a music-loving patron was surely active in persuading Georg Friederich's father to let him follow where his inclination led. He may, of course, have envisaged training the lad as a house musician. At any rate the boy was able to return to Halle with a gift of money from Duke Johann Adolf and a sense that princely encouragement was behind him.

He was even more fortunate in that his home town contained one of the finest musical teachers of the day. Friedrich Wilhelm Zachow was born in Leipzig in 1663, appropriately in the Stadtpfeiffergässlein (Town Piper Lane), where his father lived as a violinist. He had succeeded the talented Samuel Ebart as organist of the Halle Marienkirche in the year before Handel's birth, probably owing to the influence of his grandfather, head of the city waits. He was a noted composer and performer; among the many testimonies to his skill, the most charming is Martin Fuhrmann's comment in *Die an der Kirchen Gottes gebauete Satans-Capelle*: 'In my time, when in 1692 I was studying in Halle, Zachau was flourishing, whom I heard on Sundays with a true hunger and thirst. If I had to travel there, and there were no bridge over the Saale, and I could not reach the city, then truly I would swim across the river like Leander for his Hero, even to hear famous pupils of his such as Herr Kirchhoff.'

Gottfried Kirchhoff, Zachow's successor at the Marienkirche, was one of several eminent students, and Fuhrmann's praise clearly suggests the enduring effect on them of excellent teaching by an original musical mind. This is borne out by Zachow's surviving compositions, all of them, with the exception of a trio sonata and a handful of keyboard pieces, religious works designed for incorporation in Lutheran church services. From Zachow Handel learned not only a great deal about the line and shape of an aria, about strong, adventurous bass lines and solid choral writing, but also about those delicacies of instrumental colouring which he later perfected in his own style.

It is worth noting, too, that Zachow, like his famous pupil, seldom falls easily into a traditional mould. The musical language of his cantatas, with their formal anticipations of Bach, is a strikingly personal blend of German with Italian. A commonplace book belonging to Handel while under Zachow's tutelage which has since, alas, disappeared is known to have contained examples culled from works by Kerll, Froberger and Krieger whose compositional styles bore a markedly international stamp.

What sort of lessons were actually offered? Zachow seems to have begun by giving Handel a solid grounding in harmony, and then exposing him to various contemporary styles by providing scores for analysis and discussion from his own extensive library. In addition the boy learned to work fugue subjects and copy out music, as well as taking his master's place now and then as organist and composer. Whether he 'actually did compose a service every week for three years successively' is doubtful. At any rate not one of these 156 services survives, and no single work of his can positively be ascribed to this period, though a good case can be made out for some of them. One is a setting for soprano and strings of Psalm 112, *Laudate Pueri*, in F, a work which reveals little in the way of future promise. The vocal lines feature inelegant, overlong melismatic passages and awkward word setting (for example of '*Suscitans a terra inopem*') and the piece ends with a 53-bar Amen. Some typical Handelian features are there, however, in the opening string figures and the germ of a melody which later became 'O had I Jubal's lyre' in *Joshua* some 40 years later.

Handel's progress as student and composer was to be halted in 1697 by the death, on 17 February, of his father at the age of 75. Late in the previous year Dr Händel had developed a fever and slowly sank under it, despite consultation with medical colleagues, until a final relapse '*war gleich Dom. Estomihi früh 3 uhr*'. The respected figure was given a dignified funeral, with an oration delivered in the family house by the distinguished pastor Johann Christian Olearius. Following contemporary custom, it was published alongside a clutch of mourning elegies, including a turgid 68-line effusion by Andreas Roth, '*Pfarrer zu Grosskugel*', a rather jolly poem in tetrameters by a certain J.G., and, from the dead man's father-in-law Pastor Taust, an affecting dialogue between the '*selig Verstorbenen*' and the miserable mourners. 'Ah sorrow, ah misery, how shall we begin?' they cry, to which the parting soul rejoins, 'Be still, children, do not weep, I live in a thousand joys,' rounding off with an abrupt '*Nun, gute Nacht*'.

Of more immediate interest are the verses by the twelve-year-old Handel himself. Though these may well have been retouched by a kindly adult, there is no good reason for doubting Handel's authorship. This was an age of forward children — limited life expectancy could scarcely make it otherwise — and the idea of the composer as poet is no odder here than it is in the era of Wagner and Berlioz. We may note that the boy signs himself impressively 'Georg Friedrich Händel, dedicated to the liberal arts'.

February was a significant month for him. Five years later, a week or so before his seventeenth birthday, he signed the register of Halle university. His chosen faculty is unknown, and whether he actually pursued any studies at all is a mystery. Perhaps the gesture was made to please his family, who must in any case have been delighted when, on 13 March 1702, he was appointed to the prestigious post of organist of the Domkirche to succeed the unsatisfactory Johann Christoph Leporin. This cathedral church was Calvinist, but the elders seem not to have objected to the Lutheran appointment. The job was tenable initially for a single probationary year, and the stipulations, besides requiring Handel to 'perform such duties in a way that will seem to an upright organist suitable and fitting', and 'to have due care for whatever might be needful to the support of beautiful harmony', also included keeping the instrument in good repair and leading 'a Christian and edifying life'. He was granted a salary of 50 thalers a year in quarterly instalments and free lodgings.

Handel fulfilled the terms of this contract satisfactorily, as documents make plain, and might well have gone on to pursue a career similar to that of his direct contemporary, Johann Sebastian Bach, serving as organist in

18

some other cathedral city or as *Kapellmeister* at one of the princely courts, and following the accepted pattern of professional life for a German musician. However, as with his two other significant musical journeys, we do not know exactly why he took the decision, at some time during the early spring of 1703, to leave for Hamburg. He is known to have met the ebullient and companionable Georg Philipp Telemann during this period, and it may have been that this gifted fellow-Saxon, who became one of Handel's warmest admirers and friends, suggested Hamburg as a lively place in which an aspiring musician could develop his skills. Or it may simply have been that Handel felt restless and wanted somewhere a little less restricted than Halle. By the summer he had left his native city and would thereafter return only as a distinguished visitor.

Hamburg's jealously guarded privileges as a free community were maintained against a background of constant bickering among the various groups and factions involved in its administration. Smart, rich and sybaritic, its citizens were noted as deep drinkers, a fact which must have appealed to Handel, always fond of his bottle. Joseph Addison, arriving more or less at the same time as the composer, wrote to Lord Winchelsea: 'the great Business of the place is commerce and Drinking: as their chief commoditie, at least that which I am best acquainted with, is Rhenish wine. This they have in such prodigious Quantities that there is yet no sensible diminution of it tho Mr Perrot and my-self have bin among 'em above a Week. The principal curiositie of ye town and what is more visited than any other I have met wth. in my Travails is a great cellar filld with this kind of Liquor. It holds more Hogsheads than others can bottles and I believe is capable of receiving into it a whole Vintage of ye Rhine.'

Increasing wealth and international importance brought sophistication to the city. What money could buy Hamburg must have, and the result was one of the earliest civic opera houses in northern Europe. The theatre in the Gänsemarkt, built in 1677 to a design by Girolamo Sartorio, architect of similar buildings in Leipzig and Amsterdam, opened its doors a year later with an opera on the story of Adam and Eve by Johann Theile. It was only gradually that pieces of a more obviously French and Italian cast began to make their appearance, as Parisian and Venetian influences filtered into German music, but at the century's close Hamburg opera had established its own distinctive, if occasionally rather bizarre characteristics.

French taste introduced elements of ballet and spectacle, and the powerful impress of Venetian opera conditioned the handling of texts and subject matter (several Hamburg operas were adaptations of recent

19

Italian stage successes). German composers and librettists took readily to the drift towards a species of extravagant theatrical realism which had characterized late seventeenth-century Venetian opera. In Morselli's *L'Incoronazione di Dario*, for example, a scene in a philosopher's study, showing '*Globi, libri, stromenti chimicie, matematici, e da musica*', has the sage Niceno composing a cantata subsequently sung by Queen Statira. In Pietro Dolfin's libretto for Antonio Sartorio's *L'Adelaide* the heroine seeks refuge in a marble quarry, where the quarrymen sing as they work. One of the blast-charges goes off prematurely, killing several of the workmen who are standing too close, and the foreman later threatens to rape Adelaide: Sartorio omitted the first of these episodes from his musical setting. The prime Venetian exponent of this trend was Matteo Noris, whose lyric dramas demand a technical expertise worthy of Bayreuth, and certainly imply that in the annals of opera there is nothing new under the sun. His *Marcello in Siracusa* features such *coups* as a ray of sunlight cast on the Roman ships by Archimedes's burning-glass and a dance by his scholars wielding geometrical instruments. In *Il Totila*, written for Giovanni Legrenzi, the heroine Marzia jumps off a balcony into the arms of the eponymous Ostrogoth — '*Cieli, dove mi trovo?*' '*Fra le braccia d'un Re*' — but the ultimate absurdity is plumbed in the presentation to Totila of a huge gilded elephant which, unbeknown to him, contains the general Belisarius and an entire army, all soon disgorged.

Such things held an evident appeal for Hamburg audiences and composers, and the German librettists were not slow in providing appropriate material. Some operas were actually based on recent European political events, such as the Neapolitan revolt of 1647, which turned up at the Gänsemarkt as *Masagniello-Furioso, Die neapolitanische Fischer-Emporung*, with music by Reinhard Keiser. A record (hitherto unbeaten?) for bringing current affairs to the operatic stage was set by Lucas von Bostel, who dramatized the siege of Vienna by the Turks only three years after it took place. His *Cara Mustapha* introduces King John Sobieski of Poland, the Electors of Saxony and Bavaria and the Duke of Lorraine, mute components of a scene accompanied by an aria from *ein in der Lufft schwebenden Engel*.

Nothing was wanting to make the Gänsemarkt productions as handsome as possible. The stage, larger than in most other European theatres of the day, was capable of immense perspective effects and set design reached a peak in the work of Johann Oswald Harms, who had trained in Italy and reflected the slightly eerie influence of Salvator Rosa.

The orchestra was naturally superb and here Handel was able to gain valuable experience as a violinist: since his writing for the instrument is very much an experienced player's rather than a mere listener's, some critics have been led to suggest that this conditioned his vocal writing as well.

With one of his most talented fellow musicians at the opera Handel made contact: almost as soon as he arrived in Hamburg. The city's churches fostered a thriving musical life, and on 9 July 1703, in the organ loft of the Magdalenakirche, Handel met Johann Mattheson. Mattheson is what is sometimes referred to, rather ambiguously, as a 'crucial' figure in the history of musical criticism. Writings such as his *Untersuchung der Singspiele*, with its spirited defence of opera, and *Das Neueröffnete Orchester* offer invaluable clues to eighteenth-century awareness of changing musical trends. Besides producing a spate of theatrical, religious and instrumental pieces and translating extensively from contemporary English literature (works, for example, by Defoe and Richardson) Mattheson held the post of secretary to Sir John Wyche, English resident at Hamburg, and became tutor to his son Cyril. Residual Anglophilia led him to marry Catherine Jennings, daughter of a Wiltshire clergyman, of whom he says: 'She bore no children, but offered a thousand of those pleasures often lacking in children themselves.'

The two young men at once became great friends. They went boating together and made music, and Handel must have profited from professional criticism which, if not always free of envious pedantry, was at any rate candid and intelligent. Mattheson enjoyed his friend's deadpan humour — 'at first he played second violin in the opera orchestra, and behaved as though he did not know how many beans made five, for he was inclined by nature to dry jokes' — but noted that 'he knew very little about melodic writing before he got to the Hamburg Opera. . . . ' Handel was also able to avail himself of free meals at Mattheson's house 'and he repaid that by imparting to me several choice touches of counterpoint'.

During that summer both of them were attacted by the prospect of a plum post as organist of the Marienkirche at Lübeck, news of which had reached Mattheson through Magnus von Wedderkopp, President of the Holstein Privy Council and related to the Wyches by marriage. The current holder of the job was the eminent Danish composer and performer Dietrich Buxtehude, who had taken it under a condition familiar enough in Baroque Germany but altogether more odd to us. This was the stipulation that the prospective organist should marry the daughter of the incumbent, presumably a bonus to his apprenticeship.

Buxtehude's wife was indeed the daughter of his predecessor Franz Tunder, and Margreta Buxtehude now awaited the chosen candidate.

On 17 August Mattheson and Handel set off in the coach to Lübeck. It was a pleasant journey, made the jollier by the antics of a travelling pigeon-seller and because, as Mattheson says, 'we made up many double fugues together, *da mente non da penna*'. When they arrived they enjoyed themselves well enough in trying out the best of the city's keyboard instruments, but jibbed at poor Margreta, who had to wait another couple of years until Johann Christian Schiefferdecker was prepared to fulfil the terms of the contract in which she was the sticking point. Bach's visit to Lübeck in 1705, incidentally, was probably not unconnected with the same issue.

Handel's rejection of marriage to Margreta Buxtehude raises the general and hitherto unresolved issue of his relations with women. There is, alas, practically no documentary evidence regarding this aspect of his private life, and he is the only major composer of the last three centuries firmly to have barred the doors on the subject. We must make what we can of Paolo Antonio Rolli's comment to the Abbate Riva in 1719 that Handel was secretly in love with a certain 'Denys woman, alias Sciarpina' and of George III's annotation in his copy of Mainwaring's biography: 'G. F. Handel was ever honest, nay excessively polite, but like all men of sense would talk all, and hear none and scorned the advice of any but the Woman He loved, but his Amours were rather of short duration, always within the pale of his own profession, but He knew that without Harmony of souls neither love nor the creation would have been created and Discord ends here as certainly as the last Trumpet will call us from our various Pleasures. . . . ' Earlier the king had remarked (this time in German) apropos of the author's observing that the ladies would have preferred Senesino to Handel: 'that is not so obvious; Handel was very well built and lacked nothing in manliness; the other fellow was just a mule'. Which more or less sums everything up. We can surmise that while in Italy he fell in love with the soprano Vittoria Tarquini, and it is not unreasonable to suppose that he may have felt attracted to certain of his leading singers such as Margherita Durastanti, Anna Strada and, in later years, Kitty Clive and Susannah Cibber. The assumption that as a lifelong bachelor he must perforce have been homosexual is untenable in an eighteenth-century context, when the vagabond life of so many musicians made marriage a distinct hindrance. Given the fact that much of the music of his operas, cantatas and oratorios constitutes a mature and complex expression of love worthy to rival Mozart and Wagner, the statement by

Newman Flower that Handel was 'sexless and safe' seems strikingly misjudged. So much, apparently, for the creator of Semele, Rodelinda and Alcina. Safe, in any case, from what?

A letter to Mattheson urging his return from Amsterdam, where he was being feted by the Jews, 'for the time is coming when nothing at the Opera can be done in your absence', indicates Handel's growing involvement with the theatre's affairs. Musical director at the Gänsemarkt was Reinhard Keiser, the leading German operatic master of his day, a pioneer spirit of boundless inventiveness, with a lasting effect on Handel's sense of priorities in the creation of a dramatic style. His enormous output embodies Hamburg eclecticism, with its continuing sensitivity to changing international trends, and shows a typical capacity for incorporating a whole range of musical genres within a single work. *Der Hochmüthige, Gestürzte und Wieder Erhabene Croesus*, for instance, not only contains scenes of tragic intensity, such as Croesus's aria 'Götter, übt Barmherzigkeit', but includes an extended peasant interlude adapted from Minato's Italian original by Bostel, and cast in authentic German folk idiom. Rough-edged and naïve as Keiser's music may seem to us against a wider eighteenth-century background, there is no denying the inspiration it continued to give to younger talents. His pupil Johann Adolf Hasse, who brought *opera seria* to a functional perfection, regarded Keiser as the greatest master of the days, and years after his death Scheibe in his *Musiklexikon* described him as 'perhaps the greatest original genius Germany has ever brought forth'.

Handel's admiration for Keiser shows itself best in the many allusions to the Hamburg operas to be found in works as early as *Agrippina* and as late as *Joshua*. In at least one case Handel was veritably haunted by a Keiser motif. The latter's *Octavia* of 1705 contained an aria for Seneca, *Ruhig sein*, based on a pattern of repeated string quaver phrases. Handel carried this wholesale into two Italian works, *Il Trionfo del Tempo e della Verità* and *Agrippina*, into a London opera *Muzio Scevola* and into the ravishing G minor trio sonata customarily grouped as 'number 1' with the Opus 2 set (though originally published in B minor — the G minor version, possibly the authentic one, is first known from a Dresden manuscript). In addition, reminiscences of it turn up, adapted but recognizable, in Tassile's aria 'Sempre fido e disprezzato' in *Alessandro*, and the merest ghost of the idea hovers through three bars of 'Va, perfido' in *Deidamia*.

A sense of professional rivalry between the two composers was unavoidable, but Keiser seems never to have felt seriously threatened by the younger master. It was on the friendship of Handel with Mattheson that sooner or later the enclosed, contentious world of the opera house, with its bickering and scandal, was bound to tell. On the evening of 5 December 1704, Mattheson's opera *Cleopatra* was being given its second performance at the Gänsemarkt. The composer not only figured as conductor, but as one of the stars, in the role of Antony (the libretto follows the well-known historical outline). Having fallen on his sword, and had his death scene, he was then at liberty to slip into the pit and take over at the harpsichord. Handel, who had migrated from second fiddle desk to the keyboard, now refused to budge, though Mattheson, as director of his own opera, had an acknowledged right to take over.

Furious with each other, they managed to get to the end of the show, while several of the orchestral players egged them on. There was a challenge at the stage door, a crowd gathered, the two men drew their weapons and set to in the open market place outside the theatre. It was a duel which, as Mattheson tells us, 'might have passed off very unfortunately for both of us, had God's guidance not graciously ordained that my blade, thrusting against my opponent's broad metal coat-button, should be shattered'.

Saved for posterity by a button. It was not like either of them to bear grudges for long. One of Handel's most endearing qualities as a man was the strength and diversity of his friendship, and in less than a month, through the intervention of a Hamburg councillor and one of the Gänsemarkt shareholders, he and Mattheson were reconciled. After a celebratory meal, they went to the rehearsal of Handel's first opera, *Almira*, better friends than ever. Cynics must make what they can of the fact that Mattheson took one of the leading roles.

Almira received its première on 8 January 1705. It was an instant success, with some 20 performances, but it is impossible to be more than lukewarm about Handel's unique surviving essay in Hamburg opera. Keiser and Mattheson both did this kind of thing better, but to pick through the 42 German and 15 Italian arias for flashes of Handelian brilliance is an absorbing task.

The libretto, whose full title is *Der in Krohnen erlangte Glücks-Wechsel, oder Almira, Königin von Castilien*, is an adaptation by Friedrich Christian Feustking of a Venetian text by Giulio Pancieri based on the familiar seventeenth-century dramatic situation of the queen who secretly loves a commoner (Webster's *The Duchess of Malfi*, Corneille's *Dom Sanche de Navarre* and Dryden's *Secret Love* contain similar plots). The whole thing belongs very much to its Venetian Baroque operatic world, with a loose plot full of intrigue interlaced with comedy and ballet. Besides the three female and three male leads, the story introduces a *buffo* servant Tabarco, a Papageno-like figure first seen setting out the card tables for an evening's gaming at the Castilian court. The princes and princesses, by now neatly entangled, sit down to a fraught set of ombre (the game immortalized in Pope's *Rape of the Lock*) followed by a ball during which the horrified Queen Almira sees her secretary Fernando happily dancing with the Princess Edilia. After a multitude of plot twists all comes right in the end, however, and to save the queen from betraying her class by marrying a mere person, Fernando is discovered to be the long-lost son of the Count of Segovia. Tabarco enters on horseback, and Almira says that she will be delighted to share the throne with her quondam secretary.

Handel was evidently powerless to do much towards modifying Pancieri's rambling drama (Feustking was justifiably slated for his performance by rival Hamburg theatre poets) and the authoritative presence of the composer which we sense throughout the mature operas and oratorios is sometimes lacking in *Almira*. Despite imaginative daubs of instrumental colour (some lessons well learned from Keiser here) the writing, especially in the vocal lines, is often mannered and ungrateful. Moments of florid grandeur in the word setting, a strong French idiom and a generally uncritical subservience to the Hamburg style are elements bundled together rather than assimilated, and the total effect, even if we suppose that Handel would have become as adept a practitioner of this kind of opera as Mattheson and Keiser, is like looking at the ambitious façade to a provincial corn-exchange.

Hamburg's enthusiasm for its new composer was greeted with a second collaboration between Handel and Feustking, hurried into production on *Almira*'s heels and ready for performance in February. The title followed the usual German Baroque practice of giving the theme first, in the ungainly form then favoured of article and noun split by an adjectival phrase, so that it reads, literally translated: 'The Through Blood and Murder Acquired Love, or: Nero'. Handel's music has disappeared, but Feustking's text survives, and we can note that the opera's subject is akin to that of *Agrippina* with which the composer triumphantly concluded his Italian journey in 1709. Among characters common to both pieces are Nero and Poppaea, while Agrippina, true to history, is instinct, in Hamburg as in Venice, with jealousy and cunning. Seneca and Octavia are also present, to remind us of Monteverdi's imperishable treatment of the theme nearly a century earlier. There are plenty of duets and choruses, and comedy is provided by Anicetus, *des Kaysers Mignon oder*

25

Liebling, and Graptus, Claudius's freedman, whose long mock-meditation on philosophy is followed by an aria in which he declares that he will be a *Stagiritisch*, a *Stoisch*, an *Epicurisch* and an *Eclectisch*.

Perhaps the total loss to us of Handel's music has something to do with the fact that *Nero* was a complete flop, withdrawn after one, or perhaps two performances. Discussing the libretto, one of the Hamburg poets who had earlier pitched into Feustking exclaimed: 'How is a musician to create anything beautiful if he has no beautiful words? Therefore, as in the case of the composition of the opera *Nero*, someone has not unjustly complained: "There is no spirit in the verse, and one feels vexation at setting such a thing to music."'

The someone was probably Handel, who promptly vanished from the Gänsemarkt stage. A third opera, *Florindo*, ultimately divided into two by its librettist Heinrich Hinsch on grounds of length, was given two years later as *Der beglückte Florindo* and *Die verwandelte Daphne*, but of the score only a handful of orchestral pieces has survived. He presumably went on playing in the opera band, and eked out his income by giving lessons to the children of Hamburg citizens. A sizeable amount of his keyboard music can be conjecturally dated to this period on stylistic and other grounds, and several voluminous chaconnes and pieces containing ideas figuring more solidly elsewhere may have been written as teaching exercises.

Handel was not temperamentally cast in the mould of a great teacher. Sir John Hawkins is a little too partial in saying that he 'disdained to teach his art to any but princes', but he was not one to dazzle his audience with musical science and was far too impatient and quick-tempered a man to suffer fools or slowcoaches gladly. Profoundly educative though it is to the spirit and the imagination, his music is notoriously resistant to textbook exemplification. Thus it is almost impossible to imagine him writing an *Orgelbüchlein* or an *Art of Fugue* or even compiling a notebook for some notional Anna Magdalena. Like Beethoven or Elgar, he took pupils because he needed the money. And when he had scraped enough of it together, he set off in the winter of 1706 for Italy.

Caro Sassone

We enter upon the one period in Handel's life in which the words 'perhaps', 'probably', 'possibly' and 'presumably' are exasperatingly paramount. We can guess why he should have wanted to go to Italy, since, as the nursery of established musical form, terminology and style during the period, it was the logical goal of young composers from all over Europe, but whether he was, as tradition has it, invited by Prince Ferdinando de' Medici, son of Grand Duke Cosimo of Tuscany, is altogether more questionable. Ferdinando was indeed out of Florence at some stage immediately before Handel's departure from Hamburg, could certainly have been visiting some of his German princely connexions, and might perhaps have met Handel on one such visit — but there is no proof that he did so.

Finances are a somewhat simpler issue. As a rule Baroque artists travelling in Italy were paid for by their patrons, who saw the tour as a species of talent investment, paying off in the resulting sophistications of style. Handel had no need of this. Money was forthcoming from his father's estate, friends and family connexions rallied round, and Handel was able to set off for Italy, to use Mainwaring's immortal phrase, 'on his own bottom'. The word 'bottom' has the English eighteenth-century sense of 'initiative', 'enterprise' or 'substance'. Once in Italy itself, the necessary bottom would have to be provided by his own creative resources, directly linked to the enormous network of patronage and acquaintance hardly less essential to Italian life now than it was in those days.

His journey may have taken him through such musical centres as Munich, Turin and Milan, all of them with resident composers and flourishing operatic traditions, but he is first supposed to have halted for any length of time at Florence. The capital of the Grand Duchy of Tuscany under the rule of Cosimo III, obsessively religious and increasingly preoccupied with the issue of a likely successor among his brood of wayward children, was hardly an exciting city, but music of all kinds gained enthusiastic support from his eldest son Ferdinando. The prince had received a broad education, comprising, among other subjects, geometry lessons from the great mathematician Viviani, natural sciences and philosophy instruction from Francesco Redi, and practical courses on the violin and harpsichord from the Genoese composer Giovanni Maria Pagliardi. An anonymous contemporary notes that 'he also sang most gracefully . . . he liked operas, sad and serious ones for preference . . . he had his amusements for each season: in the spring he went to Poggio a Caiano, where he kept a troupe of comedians on purpose to act for him. Then he went to Villa Imperiale, where . . . the pages and courtiers improvised entertainments. . . . In the autumn he went to his favourite villa at Pratolino . . . there he went hunting and there he had a musical drama acted by the choicest singers, with a great crowd of spectators. Other operas under his patronage were given at Leghorn, where he "gently obliged" the richest merchants to buy all the tickets, lending his own orchestra, led by the virtuoso Martino Bitti. Besides this he was active in encouraging special performances of music for Holy Week in the Florentine churches, featuring new commissions. No wonder that when he died it was said of him that 'the most musical prince in all the world is dead'.

Nothing Handel composed on this first visit to Florence has survived, and in the last days of 1706 we find him already in Rome. On 14 January 1707, the diarist Francesco Valesio noted that 'there has arrived in this city a Saxon, a most excellent player on the harpsichord and composer, who today gave a flourish of his skill by playing the organ in the church of S. Giovanni* to the amazement of everyone present'.

It must have been at this time as well that he first heard the music of the *pifferari*, the Abruzzi shepherds whose tradition it was to play their bagpipes in the Roman streets during December and January. The simple tunes over their drone clearly made a deep impression: though this kind of one-note bass is a cliché of Baroque musical rusticity, the merest mention of sheep or shepherds, whether in 'Quanto voi felici siete' in *Ezio* or 'But as for his people' in *Israel in Egypt*, is enough to set the pastoral Handel going and a symphony labelled *pifa* duly introduces the shepherds of *Messiah*.

From a musical point of view Handel could not have chosen a more interesting moment at which to visit Italy. From a political aspect he could scarcely have hit on a worse. Popular historical awareness in England tends all too readily to forget that the War of the Spanish Succession

*Perhaps S. Giovanni dei Fiorentini or even the basilica of S. Giovanni in Laterano itself.

embraced far wider issues and more diffuse theatres of activity than the plains of Flanders and the Danube on which Marlborough gained his victories. The conflicting Bourbon and Habsburg interests were heavily engaged not only on France's eastern borders but also in Spain and, following a classic pattern, throughout the entire length of Italy. Handel's arrival was on the heels of a huge imperial push made possible by the brilliant operations of Prince Eugene, culminating in his victory at Turin and the surrender of Milan, both during the September of 1706. With the exception of Venice, which adopted its customary position on the diplomatic fence, all the Italian states were heavily committed, either through enforced levies as imperial fiefs, or through direct political and military involvement.

In terms of prestige the severest losses were suffered by the dominions of the Pope, whose support of the Bourbon cause in Spain and of the family of the exiled James II of England outweighed his efforts towards peace as far as Austria and her allies were concerned. Raised to the papacy in 1700, as Clement XI, Gianfrancesco Albani was destined to a term of office as miserable as it was long. Unlike his immediate predecessors, who had interpreted their responsibilities in a spirit of self-seeking worldliness, Clement was a worthy and conscientious pontiff, whose idealistic attempts to do right were perpetually frustrated by the cynical turn of European great-power politics.

Early in his reign he had seen his capital devastated by a succession of natural disasters. The Tiber flooded the city three times in as many years, and on 14 January 1703 there began a series of violent earth tremors which lasted with a more or less consistent intensity for nearly two months. Special prayers, fasts and processions took place to ward off what was seen as a fitting punishment for the decadent luxury of Roman society: 'Faith is not dead in Rome,' said an eyewitness, 'the earthquake, in fact, has been a great preacher.' Terrible cracks appeared in the Vatican and the Colosseum and the pillars of Bernini's great baldacchino in St Peter's were seen to tremble. Perhaps the most amazing scenes took place on the night of 2 February, when a rumour spread that the city was to be destroyed within two hours. Streets, squares and gardens quickly filled with people, many of them half dressed, flinging themselves on their knees, making public confession and embracing each other as if for the last time, and it was almost morning before a relative calm was restored.

Clement was instrumental, not only in sustaining Roman morale during such periods of intense crisis, but in reaffirming the city's metropolitan character through his extensive restoration of its older basilicas and his reconstruction of walls, aqueducts and fountains. The Rome in which Handel arrived was thus in one of its signal moments of renewal, even though its population was decreasing and in area it was little more than a magnificent market town among a scatter of impressive ruins.

Roman society was naturally dominated by ecclesiastics and by the noble families from whose ranks many of them were recruited. The machinery of patronage was controlled by these two heavily interlinked groups, and the city's flourishing artistic life depended exclusively upon their support. Alone among the major Italian cities, however, Rome boasted no opera house. The puritanical zeal of Innocent XII had closed the Teatro Tor di Nona in 1697 and no new theatrical enterprise was to be set on foot until the opening of the Capranica in 1709. Musicians nevertheless continued to flock to the city. Besides the inevitable demand for new music to accompany church celebrations of every kind, there was enough continuing impetus from wealthy and distinguished amateurs among the cardinals and their noble relatives to promote an exciting musical culture, whose influence was to condition Handel's style more strongly than any other he had encountered before or was to meet again.

Several of the leading ecclesiastics maintained their own domestic bands and, if not actually composing themselves, wrote texts for the musicians they patronized. Pietro Ottoboni, for example, appointed a cardinal at the age of 22 by his great-uncle Pope Alexander VIII, seems to have laid out most of an enormous income in indulging a passion for music. Before Innocent's ban on theatres, Ottoboni had staged operas by promising young composers such as Alessandro Scarlatti, Giovanni Bononcini and Francesco Pollarolo, in his huge Palazzo della Cancelleria, which also had a little stage for marionette operas.*

As a welcome visitor at Ottoboni's Wednesday music meetings, Handel could make valuable contacts here with some of Italy's leading masters. The atmosphere is well summed up for us by the French traveller Blainville, who was in Rome at the same time. 'His Eminence keeps in his pay the best musicians and performers in Rome . . . so that every Wednesday he has an excellent concert in his palace. We were there served with ices and other delicate liquors . . . but the greatest inconveniency in all these concerts is that one is pestered with swarms of trifling little Abbés, who come thither on purpose to fill their bellies with these liquors, and to carry off the crystal bottles with the napkins into the bargain.' The Ottoboni connexion in fact bound together practically all

*Ottoboni wrote librettos, including a lyric drama on the subject of Christopher Columbus's discovery of America.

The Bowes Museum, Barnard Castle, Co. Durham

Cardinal Pietro Ottoboni *c.* 1690 by Francesco Trevisani

Rome in Handel's day; the Piazza di Spagna

the musical Italians who later made their way to London while Handel was there. Nicola Haym (already in England) and Paolo Antonio Rolli, Handel's King's Theatre librettists, for example, had both been part of the cardinal's circle, as had Pietro Castrucci, leader of the opera band, and Filippo Amadei (Pippo Mattei) a collaborator in *Muzio Scevola* and a brilliant cellist whose career foundered in a syphilitic decline.

Handel's most significant encounter at the Cancelleria was with the orchestra's leader, Arcangelo Corelli. Corelli is one of those artistic figures whose effect on their contemporaries is out of all proportion to the volume of their output. He wrote and published nothing save six instrumental collections, but in so doing he profoundly altered and deepened the whole character of European music. His influence pervaded everything from a tiny trio sonata to a full-blown opera, and with those of Vivaldi and the elder Scarlatti his musical personality dominates the central phases of the Italian Baroque.

Among the many things which Handel learned from him must surely have been the technique of controlling an orchestra, in an age before baton conducting, well enough to produce a clean sound. Domenico Scarlatti once told the violinist Francesco Geminiani that he was especially struck by Corelli's 'nice management of his band, the uncommon accuracy of whose performance gave the concertos an amazing effect . . . for Corelli regarded it as essential to the *ensemble* of a band, that their bows should all move exactly together, all up, or all down; so that at his rehearsals, which constantly preceded every public performance of one of his concertos, he would immediately stop the band if he discovered one irregular bow'. This was an invaluable legacy to Handel, whose insistence on the highest professional standards in performance owed much to Corelli's example.

The effects of the older man's music itself upon Handel's own style are not so much heard as felt within the framework of the pieces he composed during this period, through the creation of structures immediately recalling those used in Corelli's concertos (which, though not published until 1714, may already have been known in manuscript). Nowhere is this more apparent than in the setting of the *Dixit Dominus* which Handel completed in the April of 1707. The freedom and suppleness of the string writing determine the character of the entire work, essentially a series of vocal concerto movements, relentless in its momentum and dazzling in its grandeur of design.

The stylistic synthesis is not only between Handel and Corelli but draws together elements from the composer's German church training of

Halle days and features which suggest that he must have begun to study the work of earlier Italian masters, Stradella, Carrissimi, Giovanni Paolo Colonna (in whom Boyce was later to detect an obvious Handelian model) and maybe even Monteverdi and his accomplished assistant at St Mark's, Alessandro Grandi, whose own brilliantly idiosyncratic setting of the *Dixit Dominus* was published in 1629. The sturdy *cantus firmus* of '*donec ponam inimicos tuos*' in the first movement could pass as easily for a Latin psalm tone as for a Lutheran chorale (it is not unlike *Wachet auf, ruft uns die Stimme*) but the pattern of contrasts between soli and five-part chorus, and the double fugue setting '*Tu es sacerdos in aeternum*' marching against the rushing semiquavers of '*secundum ordinem Melchisedech*' are quintessentially Italian in idiom. This very movement Handel was to use again, more than thirty years later, in *Israel in Egypt*, a work which achieves the same sort of fusion, albeit on a far grander scale, through the remarkable diversity of its allusions.

There is no record of a first performance for the *Dixit Dominus*, but since it forms part of the Vesper Offices, the ingenious suggestion has been made that Handel intended it as part of a far larger service, at which his settings of two other vesper psalms, *Laudate Pueri* and *Nisi Dominus*, would also be given. A Handelian Vespers, to place beside Monteverdi's set of 1610 and Mozart's *Vesperae Solennes de Confessore* is an attractive idea, though nearly three months divide the composition of *Dixit Dominus* and *Laudate Pueri*, finished on 8 July. Together with the motet *Saeviat tellus inter rigores*, they may all have been given at the church of Santa Maria di Monte Santo, in special commemoration of deliverance from the earthquakes. The only piece of Handel's, however, which has a definite link with such a commemoration is the motet *Donna che in ciel* for soprano, chorus and orchestra.

Whatever their purpose the two other psalms show us that the Roman Handel had begun as he meant to go on. The *Laudate Pueri* uses the same technique of contrasting masses and build-ups (a florid solo soprano opening, for example, balanced by some admirably rich choral writing) and explores a bewildering selection of keys (including a doom-laden switch from F to F sharp in the 16-bar *Quis sicut Dominus*) before homing to the original D major in the Gloria. This final movement repeats the old 'As it was in the beginning' trick, more deftly used in the *Dixit Dominus*, in which the sense of the words is mirrored in a reprise of the opening material. A similar ploy marks the close of *Nisi Dominus*, whose ostinato string figure is used again to thrilling effect at the beginning of *Zadok the Priest*. The psalm is a tiny capsule of perfectly staged *coups de théâtre* (note the miraculous stillness, for example, of *Cum dederit delectis suis somnum*, in which the voice floats above the ghostly accompaniment like a winter sun) ideally Roman, ideally Baroque, in form and idiom.

During the spring of 1707 Handel was busy in other directions. As well as his entree to the Ottoboni household he had gained an introduction to an equally rich and influential amateur who very soon became a devoted admirer of his music. Like Ottoboni, Benedetto Pamphilj was both a cardinal and the great nephew of a pope. Innocent X raised him to the purple in 1681, and his musical patronage embraced several of those who performed at the Cancelleria, including Corelli and Scarlatti, for whom he wrote librettos. As a poet he was not without talent. Handel clearly appreciated the musicality of his verses and various cantata texts are certainly his. On a much larger scale Pamphilj produced an entire secular oratorio *Il Trionfo del Tempo e del Disinganno* ('The Triumph of Time and Truth') to be set by Handel for one of Ottoboni's concerts.

Il Trionfo has never really received the attention it deserves from Handelians. The fact that Handel returned to it on two subsequent occasions, 30 and 50 years respectively after the first version, suggests that he maintained some sort of special interest or involvement in the work. At any rate the libretto is certainly no worse than many others he came to set, and in overall smoothness and elegance often a good deal better.

The underlying idea is the kind of moral abstract cherished by the Baroque imagination. Time and Truth oppose Pleasure in a combat for the allegiance of Beauty, who eventually yields to them after being offered visions of what will happen if she chooses the alternative. A case indeed of everything being done by mirrors, and Pleasure is finally sent packing, in a burst of G major resentment, when Beauty casts her away after another look in the faithful glass, which she has invoked in the opening aria. As dramatic material there is nothing especially promising in all this, but it gave Handel the chance to develop a distinctive aria style, which, though it absorbs material from the Hamburg years, is very different to anything he had evolved earlier. Something of the sweep and exuberance of his mature operatic manner is here already, underpinned by a rich scoring, which includes paired recorders, plentiful work for solo oboe and violin, and a sinfonia with an organ solo, whisking a somewhat bewildered Beauty into the Domain of Pleasure. Several of the numbers have, besides, a genuine distinction which transcends the imaginative limits of Pamphilj's text. There is an extended quartet, in which Handel plays with the word *tempo* as Beauty pleads for time to consider her choice, while

Time, Truth and Pleasure throw in their arguments. Among the arias 'Urne voi', Time's exclamation of dignified outrage at the insolence of '*a frail beauty*', is justly admired for its harmonic boldness. F minor (one of Handel's favourite 'special effect' keys) is a mere starting point for what ultimately becomes a shattering vision of anarchic gloom, as the urns of dead beauties are commanded to yield up their grisly treasures.

The overture to *Il Trionfo* may well have been the source of a famous bone of contention between the young composer and Corelli. As leader of the Ottoboni band, Corelli had some difficulty in satisfying Handel's demands as to style and execution; impetuous as ever, Handel snatched the violin from the master's hand and the Hamburg second fiddle tried to show one of Europe's finest instrumentalists how to play. Corelli, whose typical modesty hid a sly sense of humour, answered: 'But my dear Saxon, this music is in the French style, and I don't understand that sort of thing at all.' In fact, as his own compositions show, he understood it very well, and if the remark was intended to put Handel gently in his place it probably succeeded.

Under the name of Arcomelo, Corelli was a member of the prestigious Accademia Arcadiana, founded in 1690 and including Ottoboni, Pamphilj and the bizarre figure of Queen Maria Casimira of Poland, a disappointing substitute for the lamented Queen Cristina of Sweden, whose patronage had been so valuable to seventeenth-century Roman musicians. The Arcadians, led by influential critics such as Giovanni Maria Crescimbeni and Carlo Gravina, set out to refine literary expression among contemporary Italian writers: as apostles of order and dignity in art they represent a significant element in a more general trend which was to carry opera along with it and which inevitably had its effect upon Handel. The whole cast of Accademia Arcadiana was emphatically pastoral. The members were all pseudonymous classical shepherds and the annals of the society were written up in a quaintly rustic fashion — for example, Ottoboni's enormous palace becomes 'the hut of the famed Crateo'. In 1706, together with Corelli, Scarlatti and the harpsichordist Bernardo Pasquini joined the exalted swains, as Terpandro and Protico respectively.

Handel was too young to be a member, but was undoubtedly a welcome guest. The Roman climate was then agreeable enough for meetings to take place out of doors, in an attractive amphitheatre, the Bosco Parrasio, which can still be seen within its garden on the Janiculum. The grounds belonged to one of the society's most eminent members, Francesco Maria Ruspoli, who rapidly became an important patron of Handel.

The Marchese Ruspoli, son of Count Alessandro Marescotti, had inherited the title and fortunes of his uncle Bartolommeo, and now lived in some splendour in the Palazzo Bonelli, on the south side of the Piazza SS. Apostoli, east of the Corso. His love of music and his wealth rivalled those of the two cardinals, and his Sunday *conversazioni* were notable for launching new compositions. Handel may actually have lived in the Palazzo Bonelli during 1707, as documentary evidence shows him doing the following year. It was for the Marchese, in any case, that he produced a series of chamber cantatas to Italian texts which are among the most polished examples of the form.

Developed during the early seventeenth century by such masters as Marc'Antonio Cesti and Luigi Rossi, the cantata was related to opera, though independent from it, using the same expressive alternation of recitative and aria, but exploring a simpler and more intimate world. It offered the composer excellent practice in constructing a sequence of linked numbers and rewarded the singer with opportunities for vocal display. The texts are, of course, mainly of the familiar pastoral kind, in which shepherds or shepherdesses complain of a lover's faithlessness or berate Cupid for his caprices.

During his stay in Italy Handel produced nearly a hundred works of this type. The existence of several manuscript copies of selected cantatas in various Italian libraries suggests that it was precisely these compositions for which he became first noted (a collection of 23 of them in the Biblioteca Marciana at Venice features two portrait caricatures, developed from the initial 'C' of *cantate*; one of which may even be of the composer himself). Respect for his handling of the *genre* is shown in the number of contemporary copies of individual examples, such as *Sento la che ristretto* and *Se pari e la tua fe*. Admiration was well founded. The cantatas are an extensive sampler of Handel's skill in capturing a range of different moods, besides underlining that essentially human dimension which never failed to stimulate his musical imagination.

Many of them are carefully-observed character portraits, by turns passionate, ironically humorous or tenderly pathetic, but tinged with a characteristically broad sympathy. Some exploit that favourite feature of Italian lyricists, the simile aria, in which the lover's state of mind is paralleled with a ship in a storm or a swallow seeking her nest. Others take us through the various phases of an emotional drama. *Tu fedel, tu costante*, for instance, shows an integration of numbers so absolute as to make the mocking simplicity of the final aria a logical counterpoise to the hysterical turbulence of the opening sinfonia. Handel was to use pieces of identical form (abrupt staccato chords followed by volleying semiquaver sequences) in *Partenope* and *Alcina* for the obviously similar purpose of precipitating crises of feeling. In the cantata we watch the jilted girl's sense of injustice at her Fileno's sexual effrontery turn to a frank cynicism as Handel progressively lightens the music's intensity.

What most clearly appealed to him was the form's dramatic potential. Three of his finest cantatas are cast in the shape of tragic scenas, the heroine in each being a woman driven by circumstance to the brink of despair. *Agrippina condotta a morire* ('Agrippina led to her death'), whose title encapsulates its theme, is a striking essay in structural control and an excellent illustration of the way in which the Baroque recitative and aria form are designed to work. Initially Agrippina is still the vigorous Roman matron of history, properly outraged at the way events have overtaken her, but as her nerve starts to crack, so does the rigidity of the cantata's outlines. Her third air collapses into *recitativo semplice* after fourteen bars, briefly resumes with her resolve, then peters out again, a pattern continued through the scene with an aria whose middle section changes from quadruple to triple time. The whole piece ends with superb abruptness on four bars of unadorned recitative. *Armida abbandonata*, of which J. S. Bach made himself a copy, opens with an extraordinary stretch of declamation introduced by a vocal line supported on two *arpeggiando* violins and featuring one of the earliest of those plangent sicilianos Handel enjoyed devising for his lovelorn heroines, while *O numi eterni*, for soprano and continuo, carried his fame out of Italy under its better known name of *La Lucrezia*.

The best of them all, however, was probably written after Handel's return from Germany. *Apollo e Dafne* or *La terra e liberata* is almost an opera in itself. Its technique is beyond praise, but its supremacy springs less from mere polish of line and surface than from Handel's penetrating sense of the realities of feeling which lie beneath the mythological framework. The simple harmonies and cheerful ditties of the sun god, bumptious after strangling the Python, are answered by the gentler, more reserved cast of Daphne's music as in 'Ardi adori' she meets his advances not so much with anger as with detached remonstrance. The duet 'Deh! lascia addolcire' emphasizes their separateness by the use of glacial flute tones, a different tempo for each of them, and the fact that their voices are never allowed to blend. Apollo's final pursuit is brilliantly realized in an air with concerto grosso accompaniment which dissolves into alarmed recitative as Daphne is transformed into the laurel he ultimately hails in a dignified lament.

The principal soloist at the first performances of many of these cantatas was Margherita Durastanti, who had made her earliest appearance at the Ruspoli concerts in January 1707. She was evidently an able linguist (her farewell to the London stage was in English) and Handel composed cantatas for her in Spanish and French. More important, she was the first singer we know of whose individual vocal qualities were directly related to the music Handel wrote for her. She was not particularly attractive — a contemporary caricature stresses her jutting 'singer's chin' and large breasts — but though not in the same rank as divas like Faustina and Cuzzoni, she was a loyal Handelian trouper, and her dependable musicianship helped to ensure the success of several of his operas with the London public. The two of them were much in each other's company during this Roman spring and summer, but documents are impenetrably silent on any supposed liaison.

In late May the Marchese Ruspoli and his entire household set off for the *villeggiatura*, always a part of the seasonal rhythm of Italian life. Nowadays the summer exodus takes place in August and is generally a dash to the seaside, but in the eighteenth century it was a slow, stately progress to the country villa, where the sweltering days were spent in gossip, flirting and *ennui* and pottering about the estate. Handel, with his love of the country, must have enjoyed a two-month sojourn at the moated palace in the little town of Vignanello, in the foothills of the extinct volcano Monte Cimino, between Rome and Viterbo. He was busy in any case with *Armida abbandonata* and a motet, *Coelestis dum spirat aura*, composed for St Antony's day, 13 June, on which the cathedral was presented with a new altarpiece by Michelangelo Ceruti. The Marchese was well pleased with the music and its performers. Handel got a jewelled ring and so did Durastanti, which suggests either that as a woman she was given the then exceptional privilege of being allowed to sing in church, or, more likely, that the motets must have been given in the Ruspoli palace.

It seems reasonable to assume that a more important commission than either of these was preoccupying Handel during the torrid days in the Latian countryside and in the weeks following his return to Rome. The exact circumstances under which he came to compose his first Italian opera are unknown, and for many years even its actual performance history was in question. It has now been discovered that it was given in Florence during the early autumn of 1707, and that its title (it has always been called *Rodrigo* for convenience) was *Vincer se stesso e la maggior vittoria* ('The greatest victory is over oneself'). It was probably given in the Teatro del Cocomero, which since 1652 had been the seat of the Accademia degli

Infuocati, a splinter group of members of the original Accademia degli Immobili, established under the protection of Cardinal Giovanni Carlo de' Medici.

One of numerous such learned bodies in Florence — there were also the Sorgenti, the Cadenti and the Nascenti, as well as the Conversazione del Centauro and various smaller ones — the Infuocati had their theatre, now known as the Nicolini, in the Via dei Servi by the Duomo. Its name was taken from the sign of a water-melon — *cocomero* — hanging outside; much rebuilt, it has nevertheless the distinction of being one of the four surviving houses associated with Handelian first nights.

One of the academy's number, Antonio Salvi, was well known as a librettist, and may have supplied Handel with the text, a revision of Francesco Silvani's *Il duello d'Amore e di Vendetta*, written for Venice in 1699. The story is very loosely based on events and characters from the last days of Gothic Spain, but though the historical figures of Roderick and Julian both appear, the invading Moors they were responsible for letting in do not and the drama ends with a lively *coro*, the customary closing ensemble for all the singers which rounded off a Baroque opera. There is some distinguished poetry here, and among two or three highly effective dramatic moments the finest is undoubtedly the scene in Act III when, as Giuliano and Evanco are about to kill the tyrant Rodrigo, Florinda rushes in to claim vengeance for herself and is in turn stopped by the appearance of her infant son in the arms of Esilena, brandishing the child as an object of moral blackmail.

Although recently performed in a modern reconstruction, the complete text of *Rodrigo* is not yet published. Part of the first and third acts is missing from the autograph score, though it has been suggested that we might be able to discover some of the lost material in the music used by John Christopher Smith, son of Handel's assistant, Johann Christoph Schmidt, for some of the additions to the oratorios made during the composer's blindness in the 1750s. Enough remains for us to appreciate the piece as a fascinating transitional step in Handel's development as a dramatic composer, linking the Hamburg manner of *Almira* with the Venetian style of *Agrippina* to which he remained loyal throughout his subsequent career. For the first time he encountered the established form of Italian *opera seria*, freshly evolved during the last decades of the preceding century and destined to still further modification during his own lifetime. He was required to handle long passages of plain recitative (in which the voice is accompanied only by continuo instruments) to create exit numbers, in which the drama allowed the singer, after applause for vocal display, to leave the stage (over half the arias here observe this convention) and to show the mastery he had acquired, through cantata-writing, of the *da capo* air, the standard operatic unit of the day, with its A and B sections and chances for ornamented reprise.

The result is an absorbing mixture. There is a fully developed French overture with dance suite (rearranged as incidental music for performances of Ben Jonson's *The Alchemist* in London in 1710) and a series of arias whose brevity and prevailing manner show that Handel was making a conscious effort to imitate the style of Giacomo Perti and Alessandro Scarlatti, then the approved models in Florence. Very few of the individual numbers have that expansiveness which stamps a work like the *Dixit Dominus* as inalienably Handel's own. The recitatives are nervously handled, and the role of Esilena is burdened periodically with prolix paragraphs of declamation, the longest single utterances by any one Handelian character.

A glance at *Rodrigo* suggests that Handel had made a careful study of Scarlatti in particular. The two could not have met at this time, however, as Scarlatti was in Urbino during the summer and autumn of 1707, and writing miserable begging letters from there to Prince Ferdinando, depicting himself and his family, accurately enough, it seems, as being on the bitterest edge of poverty: 'I throw myself at the feet of Y.R.H., as though to my tutelary god, the perennial source from which, on so many occasions, I have received the precious waters of such exalted and benign grace.' Ferdinando sent a remittance accompanied by a curt, though polite reply. The relationship between patron and composer, which a year before had brought *Il Gran Tamerlano* to the Pratolino stage as the fifth of Scarlatti's works to be given there, now cooled disastrously, as the prince looked to Perti for the new Pratolino opera, *Dionisio, Re di Portogallo*, to a libretto by Salvi. As *Sosarme* it was to be set by Handel in 1732.

None of Handel's surviving music was provided for Ferdinando himself, though the *Rodrigo* libretto notes that the performances were 'under the protection of the Most Serene Prince of Tuscany'. Political analogies between the opera's plot and the current political situation in Spain have recently been suggested, and Ferdinando, whose mother was a French princess and whose father, Grand Duke Cosimo, was pro-Bourbon, no doubt appreciated these. How Handel spent his time otherwise at Florence is sketched in for us by a nugget of gossip retained by Mainwaring, who, besides remarking that he received a present of 100 sequins and a service of plate for *Rodrigo*'s composition, says 'VITTORIA, who was much admired both as an Actress, and a Singer, bore a principal part in this Opera. She was a fine woman, and had for some time been much in the good graces of his Serene Highness. But, from the natural restlessness of certain hearts, so little sensible was she of her exalted situation, that she conceived a design of transferring her affections to another person. Handel's youth and comeliness, joined with his fame and abilities in Music, had made impressions on her heart. Tho' she had the art to conceal them for the present, she had not perhaps the power, certainly not the intention to efface them.' The soprano Vittoria Tarquini was certainly in Florence during this period, as a star of the Pratolino operas, but she was not among the *Rodrigo* cast. How far her amorous designs succeeded with Handel we can never know, but a letter from the Electress Sophia to the Queen of Prussia in 1710 bears out the existence of a rumoured liaison.

Poor Scarlatti, sorely in need of commissions, had meanwhile retreated to Venice, then the liveliest musical capital in Italy and a place where composers and performers could inevitably glean information as to job prospects in the courts, churches and theatres of Europe. We know nothing of Handel's movements between September 1707 and March 1708, but a Venetian visit seems not unlikely, especially since the text of his opera *Partenope* (1730) is basically that used for performances given in Venice during the winter opera season of 1707–8. More important as being a direct influence on his musical style was Scarlatti's opera *Mitridate Eupatore*, a bold and experimental work which met with a noisy and generally hostile reception from the Venetians.

There was a chance as well to meet other composers in the bustling, competitive world of the four opera houses at San Cassiano, San Fantin, Sant' Angelo and San Giovanni Grisostomo, of the pious orphanages, each with its orchestra of teenage pupils, of private concerts in patrician palaces and of the great basilica of St Mark's. Yet it was not to the works of the nowadays better-known Venetian masters such as Vivaldi, Albinoni and the Marcello brothers that Handel most eagerly responded, but to the music of Antonio Lotti, organist at St Mark's, and Francesco Gasparini, Vivaldi's predecessor as director of the redoutable band of girl instrumentalists at the Pietà foundling hospital. The former not only became a friend and supporter of Handel's music (he and his wife were among the most vociferous partisans of *Agrippina*, written for Venice two years later) but left a very strong mark upon the young man's aria style and even on his choral writing: the latter, already well known in Roman and Florentine circles which had welcomed Handel, was to furnish a significant model for the composer's subsequent handling of recitative and air, most notably in *Tamerlano* and *Faramondo*, both operas making use of Gasparini's treatments of the same subjects.

The spring of 1708 found Handel returning to Rome and the Ruspoli palace, where an exciting and ambitious new commission was awaiting him. For Easter Sunday and Monday of that year the Marquis was planning to present a large-scale oratorio on the theme of Christ rising from the dead, to a text by his fellow Arcadian Carlo Sigismondo Capece. Extensive preparations were begun in the palace itself, where a special stage was set up in the largest of the *saloni*. Its principal decoration was a large painting of the Resurrection by Ceruti, framed by the Ruspoli arms, with an ornate frontispiece showing the work's full title, *Oratorio per la risurrettione di Nostro Signor Gesu Cristo* in letters cut out of transparent paper and lit from behind by 70 lanterns. Crimson, yellow and scarlet hangings in damask and velvet adorned the hall, where light from sixteen candelabra allowed the immense audiences to read their wordbooks (1,500 of them, suggesting packed houses on each day).

For the orchestra special music stands were made, their legs shaped like fluted cornucopiae, painted with the arms of Ruspoli and his wife Isabella, and a platform was devised for the concertino strings, led by Corelli. The full band consisted of 38 string players, two trumpets and four oboes, who could presumably double on flute and recorder. Handel himself was taken good care of by the marchese, as the household accounts reveal in their details of a bed and bedcovers hired from the Jews of the ghetto, whose chief line of business this was, and of the enormous bills for his food — a healthy indulgence in the pleasures of the table would stay with him till the end of his life.

The first of the sumptuously stage-managed performances (non-dramatic, of course) went off successfully in a fashion typical of Ruspoli concerts, but news that Margherita Durastanti had taken one of the solo roles was quick to reach the ears of the Pope, who issued a scandalized admonishment to the marchese for employing a female singer in an Easter oratorio and threatened the wretched soprano with a flogging. She was promptly replaced by a castrato called Filippo. Otherwise Ruspoli's satisfaction expressed itself in the customary lavish gifts to the performers of diamond, emerald and ruby rings.

As the grandest work Handel had so far attempted in Italy, *La Resurrezione* reflected even more powerfully than the Latin psalms those qualities of opulence and sensuality pervading the religious atmosphere of late-Baroque Rome. The oratorio form itself had been evolved in the city during the preceding century and brought to maturity in the works of composers like Carissimi and Stradella, whose sacred dramas reached out to embrace the language of the theatre without abandoning an essentially devout aim. Once again, therefore, the young Saxon master was being called upon to provide music in a genre of which his audience would have considered itself the best judge in the world, and to strike a perfect balance between orthodox religious posture and the tastes of those to whom secular lyric drama was currently forbidden.

Thus we should not expect to find in Handel's first oratorio qualities similar to those we look for in the great English works of his maturity. The two choruses were sung by the soloists and there is nothing especially dramatic in the outline of the text. An angel champions Christ's harrowing of hell against the *braggadocio* of the arrogant Lucifer, while on earth Mary Cleophas and Mary Magdalene, lamenting their lost Saviour, are consoled by St John with the assurance that He will rise again on the third day. Lucifer and the angel try conclusions once more and the last scenes of the work elaborate on the women's discovery of the empty sepulchre and the joyful news brought to the Apostles.

If there is little in all this to recall the sublimities of *Messiah*, *Saul* or *Israel in Egypt*, Capece's excellent poetry is transfigured by a score of unabashed richness, in which Handel concentrates on arias which are effectively a series of detailed emotional studies, designed to heighten our awareness of individual moods, as opposed to adding anything to a composite character portrait or to illuminating a central theme. Even by the standards of the Ruspoli-Ottoboni-Pamphilj world there is an exceptional reliance here on the varying strands of orchestral sound. In Maria Maddalena's 'Ferma l'ali' we are invited to admire the suppleness of the vocal line while simultaneously being wooed by a pair of recorders, muted violins and viola da gamba. Trumpets add lustre to Cleofe's 'Vedo il ciel', but the rising sun evoked by Giovanni in 'Ecco il sol' is portrayed with an elegant economy through simple use of an ornate continuo line — in the end Handel's trust was founded upon his basses.

With the success of *La Resurrezione* still reverberating, Handel left Rome for Naples in May 1708. His departure was doubtless hastened by the unexpected intensity with which the war in Italy now gathered momentum. Encouraged by a gradual weakening in political support for England's share in the conflict, the French had stepped up their military effort in Flanders and Spain, and the Austrians were now constrained to follow suit. The fall of Mantua to the imperial troops the previous year had not simply served to enrich the cast of *Vincer se stesso e la maggior vittoria* with the singers of its dethroned duke. Pope Clement's wavering neutrality was now severely threatened and an army under Marshal Count Daun actually appeared at the gates of Rome itself en route to Naples. The point has been very well made that the situation in Italy during these years was bad enough to undermine the traditional sources of local patronage towards musicians of all kinds and to create the *diaspora artistica* which sent many composers and instrumentalists of the highest quality wandering through Europe in search of secure employment.

Naples was hardly the safest of places. A strong Austrian military presence under the command of Prince Philip of Hesse Darmstadt upheld viceregal rule in the name of Archduke Charles as King of Spain. While Handel was there the rough and ready Count Daun was superseded as viceroy by a man of very different stamp, to whom the composer was probably recommended by Cardinal Pamphilj. One of the most powerful figures in the whole of Italy, Vincenzo Grimani came of a Venetian noble family, several of whose members had held high offices of state and two of whom were actually doges. Related to the Mantuan Gonzagas through his mother, he had used his connexions in tireless political activity on Austria's behalf. The cardinal's hat he had gained from Innocent XII in 1697 was probably a good deal less important to him than the gift of abbeys in Lombardy and Hungary from the Emperor. 'No one was abler than he at making alliances', says one historian. 'No one understood better how to secure allies through promises and eloquent descriptions of the benefits accruing.'

Grimani had already been heavily involved in the *Congiura di Macchia*, a conspiracy of Neapolitan nobles in 1701 to assassinate the Spanish viceroy Villena, but it is a measure of his extraordinary force that he had so far kept his hands clean as to be appointed imperial ambassador to the Vatican, thus embarrassing and affronting Pope Clement, whom he seems to have despised. He himself arrived in Naples in 1708 and was at once faced with the challenges presented by a profoundly divided community, its rifts widened still further by the presence of an Austrian garrison whose discontent over pay was ultimately taken out on the civilian population. Grimani failed to solve such problems, but was at any rate able to make capital out of local resentment at the enormous financial exactions of the church, so as to further his campaign against Clement.

His path and Handel's were shortly and significantly to cross. The cardinal must have been responsible for securing the young man his one important Neapolitan commission, the serenata *Aci, Galatea e Polifemo*, probably written for the wedding of the Duke of Alvito to Donna Beatrice di Sanseverino, daughter of the Prince of Monte Mileto, in June. The

43

Duke was markedly pro-Austrian, having sent his servants to do homage to the imperial authority when the troops first arrived in Naples, and was to celebrate the archduke's conquest of Sardinia that September with a serenata by Domenico Sarro, but the natural urge to find political allusions in everything Handel wrote at this time can be carried to excess. *Aci, Galatea e Polifemo* is neither more nor less than what it pretends to be, a dramatic cantata with instruments to adorn an aristocratic wedding feast.

Its interest for us, of course, lies partly in the fact that one of Handel's best-known works was written on the same subject, drawn from Ovid and Theocritus, exactly ten years later. The outline of the anonymous libretto is similar to that of *Acis & Galatea* itself, save that here there is none of the jubilation which rounds off the later work after Galatea has turned Acis into a river god, partly because there is no chorus to tell her to dry her tears. She simply runs off to indulge her sorrows on the seashore, and the work closes with a trio, scored for two trumpets, oboes and strings, in which all three characters, directing their words presumably at the newly-wed duke and duchess, declare that 'he who loves best has truth and constancy as his objects'.

However modestly proportioned, the piece attracts by virtue of its attempts at musical characterization and diversity of orchestral shadings. Galatea, even if she lacks the strength of will with which her English avatar so wonderfully triumphs, is a figure fully rounded in her two simile arias and the languishing 'Se m'ami, oh caro', an affecting miniature with a tiny middle section, in which two cellos paint her passionate sighs in quavers punctuated by rests. Polifemo is the Polyphemus of 'O ruddier than the cherry' but both more grotesque and more menacing through the versatility demanded of him in the enormous compass of 'Fra l'ombre e gli orrori', for instance: it is noteworthy that Handel refurbished this aria many years later to give to his ablest Italian bass, Montagana, in *Sosarme*. None of the airs, in any case, exactly reproduces the orchestral balance of another, so that the ear is continually engaged by shifting sonorities.

The serenata apart, Handel's Neapolitan visit was more of a prolonged summer holiday than anything else. He composed very little during these months, but despite the background of political unrest there was plenty to interest him on the city's musical scene. The famous conservatories, such as that nursery of great castrati, the Poveri di Gesu Cristo, were already acquiring the reputation for fine teachers and performers which so allured travellers of later decades; there was the Royal Chapel, of which Scarlatti himself became master, there were churches humming with every sort of sacred music, and a notable operatic tradition, incorporating those touches of popular comedy so characteristic of the true Neapolitan spirit.

In August, however, it was time for him to return to Rome, where Ruspoli and the cardinal patrons awaited him. Refreshed by his southern jaunt Handel turned, with that energy which never left him, to cantata composing, producing almost a third of his entire output in the medium during this busy autumn of 1708. There were pieces of all kinds for the copyist Angelini, nicknamed 'Panstufato' (literally 'stewed bread') to write out from the composer's vigorously sketched manuscripts — amorous remonstrances like *Se pari e la tua fe* and *Dite mie pianti*, cantatas with instruments, such as *Amarilli vezzosa*, and one oddity, a work in praise of the master himself, *Hendel, non puo mia musa*, by no less than the admiring Pamphilj. The words and music were apparently improvised at an Arcadian assembly, as the opening makes clear. 'Handel, my muse cannot in an instant make verses worthy of your lyre,' says the cardinal, comparing the composer to Orpheus, as he was to be compared *ad nauseam* in England, and celebrating his ability to draw poetry from 'a plectrum which has lain so long unused upon an aged tree'. Thanks to a marginal jotting made decades later by his friend Charles Jennens on a copy of Mainwaring's biography we know exactly what Handel thought of such fallall. '"An old Fool!" I ask'd "Why Fool? because he wrote an Oratorio? perhaps you will call *me* fool for the same reason!" He answer'd "So I would, if you flatter'd me, as He did."' But that did not stop him from setting Pamphilj's little *jeu d'esprit* to music.

The most serious assignment in the midst of all this may reflect the Marchese Ruspoli's growing political involvement. Late that summer the continuing squabbles between the Pope and the Austrians over the lagoon of Comacchio and the territory around Ferrara developed into open conflict and the Marchese raised an army of 1,200 men to defend the city for the papal cause. He was not a particularly competent commander, but it seemed only right that the event should be celebrated in fine style with a Handel cantata on the grand scale. *O come chiare e belle* is, by its very nature, not among his most memorable examples of the genre, an occasional piece in which the spirit of the river Tiber, invoked by the shepherd Olinto (Pamphilj's Arcadian name) is urged by Glory (soprano) to shed his fears of Austrian arms, with promises of historical fame. Olinto, making an oblique reference to universal papal supremacy, prepares to change 'the humble bagpipe into a trumpet', and the trio hail Ruspoli's favourable star. The music, a series of facile, short-breathed arias, has all the signs of having been put together in a considerable hurry.

What Handel's immediate reasons for leaving Rome were we cannot tell, but we know that he returned to Florence at some time in March and stayed there until December. During this Florentine visit he was busy assembling the materials of what was to become the very finest of his Italian works, a piece which, besides consolidating a style which was emphatically his own, looks forward to the compositions of his maturity in a way unparalleled by anything he had written earlier.

The libretto of the opera *Agrippina* had been provided by none other than Cardinal Grimani, Viceroy of Naples, with a view to performance at the San Giovanni Grisostomo theatre during the Venice winter season of 1709–10. All the Venetian theatres belonged to patrician families and the Grimani themselves owned this one, among the newest and grandest, next to the church of the same name to the north of the Rialto and close to the house where Marco Polo 'el milion' was supposed to have lived. The French *Mercure Galant* described it as 'the finest and richest in the city. The room for the spectators is surrounded with five rows of boxes one above the other, thirty-one to a row... enriched with sculptured decorations.' The ceiling showed the Grimani arms cradled among garlands held by cherubs in a *trompe-l'oeil* gallery. There was a drop curtain painted with Venus and Cupid, raised an hour before the overture, when a big chandelier and four candle-brackets came down to illuminate the audience. Thanks to a barely legible inventory of the family effects made in 1714 we know something of the stage and the sets, from details such as 'perspective backcloths', 'sky-borders' and 'a tin moon' (*Ariodante*, incidentally, features a stage moonrise) and the six wings on either side. All of this has now disappeared, and the theatre, much rebuilt, and fitted out in the 'Liberty' style at the beginning of the century, is now the Teatro Malibran — but its back view from the bridge across the canal on to which it abuts can have altered little since Handel's day. The inventory, by the way, also mentions a house annexed to the theatre, where the composer probably stayed while in Venice.

That season was an especially good one, with new operas by Gasparini and Albinoni at San Cassiano, and two by Lotti, *Ama piu che men si crede* and *Il comando non inteso ed ubbidito*, scheduled for San Giovanni Grisostomo on either side of *Agrippina*. Handel's cast, what is more, was one of the best he ever mustered: Durastanti was there as Agrippina herself, Valeriano Pellegrini sang Nerone and Poppea was the outstanding Diamante Maria Scarabelli. Even the smaller roles carried distinction, if the presence of the bass Giuseppe Maria Boschi as Pallante is anything to go by. Success, of a sort Handel was hardly ever to know again, was inevitable and richly deserved. There were apparently 27 performances, and we may surely believe Mainwaring when he says that 'the audience was so enchanted with this performance, that a stranger who should have seen the manner in which they were affected, would have imagined they were all distracted. The theatre, at almost every pause, resounded with shouts and acclamations of *viva il caro Sassone* and other expressions of approbation too extravagant to be mentioned. They were thunderstruck with the gravity and sublimity of his stile . . . '

They were just as likely to have been impressed by its wit, for so far from being grave and sublime *Agrippina* is a wickedly satirical comedy of sex, politics and female ambition, in which hardly a single character escapes Grimani's barbed pen. The story uses the same protagonists as Monteverdi's more familiar *L'Incoronazione di Poppea* (Seneca is a conspicuous absentee, though maybe the Cardinal had turned over Busenello's libretto) in dealing with the machinations of Agrippina to secure the imperial succession for her son Nero and to thwart the amorous designs of her husband Claudius on Poppea, who is loved by Otho. Throughout the libretto Grimani stresses the atmosphere of conspiracy and intrigue with which he himself was so familiar. Several of the dramatic situations, requiring characters to overhear secrets or to deliver a series of asides, show clear debts to the 'prose' theatre, but a genuine consistency governs the management of plot and participants to the extent that the piece could almost be given independently of its music.

It is to Handel's credit, of course, that this should not be allowed finally to obtrude. The integration of aria and recitative is ideally complete, so that a self-generating momentum is set up from the start. Many of the numbers, besides, are very short and each is perfectly shaped to fulfil a dramatic function. The tiny trio 'E quando mai', which follows on Lesbo's announcement to the startled Claudio and Poppea of Agrippina's impending arrival, is farce *par excellence* and marvellously economical in doing no more than is necessary to create an air of total confusion. Equally just in their positioning are the brief bursts of song, scarcely more than vocal dances, with which Agrippina, Poppea and Nerone reject the unfortunate Ottone, destined to wander through the opera in an atmosphere of misunderstanding and foiled good intentions.

He is given, in compensation, some of the score's truly eloquent moments, when Handel pauses to dwell upon his integrity, and asks us to do the same as we listen to the flutes and muted violins of 'Vaghe fonti' (Keiser's 'Ruhig sein' again) or the poignant G minor of 'Pur ch'io ti stringa'. Yet it is Agrippina who dominates her own opera, a complete study in power, on whom all the other characters depend, but, for all her resourcefulness, gnawed by continuing doubts, obsessively enjoining everyone to 'follow my advice and you shall prosper', but revealed in her essential weakness in the deliberately formless 'Pensieri voi, mi tormentate', a splendid demonstration of the flexible language of recitative.

Everything in *Agrippina* counts, and we catch, for the first time in Handel's work, that skill in mingling musical idioms of all kinds, from the pompous French overture to the infectious Venetian rhythms of 'Ogni vento'*, which was to become a trademark of his style. Nevertheless, practically every number is a re-creation of something he had written before, so that the entire opera sounds like a guide to Handel's singular memory. His technique of self-borrowing is not the result of a lack of originality. There were some 35 operas yet to spring from his pen, all of them crammed with new melodies. It is rather that he appears to have seen composition in terms of appropriate solutions to the demands of a given circumstance, and to have worked continuously at the fresh application of his initial ideas. Old beginnings and old endings (and one or two of the latter turn up everywhere in his work) do not necessarily enclose the same old in-fillings, and the effect of *Agrippina* on those who have grown familiar with his earlier pieces must inevitably be like that of re-reading a much-loved novel of which we already know the story and can now appreciate the finer touches.

His Venetian triumph did not serve to keep him in Italy, but by any standards it was unforgettable, and must often have consoled him in some of the darker years to follow. As a sardonic footnote, let it be said that Vincenzo Grimani died the following year, loathed by the Neapolitans he governed, who saw a divine portent in the fact that when he touched the miraculous phial of San Gennaro's blood it changed colour and congealed. The day afterwards he was supposed to have fallen ill and languished for five months, but according to Prince Philip of Hesse Darmstadt it was only a fortnight's kidney disease and a stoppage of the bladder.

*Derived from a Roman cantata.

3

Popery in Wit

They did not forget Handel in Italy. Later in the century several of his works found their way there from London. *Rinaldo*, for example, was given at the Palazzo Reale in Naples in 1718, to celebrate the birthday of the Emperor Charles VI, with additional music by the 24-year-old Leonardo Leo, himself destined to influence Handel's operatic style. At Florence, during the early 1770s, two ardent Handelians, Lord Cowper and the Marquis de Ligneville, arranged performances of *Alexander's Feast, Acis and Galatea* and *Messiah*, all in Italian translations, and still later the death of the Empress Maria Luisa, wife of Leopold II, was commemorated by an elegy with music compiled from a variety of Handel's works.

Those who had known him vividly recalled his wit and talent. On 15 February 1711, for example, Prince Ferdinando spoke of him to a group of friends gathered at the Pitti Palace. He wanted to include the *Pianto della Vergine Maria*, which Handel had written two years previously, in the forthcoming Sienese Good Friday celebration: 'His Highness, though he thought it a beautiful piece, considered it at the same time disconnected and rather rough, as he is accustomed to say of music which is not wholly new. . . . Signor Perti then said that the young Saxon would perhaps turn out to be the greatest of them all when he ceases to imitate others in order to compose as quickly as he can. To this Father Cassini rejoined: "I found him a miracle of talent, but altogether too mischievous, as you all say. In this his youth partly absolves him, and the fault will pass quickly enough."'

Handel returned from Italy with Ferdinando's letters of recommendation in his pocket. One was addressed to Prince Carl of Neuburg, Count Palatine and Governor of the Tyrol, and dated 9 November 1709. 'During his stay here,' wrote Ferdinando, 'Georg Friedrich Händel, native of Saxony, has shown himself so endowed with honourable sentiments, civil behaviour, a great gift of languages and a more than ordinary talent for music, that since he has striven to earn my good will, I cannot refrain from trying to procure, on his behalf, the most useful support for him on his return to Germany. More especially, your Highness's favour, destined by the promptings of your lofty genius to honour merit and virtue. . . . ' Handel arrived at Innsbruck in March 1710, but did not stay to court the patronage of Prince Carl, who replied to Ferdinando that though the composer had presented his introduction, 'the aforementioned had no need of my assistance'.

He must already have settled on a destination and a job to go with it. By all accounts it was Ernst August and Baron Kielmansegg, during that first Venetian winter, who suggested Hanover to him, and it was probably their recommendations, rather than Ferdinando's, which he made up his mind to use. He arrived at Hanover some time during the spring of 1710, and though the Elector officially appointed him *Kapellmeister*, with a salary of 1,000 thaler, on 16 June, we find the old Electress Sophia writing to the Queen of Prussia two days earlier: 'Here there is no news save that the Elector has taken into his service a *kapellmeister* named Händel, who plays the harpsichord marvellously to the enjoyment of the Electoral Prince and Princess. He is a good-looking man and the talk is that he was the lover of Victoria.' Both these last comments are worth noting. The first bears out the impression conveyed by the earlier portraits and underlined by George III's German manuscript comment that 'Handel was extremely well built and lacked nothing of manly charm'; the second makes far more convincing the allusion to Vittoria Tarquini by Mainwaring.

The Elector was, of course, later to become our own George I, and the Electoral Prince and Princess who so delighted in Handel's playing would rule as George II and Queen Caroline. Few royal figures of the period have been so deliberately misunderstood as these three, and we are even now moving only very gradually towards a proper appreciation of them as rational, cultivated individuals. The idea of George I as the 'wee Jairman lairdie' of Jacobite propaganda, a boorish Teutonic squire, is no longer tenable when we look closely at the personality and attitudes of this refined, astute and often admirable man, whose mature political awareness earned him the loyalty of his English ministers and the respect of two such bitterly opposed contemporaries as William of Orange and Louis XIV. As for his supposed philistinism, in a court which had nourished Leibnitz, it is enough to dismiss this old *canard* by instancing George's evident delight in his brilliant new *Kapellmeister*, a lifelong enthusiasm.

Like all German courts of the period Hanover gave employment to visiting Italian virtuosi in the various arts, and among the most intriguing of these was the Abbate Agostino Steffani. Born at Castelfranco, already famous for Giorgione, he became a choirboy at St Mark's, Venice, and was ordained in 1682. By then his fame as musician was considerable enough for Duke Ernst August of Hanover to invite him to Germany, and while there Steffani developed his notable talent for diplomacy. He became an important negotiator in the duke's ultimately successful efforts to secure himself an electorate, and, as a familiar presence among the princes of northern Germany, he was later made responsible, as Pope Clement's Vicar Apostolic, for overseeing the welfare of Catholics in the various Protestant states and for sterling attempts to convert various wavering heretic royalties. Despite a handful of illustrious proselytes, he was doomed to almost constant failure in his drive to re-establish a Catholic presence in solidly Lutheran and Calvinist communities (though he did set up a mission in Halle).

As a musician he has justifiably been termed 'the greatest Italian master between Carissimi and Scarlatti' and his truly international experience, studying in Padua, Rome and Munich and visiting the French court, significantly foreshadows Handel's. There is no doubt that he used his enormous musical gifts as a diplomatic passport to places which might otherwise have been more impervious to him. His influence on Handel bit far more deeply than that of any other living Italian musician and a mere glance at one of the operas he wrote during his Munich and Hanover years will show how much, in the shape of melodies, the general layout of arias and the pervasive Gallic accents of music many of whose actual dynamics are written in French, Handel owed to him.

It is possible that Handel and Steffani, who must already have met in Rome, may first have made each other's acquaintance as early as 1703, when the younger composer perhaps paid a brief visit to Hanover on his way to Hamburg. Besides having the obvious advantage of Steffani's commendations, Handel was soon able to show himself an accomplished practitioner of the particular musical form of which the older composer was regarded as master *par excellence* — the vocal duet with continuo accompaniment. Steffani's duets are the classics of the genre, closely rivalled by Franceso Durante's superb improvisatory elaborations of Scarlatti's recitatives, favourites with eighteenth-century singers in need of warming-up exercises. Handel's earliest essays had been composed in Italy and he was to return to the form in the 1740s. It was the Princess Caroline who spurred him to write further duets during his Hanover visits, and another Italian diplomat, Ortensio Mauro, a Veronese in

Venetian service and well regarded as a poet, who supplied him with their witty and polished texts. Their combination of engaging directness, vocal display and effortlessly skilful counterpoint is irresistible, and it seems a pity that they do not more often enter the modern recital repertoire.

We know nothing of Handel's other duties as *Kapellmeister* or of his execution of them. The more we examine the circumstantial details surrounding it the more the appointment comes to seem like an inspired stop-gap on the part of the Elector, probably assisted by the enthusiasm of his son and daughter-in-law, with whom he was still on good terms. This is borne out by his readiness to allow Handel to leave the court almost as soon as he had taken up his position, with the apparent intention of visiting England.

The traditional view that he was invited to London by the Duke of Manchester, who had just returned from an unproductive mission to Venice, is not supported by evidence of further contact between them. Another theory proposes his former Hamburg music pupil Cyril Wyche as having made the suggestion, though it could as easily have been one or other of the various Italian and German musicians then in England to whom his growing reputation had become known. Relations between Hanover and the court of St James's, however, were now closer than ever, albeit on an unofficial level, as Queen Anne, after a dozen unsuccessful pregnancies and the deaths of the hydrocephalic Duke of Gloucester in 1700 and of her husband Prince George eight years later, was now seriously concerned with the impending succession crisis. There was, it is true, no love lost between her and the Hanoverians, and the collapse of the Whig ascendancy following the fall from favour of the Marlboroughs easily exacerbated this, but already shrewder politicians were looking towards Hanover with a view to feathering their nests, while at the same time keeping an eye cocked in the direction of Saint Germain and the Pretender. Politics may thus have swept Handel along; in one form or another they were to dog his English enterprises for the next 30 years.

Before leaving Germany he went south to Halle to visit his mother. 'Her extreme-old age . . . tho it promised him but a melancholy interview, rendered this instance of his duty and regard the more necessary', says Mainwaring. Dorothea Händel was then 59, even by eighteenth-century standards not excessively old. He visited friends and relatives, 'among whom his old Master ZACKAW was by no means forgot', and then set off for Düsseldorf, where he had been invited some months before by the Elector Palatine Johann Wilhelm. The ubiquitous Steffani had for a time acted as Johann Wilhelm's chief minister and had managed to carry the

Palatinate successfully through the toils of the war, now in its ultimate phase. A further recommendation had been made by Ferdinando de' Medici, whose sister Anna Maria was married to the Elector Palatine. Delighted with the young composer, the latter wrote to Florence: 'I have found in the *virtuoso* Georg Friedrich Händel all those singular talents for which he enjoyed a justified place in Y.R.H.'s favour, whose kind letter he has given me. I am, moreover, Y.R.H.'s debtor for the satisfaction I have received from his several weeks' stay here', signing himself 'Your Brother and Servant even in the Grave'.

The years before Handel's arrival in England had seen startling changes in the nature of London's flourishing theatrical life. At the start of the century there were two playhouses open in the city, the Theatre Royal in Drury Lane and the house in Lincoln's Inn Fields. In 1705 a new theatre was built at the bottom of the Haymarket to designs by Sir John Vanbrugh, on a site now partly occupied by New Zealand House and Her Majesty's Theatre. 'Van's tott'ring dome', as Nicholas Rowe called it, was an ambitious affair and the acoustics, according to the sardonic Colley Cibber, were generally inadequate: 'the Tone of a Trumpet, or the Swell of an Eunuch's holding Note, 'tis true, might be sweeten'd by it; but the articulate Sounds of a speaking Voice were drown'd, by the hollow Reverberations of one Word upon another'. This was corrected some four years later, by which time audiences had had ample opportunity to judge both sorts of entertainment in their new setting. Meanwhile opera, for better or worse, had arrived in England and altered the entire spectrum of stage entertainment in the capital.

Its appearance was not altogether a surprise. London audiences had grown increasingly accustomed to musical interpolations in comedy and tragedy performances, and all plays were in any case given with 'act music' designed to cover scene changes, quieten the spectators and introduce the forthcoming stages of the drama. During the 1690s Purcell had brought out his *ambigus* or 'semi-operas', plays heavily larded with dramatic music of the highest calibre, though not all the speaking roles were expected to sing as well. The growing number of young noblemen spending long periods on the continent to complete their education inevitably made for a greater sophistication in the taste of at least one important sector of the metropolitan public. Thus Italian singers and instrumentalists started by degrees to figure in theatrical programmes, and operatic arias were inserted at appropriate moments.

The Queen's Theatre in the Haymarket opened under Vanbrugh's direction on 19 April to a prologue spoken by Anne Bracegirdle, the outstanding actress of her day, written by the royal physician Sir Samuel Garth:

> Your own magnificence you here survey,
> And cars triumphal rise from carts of hay.
> Swains here are taught to hope, and nymphs to fear,
> And big Almanzors fight mock Blenheims here.
> Descending goddesses adorn our scenes,
> And quit their bright abodes for gilt machines.

At the beginning of the year the first opera in the Italian manner to be performed in England had been given at Drury Lane. The text was an English adaptation of Stanzani's *Arsinoe*, originally written in 1677, and the music was provided from various sources by Thomas Clayton, a member of the Queen's band. It is a measure of the naïvety of London audiences that anything so woefully inadequate as *Arsinoe* should have had the success it did. The first run reached 24 performances and a 1706 revival ran to eleven. Neither music nor text achieves memorability, and the success of the piece must have depended largely on its novelty value and the fact that the exceptionally handsome sets were designed by Sir James Thornhill, one of the most accomplished decorative artists of the age.

London had not heard the last of Clayton. Two years later, zealous for the triumph of vernacular opera, Joseph Addison, by now one of the most respected components of the Whig propaganda machine, brought out *Rosamund*, based on the life of Henry II's wretched mistress, to Clayton's settings. Addison's high-flown muse was unsuited to lyric-writing, and matters were made worse by his attempt to imitate the by-now outmoded Venetian habit of introducing low comedy characters. He can hardly be blamed outright for *Rosamund*'s failure (a miserable three-night run) since he seems to have known little about music and the operas he saw on his Italian travels in 1701 included Pollarolo's *Cato Uticense*, another of Matteo Noris's surreal lyric farragos. Ironically, nevertheless, he was able to note among the Venetian theatre poets 'a multitude of particular words that never enter into common discourse. . . . For this reason the Italian Opera seldom sinks into a poorness of language, but amidst all the meanness and familiarity of the thoughts, has something beautiful and sonorous in the expression.'

The *Rosamund* fiasco soured Addison's view of Italian opera for good. His comments, distributed to London breakfast tables in the *Spectator*, set

54

the tone for an opposition to the genre so rootedly English in its xenophobic, philistine simple-mindedness as to have survived in certain quarters almost unchanged to this day. One of the chief objections, in a decade during which Englishmen saw themselves as embattled champions of liberty, was the fairly basic one that it was foreign:

> No more th'Italian squalling tribe admit
> In tongues unknown: 'tis Popery in wit,

wrote Steele, neatly summarizing the common view. Writers, what is more, saw their public being snatched away by the new craze. In a letter to Ambrose Philips, Swift, as proud as other Augustan literary men of not being musical, says: 'The Town is run mad after a new Opera. Poetry and good Sense are dwindling like Echo into Repetition and Voice. Critick Dennis vows to G— these Opera's will be the ruin of the Nation and brings Examples from Antiquity to prove it. A good old Lady five miles out of Town askt me tother day, what these Uproars were that her Daughter was always going to.'

High-minded and humourless, John Dennis pitched into opera with a blinding obtuseness. It could not, he said, 'inspire publick Spirit and publick Virtue, and elevated Notions of Liberty'. Music, unless subservient to Reason, encouraged vanity, selfishness and stupidity. Opera was 'Barbarous and Gothick' and unpatriotic. 'If any Yeoman of Kent or Sussex should neglect to sow his Wheat or his Barley, should grub up his Fruit-Trees, and demolish his Hop-Grounds, and fall a planting the Olive of Lucca, the Orange of Naples, and the Muscatello of Monte-Fiascone, or of Mont-Alchin, what would his Neighbours think of such a Proceeding?' — and it promoted homosexuality — '. . . if our Subscriptions go on, at the frantick rate that they have done, I make no doubt but we shall come to see one Beau take another for Better for Worse, as once an imperial harmonious Blockhead did Sporus'.

Heedless of such warnings, the public avidly embraced the new form. The earliest complete Italian opera given in London was Giovanni Bononcini's *Camilla*, originally for Naples to a text by the popular poet Silvio Stampiglia, now translated for the English production. The *buffo* characters Linco and Tullia were retained as roles for the popular playhouse singers Leveridge and Salway (who sang the part *en travesti*) and the opera's triumph was reflected in its 64 performances between 1706 and 1709. An apparently deathless controversy over singing opera in the original language found a compromise in the half-English, half-Italian version of Scarlatti's *Pirrho e Demetrio*, but Italian finally conquered with *Almahide* and *L'Idaspe Fedele*, given at the Queen's Theatre with almost exclusively foreign casts.

By 1710 opera had dug its heels in, and the Haymarket management, after an increasingly acrimonious relationship with the actors which culminated in a dangerous brawl at the theatre door, saw them off to Drury Lane, 'leaving the opera house wholly to the lyric Muse'. The managers themselves cannot have been easy to deal with and the story of the theatre is the classic chronicle of expensive triumphs and ruinous flops, supervised by a bunch of singular 'characters', which has distinguished the running of opera houses throughout the ages. Vanbrugh still had a finger in the pie, having used his influence with Marlborough and the Queen to get rid of the players, but his misgivings had a timeless ring: 'you are sensible the daily Recepts of the Operas are not near sufficient to answer the Daily and monthly demands and whenever they fail there will be a full stop. . . . ' Somebody else who foresaw this was Owen Swiney, an Irishman fluent in Italian and familiar with the unique problems attached to operatic enterprise.

His fellow managers were Aaron Hill and John Jacob Heidegger, both already noted figures in the London of their day. Hill was of an age with Handel, the adventurous son of a Malmesbury lawyer, who had set off, when only fourteen, to visit his cousin Lord Paget, ambassador at Constantinople. Properly respectful of the boy's pluck, Paget sent him to travel through Greece and the Levant. He visited Jerusalem and Mecca, explored the site of ancient Troy, and entered one of the Egyptian pyramids where he was nearly finished off by a party of bandits. Appropriately, he became secretary to the eccentric, schoolboyish Lord Peterborough, daredevil hero of the siege of Barcelona, and followed up a literary career with a series of disastrous moneyspinning projects, including a scheme for making a cheap substitute for almond oil from beechmast, exporting Scotch timber and sinking coal and copper mines. Heidegger, an ex-guards officer known as 'the Swiss Count', was as famous for his entrepreneurial flair as for his villainous looks (Mrs Delany called him 'the most ugly man that ever was formed' and he was a favourite butt for caricaturists). Among impresarios he was destined to loom the largest in Handel's career.

Vanbrugh's warning note to Coke, the Lord Chamberlain, about the likelihood of 'a full stop' was borne out by Swiney's own calculations of the expense of mounting an operatic production. Singers and dancers were rated at £44. 17s. 6d. and the orchestral players were given wages totalling £17. 'Office Keepers & Attend^s–.' took £9. 19s. 2d. and £6 was laid out on candles and wax lights. A guinea on 'oil' was presumably for the special-effect lighting which was occasionally needed. The printer had to be paid for the word-books, handbills and tickets, and the managers themselves took the modest fee of £8. 5s. The entire sum for a single performance was estimated at £110. 17s. 6d., a staggeringly expensive outlay for the period. Given this, and the continuing need to retain a public 'among the better sort of people' by the engagement of expensive foreign stars, it is hardly surprising that none of the three managers lasted the course for very long.

Handel's arrival in the autumn of 1710 was at any rate calculated to provide the Haymarket with a box office novelty. If the interpolation of the Corellian 'Ho un non so che nel cor' from *Agrippina* into a *Pirro e Demetrio* performance on 6 December was meant as advance publicity, then it apparently succeeded. Evidently raring for an opera, Handel fastened eagerly on the text supplied by Hill, and a new piece, *Rinaldo*, the first Italian lyric drama expressly composed for the London stage, was completed by the middle of February 1711. The story, based on an episode in Tasso's *Gerusalemme Liberata*, in which Rinaldo is freed from the amorous snares of the sorceress Armida, was sketched out by Hill as the basis for an Italian libretto by Giacomo Rossi, one of the theatre's staff poets. Hill himself provided a verse translation, for whose inconsistencies he offered the lame excuse that ''tis for want of Power to reach the force of his Original'.

According to Rossi, Handel, 'the Orpheus of our century', knocked up *Rinaldo* in two weeks, at a speed which hardly gave him time to supply the text to order. Tickets and word-books were sold at White's Coffee House in St James's Street, a leading Whig forum patronized by Addison and his cronies, and on Saturday 24 February the first performance took place.

It could scarcely have failed to be a hit. The cast, besides Giuseppe Maria Boschi and his wife, whom we have already met with in Italy, and Elisabetta Pilotti, whom Handel had known in Hanover, included Niccolo Grimaldi, 'Nicolini', as the eponymous hero, one of the century's finest singing actors. Born in Naples and early employed in the Royal Chapel, he starred in three of Scarlatti's most successful operas and went on to spectacular triumphs in Bologna and Venice. He arrived in London in 1708 and gained instant popularity for the extraordinary grace and dignity of his stage presence. Steel, who saw him in *Pirro e Demetrio*, could not forbear praising him. 'Every limb and every finger,' he wrote, 'contributes to the part he acts, inasmuch that a deaf man may go along with him in the sense of it. There is scarce a beautiful posture in an old statue that he does not plant himself in, as the different circumstances of the story give occasion for it.' Even more striking was his combat with a lion in Mancini's *L'Idaspe fedele*, the singer having apostrophized the brute in an aria 'Monstro crudel, che fai?'. This frequently got an encore, and the lion, admired by one foreign visitor because his human hands and feet were properly concealed, had to live to fight another day, like the dragon in a mummers' play. Addison thought it all very silly and unworthy of Nicolini's talents, but Mary Wortley Montagu particularly commended the way that he 'represented nakedness so naturally'.

Rinaldo's success was not solely due to its exceptional cast. Hill had recently made some technical improvements to the Queen's Theatre stage and the results were evidently meant to figure in the performances. The *Spectator* found the opportunities for ridicule irresistible: 'the Opera of *Rinaldo* is filled with Thunder and Lightning, Illuminations and Fireworks; which the Audience may look upon without catching Cold, and indeed without much Danger of being burnt; for there are several Engines filled with Water, and ready to play at a Minute's Warning, in case any such Accident should happen.' Steele and Addison recommended Hill to insure the theatre and poked fun at the promises made in his printed stage directions which the *mise-en-scène* failed to carry out. There was no chariot with white horses for the pagan champion Argante, and the live sparrows and chaffinches in the 'delightful Grove' of Act I flew out into the pit and shat upon the audience, while inefficient stagehands forgot to move the wing flats, so that the sea suddenly appeared among the trees and Steele saw 'a well-dressed young Fellow, in a full-bottom'd Wigg . . . without any visible Concern taking Snuff'.

But London was well pleased, and the piece, which was given several subsequent revivals, became a firm favourite. It is not hard to see why. Though nearly all the music is drawn from earlier works (the famous sarabande 'Lascia ch'io pianga', for instance, began life as 'Lascia la spina' in *Il Trionfo del Tempo*) the effects of Handel's re-cycling are cleverly calculated throughout, and it is important to realize that, as far as English audiences were concerned, this was new music in the newest style, designed to show the young composer's technical and dramatic ranges at their most expansive. The libretto, although far removed from Tasso's Mannerist gravities in its primitive array of sensational set-pieces, at least helped Handel to achieve this as directly as possible, and it is precisely this quality of immediacy which makes the opera among his most attractive.

For *Rinaldo* is hardly to be compared as a unified dramatic organism with such later masterpieces as *Rodelinda* or *Orlando*, or even with the earlier *Agrippina*. It contains a string of magnificent numbers, from 'Cara sposa', 'one of the best airs in that style that was ever composed by himself or any other master, and by many degrees the most pathetic song, and with the richest accompaniment, which had then been heard in England', the ideal utterance of intensely private grief, through the wrily comic lovers' tiffs of the warrior Argante and the sorceress Armida, to the pantomime episodes of battle, magic and mythology, with seductive sirens, fire-breathing dragons, 'ugly spirits' and parading armies. Yet the music, owing perhaps to the uses Handel has already made of it, never seems wholly involved with the text, either as something arising quite naturally and necessarily from a given situation or as an element supplying a needful momentum.

With the exception of Armida and Argante, who bring a species of crude energy to all their scenes, the characters are conventional enough, yet theirs is the charming woodenness of the Sicilian puppet plays based, like Rinaldo, on Italian Renaissance epics. If Handel explores no profundities here, he shows in recompense an unflagging inventiveness, consolidating upon that sense of theatre he had developed in *Agrippina*, for which the opera's triumph was a well-merited reward.

Performances went on at intervals till the end of May, the later ones apparently at the desire of various aristocratic theatre patrons. *Rinaldo* was printed by the firm of Walsh and Hare, the first major work of Handel's to appear in England and foreshadowing a later publishing connexion which was to last until the composer's death. The third issue of '*All the Songs set to Musick in the last new Opera call'd Rinaldo*' contained Handel's own harpsichord ritornellos to Armida's aria 'Vo' far guerra' concluding Act II. Six years afterwards the orchestra bassoonist William Babell had grown so impressed by the composer's keyboard improvisations at the various revivals that he published a reconstruction of them (Burney dismisses it as 'wire-drawing the favourite songs . . . into showy and brilliant lessons') which is perhaps the nearest we shall ever come to appreciating the impact made by Handel as an instrumental performer.

The obligatory return to Hanover can scarcely have been made with much willingness. At Düsseldorf, Elector Johann Wilhelm, reluctant to let Handel go, apologized to George and made doubly sure by sending the composer with a similarly contrite note to the old Electress Sophia. The music-loving John Hughes, friend of Pope and Gay, had made himself known to Handel in London, and now he was asked, through a mutual acquaintance, the German Andreas Roner, to send him an English poem to set. 'Since I left you,' wrote Handel to Roner, 'I have made some progress in that language.' Two surviving arias from Hughes's cantata *Venus and Adonis* must represent his first setting of English words. A visit to Halle in November coincided with his niece's christening; she was given the names Johanna Friderica and her uncle 'Herr Georg Friedrich Händel, Court *Kapellmeister* to the Elector of Hanover' was one of the godparents (since another was called Friderica Amalia Schwartz von Oppin, the baby was probably given her second name with this in mind).

English musical patriotism, meanwhile, was having a final fling with a series of *Spectator* advertisements by the egregious Clayton, aided by his fellow musicians Nicola Haym and Charles Dieupart, who ought to have known better, for 'exhibiting Entertainments of Musick in *York Buildings*'. Despite its fine painted ceiling by Verrio, York Buildings, south of the Strand, was more like a circus than a concert room, its programmes enlivened by diversions such as 'an extraordinary Performance on the Manag'd Horse by the greatest Master of the Age, exceeding whatever has been done by any other, especially his resting on one hand with his whole Body extended, while he drinks several Glasses of Wine, and then throwing himself a Somerset over the Horse's head. And the most excellent Danceing on the Rope with and without a Pole, by the two famous French Maids.' Steele had begun a disastrous two-year tenure in 1710 and the note of hectoring desperation in the advertisements of which he was probably the author is quite understandable. The scheme foundered, foreigners were here to stay, and Handel came back to London in the autumn of 1712.

His new opera for that season, finished on 24 October, was a musical version of Guarini's classic Italian pastoral *Il Pastor Fido*. The genre held an enduring popularity among the English, though it was already in the process of transforming itself into something altogether less artificial and more directly related to modern rural life, in works such as Gay's burlesque *The Shepherd's Week* or Somerville's *Hobbinol*. Of Handel's two surviving essays in dramatic pastoral, the one, *Acis and Galatea*, is as full-blooded as the other, *Il Pastor Fido*, is generally vapid.

Various modern revivals have enabled us to see that the fault does not lie wholly with the composer. Though several of the arias are based on music from the Italian years (Eurilla's 'Di goder il bel ch'adoro' is the last number of the cantata 'Tu fedel, tu costante') and the by now rather hoary favourite 'Ho un non so che nel cor' turns up at the beginning of Act III, a characteristic sensitivity has gone into the creation of a series of rustic miniatures whose lightness of texture is wholly suited to the gauze and

Handel painted by Balthazar Denner, 1721

The 1st Duke of Chandos, *c.* 1730–40. Attributed to H. van der Myn

tinsel of romantic tragi-comedy. At least six numbers are accompanied by figured bass alone, contrasted attractively with others using flutes, paired oboes, solo violin and pizzicato strings. By such skilful variations in the weight of his accompaniments Handel is able to make an effective differentiation between the various pastoral stereotypes. Dorinda and Silvio, the soubrette couple, are slenderly supported throughout, either by a simple bass or unison violins. Mirtillo alternates between the continuo and the full band. Amarilli, with whom the Act III duet finally unites him, achieves deepening perspective culminating in her sustained G major outburst 'No! non basta un infedele', but much of the best music goes to the scheming Eurilla, whose 'Ritorna adesso Amor', an elegantly scrupulous piece of fuguing, is a splash of Handelian academic wit.

Francis Colman, later English envoy at Florence and a useful Italian contact for Handel, saw the 'New Pastorall Opera called the Faithfull Shepherd' at its second performance on 26 November 1712, and noted curtly: 'The Scene represented only ye Country of Arcadia. ye Habits were old. — ye Opera Short.' Pilotti and Valentini starred once more, and Handel's company was joined by Valeriano Pellegrini (the creator of Nerone in *Agrippina*) and Margherita L'Epine as Eurilla. Known as 'Signora Margherita' or 'Greber's Peg' from her association with a German impresario, she was notorious for having seduced Lord Nottingham, First Lord of the Admiralty, so successfully that, according to one epigrammatist:

> Treaties unfinish'd in the office sleep
> And Shovel yawns for orders on the deep.

Later on she settled down to a happy marriage with Johann Christoph Pepusch, who nicknamed her Hecate for her swarthy complexion.

The excellent overture, one of Handel's longest and really an orchestral suite, at once became popular, but *Il Pastor Fido* had thin houses, and it was time for something altogether more spectacular to bring back the audiences. Somebody hit on the ambitious project of staging an Italianized version of Philippe Quinault's five-act *tragédie lyrique Tésée*, written for Lully at Versailles in 1675. As far as the staging was concerned the piece, loosely based on the story of Theseus and Medea and introducing a companion pair of lovers Arcane and Clitia offered splendid opportunities for mechanical effects and handsome costumes, but to adapt anything so diffuse as a French lyric drama to the conditions of Italian opera proved too much for Handel's librettist, Nicola Haym, and for Handel himself. While Haym occasionally cut out pieces of Quinault's original text upon which a clear appreciation of the dialogue depends, Handel impatiently lopped chunks from Haym's version in his efforts to mould the thing into as manageable a form as possible.

Handel's only essay in five-act structure, *Teseo* is archetypally the work of a young experimenter. Despite the intrinsic delights of individual arias, an uneven concentration of plot and character interests and the overall lack of unity created by the very nature of the libretto hardly make for effective balance. Burney, however, rightly emphasizes the 'bold and piquant' quality of the overture, 'which must have been very new at this time to all ears but those accustomed to the cantatas of the elder Scarlatti'. Such novelty is further reflected in a sort of French accent which transcends the opera's origins, with aria and arioso here and there integrated with recitative to form scenes whose continuity recalls Lully and Charpentier.

The opera's outcome is resolved by the comparatively rare appearance in Handel's work of a *dea ex machina* in the shape of the goddess Minerva. Much of the glory of the first night, however, must have been reaped by the orchestra, for whom the score provides a real feast. For most of the instruments (though not, interestingly, the violin) it is a sustained technical display. Nine arias have oboe solos, Agilea's 'Deh! v'aprite' has exquisitely sensuous writing for flutes over a drone, there are divided violas in Medea's quarrel duet with Egeo and the strings throughout are handled with consummate delicacy and verve.

'A New Opera, Heroick, all ye Habits new & richer than ye former with 4 New Scenes, & other Decorations & Machines', is Colman's description of *Teseo*. It was plainly Owen Swiney's last desperate shift as theatre manager, but his attempt to secure the tottering Haymarket finances with a subscription scheme foundered and he had to be content with tickets at half a guinea each. 'After these Two Nights' (the première was on 10 January) 'Mr Swiny Brakes & runs away & leaves ye Singers unpaid ye Scenes & Habits also unpaid for. The Singers were in Some confusion but at last concluded to go on with ye operas on their own accounts, & divided ye Gain amongst them.'

Swiney's panic is entirely forgivable. He was not a bad fellow, as Handel must have known, as they kept in touch after he had levanted to Italy with the Haymarket funds and become an entrepreneur in deals with such painters as Canaletto. In 1735 he was allowed to return to England, having changed his name to the more obviously Hibernian MacSwiney, was given a couple of sinecures to keep him going and became the patron of the actress Peg Woffington.

The gallant musicians' collective advertised further performances of 'the Opera of Theseus composed by Mr Handel' in the *Daily Courant*: 'the Performers are much concerned that they did not give the Nobility and Gentry all the Satisfaction they could have wished, when they represented it on Wednesday last, having been hindered by some unforeseen Accidents at that time insurmountable'. Heidegger stepped in as manager to check the accounts and detail the payments, but the company's state of affairs was made clear in his dedication to Lord Lonsdale of the libretto of the pasticcio *Ernelinda* given during February, where he speaks of 'a time when we labour under so many unhappy circumstances. . . . By these means, we may retrieve the reputation of our affairs, and in a short time rival the stage of Italy.' There were the inevitable *Rinaldo* nights and *Teseo* had a revival in May with the bonus of 'an Entertainment for the Harpsichord, Compos'd by Mr Hendel on purpose for that Day'.

Handel got a benefit on the season's last evening, from which, as Heidegger's accounts show, he made £73. 10s. 11d. During the previous two seasons he had received a total payment of £811 and his overall gains in 1713 were £430. There was nothing specially disappointing about this, but Swiney's absconding and 'the poor proceedings at the Haymarket' in general offered a bleak prospect for any further operatic ventures in London under the existing system.

Nevertheless the taste had caught on. New, expensive and foreign, dealing with a world of broad gesture and emotion, shamelessly exploiting versatility and display, opera was bound to appeal most of all to the aristocracy, many of whom had already sampled it on their Italian travels and who were able to retain performers and composers in their households. However, attractive though the notion is of a Handel opera written for private performance, there is no solid evidence to support the recently canvassed theory, based on Giacomo Rossi's dedication of its printed libretto, that *Lucio Cornelio Silla* was given at Burlington House. Probably planned for the King's Theatre, it seems never actually to have taken the stage.

Rossi's text, based on incidents in the life of Silla, is, to say the least, unsatisfactory. Much of the dictator's time is spent in making inept sexual assaults, on Celia, during which he is intercepted by his wife Metella, and on Flavia, who is temporarily saved by the intervention of four ghosts who replace Silla's statue with a cypress tree, only to be groped at once again and rescued finally by Lepido with a drawn sword (though Silla promptly has him arrested). None of the *dramatis personae* is given time in which to develop, though Handel shows his unrivalled ability to display complete empathy with his characters in numbers such as Claudio's tiny eighteen-bar aria as he is about to be thrown into a cage full of wild beasts or in the central duet in which Flavia and Lepido declare their love for one another. The music for the opening triumph scene, with Silla being drawn in a chariot by black slaves to the sound of *stromenti militari*, has disappeared (if it ever existed) and a storm at sea, during which the eponymous hero swims to safety, exists merely as a stage direction between two bars of recitative.

Though *Silla* may not after all have been performed at Burlington House, it was as a guest of Lord Burlington that Handel now lived for the next three or four years. Richard Boyle had succeeded his father in the earldom (together with that of Cork) in 1703 at the age of eight, and carried the family penchant for intellectual pursuits to a degree which made him one of the most noted patrons and connoisseurs of the age. His avid enthusiasm for architecture left a permanent impression on trends in English design, though his submission of a set of unrealized plans by Palladio to the aldermen of the City as a potential Mansion House was rebuffed with the amazing but wholly characteristic objection that as there was no evidence that the great Italian architect had ever been a freeman of London they could not possibly consider him. Burlington's immense wealth, what is more, made him lavish of hospitality to artists and men of letters, including Alexander Pope and Queen Anne's doctor, John Arbuthnot, as well as the feckless but charming John Gay, who, having overstayed his welcome and fallen ill into the bargain, was once discovered by Arbuthnot, on a visit to the earl, gnawing his poultice for sustenance.

In happier times Gay brought Burlington House into his *Trivia: or the Art of Walking the Streets of London*:

> There Hendel strikes the Strings, the melting Strain
> Transports the Soul, and thrills through ev'ry Vein;
> There oft I enter (but with cleaner Shoes)
> For Burlington's belov'd by every Muse.

The earl's penchant for music, however sincere, seems to have been merely a part of his eager assumption of his role of the Man of Taste. Handel in 1713 was new and exciting, but we must recall that it was Burlington who, after his Italian tour the following year, was instrumental in cultivating a taste for Bonocini, Handel's competitor at the Haymarket, and who was one of the first to desert his former protégé when the Opera of the Nobility was set on foot in 1733.

For the moment the composer was secure in the young peer's approbation. Their relationship seems not to have been the traditional one of patron and house musician; Handel, so far as is known, maintained as much independence as he was able during this period and his association with Lord Carnarvon's household which followed it. Burlington House, in which, according to an unsubstantiated tradition, he occupied a room looking out into grounds soon to be laid out as Cork Street, Old Burlington Street and Burlington Gardens, offered a congenial atmosphere in which to complete his next opera, *Amadigi di Gaula*, brought out on 25 May 1715 (Heidegger's dedication to the earl notes that 'this Opera more immediately claims Your Protection, as it is compos'd in Your own Family).'

The author of the actual Italian text remains unknown, but since the source is yet another French *tragédie lyrique*, Houdar de la Motte's *Amadis de Grèce*, originally set by André Destouches and first performed in 1699, the adaptation was probably the work of Nicola Haym. Once again magic, romance and the figure of a jealous sorceress play their part, and Heidegger was evidently looking to the trusted formulas of *Rinaldo* and *Teseo* to shore up the uncertain fortunes of the King's Theatre. Leading the cast (with five characters the smallest of any Handel opera) was Elisabetta Pilotti, repeating her triumphs as Armida and Medea in the role of the enchantress Melissa, but the work met with an unexpected check to success in the outbreak of the Jacobite rising in Scotland during the summer of 1715. 'No Opera performed since ye 23 July, ye Rebellion of ye Tories and Papists being ye cause,' noted Francis Colman, ' — ye King and Court not liking to go into such Crowds these troublesom times.' Engaged in quelling the Old Pretender's ill-starred attempt to recover his father's kingdom were soldiers such as John Duke of Argyle and Generals Wade and Dormer who were later to be associated with Handel's musical ventures, while at Hamburg Mattheson, in his capacity as secretary to the English Resident, was busy searching Scotch ships for suspect cargo. *Amadigi* was thus not revived until the following year and given further performances in 1717, after which it was not heard again until the present century and remained among comparatively few Handel operas whose 'favourite songs' were never published.

Such neglect is unjust, for though *Amadigi* is no masterpiece it represents a more cohesive attempt than *Teseo* to reconcile French and Italian styles in its dramatic layout, and the pronounced Gallic accents of

Handel's music often have a more than simply coincidental appropriateness. The plot, based on one of those old Spanish knightly romances beloved of Don Quixote and involving the machinations of Dardano and Melissa to frustrate the union of Amadigi with princess Oriana, offers little chance for subtle characterization but plenty of occasion for colourful alternations of mood. Handel was again able to flourish his orchestral palette to powerful effect in numbers featuring solo trumpet, oboe, recorders and bassoons. The work is tonally dominated by flat keys, to the extent that from the overture to the end of the first act only two out of thirteen numbers break with this, and C minor, G minor, B flat and E flat major continue preponderant in Acts II and III.

Mechanical as the reflexes of its plot and characters appear, *Amadigi* provides an excellent illustration of the ideal functioning of the Baroque recitative-and-aria form in the hands of a master. Take, for example, the sequence which opens Act II. Amadigi, searching for Oriana, gazes into the waters of True Love to examine her faith. His F major air, accompanied by paired recorders, suggests that in the end it is less Oriana's constancy which preoccupies him than his own solitude. There is no middle section, for he is jerked back into the present by a vision of her making up to Dardano, and faints with half the word *moro* ('I die') still on his lips. Melissa, stirring the pot avidly, commands her attendant spirits to bring in Oriana, who, believing her lover dead, throws herself into one of those F minor outbursts Handel saves for special moments of anguish. The resulting tiff when Amadigi awakes leads naturally into an air whose alternation of slow and fast tempi reflects his muddled state of mind. Oriana ripostes in an impatient accusation of injustice, and Melissa's eager attempts to make capital out of the situation after her rival has left the stage are furiously rebuffed by Amadigi. 'Let me die, I don't love you,' he cries, whipping up her anger by his scorn. The duet which follows, edgily patterned with dotted quavers, is the inevitable outpouring of their rage at each other. In the face of dramatic music of this calibre, can it still be said that nothing happens in a Handel aria? So far from invalidating the form, its very artifice enhances its supreme ability to communicate the atmosphere of those all-too-familiar moments when civilized human beings are driven to break out of their emotional reserve.

The 1716 season ended with an *Amadigi* performance on 12 July, featuring a solo on the viola d'amore played by Attilio Ariosti, later to join Handel as composer of the King's Theatre operas, following which Handel himself left for a trip to Germany. He visited his family and friends at Halle and went on to Ansbach, apparently charged with a mission by the Princess of Wales, who perhaps thought to find in him another Agostino Steffani, though the nature of his errand is unknown. Doubtless it was while on this journey that he came across the text of the Passion oratorio *Der für die Sünden der Welt gemartete und sterbende Jesus* (Jesus martyred and dying for the sins of the World) by the Hamburg littérateur Barthold Heinrich Brockes, subsequently made a senator of the city and highly regarded throughout the Germany of his age as a gifted poet and translator. His Passion drama, an alternation of biblical paraphrase, highly coloured reflective aria and arioso verses and *turba* (crowd) choruses and chorales, with inset recitative and air sequences designated as *soliloquia*, was first published in 1712 and soon became a favourite with German composers during the next three decades. Bach himself incorporated sections of it in the *St John Passion*, and complete settings were made by Telemann, Mattheson, Fasch and Stolzel.

Part of its appeal lay in the flamboyantly dramatic imagery employed by Brockes as a sort of literary homage to the seventeenth-century Italian poets he so admired. His conceits, belonging to a vanished early Baroque world, seem to have left Handel comparatively cold, however, when he embarked on his version of the *Brockes Passion* at some stage between 1716 and 1717. As with the *Chandos Anthems* in certain of their aspects, he appears curiously unmanned by the nature of the work. Where we might expect the chorus to receive the kind of treatment afforded it in pieces such as the *Utrecht Te Deum* or the *Dixit Dominus*, its role is reduced to relative insignificance by the brevity of the *turba* moments and the plainness of the chorales. The contemplative soloists, Daughter of Sion and a trio of Believing Souls, are given arias of accomplished but faceless character, essentially operatic in feeling to the extent that we should hardly have guessed them, save on a purely technical basis, to be the work of the man who wrote *Messiah* and *Israel in Egypt*. Only with Jesus, Peter and Judas does Handel respond to emotions of agony and guilt with music of genuine substance, as in Peter's contrasted meditations on his denial in 'Heul, du Schaum' and 'Schau, ich fall', and in Christ's 'Mein Vater, mein Vater', its vocal line carried on a typically Handelian dotted accompaniment.

Highly finished and yet somewhat aimless as the piece now seems, it achieved considerable popularity in north Germany after its first performance under Mattheson's direction in Hamburg on the Monday of Holy Week (Handel had sent him the 'unusually close-written score' from London) and Bach himself copied out part of it in manuscript. Facile assumptions as to an absence of some sort of nebulously conceived 'spirituality' in Handel are too easily made by comparing the *Brockes Passion* with the two masterpieces in the same genre of his great contemporary. That the former work should come off very much the loser means nothing in the face of that encyclopaedic analysis of human spiritual experience, complete with its doubts and terrors, manifested to us by the oratorios and (paradoxically, some may feel) the operas. Handel's study, scarcely an unworthy one by any standards, was the compassionate scrutiny of his fellow men.

4

Noble Oratories

The musical London in which Handel arrived in 1710 was far from being the desert that has occasionally been portrayed. True, the death of Purcell in 1695 had deprived English music of a central figure, versatile, prolific and highly regarded by his contemporaries, to whom he seems to have given the kind of co-ordinating inspiration which was only to be renewed by Handel himself. But as the seat of a royal court and noble patrons, a flourishing centre of church music and host to a lively tradition of amateur performance, London could hardly be considered a dull or backward capital.

Among the official musicians at court and in the Chapel Royal were several whose distinction was likely to have commended them to any composer such as Handel, in search of competent and experienced professionals. The worthiest of these was William Croft, an ex-chorister of the Chapel and a protégé of Purcell's mentor John Blow. In 1708, following Blow's death, Croft had been made Master of the Children of the Chapel Royal and organist of Westminster Abbey, which meant that he had to provide music for all the various state occasions celebrated by the court. Though he notably lacked a melodic gift, his anthems and keyboard music show a lucidity and expansiveness of design unrivalled by any of his English contemporaries.

He clearly took his functions as teacher, composer and performer very seriously, which is more than can be said for the eccentric, though undeniably talented John Eccles, who had been made Master of Music by King William in 1700. He had started as a sympathetic song-writer for the actress Anne Bracegirdle, who appointed him her music director at Lincoln's Inn Fields theatre, and had joined Daniel Purcell, John Weldon (candidate for authorship of 'Purcell's' *Tempest* music) and Gottfried Finger, who had done so much to promote new instrumental styles among English players, in a competition for setting Congreve's *The Judgment of Paris*. Two hundred guineas was divided among the competitors, Weldon being the winner, Eccles runner-up, Daniel Purcell third, and Finger a disgruntled fourth who promptly left England in justifiable chagrin. It was Eccles who provided the earliest setting of Congreve's *Semele*, later to be treated more elaborately by Handel. Though it may have been planned as an inaugural spectacle at the opening of the Queen's Theatre, Haymarket, in 1705, the composer did not complete it till two years later and it was never performed.*

Linked with the world of court and theatre music was the more obviously social pleasure of the various concert clubs. Following the lead given by promoters like John Banister, with his curtained music gallery in a large room opposite the back gate of the Temple, the vogue for convivial meetings at which the players were a mixture of well-known professionals and talented amateurs quickly became an established feature of London life. Many of the concerts took place at taverns, such as the Angel & Crown in Whitechapel, the Devil near Temple Bar, and the Castle in Paternoster Row. Such was the enthusiasm that several private individuals threw open their doors for music meetings, including the printer William Caslon, whose houses in Ironmonger Row and Chiswell Street were the venue of the 'Lunatics', so called because their concerts took place on the Thursdays nearest the full moon, so that the guests could walk home in safety. 'In the intervals of the performance the guests refreshed themselves at a sideboard, which was amply furnished; and when it was over, sitting down to a bottle of wine, and a decanter of excellent ale, of Mr Caslon's own brewing, they concluded the evening's entertainment with a song or two of Purcell's sung to the harpsichord, or a few catches, and about twelve retired.'

The most remarkable of all these regular meetings were those taking place in the house of Thomas Britton 'the musical small-coal man' in a house in Aylesbury Street, off Clerkenwell Green. Encouraged by that Royalist Methuselah Sir Roger L'Estrange, 'a very musical gentleman, and who had a tolerable perfection on the bass viol', Britton, who dealt in coal from the ground floor, turned the upper storey into a concert room notoriously long and narrow and reached by some rickety stairs. In a tiny and highly effervescent artistic community like that of eighteenth-century London, Britton's meetings, featuring the finest musical hands in the city, attracted a glittering patronage: among others, 'a lady of the first rank in this kingdom, the Duchess of Queensberry, now living, one of the most

*The jaundiced Eccles retired to Hampton Wick, where he took up fishing, cut off his daughters with a shilling and left his estate to his housemaid.

celebrated beauties of her time, may yet remember that in the pleasure which she manifested at hearing Mr Britton's concert, she seemed to have forgotten the difficulty with which she ascended the steps that led to it'.

Handel himself is said to have taken part in Britton's concerts, and among the performers were several who became his friends. John Hughes, who had supplied him with cantata texts, played in the band and so did Henry Needler, civil servant and violinist, instrumental in popularizing Corelli's concertos in England. The great fiddle virtuoso Matthew Dubourg, who was to lead the orchestra at the first performance of *Messiah*, played his first solo in Britton's concert room, a small boy standing on a joint-stool.

Not far away, within the City itself, music of a different kind was offered. The new cathedral of St Paul's, still incomplete and the centre of heated controversy between the various parties involved in the rebuilding, boasted a splendid organ, and Handel, attending evensong, used to stay behind to play on it himself. Afterwards he and the choir lay vicars would adjourn to the nearby Queen's Arms in St Paul's Churchyard, a tavern which, like so many others in London, maintained a harpsichord for its patrons. 'It happened one afternoon, when they were thus met together, Mr Weely, a gentleman of the choir, came in and informed them that Mr Mattheson's lessons were then to be had at Mr Meares's shop; upon which Mr Handel ordered them immediately to be sent for, and upon their being brought, played them all over without rising from the instrument' — a moment of very Handelian impetuosity.

Samuel Wheeley, the bass lay vicar who brought the news to the company at the Queen's Arms, was already well known to Handel, who had made use of him in his first major work to an English text, the Birthday Ode, *Eternal Source of Light Divine*, designed for performance at court on 6 February 1713. Lovers of English Baroque music in general will be familiar with this annual custom, which was allowed to die only during the latter part of the eighteenth century, and which produced, amid much that was trivial and sycophantic, some splendidly imaginative solutions to the problem of having annually to reassure the monarch that his or her existence was a thing to be treasured by mortals and by gods. The effect of the birthday odes is somewhat like the work of contemporary fresco painters such as Thornhill, Verrio and Laguerre, splashy, over-blown and surreal in its degrees of flattery.

Queen Anne's birthday odes had mostly been supplied by John Eccles, who presumably left off fishing in order to earn his keep. The texts were generally provided by the poet laureate Nahum Tate, best known as writer of the excellent libretto for *Dido and Aeneas*. Before Handel's the last ode had been provided for 1711: there had been no 1712 ode, perhaps because the queen was too busy on her birthday welcoming her cousin Eugene of Savoy. No one knows why Handel should have been selected for the unique contribution of 1713. Though the queen was not noted as a practical musician she had all her family's love of music, and, given Handel's rising popularity among her courtiers, may have wanted something of his for herself. His recommendation might also, like the *Silla* commission four months later, have had faintly political overtones.

Tate was not asked for the ode that year. According to Charles Jennens, arranger of *Messiah*'s text, the author of the seven stanzas, each ending:

> The day that gave great Anna birth,
> Who fix'd a lasting peace on earth

was Ambrose Philips, author of the successful tragedy *The Distrest Mother*, of a series of pallid neo-Spenserian pastorals, and of that truly ineffable line 'O Property, thou goddess English-born!'. A zealous Whig in the Addison circle, he seems rather an odd candidate for making a triumphant Tory proclamation of the virtues of a peace with France.* Still, Philips was the original half-crown hack, and the style of the piece is not unlike that of his other poems. The birds are called upon to pay 'their winged homage', the beasts, in a singular fling of impiety, are made to renounce their natural instincts, Envy conceals her head, blasted faction glides away, and united nations combine to convey to distant climes the news that 'Anna's actions are divine'.

Philips's allusion to 'Kind Health' bringing new life to the queen is highly topical, since she was severely ill during early February 1713, with a renewed attack of the chronic gout which, culminating in acute erysipelas, carried her off in the summer of the following year. If she ever heard Handel's ode it was not on her birthday; she may indeed never have heard it at all. The names of the singers sketched in by the composer indicate an exceptional line-up. Joining Wheeley as bass soloist was Bernard Gates, later master of the Chapel Royal children and notorious for his extravagant vocal shakes, the altos were Hughes, who had taken a leading role in *Arsinoe*, and Elford, who was so good that £100 had been added to

---

*By no special accident, indeed, the current East German edition of the piece has transmuted it easily into a *Friedensode*, banishing all mentions of the sovereign.

his Chapel Royal salary, and the soprano and contralto were Anastasia Robinson, later a Handel opera star, and Mrs Barbier, who had sung in *Il Pastor Fido* and *Teseo*.

Philips had no doubt imagined, in writing the ode, that Handel would set the two-line refrain of each stanza to the same music throughout. In fact the skill with which the composer varies his treatment of it at each appearance is one of the noteworthy features of this charming and thoroughly accomplished piece. The sensitivity with which he handled such banal material looks forward to the extraordinary transformations of the Morell oratorio texts of the 1740s. His essentially pictorial imagination fixes on the simplest of images, enriching it with what, for a bare 25 minutes of music, is an astonishing array of textures. The piece's organic quality is enhanced by the scoring; it seems a perfectly logical progression from the translucent opening *largo*, a dialogue between alto and trumpet solos, to the joyous closing antiphonies, in which the trumpet, held back since the first number, returns, and whose double choir effect and reprise of the earlier chorus recall the Venetian *cori spezzati* and the *Sicut erat in principio* trick, surely reflexes from the Italian years.

Much has been made of a Purcellian influence in the Ode, but this is never particularly striking. A glance at Purcell, and at other court composers, perhaps affected the external structure, in Handel's use of interlocked solo and chorus and the dance rhythms, passacaglia, siciliano and minuet, which appear. There are more especially Purcellian touches in his next English piece, written before the Ode but performed after it.

Handel composed the *Utrecht Te Deum and Jubilate* during January 1713. This and the Ode must have been part of a package, both in their different ways intended to celebrate a peace which was almost inevitable, owing largely to the political manoeuvres of the queen's ministers, Oxford and St John, to the successful propaganda of works such as Swift's *Conduct of the Allies*, and to the notably fainéant character of English military commitment in Europe following Marlborough's dismissal. To suggest that Handel was in some way party to secret political developments is a gross exaggeration. It was common knowledge that peace negotiations were pending: the Queen's Speech of 1711 had contained a controversial reference to 'the opening of the Treaty of a general peace' and though the Whigs had initially combined to carry a motion rejecting the proposals, the government finally won through, and the Utrecht conference began on 18 January 1712.

Obviously Handel's brief was to get the *Te Deum* and *Jubilate* ready for the final festivities for the treaty, delay over whose completion involved the queen in repeated proroguings of Parliament. More interesting than speculation over 'Handel-the-secret-agent' is the question, hitherto unresolved, of why, as official *Kapellmeister* to the Elector of Hanover, he should have been involved in writing a work designed to proclaim a political *fait accompli* to which George was openly opposed (his protest had been published in England as early as December 1711). It was a risk Handel was prepared to take in the interests of professional advancement and George's later actions show that he was not inclined to blame him.

The two canticles were given in St Paul's at the thanksgiving service on 5 July. The queen, who had announced the news of the treaty's signing to Parliament on 7 April, did not attend. 'I find myself soe much tyerd with the little fatigue of yesterday,' she wrote to Oxford, 'that it will be impossible for one to undertake that of going to St Paul's; but however I think both Houses should go thither and I will perform my devotions at St James's and be contented without a sermon. It is really very uneasy for me that I cannot go, which I hope all my friends beleeve.'

What the queen did not hear was once again music of tremendous authority and distinction, which must have given substantial pause to the composers present at the occasion. Handel resorted to the comparatively rare expedient in contemporary English church music of introducing oboes and a flute into the score and saving the trumpets and timpani in the *Te Deum*, despite festal associations, for a spectacular appearance some three quarters of the way into the piece. Much more important than these factors, in view of his later development, is his free handling of the chorus. The temptation in both pieces must have been to divide the verses into distinct solo and choral episodes, but in the *Te Deum* Handel avoids this in favour of a far more complex fusion of the two, seen at its best in the cumulative treatment of the several lines in the 'Glorious company of the apostles' section, where the chorus represents 'the holy church throughout all the world' and in the highly dramatic 'When thou took'st upon thee', in which the solo lines jarring and bumping against each other for 'the sharpness of death' are overwhelmed by the choral 'Thou didst open the kingdom of Heaven to all believers'. Thus the choir is a positive participant in a work whose formal aspects strikingly anticipate the world of oratorio.

The commissions for both the Ode and the two canticles were perhaps obtained through the good offices of somebody in the Burlington circle, possibly the dowager countess herself, as one of the bedchamber women who had managed to weather the storms occasioned by the queen's transfer of favour from the Marlboroughs to the Mashams. Anne's granting of a £200 pension to Handel, though a royal breach of the law (foreigners were not permitted to receive such emoluments) was probably not, as has been suggested, a snook cocked at the Elector so much as an oblique compliment to the man on whom the queen had already, in her mind at any rate, settled the succession.

At a quarter to eight in the morning of Sunday 1 August 1714 Queen Anne died, at the age of 49. In the last stages of her long illness, of which Arbuthnot wrote to Swift 'I believe sleep was never more welcome to a weary traveller than death was to her', she had handed the white staff of Lord Treasurer to the Duke of Shrewsbury, a symbolic rebuff to Jacobite hopes. The kingdom was put in readiness to welcome the Elector: the ports were closed, regiments were moved to London and a watch was set on suspected persons, while the horses and arms of Papists throughout the nation were commandeered, a naval squadron was sent to Holland to escort George to his kingdom, and James Craggs, later a secretary of state, was despatched to Hanover with news of the great change.

Nearly every writer on Handel (there are a few honourable exceptions) has made much of the supposed disfavour under which the *Kapellmeister* now laboured with his royal master. The idea that he was compelled to appease George I for having spent some three years away from Hanover is, in fact, pure invention. It has justly been pointed out that economic reasons connected with George's commitment to the war made it necessary for him to reduce the Herrenhausen musical establishment and that there would thus have been little for Handel to do there beyond composing duets for Princess Caroline or writing instrumental pieces. So far indeed was George from begrudging his *Kapellmeister* any English success that he heard a *Te Deum* of Handel's, presumably the so-called 'Caroline', in St James's Chapel on 28 September and commanded (but did not attend) a *Rinaldo* revival on 30 December.

Reconciliation between king and composer took other forms besides. For musical Londoners 1714 was remarkable as the year which brought to England the two star Italian violinists of their generation, Francesco Maria Veracini and Francesco Geminiani. Veracini gave solo performances between the acts at the opera, but his compositions and performing style were not to the audience's taste and he soon left, to return in 1735 as leader of the Haymarket band and composer of various operas, among them an Italianate version of *As You Like It*, which Burney calls 'wild, awkward and unpleasant'. He was a vain and difficult man, with little tolerance of other musicians, but though he criticized Handel he was not ashamed to take part in concerts with him, and the exceptionally full and rewarding Opus I violin sonatas of 1721 have enough in them to suggest that the two masters took due note of each other's work.

Geminiani commanded a comparable respect from string players as the pupil of Corelli's who had most successfully absorbed his teacher's traditions both as player and writer for the instrument. He remained for so long in this country that it is safe to say that no proficient English performer of the period could possibly have disregarded his influence, and his style, as conveyed to orchestral players such as Matthew Dubourg, must directly have conditioned the nature of early performances of Handelian oratorio. In certain respects the music of his sonatas and concertos seems as much a determined effort not to emulate his great German contemporary as to renew Corellian models; such a dogged independence won him the advocacy of Charles Avison, one of Handel's severest critics.

His regard for Handel as a performer, however, was considerable (the two may have met at some stage on the Italian journey) and to the king's request that he give some of his Opus I violin sonatas before a select court audience he assented on condition that Handel was the accompanist. Geminiani's sonatas, published in 1716, were dedicated to Baron Kielmansegg, whose influence with the king owed something to the fact that the Baroness was one of George's two mistresses. The other, on whom he fathered two illegitimate daughters, was Melusine von der Schulenburg, whose younger child Petronilla Melusine, later wife of the letter-writer Lord Chesterfield, was one of Handel's pupils. Thus the composer was directly linked with the court circles of Kensington and St James's, and it comes as no surprise to find the king doubling his pension quite soon after coming to the throne.

Besides producing Handel for Geminiani's recital, Kielmansegg is traditionally credited with having brought about the performance of one of the handful of Handel pieces known to the average concertgoer — *The Water Music*. The old tale has it that George 'forgave' his former *Kapellmeister* after hearing this performed on a river outing to Greenwich. In fact the circumstances surrounding the work's first hearing are far from clear, but a report, in three different forms, shows that a complete performance took place on Wednesday 17 July 1717.

Fond of attending Heidegger's novel if slightly disreputable winter masquerades, which alternated with opera nights during the season, the king had the idea of getting him to provide a summer river concert on a similar subscription basis. Kielmansegg, as intermediary, forced to bring back reasonable economic objections to the scheme from Heidegger, undertook to lay on the entertainment himself, and at eight in the evening the king 'took Water at Whitehall in an open Barge' accompanied by a seraglio of ladies and set off towards Chelsea, followed by a second barge 'wherein were 50 Instruments of all sorts, who play'd all the Way from Lambeth (while the Barges drove with the Tide without Rowing, as far as Chelsea) the finest Symphonies, compos'd express for this Occasion by Mr Hendel; which his Majesty liked so well, that he caus'd it to be plaid over three times in going and returning. At Eleven his Majesty went a-shore at Chelsea, where a Supper was prepar'd, and then there was another very fine Consort of Musick, which lasted till 2; after which, his Majesty came again into his Barge, and return'd the same Way, the Musick continuing to play till he landed.' The musicians alone cost Kielmansegg £150, and his wife was the hostess at the super party at Lady Ranelagh's villa.

The Water Music's Gallic charm has endeared it to twentieth-century listeners largely through the medium of Sir Hamilton Harty's well-known re-orchestrated selection. The complete piece, however, falls into three distinct suites, whose diversity of key and orchestration makes plausible the suggestion that they may have been designed for separate moments during the evening, though finally the whole thing, as we have seen, was played at a stretch and then given twice more. Handel's choice of mood, colour and tonality in these suites creates a potent contrast. King George's cousin, the Duke of Orleans, as a pupil of Marc Antoine Charpentier, had once been given a list of the composer's ideas on tonal 'affects', under the heading '*Energie des Modes*', and it is interesting to match this, as one of many examples of the importance attached to key signature by Baroque musicians, with a piece which, more than many others, shows Handel as 'a complete Monsieur'.

In what is effectively an early example of a *galant* orchestra, horns, oboes and bassoons are blended with strings for the opening group of pieces, in F major. Charpentier thought this key to be '*furieux et emporté*' but any musical carrying-away is with all the serenity appropriate to the royal embarkation. From the outset Handel's matchless delicacy as an orchestrator (a skill which renders the efforts of Beecham, Harty and others to 'enrich' Handel's scores like the labours of cack-handed cooks thickening a savoury stock) makes him alert to the beauties of varied sonority and echo effects in the resonant clarity of a summer evening on the river. For Charpentier D major was '*joyeux et tres guerrier*', and Handel's colourful splash of trumpets, horns, woodwind and strings in the second group must have seemed an entirely suitable tribute to a

77

seasoned campaigner from his master of horse. For the final collection, in G, *doucement joyeux* is the perfect definition. With flutes and recorders shading the melodies, the pieces form an elegant anthology of French dance music.

The king's arrival in 1714, though it may not have brought Handel into any sort of disfavour, left him in effect without a job. George inherited the court and chapel establishments created during Anne's reign and Handel was destined never to occupy any of the offices filled by composers such as Croft and Eccles. Burlington's patronage seems to have been more like the friendship of an influential host than the sort of supply-and-demand relationship exemplified by Prince Ruspoli or the Neapolitan nobility. The Italian opera at the Haymarket folded after the 1717 season and, apart from the *Water Music*, there were no other commissions forthcoming for Handel. In November, to make matters somewhat harder, as *The Political State of Great Britain* reported, 'on the 15th, in the Morning, dy'd the Baron de Kilmanseck, Master of the Horse to his Majesty . . . a Gentleman of Parts, who had a good Taste of Literature and Learning, and great Skill in Musick and Painting, and who was a great Encourager of Arts and Sciences'.

It is possible that at this juncture Handel may have entertained serious thoughts of becoming a resident composer on the pay-roll of a noble household, a dignified and lucrative professional outlet for a young musician. Several of his associates took on such work: Haym, for example, had been composer and performer in the family of the Earl of Bedford in Bloomsbury and Covent Garden, and Bononcini was to become the protégé of the eccentric Henrietta Spencer, Duchess of Marlborough. Handel's fellow artist at the Britton concerts, Johann Christoph Pepusch, had meanwhile secured the plum post of music master in one of the age's grandest establishments, the household of James Brydges, Earl of Carnarvon and later Duke of Chandos.

A member of a clan of minor Herefordshire gentry who, much later in the century, could claim kinship with Jane Austen through the antiquarian Egerton Brydges, he had made his fortune as paymaster of the English armies during the Spanish Succession war. He was a shameless believer in nest-feathering through skilful farming of national resources, and used public funds to buy shares and pension rights, speculated in silver, took *douceurs* from Austrian and Dutch diplomats, and fiddled the clothing contracts for the Portuguese army. Estimated to have made nearly £600,000 out of the office from 1705 onwards, he took care, on Godolphin's fall five years later, to curry favour with Harley while not losing touch with the Marlboroughs. In all this, however, he was no worse, if certainly no better, than any high-ranking government official of his day or any other.

The result was not only an earldom and a dukedom within six years of the king's accession, but a burst of opulence without serious parallel in the aristocratic life' of the period. Though never as grand as Blenheim or Castle Howard, the house Brydges built for himself at Cannons on the fringes of Edgware was sufficiently magnificent to be taken, despite all the author's denials, as the original of Pope's 'Timon's Villa', that ghastly monstrance of conspicuous waste which provides the dominant image in the first of the *Moral Essays*. Colonial connexions made during Brydges's paymastership enabled him to stock his 83-acre pleasure grounds (including fish stews and a wilderness) with exotic fauna such as flamingoes, eagles, storks, mocking birds and macaws. Guests were entertained, in what was really a museum of Augustan good taste, with a choice library and picture collection and an exceptionally fine table — drinks included Burgundy, Margaux, champagne, Samos, Tokay, arrack, usquebaugh, Hereford redstreak cider, Nottingham beer, 'Kill Priest' and 'Barbados Mordelleeno'.

The enormous household was divided into five tables in the servants' hall, one each for the Offices, Kitchen, Farmyard, 'Gentlemen of the Horse' and Musicians. We know the salaries of most of these people: while Pepusch, for example, got £100 a year, Joseph Cox the stablehand only got £2, and so did a dairymaid with the wonderful name of Eliza Squelch. Always fond of music, the earl maintained a handsome establishment and kept a small collection of musical instruments including a harpsichord made by Johann Christoph Bach. Several of the musicians appear to have doubled as domestic servants. George Monroe, later organist at St Peter Cornhill and keyboard player in the Goodman's Fields theatre band, started his career as a page at Cannons, where he was taught by Pepusch and Handel. A certain Gherardo, 'one of my Musick', accompanied Carnarvon's son on the grand tour, with the significant recommendation that 'he shaves very well & hath an excellent hand on the violin, & all necessary languages'.

Notable for sturdy independence in an age when most musicians were compelled to doff the hat and crook the knee, Handel is unlikely even to have contemplated anything quite so servile, and his position in regard to Carnarvon was as someone executing commissions rather than commands. Though the only evidence we have for his visits to Cannons is Mainwaring's, and an oblique hint in a letter from the earl to Arbuthnot, he does not re-emerge in the London musical world until early in 1719. During the previous two years it is safe to assume that he was with Carnarvon, either at his house in Albemarle Street or at Cannons itself.

Recommendations were hardly necessary. Carnarvon and Burlington were acquainted and the earl was on good terms with Arbuthnot, Swift and Pope. The pomp and grandeur of Cannons was the subject of continual comment by these and other writers, but Carnarvon was obviously pleased with his achievements. A fine new chapel was being built, with a ceiling by the Trevisan artist Antonio Bellucci and specially designed windows, though until it was finished services took place in the nearby parish church of St Lawrence, Whitchurch, and it was for this that Handel now furnished eleven new anthems. Writing to Arbuthnot, Carnarvon, delighted with the result, says: 'Mr Handle has made me two new Anthems very noble ones & most think they far exceed the two first. He is at work for 2 more & some Overtures to be plaied before the first lesson. You had as good take Cannons in your way to London.'

The so-called Chandos Anthems are Handel's first attempts at the kind of grand religious music best represented among his immediate English contemporaries by the instrumentally accompanied anthems of William Croft. Settings principally of psalm texts, their layout is for soprano, tenor and bass voice (though the Cannons concert contained an alto, Morphew, none of them features alto solos, a fact attributed to the earl's dislike of such a voice) alternating with choral episodes. They occupy a unique place in Handel's output, as his only extended pieces of church music not designed for a specific festive occasion and represent an absorbing extension of the techniques and sonorities he had already made to work so effectively in the *Utrecht Te Deum and Jubilate*.

Through the anthems the choral writing is splendidly resourceful and the exhilarating rhythmic pulse of the opening numbers of *Let God arise* or *O praise the Lord with one consent*, with its chorale-like use of Croft's 'St Anne' tune is totally infectious. In the solo items a much quieter, more restrained hand is at work, and though at times a hint of embarrassed self-consciousness sets in, almost as if religious decorum is getting the better of the composer, these movements in general form apt islands of introspection within each work.

Nowhere is this use of contrast made clearer than in *As pants the hart*, a jewel among Handel's earlier English compositions and justly admired in its own day. The spiritual balance towards which he seems to have been aiming is achieved in a way which sets at naught accusations of cynical worldliness. The essentially private, meditative atmosphere of mystical yearning makes an immediate appeal to the composer's imagination, and soloists and chorus become actors in a passionate dialogue, whose authentically Baroque intensity is heightened by such hardly English moments as 'For when I think on my God', and exquisite accompanied declamation over violin arpeggios.

All the works of the Cannons period suggest that Handel's major preoccupation at this time was with forms created by the special conditions of contemporary English religion and aesthetics. During the years 1715 to 1718 an interesting series of short operas, or 'masques' with dancing, were given at the theatres in Drury Lane and Lincoln's Inn Fields and Handel must surely have seen some of these. One of them, *Apollo and Daphne*, to music by Pepusch, had a libretto by John Hughes, and it is tempting to suppose, on grounds of comparison, that it was this piece which inspired one of Handel's best-loved dramatic works, the serenata *Acis and Galatea*, probably produced at Cannons during the summer of 1718.

The libretto, traditionally ascribed to Gay, but perhaps also worked over by other writers in the Burlington circle (there are touches of Pope and strong traces of Hughes) is, however artificial, among the finest ever written in English, a worthy successor to Tate's unjustly maligned *Dido and Aeneas* and Congreve's *Semele*. Its treatment of the myth of Acis, Galatea and Polyphemus, drawn from Theocritus via Ovid, is supple, economic and remarkably consistent, matching decorous pastoral imagery with touches of humour and achieving a dignified serenity at its half-tragic, half-visionary close. In its terse vignettes of Augustan classicism, the poetry is often strikingly memorable, in moments such as:

> Spring swells for us the grain
> And autumn bleeds the vine,

or:

> Wretched lovers! fate has passed
> This sad decree: no joy shall last.

or:

> Of infant limbs to make my food,
> And swill full draughts of human blood!
> Go, monster! bid some other guest:
> I loathe the host, I loathe the feast.

All four characters in the cast are exceptionally well drawn within the limits prescribed by the piece and receive correspondingly subtle portrayal in Handel's music. Acis is the heroic extrovert, rushing foolhardily to meet his death, and Damon is his perfect foil. Polyphemus, full of galumphing amorousness, is a proof, if any were needed, of Handel's ability to be funny without labouring the point. But the masque really belongs to Galatea, and all its most sensuous passages are hers.

Much has been made by certain commentators of Handel's supposed attempts to relate his overtures to the prevailing mood of the dramas they introduce. For the most part there is little in such a theory — consider, for instance, the opening of *Saul*, that most tragic of all the oratorios, which begins with what is, to all appearances, a concerto for orchestra in Handel's most sumptuous manner. *Acis and Galatea* is rare among the composer's works in having a sinfonia whose associations with the story are programmatic. The brio of the opening allegro (containing, by the way, an Italianate string figure of a falling sixth which turns up in the last chorus) is suddenly, shatteringly checked by a sledgehammer chord after which the oboe's plaintive minor can only be the voice of the bereaved Galatea.

The whole character of the masque (it is emphatically not, *pace* Novello vocal scores and English choral societies, an oratorio) is thus reflected at the outset, not only in dramatic terms but also as a crucial moment in Handel's artistic development. An attractive succession of arias for the two lovers and their pastoral mentor, clinched by a jolly duet, leads us deceptively enough through a world of Meissen statuettes and Watteau *fêtes champêtres*, but this is not the acquiescent world of Bach's *Hunting Cantata* or Vivaldi's *La Senna Festeggiante*. The shepherds, so joyously rustic over their bagpipes (back, as always, to the *pifferari*) at the opening, now become the masked, vatic celebrants of classical tragedy as they launch into one of the most startling uses of a chorus by any composer, the resistless, monumental 'Wretched lovers'. Built on the contrast between a series of imitative entries, slow, sombre, minatory, and the nervous, fretful anticipations of Polyphemus's arrival depicted in patterns of hurrying semiquavers, the music reaches a spectacular climax in the fusion of both ideas in the closing bars, where the initial pulse becomes a grim staccato stamp in which all the voices join before the piece dissolves in descending figures evoking anarchic gloom.

The last section of *Acis and Galatea* reinforces its claim to be Handel's finest composition of the decade. Polyphemus, that very English cyclops, is not punished for venting his jealous fury on Acis, but morality is assuaged by something altogether more sublime in its abstraction, Galatea's belated use of her powers to give her dead lover immortality as a river. The choral threnody for Acis, 'Mourn all ye muses', has the newly-acquired grandeur of 'Wretched lovers', and the chorus finally establishes its indispensable dramatic presence via the interjections of 'Cease, Galatea, cease to grieve' thrown into the nymph's Purcellian lament. Nothing else in the work, however, quite rivals 'Heart, the seat of soft delight', a piece to whose perfectly distilled erotic melancholy no words can do justice. The bouncing minuet finale is thus not so much a paean of exultation as a celebration of enduring hope and love in spite of death.

Here, as elsewhere in the piece, we catch echoes of Italy — Polyphemus's 'Cease to beauty', for example, is based initially on an aria in Giovanni Legrenzi's *Il Totila* which Handel may have recalled from a Venetian score — intermingled with memories of the *Brockes Passion* (the bass line of Damon's 'Consider, fond shepherd' is actually modelled on 'Nehm mich mit, verzagte Scharen') borrowings from *Agrippina* and the cantatas, and foreshadowings of native Englishness in 'Happy we'. Handel's eclecticism was seldom more potently displayed, yet the ultimate artistic triumph was created by tension of another sort than stylistic. The work calls for four soloists, a five-part chorus (no alto line) and a standard Handelian band of strings (without violas), oboes (doubling flutes) and continuo. It has been given as a fully-staged opera, most notably at Drury Lane in 1842 under Macready's direction, and as a monster oratorio with additional choral forces, at the Crystal Palace in 1871; ballet was added in 1829 when it shared the bill at the Haymarket with a danced version of Beethoven's Pastoral Symphony; its orchestration was revamped by Mozart and Mendelssohn, among others. Yet the evidence of Pepusch's list of the Cannons music and certain features of Handel's scoring and autograph manuscript suggest that the original *Acis* may have been given by only twelve performers, the soloists doubling as chorus and seven instrumental players. A performance according to these specifications inevitably lays emphasis on the contrast between the slenderness of Handel's resources and the increasingly lofty and expansive scope of the musical expression throughout, enhanced by a refinement in the instrumental writing, particularly for woodwind, which any re-orchestration merely stifles.

Acis and Galatea is as significant in Handel's artistic career as his other dramatic work for Cannons, the oratorio *Esther*, or 'The History of Hester' as it was sometimes called, but the two pieces are widely different in quality and consistency. Whereas *Acis* reflects a gathering confidence, *Esther*, with the most complex performance history of any Handel work, remained in an embryonic state throughout the composer's life, and he was still busy modifying it (though not necessarily with any idea of improvement) in 1757, two years before he died. There is thus no authoritative text, since the autograph is an inadequate guide, lacking the overture and the last page but including some of the attractive additions made for the 1732 revival.

No one seems quite certain when *Esther* was performed, but a recently discovered manuscript source carries the note 'The Oratorium Composed by George Frederick Handel Esquire in London 1718', so perhaps it was written either at Burlington House or at Chandos's town residence in Albemarle Street, where there were good keyboard instruments for Handel's use, and given its first hearing either in London or at Cannons, more or less at the same time as *Acis*. The two may indeed have formed part of a dual commission from Chandos himself, and it is interesting to consider whether it was he, Handel or Pepusch who initially conceived the idea for the first English dramatic oratorio.

The libretto is probably by the same Scribblerian team, Pope, Arbuthnot and Gay, who worked on *Acis*. Later advertisements attributed it to Pope, who was not at pains to deny it, and later still it was credited to Arbuthnot, but the general textual and dramatic quality suggests that several hands stirred this rather coarse, lumpy pudding. Its origins are firmly rooted in Racine's play, written for Mme de Maintenon's school at Saint Cyr in 1689 and welding Greek and French classical traditions together by the introduction of choruses sung by mixed voices offstage. Inspired as they may have been by this and by its English adaptation by Thomas Brereton published nearly 30 years later, the librettists made no attempt whatever to emulate the dramatist's mastery of structural and thematic unity, offering instead a series of characters and episodes corresponding in outline with the familiar biblical narrative but lacking in any sort of continuity or interaction. This last fact, indeed, together with the notable absence of stage directions from Handel's autograph and the unconvincing nature of recent staged revivals, leads to the conclusion, *pace* modern enthusiasts and Handel's later ideas for a staged performance, that the original was not conceived in directly theatrical terms.

Musically, the effect is that of a piece assembled in a hasty and haphazard fashion and suggesting a period of composition brief even by Handelian standards. Little attention is paid to balance and proportion and much of the score resorts to the familiar technique of recycling earlier material, in this case some of the finer moments of the *Brockes Passion*, including the concerted opening 'Mich vom Stricke' which turns up as 'Virtue, truth and innocence' and the poignant arioso 'Mein Vater', which, as Haman's last despairing plea to Esther, is one of the few transferred numbers to function properly in its new context. In many other works the composer's influence on the dramatic logic and pacing of the libretto is immediately apparent, but here he submitted tamely enough to its inconsistencies, perhaps either because he was not in direct contact with the Scribblerians while at work on *Esther* or because he was reluctant to offend them by tampering.

The 1732 revival added several freshly composed numbers, including 'Breathe soft, ye gales' with its lush scoring for paired recorders, oboes, bassoons and strings, divided at first over contrasting continuo support of organ, harpsichord, theorbo and harp, with cello and bass, all forces ultimately combining to provide the sort of rich texture which sets at naught our century's attempts to Wagnerize Handel's orchestral writing. Extra brass and timpani were brought into the final chorus and the overture was filled out, but this and a re-hashed libretto by Samuel Humphreys made little difference to the lopsided atmosphere of the original. This is not to say, of course, that individually the various pieces, old and new, fail with the listener. The sure-fire quality of mature Handel diffuses itself through choruses like 'Shall we the God of Israel fear?' and the unique rondo finale, in which, with a leisurely aplomb, the composer again demonstrates his mastery of large, elastic choral structures.

That *Acis*, *Esther* and Handel's whole concept of English musical drama were shelved for another fifteen years is as typical of the composer as the fact that his sense of their importance in relation to the way in which his musical idiom was developing caused him to parade them before a wider public than any nobleman's private concert could offer. The lessons of the Cannons period were not lost on Handel, but his adventuring spirit turned now towards the lures and perils of an altogether more incalculable world.

5

A Nest of Nightingales

Though opera at the Haymarket had languished from the Jacobite summer of 1715 onwards and died out altogether two years later, it was unlikely that it would disappear from the London stage for very long. The taste and the money were both available to fuel any new initiative, and late in 1718 a grandiose project was set in motion by a powerful group of noblemen and gentlemen to revive Italian opera at the King's Theatre on a scale designed to reflect the highest contemporary standards in production and performance.

The Royal Academy of Music was conceived as a joint stock company, with each subscriber guaranteed £200 of the £10,000 stock, an artistic venture probably unique in the history of English theatrical music and directly related to the mania for playing the market during the years of the South Sea Bubble. Every shareholder received one vote and the £1,000 subscribers were given three. The king, as an interested patron, allowed a yearly bounty of £1,000. The theatre was to be altered to accommodate so superior an audience by cutting up the first, or eighteenpenny gallery, into boxes and, as in continental houses, some of these were to be let to 'particular Companyes'. On a highly optimistic note, the writer of the original proposal, possibly Dr Arbuthnot, says: 'And it is presumed among so many Gentlemen Lovers of Musick there will be Persons of Honour found who will have Leisure and Inclination enough to afford a little of their time for the Management or at least Supervising the Affairs of the Society.'

A glance at the list of the persons of honour might at first suggest that the scheme could hardly fail. The subscribers, including seven dukes, a marquis, twelve earls and four viscounts, represented the cream of the Whig ascendancy established by the Hanoverian succession, and it is clear that a king who was noted for his personal scrutiny of every promotion in the army or in the higher echelons of the church must have vetted the list before giving royal assent. Burlington and Chandos were of course there (with the young Duke of Newcastle, Lord Chamberlain and later prime minister, they were the sole £1,000 subscribers) and so were Arbuthnot, Bothmer, George's Hanoverian aide, and the influential figure of James Craggs the younger (he and Lord Sunderland were the two South Sea company directors in the list). Notable also, especially in illustrating an age when British soldiering did not guarantee oafishness and philistinism, is the preponderance of military men. Here are the Marlborough veterans Cadogan and Limerick, together with several destined to later fame, Guise, hero of Admiral Vernon's Cartagena expedition and, like Handel, an enthusiast for painting, Wade, fresh from his successful assault on Vigo and soon to impose order on the fractious Highlanders, and Gage, soldier father of an even more illustrious son.

News of the Academy's preparations seems to have got about in the first months of 1719, when the *Original Weekly Journal* prematurely announced that 'Mr Hendel, a famous Master of Music, is gone beyond the Sea, by Order of his Majesty, to Collect a Company of the choicest Singers in Europe, for the Opera in the Hay-Market'. Handel had in fact not yet set out, having written the day before to his brother-in-law Michael Dietrich Michaelsen at Halle, complaining of being 'kept here by affairs of the greatest moment, on which (I venture to say) all my fortunes depend'. The letter, written in courtly French, reveals that he had intended to return to Halle, where his sister Dorothea had died in the July of the previous year. Someone who obviously enjoyed giving presents, he had sent some pewter to Michaelsen which had got held up at Magdeburg, and this detail, mingled with anxiety for news of his mother and the rest of the family, lends a note of glum impatience to the letter.

Three days afterwards he wrote to Mattheson, with whom he still kept in touch, on the subjects of solmization and the Greek modes. His admirably concise statements on these two subjects (dear to the heart of Pepusch, incidentally) have an absence of stuffiness and a general practicality typical of Handel as a composer. 'I do not mean to argue', he writes, 'that solmization is of no practical use whatever, but as one can acquire the same knowledge in far less time by the method in use at present with such success, I see no point in not adopting the way which leads with greater ease and in less time to the proposed goal.' Of the Greek modes he says, 'Knowledge of them is no doubt necessary for those who wish to study and execute ancient music composed according to these modes; but as we have been liberated from the narrow limits of ancient music, I cannot see of what use the Greek modes can be to modern music.' Handel was never so ignorant or improvident as to scorn assistance from the music of the past, as the oratorios make plain, but pedantic worship of the antique for its own sake was not for him.

At length, during May of that year, he was able to leave for the continent to fulfil the special orders given in a warrant issued by Newcastle on the Academy's behalf, directing him 'forthwith to repair to Italy Germany or such other Place or Places as you shall think proper, there to make Contracts with such Singer or Singers as you shall judge fit to perform on the English Stage'. He was bidden to keep in touch with the board and to tell them of any outstanding vocal discoveries and 'upon what Terms he or She may be had'. And above all 'Mr Hendel' was to 'engage Senezino as soon as possible to Serve the said Company and for as many Years as may be'.

The Academy was resolved to begin in the grandest possible style. Senesino ('the little Sienese' — this had no connexion with his stature) was the name given to Francesco Bernardi, the greatest castrato of the decade and destined to create many of Handel's most taxing operatic roles. Born in Siena about 1680, he made a name for himself in Venice, less, perhaps, as a stage presence (his features had that porcine effeminacy common to so many eunuchs) or for his musicianship than as the owner of a magnificently resonant voice, capable of a considerable expressive rage. The Neapolitan impresario, Count Zambeccari, says of him: 'Senesino continues to comport himself badly enough; he stands like a statue, and when occasionally he does make a gesture, he makes one directly the opposite of what is wanted,' but audiences in Venice and Vienna seem generally to have been delighted, and his appearance at the Saxon court opera at Dresden in 1719 was on the crest of a wave of recent Italian successes.

It was there that Handel went, by way of Düsseldorf and Halle for a visit to his family — narrowly missing, it is said, a meeting with Bach, one of the great 'might-have-beens' of musical history. Dresden itself was *en fête* in celebration of the forthcoming marriage of the Electoral Prince of Saxony to Archduchess Maria Josepha of Austria. There were performances by troupes of French and Italian comedians, firework displays, balls, masquerades and hunting parties, and if Handel needed any further inducement to stay on, it was offered by the presence of his old San Giovanni Grisostomo associates, Antonio Lotti and his wife Santa Stella.

Teofane, the opera commissioned by Lotti for the festivities, was to make enough of an impression for Handel to take home the libretto and use it for his fourth Academy opera, *Ottone*. Besides Senesino and the castrato Berselli, both to be engaged for London, the *Teofane* cast included another Italian friend, Margherita Durastanti. She was signed up for an eighteen-month contract at £1,600 and Senesino's price was £2,000. If these seem rather steep, we can scarcely wonder, for the Dresden opera, bent on financial suicide, gave its singers free lodging, food, light and heating, on top of a handsome salary. They also received carriages, and so did Lotti, who took his home to Venice to show off as a souvenir.

Lingering at Dresden, Handel entertained the court with his keyboard playing and was the subject of a slightly disgruntled letter from Count Jacob Heinrich Flemming, former Saxon minister to London, writing to King George's bastard daughter, Melusine von der Schulenburg: 'I hoped to see Mr Hendel, and intended to speak to him in laudatory terms of you, but there was no opportunity. I made use of your name to persuade him to call on me, but either he was not at his lodgings or else he was ill. It seems to me that he is a little mad; however, he should not behave to me in that way, as I am a musician — that is, by inclination. . . . '

'It seems to me that he is a little mad.' Flemming would not be the last to comment on the composer's strong dash of eccentricity. The Academy directors, nevertheless, were satisfied with the way things were going, and they had now been joined by the Duke of Montague, by the indispensable Heidegger, and by another musical soldier, Colonel John Blathwayt, who, as a pupil of Pasquini and Corelli and a regular attender at Cardinal Ottoboni's Roman concerts, may have made Handel's acquaintance during the spring and summer of 1707. The only sticking point in the negotiations was Senesino, whose initial failure to reach an agreement with Handel augured badly for their subsequent rapport. At a meeting on 30 November, the directors, determined to procure the castrato's services, asked the Modenese resident in London, Giuseppe Riva, Senesino's personal friend, to step in.

Hailing from a region which has produced more practical musicians during the last three centuries than any other part of Italy, and in constant touch with leading Italian cultural figures of the day, Riva was passionately concerned to promote an Italian interest at the Haymarket. As well as dealing with Senesino, he may have been influential in laying the ground for the arrival of the illustrious figure of Giovanni Bononcini, to whom, as 'Seignr. Bona Cini', the Academy, at the same November meeting, resolved to apply. Meanwhile Heidegger was asked to get in touch with the Venetian composer Giovanni Porta, and Arbuthnot was requested to call on Pope for 'a Seal with a Suitable Motto to it'.

Arbuthnot was less fortunate than Heidegger. Pope did not comply, but

Porta, in London as a household musician to the Duke of Wharton, produced *Numitore*, whose première, scheduled for March 1720, took place in April owing to competition from a company of French comedians popular with the court. The opera, though it only ran for five nights, clearly impressed Handel, who did not disdain to quote from it in *Samson* and *Solomon* some 20 years later. Burney describes Porta as 'one of the most able masters of his time; uniting learning with invention and fire', but *Numitore* was his sole composition for the Academy.

The librettist was Paolo Antonio Rolli, who, with Nicola Francesco Haym, was one of the Haymarket's two theatre poets, and a word or two may be said here about each. Neither was known exclusively as a versifier, though Rolli's translation of *Paradise Lost*, adapted for Catholic readers, won him fame, and in his own right as the author of some highly polished odes and epigrams and as a brilliant metrist, he ranks as the best Italian poet in the generation immediately preceding Metastasio. Haym, infinitely the less troublesome of the pair (though ready to describe himself as 'not of inferior merit to any of my Profession now in England, particularly of ye Foreigners') was born in Rome, presumably of Jewish parentage, and had received his musical training among the Ottoboni circle. He composed solo and trio sonatas, cantatas and oratorios, pieces such as *Santa Costanza* (featuring Julian the Apostate among its principal roles) which reveal him as a competent if not especially distinguished hand.

In England, as house musician to the Duke of Bedford and 'cellist and arranger for the opera in its early days, he assumed a social function similar to Rolli's as an aesthetic adviser to dilettante noblemen, figuring among the virtuosos as an editor, bibliographer and expert numismatist. Always loyal to Handel, he was a sensitive collaborator, and there is abundant evidence of close co-operation between the two men in the fashioning of such masterpieces as *Giulio Cesare*, *Tamerlano* and *Rodelinda*.

It requires no great degree of cynical penetration to understand why the works based on texts supplied by Rolli, operas such as *Alessandro* and *Riccardo Primo*, should be manifestly less successful. Naturally, as an ardent champion of Italian literature, publishing London editions of classics like Boccaccio's *Decameron*, as an F.R.S. (even if his two papers were merely translations from the work of others) he earned respect, but the more we study his work, the more we learn of a cold and rebarbative personality, determined to exploit the naïve Italophilia of his aristocratic patrons and scornful of the English who welcomed him.

Excellent poet though he was, Rolli disdained to exercise his real gifts in devising the Academy librettos. As he later implied in one of his epigrams, the librettist's task wasn't really worth the effort: 'I knock up old dramas in a new style and tack on dedications . . . if the directors lose out on them, it's the fault of the singers, since the libretto doesn't count. A good drama or a bad one, what does it matter so long as it's cheap?' Haym was perhaps not enough of a poet himself to devise an entirely new text. Thus, in the traditional manner of Italian theatre hacks of the period, they confined themselves to tailoring already extant librettos to the demands of the audience, the singers and the composer.

As copies of these dramas (in London a parallel English translation was included) were bought as a matter of course by the audience, musicians and poets could build up their own supplies for future use. Some of the Academy texts, therefore, were originally designed for operas by Handel's acquaintances, such as Lotti and Gasparini, three were derived from librettos by poets personally known to the composer, and one, *Tamerlano*, was based on a version made for a performance in Reggio by the tenor destined to sing the role of Bajazet in London four years later. With the exception of *Siroe*, which, though only two years old when Handel wrote his opera, had already been set five times (including versions by Vivaldi and Porpora) the others were old-fangled Venetian texts which needed adapting for the London public.

Italian opera had by now begun to assume the outline to which, perfected by Metastasio during the century's middle decades, it would remain more or less constant until the age of Mozart. Widow Twankey nurses and waggish lackeys were either removed to the *buffo* interludes from which full-scale comedies would soon develop, or else disappeared altogether. The number of plot interests and scene changes was cut down, the proportion of arias was reduced, choral numbers vanished almost totally, and the formal aspects of the genre became heavily conventional. In the first great age of the singer as vocal acrobat, the aria, the offloading of emotions produced by moments dramatized in recitative, became the perfect means of displaying colour and technical agility, and the exit convention, whereby a character quitted the stage at the end of the piece, inviting applause to bring him back, was a standard feature of *opera seria*, conditioning the layout of the drama. There were few ensembles (caprice and mutual resentment among Italian singing stars was, then as now, taken for granted) but the opera nearly always ended with a *coro* from all the characters left alive at the end.

The poetry of the lyric dramas is of an extreme artificiality, yet to those interested in this type of opera the high-flown clichés soon become like old friends. As scarcely anybody is below aristocratic rank and there are lots of princes and princesses, everybody is immensely refined and a spade never gets called a spade. In essence the Italian is the same literary flimflam which went on being used until the mid-nineteenth century, and it is interesting to hear Violetta, Leonora or the Duke of Mantua resorting to the same tortured syntax and ballooning periphrasis as we hear from the lips of Cleopatra, Alceste or Grimoaldo. Simile is used frequently as an aid to the composer, and the images are nearly always extracted from the same limited stock, ships in a storm or arriving in harbour, swallows far from their nests, bewildered butterflies, benighted pilgrims and sturdy oak trees. Obvious attempts are made to vary mood, since singers expected to display their talents in expressing a wide range of emotions.

Like the French neo-classical tragedies to which they so often allude, the plots of *opera seria* are heavily involved with presenting stories and situations from the past in terms which would be immediately recognizable to the audience. However encrusted with the trappings of paganism and references to the ancient historians, the world of each opera is that of a Baroque court, and the conflicts presented smack as much of Saint-Simon, Sévigné and Grammont as they do of Tacitus and Livy. One of Antonio Salvi's texts, ultimately set by Handel as *Berenice*, was originally called 'The Contests of Love and Politics', a title which effectively sums up the dilemma at the core of all such dramas. Though the audience may not always have followed the libretto closely throughout, we know that this kind of theatre, whether at Versailles or at Venice, was regarded as offering effective comment on contemporary society, and thus a visit to the opera was never (at any rate in theory) a mere escape to an idealized world.

The ultimate success of *opera seria*, however, depended upon the tension between the world of illusion created by the stage picture and the affective realism produced by the composer and the librettist. To this end the scenes were changed in full view of the audience, the smooth magic of transformation being assisted by the arrangement of flats in grooves on either side of the stage and backdrops which could be quickly drawn up to reveal the new scene in a trice. This enchantment was further emphasized by the whole nature of eighteenth-century scenic design with its stress on complexity and apparently unlimited perspective, intended to give the spectator something for his fancy continually to dwell upon. As Stefano Arteaga, most lucid and intelligent of all contemporary writers on the genre, described it: 'The secret . . . is to present objects in such a way that the imagination does not end at the same point as the senses, so that there is always something left for the audience to imagine beyond what the eye can see and the ear can hear.'

Handel remained constant to this type of opera throughout his career, and touches of it permeate practically everything else he wrote (*Messiah*, for example, contained a number of features carried over from the operatic manner, including a duet placed just before the closing numbers). The newer Venetian manner, in which heavily contrapuntal textures are abandoned in favour of lightly-moving syncopated melodies over drumbeat bases, turns up in *Agrippina* and *Il Pastor Fido*, and Handel shows himself a past master of it throughout his subsequent operas. The most eclectic of all the great composers, he took what he wanted from an immense range of musical styles and made it his own, but his 38 operas testify to his belief in the validity of *opera seria* as an art form.

His earliest Academy opera, *Radamisto*, given on 27 April 1720, at the Haymarket, is a fine demonstration of the principles to which he stayed loyal as a dramatic composer, and its consistency of intention and design make it one of the best operas he ever wrote, an outstanding example of early eighteenth-century lyric drama. There is every indication that Handel had taken full advantage of his stay at Dresden to absorb newer Italian styles and the result is a work that establishes a standard hitherto undreamt of in English theatrical music, one which reflects most, if not all, of the features typifying his methods and ideas in the operas of the so-called 'Academy' period.

The libretto, Haym's adaptation of *L'Amor Tirannico* by the Neapolitan poet Sebastiano Bianciardi, provided for the San Casciano theatre at Venice under his pen-name of Domenico Lalli, is of the type Handel preferred, in which high-born protagonists turn their backs on politics to concentrate on a world of baffled intimacy and fatal misapprehension. Briefly, Radamisto, prince of Thrace, is attacked by his brother-in-law Tiridate, King of Armenia, who desires Radamisto's wife Zenobia: Tiridate's queen, Polissena, long-suffering but ultimately provoked beyond endurance, begins with a hopeless yearning for her fickle husband which finally turns to righteous fury when she sees Radamisto condemned to execution.

Like Verdi, whom as a creative personality he so frequently resembles, Handel was clearly drawn by certain types of story, and seems to have had a special fondness for that favourite Baroque figure, the heroine *in extremis*. With such characters he could exercise his penchant for the tender-pathetic, that quality which relates him so strongly to the preromantic

93

sentimentalism of the age of Ossian and Werther, the era immediately following his own. Zenobia and Radamisto, the sundered husband and wife, are portrayed, like Rodelinda and Bertarido five years later, with the mature awareness of a relationship intense enough to survive the gravest emotional shocks.

From the stirring flourishes of the overture till the leisured close in Handel's longest vaudeville finale, there is not a dull moment in the piece. The musical characterization builds on the strengths of the text, each figure is firmly outlined in moods and aspirations, and some attempt is made, as elsewhere in Handel, to relate a character to a particular key or group of keys.

One of the most interesting of the principals is Polissena, who begins the opera with the majestic wretchedness of 'Sommi Dei'. The librettist's treatment of her is noteworthy in that she makes the briefest of appearances in Act II in order, as it seems, to have something to sing (in this case an attractive G minor aria in triplet rhythms). Handel clearly felt that, notwithstanding the distinction of her music in the first version, there was not enough for her to do, and gave Maddalena Salvai, who sang in the December revival, a scene to open Act III, transferring, in the process, one of Zenobia's most moving utterances. Tiridate's young brother Fraarte also has some engaging music, including 'Mirero quel vago volto' in Act I, with its ravishing flattened third in the vocal part's opening phrase and, even if not altogether necessary to the story, makes a character of real substance, foreshadowing Cherubino in his naïve ardour. The summit of Handel's achievement in this masterly opening to the first phase of his operatic maturity is reached in Radamisto's anguished invocation to the wife he supposes dead, 'Ombra cara', which remained a personal favourite among the composer's own works. Burney says of it: ' . . . too much praise cannot be given to that song, in which, though the composition is so artful, an inverted chromatic imitation being carried on in the accompaniments, yet the cantilena is simply pathetic throughout. I remember hearing Reginelli sing this air at the opera in 1747, among some light Italian songs of that period, and it seems the language of philosophy and science, and the rest the frivolous jargon of fops and triflers.'

After the first night of *Radamisto* Lady Cowper, in the suite of the Princess of Wales, noted laconically in her diary: 'At Night, *Radamistus*, a fine opera of Handel's Making. The *King* there with his Ladies. The *Prince* in his Stage-box. Great Crowd.' Handel had taken the uncommon step of dedicating the libretto in person to the king, and George's general enthusiasm for the Academy project is shown by Handel's implication, in his brief dedicatory epistle, that the king had already heard and approved the music. There was indeed a great crowd at the performance, which started at half-past six. 'In so splendid and fashionable an assembly of ladies (to the excellence of their taste we must impute it) there was no shadow of form, or ceremony, scarce indeed any appearance of order or regularity, politeness or decency. Many, who had forc'd their way into the house with an impetuosity but ill suited to their rank and sex, actually fainted through the excessive heat and closeness of it. Several gentlemen were turned back, who had offered forty shillings for a seat in the gallery, after having despaired of getting any in the pit or boxes.' An audience, in short, not much different from those which in our own day have jostled to hear Callas, Sutherland or Pavarotti.

The cast was an English and Italian mixture, with Durastanti as Radamisto, Anastasia Robinson as Zenobia, the soprano Benedetto Baldassari as Fraarte, and that interesting figure Alexander Gordon as the tenor Tiridate. Gordon's remarkable career had begun in the theatres of southern Italy; he was later to abandon singing for connoisseurship and his final incarnation was as secretary to the governor of South Carolina, where he died a prosperous landowner. Known as 'Singing Sandie', he was clearly well thought of by Handel, but his threat to jump on the harpsichord when irritated by the composer's accompaniments drew the stinging retort: 'Oh, let me know when you will do that and I will advertise it; for I am sure more people will come to see you jump than to hear you sing.'

At the revival on 28 December, the sole remnant of the original casting was the bass Lagarde in the minor role of King Farasmane. By this time Senesino had arrived to take over as Radamisto, Durastanti became Zenobia, and Tiridate was given to Giuseppe Maria Boschi, Handel's bass of earlier days, now firmly instated as the roarer and blusterer of the Academy stage. No wonder the young Mary Pendarves, better known to us as the Mrs Delany she later became, could write to her sister Ann Granville that 'the stage was never so well served as it is now, there is not one indifferent voice, they are all Italians'.

Things looked auspicious enough for Handel. The king granted him a fourteen-year copyright, and on the strength of this Richard Meares published a finely engraved edition of *Radamisto*, personally supervised by the composer. But the artistic direction of the Haymarket, as he must already have guessed, was unlikely to offer a smooth ride. Rolli, that incurable schemer, was already writing to Riva letters full of mysterious codenames concealing theatrical personnel. Durastanti, who had brought along her husband the impresario Casimiro Avelloni, was pregnant, to the annoyance of the directors, and Bononcini, run to ground in Rome by Lord Burlington, was taking his time to arrive, but in September Senesino at last set foot in England. 'Signor Senesino, the famous eunuch, has arrived,' said *Applebee's Weekly Journal*, 'and it is said that the company allows him two thousand guineas for the season.' Rolli, though he hurried to find him lodgings in a house near Leicester Fields (now Leicester Square) and judged him 'well-mannered, well-read, extremely kind and endowed with the noblest sentiments', also thought him 'a noisy busybody and certainly not the soul of discretion', but he had obviously marked Senesino down as a potential ally in backstage plots.

Senesino's relations with Handel began as they meant to go on. Salvai, the new Polissena for the *Radamisto* revival, had brought with her Girolamo Polani, whom, as composer for the San Fantin and Sant'Angelo theatres, Handel must already have known in Venice. Handel's idea was apparently to employ him as an assistant at the opera, working as conductor and adaptor of Orlandini's *Amore e Maesta*, a recent Florentine success. Rolli was set to tinker with the libretto, junking much of the recitative and adding fresh arias for Senesino, who naturally wanted new music for them. Inevitably, Handel and Senesino clashed over the professional involvement of Polani, a board meeting was held and the directors, particularly Blathwayt and Arbuthnot, were at pains to appease their newest star acquisition, while Rolli hovered in the background, mingling diplomacy with guile. The disputed opera eventually reached the stage the following February as *Arsace*, with additional music by the theatre's 'cellist Pippo Mattei, the discomfited Polani having quit the field.

The Academy's triumph seemed assured by the arrival that autumn of Giovanni Bononcini. This admired Italian master, a consummate operatic professional with a gift for agreeable melody, was hardly the *petit-maître* whom some of Handel's biographers have chosen to portray. His childhood had not, like his rival's, been happy or secure. In the dedication to his Opus 3 sinfonias, published when he was only thirteen, he says: 'From my parents I had as much life as sufficed to acquaint me with misery, while they, by dying, left me, still a babe in arms, to poverty.' Perhaps it was this which helped to make him the proud, arrogant figure he remained throughout his life. A native Modenese, he had trained in Bologna under Giovanni Paolo Colonna, one of the most influential figures in a rich musical tradition centred on the Accademia Filarmonica and the basilica of San Petronio. After a spell as a 'cellist and composer at

Rome he went to Vienna and furnished operas to the court for nearly sixteen years. It was during a second Roman period, beginning in 1713, that Burlington, as Rolli reminds him in the dedication, attended a rehearsal of Bononcini's *Astarto*, and it was this opera which was now chosen to open the second Academy season on 19 November 1720.

Astarto was an instant success, with 20 performances in all, and the presence of a genuinely talented composer of international repute, with the psychological advantage, among the singers, musicians and theatrical hangers-on, of being Italian, must have given Handel considerable pause. He was never one easily to bear a kinsman near the throne, and one of his few major flaws of personality was a resentment of those whose skills threatened to challenge his on his own ground. It was all very well to admire Telemann, Muffat, Clari and Habermann from a distance, but the appearance of Bononcini in London made Handel combative.

It may thus have been his idea that the pair of them, assisted by Pippo Mattei, should each set an act of one of that season's new operas. There is a possibility that the directors, several of whom were racing men, may have fancied the notion of backing one musician against another, but the fondness of Baroque composers for competition (witness, for example, Bach and the wretched Louis Marchand) makes it more likely that either Handel or Bononcini or both first conceived the project, calling in Pippo to do the first act, whose beauties would easily be forgotten once the two giants took the field.

The subject chosen (with Rolli, of course, as librettist) was one on which Bononcini had already composed two operas, the story of Romans against Etruscans in the days of the early republic. Act I concerns 'How Horatius Kept The Bridge', Act II Mutius Scevola's baffled assassination attempt on Lars Porsenna and Act III the flight of Cloelia and the female hostages. It sounds almost too pious to say that Handel's setting of the final act is better than Pippo in the first and Bononcini in the second, but such indeed is the case. Pippo's music is short-breathed, naïve and rather old-fashioned, and Bononcini's act, while sensitive, idiomatic and vivid at such moments as Mutius's burning of his hand, demonstrates his incapacity to sustain melodic lines for long enough to give them an interesting shape. Gratifyingly placed for the singers though these arias are, and sensuously pretty though many of them may be, it is Handel's music which demands to be noticed.

Everything about Act III of *Muzio Scevola* suggests a determined effort by the composer to establish his supremacy and to leave the audience suitably impressed. The whole act is permeated by an attention to details of colour and balance which, since like the others it has its own overture, gives it a disproportionate grandeur of design. The shop window aspect of the work is sustained throughout by Handel's evident desire to contrast his various singers as sharply as possible. Thus Boschi's richly rewarding aria, as Porsenna enjoining the unpleasant moments to fly faster than the winds, with its turbulent 'cellos reinforced by bassoons (the middle section, coloured by the intrusion of a solitary oboe, is a restatement of the old *Octavia* motif) is followed by an expressive adagio intended to show Senesino in his most ingratiatingly pathetic vein. The act, what is more, contains a pair of duets, one in a jubilant 12/8 and the other in a languishing 3/4, separated by an extensive recitative. The structure in each is carefully differentiated, with the voices in the first (for Berselli and Robinson) only coming together after twelve-bar solos, and those in the second (for Senesino and Durastanti) altogether more closely blended.

Muzio Scevola's première took place on 15 April 1721, with a further nine performances during the season. Rolli addressed a fulsome dedication to the king, declaring that 'liberty would have gone to ground in woods and cottages if she had not found a glorious refuge in Your Majesty's happy realms. . . . Compare this kingdom to the Roman republic and see in how many respects both are alike, whether in the glory of their arms, the fabric of their laws or the honour given to learning', and it is not difficult to catch the implied political analogies between the Romans who ejected Tarquin and the Whigs who chased out James II and suppressed the first Jacobite rising. Gay, less obsequious, penned an epigram:

> Who here blames words, or verses, songs, or singers,
> Like Mutius Scaevola will burn his fingers.

Writing to Count Flemming at Dresden, the Hanoverian courtier Fabrice described the loud huzzas of the first night audience at the announcement of the birth of a son to the Princess of Wales, and added, detailing the three composers, that Handel 'easily triumphed over the others'. To which Flemming later sent the patriotic rejoinder: 'I am very glad also that the German has been victorious in composition over all the other musicians.'

Strongly characteristic of its author as the *Muzio* music was, Handel now tried a different ploy in *Floridante*, his new piece for the early months of the 1721–22 season. Several writers on Handel have noted a Bononcinian cast in the music of this opera, and there seems little doubt that he was wanting to show the Haymarket audience that he too could lure them with a bland, facile elegance. The end product is among his least interesting operas. True, none of the arias is without charm, and a piece like Elmira's 'Ma pria vedro le stelle' shows an urbane command of the newest operatic styles, but the dramatic and emotional range of the work rarely transcends a world of pastel-shaded miniature.

This is partly owing to Rolli's wretched libretto, an adaptation from Silvani's *La Costanza in Trionfo*, first set by Ziani at Venice fifteen years earlier. The setting is changed from ancient Norway to ancient Persia; ancient Timbuctoo would have done as well, for all the difference such things make to the lame story of Prince Floridante driven from Persia by King Oronte, whose supposed daughter Elmira he is about to wed, the basis for a drama utterly empty of convincing motive (unless we except Oronte's senile passion for Elmira). The obligatory second pair of lovers, Princess Rossane and Timante, Prince of Tyre, whom a competent theatre poet could have worked neatly into the intrigue, are dramatically superfluous throughout (until III.ix. when Timante turns up to rescue Floridante with all the timeliness of the United States Cavalry). Ironically, Handel bestowed some of his most affecting music on their exchanges, including the F minor siciliano 'Oh dolce mia speranza' in which the vocal line is shaded with the lightest dapplings of orchestral sound, and the unashamedly sentimental Act II duet, in which a reference to cooing doves is made by a pair of bassoons.

One scene, however, has always deserved its admirers. The latent romanticism of Handel's genius cherished the opportunities given by his librettists for night scenes, in which darkness and moonlight enhance the atmosphere of amorous confusion, and *Floridante* features one of the best of them all. In a dark gallery Elmira awaits the arrival of her lover, who has slipped back into the kingdom disguised as a Moorish slave. She begins to apostrophize the night which will return her Floridante to her, but her aria, in the rare key of B flat minor, breaks off into accompanied recitative after twelve bars as she thinks she hears somebody approach. Could it be he, leaving the secret room and coming up the stairs ('quella furtiva scala')? 'Open the door, come in!' she cries, but 'ah, no! my passion deceives me, oh! how wretched waiting for him makes me', and the aria resumes. This is one of many such moments in Handel opera in which the composer, aided by the libretto, disturbs the formal convention to heighten dramatic immediacy.

Handel was now celebrated throughout Europe as a composer and performer. Bach's wasted journey from Cöthen is an impressive tribute to a musician for whose work he had an abiding esteem (he certainly knew

Lucrezia, Armida abbandonata and the *Brockes Passion*) and Mattheson's spate of aesthetic and critical treatises makes frequent and admiring mention of him. English music lovers had never heard a keyboard player as versatile, and as an improviser his equals were few. It is typical, if sad, that this should have been the skill for which he was mainly noted and that his surviving keyboard works should offer only slender evidence of what he could achieve in imaginative exploitation of the organ or the harpsichord. He became the arbiter among the London organists of his day, asked, for example, by the churchwardens of St Dionis Backchurch to try out their new Renatus Harris organ, along with Croft, Loeillet and Babel, in 1722, and three years later sending a fugue subject to St George's, Hanover Square, as part of the competition for the organist's job eventually won by the eccentric Thomas Roseingrave.

As a writer for the voice he must have benefited from the presence of Senesino, for whom he continued to provide magnificent music, but the line-up at the King's Theatre was scarcely of so consistent a quality throughout. Anastasia Robinson, though undoubtedly gifted, had her limitations, and that good trouper Durastanti seems to have lacked the star quality on which an opera public is always eager to feed. Audiences, however, were not to wait much longer for the genuine article, for after lengthy negotiations the Academy, in December 1722, procured its first great female soloist, a prima donna every inch of her short stature.

No writer more pithily describes Francesca Cuzzoni than Horace Walpole. He never actually saw her in her heyday, but his mother, an enthusiastic patroness of hers, must have furnished an accurate description. 'She was,' he says, 'short and squat, with a doughy cross face, but fine complexion; was not a good actress; dressed ill; and was silly and fantastical.' But that was not the point. The virtuoso flautist and composer Johann Joachim Quantz, who heard her on his visit to London in 1727, praised her clarity of voice and purity of intonation, detailed her double octave compass, but pointed out tactfully that 'her figure was not advantageous for the stage'. She was famed for her effortless divisions and, as Burney says, for 'enriching the cantilena with all the refinements and embellishments of the time . . . she had a creative fancy, and the power of occasionally accelerating and retarding the measure in the most artificial and able manner, by what the Italians call *tempo rubato*'.

So obvious an asset needed a new opera to show her off to the fullest advantage, and as Handel finished his latest work in time for the opening of the 1722–23 season Cuzzoni was presumably expected to appear for the rehearsals which began in October. 'There is a new Opera now in

Rehearsal at the Theatre in the Haymarket, a Part of which is reserv'd for one Mrs Cotsona, an extraordinary Italian Lady, who is expected daily . . . ' True to form, however, the extraordinary Mrs Cotsona was doubtless proving tough over contract terms, for the new opera had to be shelved, and the early part of the season was eked out with *Muzio Scevola* and *Floridante* revivals until she condescended to appear in the last week of the year. Sandoni, the Haymarket's second keyboard player, had been sent to fetch her over and was shrewd enough to marry her on the way. With glacial irony the *British Journal* commented: 'Seigniora Cutzoni is expected here with much Impatience for the Improvement of our Opera Performances; and as 'tis said, she far excells Seigniora *Duristante*, already with us, and all those she leaves in Italy behind her, much Satisfaction may be expected by those who of later Years have contributed largely to Performances in this Kind, for the great Advantage of the Publick, and softening the Manners of a rude *British* People.'

The new opera, *Ottone, Re di Germania*, marked a return to the level of *Radamisto*, and demonstrated Handel's reliance on the inspirations of a good libretto and a fine cast to produce first-rate music. It was to be Cuzzoni's introduction to the English public, and Handel had made a careful judgment as to the sort of aria which would go down best of all at the prima donna's first appearance as the Byzantine princess Teofane, comparing the effete Adelberto, posing as her betrothed Ottone whom she has never seen, with a portrait of the original. 'I was sent here as a token of established peace between the Greek and German empires,' she says with political disingenuousness, 'not so that there should be eternal war between my spirit and my sense of duty,' and soon launches into one of Handel's most haunting soprano arias. Constructed in the old-fangled Venetian manner with the string ritornello at the end and the vocal line strung over a slow dotted bass, 'Falsa imagine' is a mere 28 bars, yet its nonchalant artistry is breathtaking. The sense of Teofane's baffled disappointment growing towards a genuinely anguished amazement, as she contrasts supposed reality with a painted likeness which she has been led to believe is closer to the actual thing, is wonderfully conveyed by pitting the blank simplicity of the opening melody, to the words 'False image, you have deceived me, you showed me a lovely face', against the ornate dotted semiquavers of the subsequent 'and that face attracted me', ending with a melisma on the word 'allettò' ('attracted'). Through purely musical means the incipient sexual allure created by the picture of Ottone is thus depicted in the shape of the phrases, and the same alertness to the text dictates the plunging intervals on the words 'orrore' and 'affanno' ('trouble') in the little middle section.

Cuzzoni was understandably disappointed with 'Falsa imagine' and refused point blank to sing it in rehearsal. She did not know her man. Handel, unaccustomed to dictation from his singers on points of art, took hold of the fractious diva, shouting (in French, which he seems to have spoken more readily than Italian): '*Madame, je sais que vous êtes une véritable diablesse, mais je vous ferai savoir, moi, que je suis Beelzebub, le chef des diables*', and threatened to throw her out of the window. The 'little Siren of the stage' was no match for 'the Charming Brute'. She gave in, and her victory over the London audience was assured.

The whole venture was one of Handel's greatest triumphs, and its success must feelingly have recalled the *Rinaldo* nights more than a decade earlier. Much of this *réclame* was due to Cuzzoni herself. Francis Colman noted that she was 'extreemly admired' and the *London Journal* scurrilously observed: 'His Majesty was at the Theatre in the Hay-Market, when Seigniora Cotzani performed, for the first Time, to the Surprize and Admiration of a numerous Audience, who are ever too fond of Foreign Performers. She is already jump'd into a handsome Chariot, and an Equipage accordingly. The Gentry seem to have so high a Taste of her fine Parts, that she is likely to be a great Gainer by them.'

Fabrice compared the run on tickets to the South Sea Bubble. Such was the audience's critical enthusiasm for Cuzzoni that a footman in the gallery was moved to shout out: 'Damme, she has a nest of nightingales in her belly.' This was apparently not the only disturbance from that part of the house, and the Directors had to publish a warning in the *Daily Courant* that the footmen's gallery would be shut if the disorders continued. Gay, writing to Swift in Dublin, caught the mood of the moment when he said: 'As for the reigning Amusement of the town, 'tis entirely Musick. Real fiddles, Bass Viols and Haut boys not poetical Harps, Lyres and reeds. Theres no body allow'd to say I Sing but an Eunuch or an Italian Woman. Every body is grown now as great a judge of Musick as they were in your time of Poetry, and folks that could not distinguish one tune from another now daily dispute about the different Styles of Hendel, Bononcini and Attilio. People have now forgot Homer, and Virgil & Caesar, or at least they have lost their ranks, for in London and Westminster in all polite conversation's, Senesino is daily voted to be the greatest man that ever liv'd.'

An objective opera-goer, if there were any such in London, would have given *Ottone* a rather more mixed reception. The libretto, originally prepared for Lotti's *Teofane*, which Handel had seen at Dresden, is by Stefano Pallavicino, son of a noteworthy Venetian composer and appointed 'Poet in the Italian tongue' to the Saxon court when he was only sixteen. His literary gifts were considerable. Apart from such feats as translating Locke's treatise on education from its French edition into Italian verse, he had provided Agostino Steffani with a fine drama in *Tassilone*, and seems to have specialized in librettos with a political flavour, *Teofane* being designed to celebrate an Austro-Saxon marriage alliance. Though this aspect was unlikely to have interested Handel, Haym or the Haymarket, the text's prevailing style is far superior to those of many other Handel librettos, especially in the vivid language of the recitatives, and the characterization is splendidly forceful throughout.

Burney rightly praises the overture, one of whose movements was later to be used in the last of the Concerti Grossi Opus 3. Noting that 'the number of songs in this opera that became national favourites, is perhaps greater than any other that was ever performed in England', he makes the significant point that 'the passages in this and the other operas which Handel composed about this time, became the musical language of the nation, and in a manner proverbial, like the *bons mots* of a man of wit in society. So that long after this period all the musicians in the kingdom, whenever they attempted to compose what they called Music of their own, seem to have had no other stock of ideas than these passages.' This may have been so, yet Haym's adaptation of Pallavicino, though concentrating the focus of the various episodes on the crucial exit arias (probably at Handel's instigation), involved ruthless and awkward compressions and a consequent weakening of dramatic motivation. Handel himself heavily revised the first draft, cutting no less than ten arias and rewriting four others, but enough of the dash and vigour of the basic text remained for him to be able to project Pallavicino's characters in powerful and consistent musical terms, so that *Ottone*, in a sense, succeeds in spite of itself.

It was not enough for Handel to offer his public a vivid representation of real people in credible situations, the ambitious matriarch Gismonda, her son, the weedy, fainéant Adelberto, the good-natured pirate Emireno and Teofane herself, touchingly human in her devoted courage. The variety of his sympathies, which makes him one of the greatest of musical dramatists, turns the opera, for all its structural flaws, into a brilliant emotional display. Ottone alone travels much farther than the traditional ardour and languishing in which Senesino was a noted adept. Like Teofane he is introduced with an ingenuous simplicity, in the siciliano

'Ritorna, o dolce amore', and thereafter his music is a continually arresting contrast between buoyant virtuosity, in numbers such as the 'modern'-sounding 'Dopo l'orrore' (a superb illustration of Handel's structural mastery) and the introspective lyricism of pieces like 'Tanti affanni', in which the psychological confusions of the recitative are not so much subdued as concentrated within the enfolding gloom of the aria.

Ottone's triumph was a further stage in what was now, by implication at least, a battle of the Titans between Handel and Bononcini. The latter had recently added *Crispo* and *Griselda* to the King's Theatre repertoire and was now bidding fair to rival Handel, especially among the Italian party, whose rabble-rousers seem to have been Rolli, Riva and Senesino. Evidently they had been joined by Anastasia Robinson, for whom Bononcini had provided some attractive airs in *Crispo*, and who may have felt somewhat piqued at seeing herself gradually superseded in Handel's operas by Cuzzoni and Durastanti. Her role as Matilda, Adelberto's spurned love in *Ottone*, was not a particularly substantial one (though, true to the piece's character, her arias give full play to whatever vocal gifts she possessed) and being a Papist can hardly have made her sympathetic to the Lutheran favourite of the Whig ascendancy.

Griselda had a justifiable success. Its music is among Bononcini's best, and the story, made famous by Boccaccio and Chaucer, of the simple country girl who becomes the wife of a marquis, had a special meaning for Robinson in the name part, since it was during these performances that she finally submitted to the advances of the eccentric John Mordaunt, Earl of Peterborough and hero of the siege of Barcelona. Initially he had approached her in the traditional guise of a 'protector', but as an intelligent, well-bred woman she had given him his come-uppance and he was at length forced to propose to her on honourable terms. Though *Griselda* brought her to his arms and to a love-nest in Parson's Green, where she quickly won friends among the aristocracy by her charm and discretion in putting up with the crotchety warrior (Patient Grissel, we gather, was not in it), Peterborough's pride prevented him from making Robinson an honest woman until a wasting illness and the triumph of her devout Christian principles brought him to his senses.

Fascinating evidence, incidentally, exists to show that certain of Handel's singers took the dramatic aspect of their roles seriously, in a letter Robinson wrote to Giuseppe Riva during *Ottone* rehearsals. Though 'very sensible the Musick of my Part is exstreamly fine' she was sure 'the Caracter causes it to be of that kind, which in no way suits my Capacity: those songs that require fury and passion to express them, can never be performed by me according to the intention of the Composer, and consequently must loose their Beauty.' She asked for the words of Matilda's second air, 'Pensa spietata Madre', to be changed to suit her, assuring him that 'a Short Melancholly song' instead would not be out of place in the drama. Since Walsh prints a version of this air to different words, sung by Adelberto, we may suppose Robinson's request was listened to. A plea thus addressed to Riva suggests that he must have acted as an arbiter at the King's Theatre productions.

The *Ottone* cast all figured again in the first opera to be given at the Haymarket by the third of the Academy's foreign masters, Attilio Ariosti. Nearly 60, and a native Emilian like Bononcini, he was sometimes known as 'Padre Attilio' from his having been ordained a Servite friar, a fact which made little difference to his style of living, since he had resisted an attempt by his order to recall him from the Berlin court in 1703 by stopping off at Vienna, where he secured imperial patronage. Like Steffani he acted as a diplomatic agent, but at the Emperor Joseph's death he is said to have been banished from the imperial dominions for worldliness. The music of his *Cajo Marzio Coriolano*, first produced on 19 February 1723, has a colourless efficiency about it. There is a decent C minor largo for Durastanti, a simile aria about a swallow for Cuzzoni, a single bass number for Boschi, and a grand prison scene, a speciality of Senesino's. Handel seems to have liked the march, for he echoed the opening phrase in the *coro* of *Scipione* three years later.

If the Academy's productions were providing, in classic style, more bills than dividends and the directors were starting to shake fists at defaulting subscribers, the artistic and social triumph of opera in London was now complete, though the croak of experienced warning could already be heard from voices such as that of the theatre's own architect. Writing to his friend the publisher Jacob Tonson to thank him for 'the best Sider I ever drank since I was born', Vanbrugh added: 'I Suppose you don't care a farthing for the Towne, if you did; you'd look into it now and then. I can't blame you however, for you Spend your Life I believe, much as I wou'd do, had I made a good Voyage to the Messissippy. I'll tell you at the Same time that in Spight all the Misfortunes & losses, that have occasion'd more crying and wailing, than I believe was ever known before; the Opera has been Supported at half a Guinea, Pit and Boxes, and perform'd 62 times this last Season.' It could scarcely last, but meanwhile, in the currently favourable climate of Anglo-French relations plans were made for the company, under Bononcini's direction, to go to Paris. The agreement between King George and his cousin, Regent Orléans, involved taking the entire production outfit, dresses, sets, singers, orchestra and all, to France for a month. A pity that the scheme eventually foundered, since the concept of an international tour by a major company was relatively unfamiliar during the period, and it must have been interesting to see the effect of mainstream Italian opera on the xenophobia which, then as later, was such a marked feature of French musical culture.

Handel and Haym had been preparing a new piece, based on an adaptation of Matteo Noris's *Flavio Cuniberto*, originally set by the Venetian composer Partenio in 1682. The plot is one of Noris's more acceptable, laid in Lombard Italy so often favoured by contemporary librettists (six Handel operas have Dark Age settings) and pairs the love of Guido and Emilia (Senesino and Cuzzoni) with the secret amour of Teodata and Vitige (Robinson and Durastanti in a breeches part) temporarily thwarted by the roving passions of King Flavio. A further plot element, the rivalry of Emilia's father Lotario with Teodata's father Ugone for the governorship of Britain, may have appealed to composer and librettist on the basis of some contemporary political episode whose significance is lost on us. There is a possible parallel between the Ugone-Lotario fracas and the growing contention between Sir Robert Walpole and Lord Carteret, which, though Carteret was not dismissed as Secretary of State for the South till the following year, was certainly familiar to at least one of the Academy directors, Newcastle, and surely to others in the audience.

Flavio is one of Handel's most perfectly organized operas. A pervading sense of humour, apparent in the almost self-parodying mannerisms of the overture and enduring throughout the drama, conditions the response to a text which a less lively artist would have treated far more soberly. It is difficult, in any case, to accept Noris's intentions as having been wholly serious. Successive situations — Ugone entering with a red welt on his cheek where Lotario has slapped him, the concealed passions of Vitige and Teodata, the almost imbecile benevolence of Flavio himself, everything culminating in a dénouement of delightful absurdity — suggest that the writer was sending up the genre in a way which Handel appreciated even if his audience did not.

Most, though not all, of the elements in the formula do their work adequately. Lotario's death in a duel removes the bass from the opera before the end of Act II (Boschi presumably sang his *coro* part offstage) and Ugone is steadily reduced to a cipher. Otherwise the characters are admirably laid open to Handel's witty and perceptive treatment of them. Emilia is a consistent study in pathetic charm: four of her arias are in slow tempi and two of them feature the flute accompaniment whose timbre Handel liked to match with the soprano voice (the first, 'Quanto dolci, quanto care', in a favourite rhythmic pattern of triplets and dotted notes in 3/4, is an exquisite sketch of simple, almost childish happiness ultimately demanding some kind of nemesis). Guido's music is calculated to display Senesino's expressive powers at their fullest, while at the same time quietly mocking the various conventional postures adopted in the respective arias. Flavio himself is throughout a facile creature, and Handel here cleverly reinforces the impression of the simple-minded despot whose lookalike can be found in Tamerlano and Serse.

The scoring is sensitive to the need to preserve a light texture for a drama whose postures are so often the reverse of admirable or heroic. There are no horns or trumpets, but one of the versions of Ugone's 'Fato tiranno e crudo' includes an independent bass line for *violoncello e cembalo*, a solo oboe colours the middle section of Guido's Act II aria, and Flavio's 'Di quel bel che m'innamora' in Act I is enriched by a dialogue of solo oboe and violin.

As a whole *Flavio* is an artistic triumph, but its very alertness to nuance and ambiguity has prevented it from joining *Giulio Cesare* or *Alcina* among Handel's more popular operas; none of its roles is a vocal firework display and no character is allowed to steal the show. The recitatives are uncommonly interesting (especially III.iv., a rare example in Handel's work of an accompanied passage of dialogue) and it would require a director and conductor of considerable refinement and intelligence to capture the appropriate spirit of this sophisticated work. As in *Agrippina*, Handel does not laugh at the characters themselves. The absurdity, given point by the authentically Handelian sense of deadpan humour, lies not in what these people feel, but in the circumstances which produce the feelings.

Though the Directors tried to get a royal grant of an extra £200 on top of the bounty the king already allowed them, and although, in November 1723, a fortnight or so before the new season's opening night, they made their tenth five percent call on subscribers, Handel himself was not doing at all badly. At some stage during this year, as we know from the parish highway rate books, the composer, who had hitherto lived at the residence of a Mr Andrews of Barn Elms (modern Barnes), bought himself a fine new house at what is now No. 25, Brook Street, Hanover Square. The church of St George had not yet been built, and the new street lay in the enormous parish of St Martin-in-the-Fields.

The creation of Brook Street was part of a burst of speculative development on London's western edges during the early years of the decade, reaching a climax in 1725 when more deeds were recorded in the Middlesex Land Registry than at any other time for the next 40 years. The western part of the street lay in the Grosvenor estate, debouching on the newly laid out Grosvenor Square, with its circular central plot of plantations and gravel walks, and to this rather more fashionable end, alongside such aristocratic neighbours as Lord Hartington (who, as Duke of Devonshire, invited Handel to Ireland in 1741) and the Earls of Coventry and Northampton, Mrs Delany, one of the composer's most loyal friends, was eventually to move from Clarges Street.

Thanks to an inventory taken after Handel's death in 1759 we can get some idea of his intimate surroundings and judging by the state of the furniture things cannot have altered much since he first moved in. The garrets under the roof were used to store objects such as 'an Old Sadle' and 'an Old Grate' (the word 'Old' occurs continually) and the '2 pr Stairs Closset' contained '2 Old Globes & Frames & Chimney board'. The front room on the second floor was fitted up as a bedroom, complete with red curtains, tongs and poker for the fire and 'a Round Close Stool & white pann'. It was probably here that Handel himself slept, since the back bedroom was far more simply furnished. There were card tables in the dining-room and another in the next room on the first floor, where the presence of 'A Stove Compleat bellows & Brush' suggests that at least one familiar German domestic feature was never parted with in 48 years' residence in England. Downstairs in the back parlour the inventory seems to imply that Handel used it both as a study and dressing room, since we find an easy chair, a swing glass, '2 Wig block fixt' and a linen press in company with 'a Wallnuttren Desk' and a deal bookcase, with 'In the Clossett a Large Nest of drawers'. The kitchen, as we might expect, has absolutely everything from 'an Iron Plate Warmer', 'a Fish Kittle Compleat' and '2 Stue panns & Covers' to 'a Choping board', 'a Spice Drawer' and 'about 30 pss of Earthen and Stone Ware & a Towel Rowl'. All the household goods were ultimately bought up by Handel's servant John Duburk, but as there is no mention of musical instruments they must already have been removed by the legatees in the composer's will.

Handel owned two harpsichords, one of them the fine Ruckers now at Fenton House, and his keyboard virtuosity had been a byword among English musicians ever since his arrival in London. It was during these early years of the Royal Academy venture that he published his first group of harpsichord suites, largely as a result of a pirated selection having been issued under the imprint of Jeanne Roger in Amsterdam in 1719. The real buccaneering had probably been undertaken by John Walsh, as we can tell from the engraving of the plates, but though Walsh himself, by sheer competitive push, was ultimately to become Handel's publisher, it was to the firm of John Cluer, responsible for printing all the operas from *Giulio Cesare* to *Siroe*, that the composer now turned for an official edition. In a preface to the eight suites, issued on 14 November 1720, Handel says: 'I have been obliged to publish some of the following lessons because surrepticious and incorrect copies of them had gone abroad. I have added several new ones to make the Work more usefull which if it meets with a favourable reception I will still proceed to publish more: reckoning it my duty with my small talent to serve a Nation from which I have receiv'd so Generous a protection.'

Some of the music of the *Suites de Pièces pour le Clavecin* (First Set) was probably composed during the period spent in Hanover after Handel's return from Italy, some of it may belong to the Burlington years, and one or two movements can be stylistically related to his spell of teaching in Hamburg during the early months of 1706. The form of the suites is the familiar assemblage of dance movements, allemande, courante, sarabande and gigue, best known to modern keyboard players in examples by Bach and Purcell, alternated with extended fugues, toccata-like preludes, themes with variations and in one case a full-scale French overture. Their characteristically diversified styles reflect the same *mélange* of national traditions we noted in Handel's lost childhood commonplace book: echoes of Fischer and Kerll in the shorter movements are answered by those of Pachelbel in variation sequences like the famous 'Harmonious Blacksmith' set of no. 5 in E or the Frobergerish introspection of the F minor prelude to no. 8, and contrasted with the jolly Italian sinfonia offered as the second movement of no. 2. It is going a little too far to detect the beginnings of Handel's Englishness in gigues which may have been written in Italy, but that which ends the F sharp minor suite has suggestions of that most English of moments in *Acis and Galatea*, the duet 'Happy we'.

Handel's keyboard music has never succeeded in gaining the sort of popular regard enjoyed by that of Bach or Scarlatti, and labels like 'easy' and 'conventional' are all too readily applied. If he was such a phenomenal improviser as Burney, Hawkins and others would have us believe, where is the real proof of his virtuosity, or is it a case of his having jealously carried his secrets with him to the grave? The attraction of these pieces lies rather in their melodic and rhythmic affinities with the musical medium which interested him most, the world of lyric drama. The decorations opening the second suites are like the warbling divisions of a Nicolini or a Senesino, and the frowning grandeur of the G minor's overture raises the curtain on what is, in design if not in conscious intention, a dramatic sequence of alternating mood pictures culminating in a superb though wholly traditional passacaglia.

— 6 —

Discords in the State

'It seems to me that he is a little mad,' Count Flemming had written to Melusine von der Schulenburg: to Handel's contemporaries there was always something remote and awe-inspiring about the way in which his genius worked, and his career is marked by moments of torrential creative energy which produce a spate of stupendous achievement. One of the most extraordinary examples of this occurred during the period between February, 1724, and February, 1725, the twelve months which saw the composition of *Guilio Cesare*, *Tamerlano* and *Rodelinda*. Several factors must have assisted the process, including the embattled, combative nature of Handel's work at the Haymarket, with Bononcini and his cronies still showing fight, the sense of his having formed a genuinely appreciative public, and an awareness of the fund of professional experience upon which, with works like *Ottone* and *Radamisto* behind him, he could now draw. Something may also have been due to his working relationship with Haym, who was prepared to respect the composer's demands and whose adaptations, if they did not always overcome the technical problems posed by the original texts, for the most part made good dramatic sense.

With new works by Bononcini and Ariosti, the opera nights during the early months of the 1723–4 season were eked out with an *Ottone* revival, but by the end of February Handel had his new piece ready. Altering Bussani's *Giulio Cesare in Egitto*, originally set by Antonio Sartorio in 1677, Haym, doubtless at Handel's bidding, developed the characters of Pompey's widow and son, Cornelia and Sextus, and played down the typical Venetian cast of extras, cutting out the comic nurse Rodisbe and reducing Curio and Nireno to mere loyal feeds (they disappeared entirely in later revivals). To an already complex plot, centred on Cleopatra's love for Caesar and her acquisition of the throne from her preposterous brother Ptolemy, he added a poignant and dramatically arresting scene before Pompey's tomb and introduced the historical incident of Caesar's swim across Alexandria harbour.

The result, as modern performances (however musically and visually questionable) have shown, is one of those works which, whatever is done to it, refuses to lie down. Most producers make the mistake of assuming that because the story demands the appearance of a crowd of Caesar's followers as he crosses the Nile, the spectacle of Ptolemy anachronistically surrounded by his harem and the apotheosis of Cleopatra amid the nine muses in a vision of Parnassus, the stage in *Giulio Cesare* must be crowded in best MGM fashion. Yet, as in Verdi's *Don Carlos* and *Aida*, the great public moments are there precisely in order to imply an ironical contrast with the central intimacy of the private drama which a handful of characters is playing out in the foreground.

Handel's operas are not about three-ring-circus spectacle, canary fancying or visual gimmickry, though they feature elements of each. They are primarily concerned with the credible emotions of real people. The merit of *Giulio Cesare* lies in the subtlety with which the composer is able to vary his presentation of those emotions and shape vital, intensely fallible human figures from the posturing creations dreamed up in a Baroque fantasy version of Roman history, a mixture of Plutarch, Corneille, Venetian romance and the crotchets of Cuzzoni, Robinson, Senesino and the rest.

Cleopatra herself is a prime example. Though English audiences knew her best as the dignified heroine of Dryden's popular *All For Love*, Handel and Haym are somewhat closer to Shakespeare in their portrait of an ambitious and undaunted woman guided unerringly by the truth of her feelings and devoted to love. The proof that Handel the man was far from being 'sexless and safe' is here in the music, with its acute psychological penetration and glowing sensuality. She is worked lightly enough into the drama, after most of the other principals have already appeared, with a flippant E major aria full of teasing trills and mordents, as she tells her effete brother: 'Don't despair! who knows, if you're unlucky with the kingdom, perhaps you'll be lucky in love.' After exulting in the power of her beauty (disguised as Lidia, a court lady, she was wooed and won by Caesar) — 'a pretty woman can do anything', she cries — Cleopatra next figures in an invocation to hope based on 'Let flocks and herds' from the 1713 Birthday Ode (both are in B flat) exuberant but tinged with languorous expectation.

It is in Act II that Handel achieves his master stroke. Cleopatra's seduction of Caesar is not, after all, quite complete. Now she presents him with a carefully stage-managed erotic vision of herself as Virtue 'assisted by the nine Muses' on Parnassus. Handel's orchestration of this, to a leisurely sarabande melody, is incomparably seductive: on stage the band comprises oboe, bassoons, strings (including a viola da gamba *arpeggiando*), harp and theorbo, in the pit the basic orchestra supplies the gentlest of comments, as Cleopatra takes up the theme, with the full accompaniment, as sensuous as anything contrived by Mahler or Strauss, in 'V'adoro, pupille'. As Caesar rushes to embrace her, the scene shuts and she disappears.

The queen's tragic dignity of utterance when, later in the opera, she believes her hero to be dead, offers a direct contrast to the ravaged matriarchal grandeur of Cornelia. If Anastasia Robinson had ever felt hard done by in earlier works, she had no reason to complain here, in a role Handel endowed with a Roman nobility surely designed to counterpoint Cleopatra's Egyptian guile (though the two women, far from being rivals, are allies against Ptolemy from the outset). The shift in mood throughout her four arias mirrors the movement of the opera itself from crisis to resolution. Her initial misery leads to a baffled suicide attempt, following an air accompanied by a jagged string figure of dotted semiquavers, broken off at the end of the first section by her determination to do away with herself. Though her plangency finds a further outlet in the expressive E minor siciliano duet with Sextus, it is significantly cut into by Ptolemy's general, Achillas, in Act II, at a point when this vein has been sufficiently emphasized, and her subsequent arias are cheerfully optimistic.

The dazzling vocal and orchestral textures of *Giulio Cesare* won the opera an instant acclaim — though interestingly it was later noted that 'both the composer and the performers seem to have acquired even more reputation from the recitatives than the airs'. Besides handing out plums to Senesino, Cuzzoni and Robinson, Handel saw to it that Boschi, as Achillas, got a rather more substantial share in the drama than some of his earlier roles had allowed him, and provided in Ptolemy a study in cynical villainy for the beanpole castrato, Gaetano Berenstadt, who had joined the company two years before for *Ottone*. Making a farewell appearance, as Sextus, was Margherita Durastanti, who was to quit the London musical world later that year with a benefit concert at which her song of *adieux*, to words attributed to Pope, ended:

> But let old charmers yield to new;
> Happy soil, adieu, adieu!

Retiring £1,000 the richer from this one evening, she would nevertheless return as a proof of Handel's enduring confidence in her dependable musicianship.

It is difficult for us nowadays, in an age which can reproduce a carefully processed performance several thousand times, to appreciate the effect on English audiences of the outstanding professional artistry which the King's Theatre could now offer its patrons. Not only the singers but the band as well, featuring the kind of internationally renowned orchestral player whose services Handel, a stickler for the highest standards, could always obtain, represented a consistent level of excellence which any European company would have envied. The response from some of the more sensitive spectators was not confined to hailing Cuzzoni with a '*Brava, brava!*' or a '*Cara, cara!*' but found an outlet in poetry. The 'Post Boy' of 7 March 1723, for example, advertised an anonymous *Epistle to Mr Handel, Upon His Operas of Flavius and Julius Caesar*. If, with its moments of bathos and a line or two cribbed from Dryden, it was not especially good poetry, the effusion tried at any rate to express a widespread sensation. The unknown poet suggests that Handel can reconcile political factions and bring the nation together:

> Our Souls so tun'd, that *Discord* grieves to find
> A whole fantastick Audience of a Mind.

Though of course there are dissenters, followers of Bononcini and Ariosti, but look at the result:

> In Place of promis'd Heaps of glitt'ring Gold,
> The good Academy got nought — but Cold.
> Where cou'd they fly for Succour, but to You?
> Whose Musick's ever Good, and ever New.

To suggest that Handel's effect on the Academy audience was to make it more harmonious fell distinctly wide of the mark. Partisanship was too much of a fashionable novelty to be smoothed away merely by a single theatrical success and the Lancashire Jacobite John Byrom, among the less enthusiastic spectators at the first run of *Giulio Cesare*, put the case succinctly:

Some say, compared to Bononcini,
That Mynheer Handel's but a Ninny;
Others aver that he to Handel
Is scarcely fit to hold a Candle;
Strange all this difference should be
'Twixt Tweedle-dum and Tweedle-dee.

Letters from foreign observers bear witness to the squabbles among the Directors, to the intense public interest in the sides taken on behalf of singers and composers, and to the rising mania for anything to do with the opera.

It was not only Durastanti, however, who bowed out. Anastasia Robinson now left the company as well, and, significantly for Handel, Bononcini mounted his penultimate Haymarket opera *Calfurnia*. He was not re-engaged by the Academy for the following season, departed for Paris with Cuzzoni in the early summer, but was tempted to return with the offer of a £500 a year pension by the quirkish and slightly disreputable Henrietta Spencer, Duchess of Marlborough. For those who patriotically deplored the fuss being made over a parcel of squalling foreigners, these changes must have suggested an encouraging likelihood that the town would come to its senses soon enough. Ambrose Philips, under the impression that Cuzzoni's trip to Paris meant that she was going for good, felt emboldened to address her as though she were somehow responsible for tampering with the national character:

Leave us Britons rough and free,
Leave us as we ought to be.

Somebody had the idea of recasting Sir John Suckling's 'A Session of Poets' in the form of a session of musicians, which appeared as an anonymous pamphlet towards the end of the 1724 season, and presents an interesting conspectus of contemporary opinion on the London musical scene. Apollo settles on the opera house as an appropriate venue for his court, and Boschi and Berenstadt, by virtue of their loud voices, are nominated as the ushers. All the town musicians arrive, from 'the Op'ra Orchest' and the playhouse bands to waits, organists, dancing-masters and the fiddlers from riverside taverns. The composers then present themselves one by one, and are dealt with by the god strictly according to their deserts: Pepusch is slily criticized for his preoccupation with academic degrees, Galliard, Ariosti and poor mad Thomas Roseingrave are gently though patronizingly brushed aside, the Scotch violinist

William Corbett is banished, with heavy irony, 'to cleanly Edinburgh', and Greene and Croft are damned out of hand for dullness. Geminiani gets a fairer hearing:

> And since his Fame all Fiddlers else surpasses,
> He set him down first Treble at Parnassus,

and Loeillet is implicitly commended for his modest good-fellowship:

> A supper for some Friends I've just bespoke,
> Pray come — and drink your Glass — and crack your Joke.

The preference shown to Haym as opposed to Rolli, distinguished only for his 'scoundrel Op'ra Words', suggests that the writer must have been in the know as to the nature of the Haymarket factions. Bononcini, scornful to the last, appears with the Robinson on his arm, but his music simply succeeds in sending everybody to sleep. It is, of course, Handel who, by implication 'since but one Phoenix we can boast, he needs no name', wins the coveted bays:

> For who so fit for universal Rule
> As he who best all Passions can controul?

This sort of pamphleteering underlines the exposed position into which Handel's gifts thrust him throughout his English career. The assumption is a naïve one which depicts him as the uncontested king of London musical life, and he was now beginning to discover the true perils and responsibilities of fame, talent and success in a city where the public's reserves of caprice were as unlimited as its supply of cash. Professional jealousy was incessant, and it is clear that certain composers, such as Pepusch and later Charles Avison, a severe critic, were genuinely blind to certain aspects of his genius which we now take for granted. Others, notably Maurice Greene and William Croft, felt actively threatened by him, and since Handel, unlike the heroes of his operas, was not given to playing the *generoso rival*, the resentment is likely to have been mutual.

He was taking no chances with the new operas for the 1724–5 season. True victories are those quickest followed up, and the triumph of *Giulio Cesare* was an ideal springboard. The Italian diplomat Zamboni, writing to a friend in September, a month or so before the opening night, looked forward to a bumper season. Besides Senesino and Cuzzoni at the top of their form, the company, having shed Durastanti, had gained a good replacement in Anna Dotti, who had arrived from Paris presumably as an offshoot of the abortive foreign touring negotiations of the previous year.

Berenstadt had gone back to Italy, where, like others of his kind, he dabbled in picture-dealing while continuing his singing career, and his place was now taken by the versatile alto castrato Andrea Pacini.

The casts of the new Haymarket shows were further enriched by the acquisition of Francesco Borosini, one of the greatest tenors of his day. Yet another Modenese, he had been a popular singer at the imperial court (becoming, incidentally, a director of the Kärntnerthor theatre) and was an exciting find for Handel, who, as well as creating two outstanding new roles for him, recast the part of Sextus for a tenor in the revival of *Giulio Cesare* the following year. Borosini appears to have arrived, what is more, with the libretto of one of his more recent successes in his pocket. Zamboni tells his friend Gaburri that 'the first opera will be Bajazet, set to music by Handel', and it was to Agostino Piovene's *Il Bajazet* that Handel and the ever co-operative Haym were now to turn for their opening novelty.

A member of a leading family of Veneto nobility, Piovene had produced his popular libretto on the story of Tamburlaine and Bajazeth, based on an already extant text by Antonio Salvi with additional love interest worked up from Ducas's Byzantine history, in 1710. Borosini's triumph had been in the version made nine years later for the theatre at Reggio by anonymous adaptors styling themselves *Gli Interessati nel Dramma*. To this improved edition Borosini, notable in a cast which included such past and future Handelians as Antonio Bernacchi, Faustina Bordoni and Diana Vico, had caused a special scene to be added, as the Reggio title page tells us: 'the poetry is by the noble Venetian Piovene, apart from the last scene, which was composed by Zanella, a famous Modenese poet, and founded on an idea of Signor Borosini's'. The idea was evidently the spectacular onstage death agony of the wretched Bajazet, dying gasps and all, a relative rarity in Baroque opera and one which is not carried all the way, since the unfortunate sultan actually leaves the stage to die.

Tightened up by Handel, Haym and the Reggio adaptors, *Tamerlano* (note the change of emphasis indicated by the London title) emerges as one of the strongest of the Academy's librettos. As the only Handel opera of the 1720s to be predominantly tragic (the happy ending implied by the *coro* is softened by the glumness of the music), it is also his only work of this period to be firmly rooted in the world of French neo-classical drama. Apart from Ducas, its main literary source is indeed a French tragedy, *Tamerlan ou la Mort de Bajazet* by Jacques Nicholas Pradon, famous as a jealous competitor with Racine and a tool of the factions that brought about the initial failure of *Phèdre*, and the spirit of the original play has heavily conditioned the atmosphere of the opera.

It is an atmosphere very different from those of *Giulio Cesare* and *Ottone*, a sparse, bare, dark, indoor world, whose sense of hopelessness and claustrophobia, as though we were viewing it through an infinite corridor, has a far closer kinship to the sort of drama produced in our own century than to the age of Zeno and Metastasio. There is a startling absence of that element of spectacle and occasion which punctuates so many of the earlier operas, no marching armies, bird-haunted groves, jolly symphonies and dances, scenes of transformation, combat or seduction. Nor are the women, those Handelian catalysts who set the tone of each opera, characters in the mould, say, of Teofane, Gismonda or Cleopatra. Theirs is not even the majestic theatricality of a Zenobia or a Cornelia. Princesses both, Asteria and Irene are humanized to a point at which their plainness speaks more powerfully than any magniloquent gesture.

These stock figures of *opera seria* take life from the composer's firm grasp of dramatic consistency, as do the four male protagonists. Tamburlaine himself, swaggering and decadent, has all too evidently created the air of violence and corruption which overwhelms the refinement of somebody like Andronico, a Senesino sighing-lover role given a deeper irony by his articulate impotence, the baffled intellectual at the tyrant's court. Leone, the Boschi bass, has the task of emphasizing, as a marginal commentator, the crushing futility at the core of this extraordinary work. As for Bajazet, it is he who from the outset dominates the opera and offers a superb illustration of Handel's ability to portray human suffering. Monumental in quality though much of his music is in its quasi-religious vein (two of his arias, significantly, are derived from *La Resurrezione* and another is from the *Brockes Passion*), he remains the archetypal father and ruler, gradually stripped of power and authority until allowed to die in circumstances as poignant as King Lear's.

The music for this episode shows Handel working in the medium of which he had been a master since the days of *Teseo* and *Amadigi*, the free-moving accompanied recitative, in which ungoverned emotion temporarily annihilates form and tonality. The scene looks forward, in its depiction of passionate despair, to moments like Dejanira's madness in *Hercules* or 'Deeper and deeper still' of *Jephtha*, and seems to have been well appreciated from the first.

Handel's manuscripts reveal the extraordinary care he took over this and other aspects of a work which drew on his utmost creative resources.

Another example of his attention to balance and detail is the moment in Act II when Asteria, in order to save her father and her lover, has agreed to marry Tamerlano, though he is already betrothed to Irene. Bajazet, Andronico and Irene turn from her in horror as she ascends the throne, but she then discloses that she planned to stab Tamerlano as soon as he came near. The angry tyrant sentences father and daughter to death and leaves Asteria to face the recriminations of the others. Each responds to her appeal in a brief air beginning with the word 'No!' and Asteria finishes the scene alone, with a grand *da capo* piece designed to give full play to Cuzzonian versatility.

With its controlled key scheme (the three exit arias are in E minor, E major and G major respectively) and deliberately condensed forms (no ritornellos except to usher the characters off) this is one of those points which triumphantly validate the artificiality of *opera seria*. It recalls, of course, the triumph scene in *Agrippina*, where the characters drop away from Ottone one by one, and both episodes justify the use of that exit convention which was to become standardized in the mechanical dramas of Metastasio.

Haym dedicated *Tamerlano* to the first Duke of Rutland, a talented amateur violinist who had introduced the Haymarket orchestra's leader, Stefano Carbonelli, to England. The opera was a success, though it never succeeded in joining *Rinaldo* and *Giulio Cesare* among Handel favourites, and Anna Dotti as Irene caused unintentional laughter among the audience, as Lady Bristol told her husband: 'You know my ear too well for me to pretend to give you any account of the Opera farther than that the new man takes extremely,' she wrote, 'but the woman is so great a joke that there was more laughing at her than at a farce, but her opinion of her self gets the better of that. The Royal family were all there, and a greater crowd than ever I saw, which has tired me to death, so that I am come home to go to bed as soon as I have finished this.' Cluer published the score, with Handel's own corrections and figurations, 'and to render the Work more acceptable to Gentlemen and Ladies every Song is truly translated into English Verse, and the Words engrav'd to the Musick under the Italian, which was never before attempted in any Opera . . . '.

After nine performances of Ariosti's *Artaserse* and a successful *Giulio Cesare* revival, the second of Handel's new works for the season was brought on. For the first time in his English career, Handel turned to the writings of Antonio Salvi, whom he had very probably met during his visits to Florence and whose librettos offer interesting evidence of the reforms taking place in Italian opera during the early eighteenth century. Salvi's speciality was precisely the sort of 'human predicament' story which was bound to appeal to Handel. Like Piovene he had felt the influence of French drama, and had actually produced his own version of Pradon's *Tamerlan* for performance at Pratolino in 1706, introducing a character called Rossane 'so as to follow the Italian custom of bringing at least two women on to the stage'. For the libretto which Handel was later to use for *Rodelinda, Regina de'Longobardi*, Salvi turned to Corneille's *Pertharite, Roi des Lombards*, produced in Paris in 1652, but he may well have done this with an eye to the current vogue for 'Gothic' subjects among Italian librettists and composers. Looking, for example, at the list of operas given at Venice between 1700 and 1710 we can find at least nine, including such titles as *Edvige, Regina d'Ungheria, Berengario, Re d'Italia, Engelberta, Fredegonda, Ambleto* (Apostolo Zeno's version of the Hamlet story) and an adaptation of *Pertharite* made by another librettist for Pollarolo.

Salvi's treatment of Corneille is sensitive throughout to the nature of Italian opera as opposed to French tragedy, but even more interesting is the way in which Handel and Haym treated Salvi. Large amounts of recitative were whittled away (even with its word-books the English audience is unlikely to have welcomed *recitativo semplice* as a dominant element in the work) and though the proportion of arias was not seriously reduced, their distribution was adjusted so as to throw the major figures into greater relief. Certain new scenes were added which bear witness to the imaginative strength of the collaboration. We shall never know whether Haym or Handel was responsible for the interpolation of such poignant utterances as Bertarido's 'Dove sei' and Rodelinda's 'Ho perduto il caro sposo', but they make perfect sense in their dramatic context.

Rodelinda stands in complete contrast to the annihilating gloom of *Tamerlano*. From the outset Handel loads the odds in favour of the eponymous heroine, a wife who believes her husband is dead and repels the advances of the tyrant who has dispossessed him. Her music conveys all the strength of character which her opponent, the peevish, vacillating Grimoaldo, lacks. The arbitrary power which lays its threatening hand on the protagonists of *Tamerlano* is progressively weakened, in the palace of the Lombard usurper, by constancy and fortitude, so that when we reach the closing scene of Act III, in which Grimoaldo, wrung with remorse, wishes that he could change places with the shepherd of a poor flock, the conventional aristocratic hankering for pastoral simplicity is made the vehicle for a comprehensible change of heart, conveyed by the composer in one of his most melting sicilianos.

The structure of the opera is arguably the finest ever achieved by Handel, and the seamless progression of its successive episodes is clinched by the skill with which aria and recitative are integrated throughout, either by the patterning and contrast of various keys — the first scene of Act I, for example, is entirely in flat keys and the opening scene of Act II moves from wrathful G minor to optimistic G major, associated throughout with Rodelinda's triumphant fidelity — or by surprise shifts from one medium to the other, as in Eduige's intrusion into Bertarido's 'Con rauco mormorio' before the *da capo* or in the way in which his 'Dove sei' is made to grow straight out of the recitative, the vocal entry prefacing the ritornello. The four major roles were perfectly tailored to their original creators. It is certainly hard to think of another part, even Cleopatra, in which Cuzzoni's vocal and expressive range was treated so sympathetically. Handel's confidence in Borosini as an intelligent and discriminating performer is shown by his refusal to type-cast him: from a tragic father in *Tamerlano* he was transformed to a neurotic usurper in *Rodelinda*. The fact that Senesino had to play yet another ineffectual figure, the lurking fugitive Bertarido, and was awarded the statutory prison scene, leads to the conclusion that this was the sort of part he did best, admired as his stage presence was by certain of the audience.

Rodelinda, with its 'capital and pleasing airs', ran for thirteen nights, and was the first Handel opera to be published on a subscription basis. Its success with the ladies at the King's Theatre was partly attributable, according to Burney, to Cuzzoni's stage costume: 'on her appearing in this opera in a *brown silk gown*, trimmed with silver, with the vulgarity and indecorum of which all the old ladies were much scandalized, the young adopted it as a fashion, so universally, that it seemed a national uniform for youth and beauty'. But is he correct? The stage direction in scene four of the last act of *Flavio*, calling for an Emilia *vestita a bruno*, suggests that Cuzzoni's trend-setting may have taken place two years earlier. She was three months pregnant, timing her delivery nicely for the inter-season break in August. Mary Pendarves (Mrs Delany) wrote snobbishly to her sister: 'Mrs Sandoni (who was Cuzzoni) is brought to bed of a daughter: it is a mighty mortification it was not a son. Sons and heirs ought to be out of fashion when such scrubs shall pretend to be dissatisfied at having a daughter: 'tis pity, indeed, that the noble name and family of the Sandonis should be extinct. The minute she was brought to bed, she sang "La Speranza", a song in Otho. . . . ' Well, maybe, though it wasn't originally written for her.

Her ascendancy with the public was not to go unchallenged for much longer. A cloud no bigger than a man's hand, threatening dissolution not merely to Cuzzoni's English triumphs but to the entire Academy, emerged in the form of several newspaper paragraphs which began to appear during the autumn of 1725. On 31 August the *Daily Journal* announced that 'the Royal Academy . . . have contracted with a famous Chauntress for 2500 l. who is coming over from Italy against the Winter'. A week later the *London Journal* put things a little more bluntly: 'Signora *Faustina*, a famous Italian Lady, is coming over this Winter to rival Signiora Cuzzoni'; while *Parker's Penny Post* told its readers that 'the famous Italian Singer, who is hired to come over hither to entertain his Majesty and the Nobility in the Operas, is call'd Signiora Faustina; whose Voice (it is pretended) has not yet been equall'd in the World'.

The engagement of the celebrated Faustina Bordoni had in fact been a rumoured possibility as early as March 1723, when the inimitable *London Journal* had commented: 'As we delight so much in Italian Songs, we are likely to have enough of them, for as soon as Cuzzoni's Time is out we are to have another over; for we are well assured *Faustina*, the fine Songstress at Venice, is invited, whose Voice, they say, exceeds that we have already here; and as the Encouragement is so great, no doubt but she will visit us, and like others, when she makes her Exit, may carry off Money to build some stately Edifice in her own Country, and there perpetuate our Folly.'

She was certainly a notable acquisition. Daughter of a noble family, she was born in Venice in 1700 and, as an orphan girl, protected by the patrician composers Alessandro and Benedetto Marcello. Her debut at the age of sixteen in Pollarolo's *Ariodante* brought her immediate success, and she had gone on to become one of the most popular singers of her day, and perhaps the first great prima donna in the star tradition which has lasted into our own time. Princes and ambassadors showered gifts on her, but as the librettist Apostolo Zeno significantly observed: 'whatever good fortune or encouragement she meets with, she merits it all by her courteous and polite manners, as well as talents, with which she has enchanted the whole (imperial) court'. Like Cuzzoni she was small, but could carry this off very well and had the advantage, not only of great beauty but of being a very good actress. Unlike her rival she was endowed with common sense and a secure awareness of her supremacy. She was famous, as a singer, for her sustained notes, the result of perfect breath control, her fine trills and excellent diction. 'In short,' as Quantz remarked, 'she was born for singing and for acting.'

It is hard to imagine what the Directors thought they were doing in bringing the two leading Italian prima donnas of the decade on to the

Haymarket stage together. The desire to load an operatic organization with expensive foreign stars is a well-known phenomenon, and will go on attracting audiences and wrecking theatrical bank accounts until barbarism suppresses the adornments of civilized living. Common, too, is the fallacy that by flinging together a host of 'names' an evening's performance will somehow render greater justice to the music. Add to these familiar notions the presence of that other habitual figure the opera-buff, with which London society was now teeming, and the eagerness to welcome Faustina is easily explained, however foolish the decision to invite her. The history of the Academy from the early summer of 1726 onwards is one of prolonged artistic and financial suicide.

As it happened, Faustina did not turn up until the season was very nearly over. It had opened on 30 November 1725 with a revival of the pasticcio *Elpidia*, which had been brought on to finish the previous season in May and June. A Haym adaptation of Zeno's *I Rivali generosi*, its music was selected by Handel from the newest Venetian operas of the previous year. As these were all from the current S. Giovanni Grisostomo repertoire, this confirms an idea that Handel kept in touch with the theatre's personnel long after *Agrippina*. London audiences could now hear bang-up-to-date Italian music in the shape of three arias by Giuseppe Maria Orlandini and thirteen by the young but highly influential Neapolitan Leonardo Vinci. Five of Cuzzoni's arias in *Elpidia*, incidentally, had been composed for her future competitor Faustina. Did Handel come to savour this irony later on?

Borosini and Pacini starred in these performances, but left the company before the new season began. Handel's failure to bring on a fresh opera may have had something to do with the difficulty of finding replacements. None of them was in any case especially remarkable. When the new work was finally completed, in March 1726, it was hurried into rehearsal and produced within ten days. Much practice would not, in any case, have been necessary as the singers, Senesino, Cuzzoni and Boschi at least, knew the theatre perfectly by now and there was no such thing as a separate producer in early eighteenth-century opera (the production detail, of the simplest, was up to the singers, occasionally helped by the librettist). Entrances, exits, gesture and movement were at the performer's discretion, and stage properties were limited to the odd table or chair. Large sections of the music may have been issued to the artists as the opera was being written, and domestic rehearsal was a commonplace (Zamboni, in a letter to Riva, mentions 'a clandestine rehearsal in your house' of Ariosti's *Vespasiano*, a 1723 novelty).

The new opera, *Scipione*, was the result of a hastily revised schedule owing to Faustina's late arrival. Handel had originally planned to feature her in a version of Ortensio Mauro's libretto *La Superbia d'Alessandro*, whose composition he now broke off, turning instead to one of his stock of Florentine texts, *Publio Cornelio Scipione*, originally for the Leghorn carnival season of 1704 and probably by Antonio Salvi. Rolli, who took up as Handel's librettist after a break of some three years, retained most of the recitative material but rejected the arias in favour of his own. The story concerns the famous 'continence of Scipio' in sacrificing his love for a Spanish princess to her happiness in the arms of his rival.

Rolli's restitution was like the return of an ill-boding fowl. Why, after three consummate successes, the partnership with Haym should so suddenly have been dissolved is not yet clear. What is obvious is that Handel and Rolli did not work well together, and that the works they produced during these last troubled years of the Academy's existence were each flawed by a dramatic ineptitude which a more responsive librettist could have smoothed away.

Scipione is a case in point. Admittedly the circumstances in which it was put on were distinctly unsatisfactory. A part for the heroine's mother Rosalba (suggestions here of some comedy matriarch from seventeenth-century Venice), perhaps intended for Dotti, was cut, and the third act was comprehensively reshuffled, so that Costantini, in the soubrette role of Armira, got no aria at all. But the libretto itself it weakened, partly by the unattractive nature of Scipio himself, whose continence is made the result of a last-moment change of heart unconvincing here, whereas, in *Rodelinda*, Grimoaldo's *crise-de-conscience* seems psychologically quite justifiable, partly also by the atmosphere of *ancien régime* courtly trifling in which the successive amatory situations are contrived.

These factors are all evident in Handel's musical response. For the first time since *Floridante* we can sense the composer going through the motions of making an opera. As we should expect, the music is often pretty and tuneful, the recitative is handled with characteristic flair, and attention is paid to a governing tonal framework, in which G, B flat and related keys predominate. There is a good showpiece in Berenice's 'Scoglio d'immota fronte', placed, according to custom, at the close of an act, and richly scored for two oboes, an independent bassoon part and three violins. Yet, for all this, the work sags under the pressure of composition and Handel's occasional loss of interest. There is a predominance of 3/8 time (eleven airs out of 23 in a piece dominated by triple time) which so often spells triviality in the operas. A still stronger indication of the composer's half-hearted approach is given by his reliance in the ritornellos on a particular kind of formulaic semiquaver passagework which those who accuse late Baroque music of facility associate with the influence of Vivaldi and his Italian contemporaries. We can find this scattered throughout, not only in the more lightweight pieces, but embedded in grander concepts such as the symphony opening Act II, Lelio's first number, Lucejo's bird simile aria 'Come al nazio boschetto' and even in 'Scoglio d'immota fronte' itself.

The work was initially successful. 'The march which was played on the drawing up of the curtain, for Scipio's triumph, was a general favourite, and adopted by his Majesty's life-guards, and constantly played on parade for near forty years.' It was later to provide Cowper with the rhythms for his 'Loss of the Royal George', and has since become the official anthem of that pocket sovereign the Lord Mayor of London. Handel, however, had bigger fish to fry, for Faustina, 'whose arrival forms an aera in the annals of musical contests', soon afterwards landed in England and the dangerous fun began in earnest.

His choice of an opera designed to show the Haymarket stars in all their unabashed virtuosity had fallen on a piece originally written by his old Hanover acquaintances Agostino Steffani and Ortensio Mauro. Of all Handel's dramatic works, *Alessandro* belongs most irredeemably to the vanished operatic world of the early eighteenth century. Serious producers and conductors, imbued with the ideals of Felsenstein and Strehler, meet their challenge in this romantic confection, with its scenario of scrambled incidents from the life of Alexander the Great, interwoven with a 'love interest' for the hero and a pair of Indian princesses. Its techniques are those of cinema (indeed it recalls one of the more florid Cinecitta epics of the late 1950s) with swift cuts from one exotic location to the next and a grandiosity of musical gesture which brings us closer to the magic and spectacle of *Rinaldo* and *Amadigi* than to the antechambers and garden-walks of *Ottone* and *Rodelinda*. The language of the whole work is that of careful overstatement, a shining heap of stunning effects.

The opening battle scene, describing the siege of Oxidraca, is the most elaborate in any Handel work, with its 62-bar symphony taking life, as it were, from the crude heroics of Alexander's defiant:

> *Ossidraca superba, contra l'ira del Cielo in van contrasti:*
> *Son prole del Tonante, e tanto basti.*

'I'm a descendant of Jove, and that's enough!' The band, which, with players like Geminiani, Dubourg and the Castrucci brothers, was now on topping form, was given its head throughout the work, and, as in his next opera, *Admeto*, Handel works a second French overture into the fabric of the drama by opening the scene in the temple of Jupiter Ammon with the initial flourishes and following up the subsequent recitative with the fast fugato section. Act II is introduced by a recitative and arioso scored for a brilliantly augmented orchestra of paired flutes, oboes, bassoons and divided strings. Horns colour the jolly six-part *coro* and appear in the unusual, not to say unique ensemble movement which accompanies the returning victors after the battle.

This is just one of many moments in the piece when Handel abandons the rigid sequence of aria and recitative which forms the traditional basis of *opera seria*. Perhaps the best example of this unhampered treatment of formal resource occurs in Act II. After eight bars of orchestral introduction for wind and strings Rossane invokes protective solitude to the accompaniment of two violins, viola and 'cello, and thence breaks into an arioso with added flutes, which she fails to finish, falling asleep instead. Alexander enters, finds her asleep, praises her face and bosom, and launches into a miniature aria as he intends to kiss her. But he has been overheard by Lisaura, whom he now has to pacify. Rossane, meanwhile, wakes up to find him dallying with her rival, to whom, in turn, he gives a little ditty. In reply, each lady mocks him by quoting the song he has sung to her rival. His subsequent full-scale aria, a Senesino showpiece, has the added interest of a 3/4 first section and a common-time middle section.

Handel's radiant sense of humour suffuses not only such Mozartian scenes as this, but his entire treatment of the two ladies. He must have foreseen the rivalry of the divas from the outset and the pair are treated with an even-handedness which is in itself richly farcical. Who can have avoided a wry smile at the mathematic formality with which Rossane and Lisaura, 'each one emerging from her pavilion', survey the progress of the siege and later join in a duet whose solo passages are of exactly equal length? In fact, however, it was Faustina as Rossane who was given the edge over Cuzzoni as Lisaura. Her music demands a ferocious virtuosity, rising to a pitch in her Act III aria 'Brilla nell'alma', one of the opera's conscious allusions to newer musical styles and a piece doubtless partly intended to make Faustina feel at home in the Italian operatic province which now greeted her so enthusiastically.

Alessandro is not a great opera. There is too much bustle and confusion, aided by an otiose subplot and a coarse-grained libretto, added to which the division of the spoils between the two ladies rapidly becomes jejune and irritating. Yet its brashness is the vulgarity of genius. It is one of those works whose gestures caution us against the validity of good taste in the criticism of art. Somehow the whole nature of the piece seems encapsulated in the fact that, at its first performance, the noise of the battle scene could be heard carrying from the Haymarket as far off as Charing Cross.

Its popularity — eleven performances in May and two more before the season closed on 7 June, owing to Senesino's illness — was guaranteed by the starry cast. In a city small enough to thrive on gossip and scandal, the pleasure of opera-going was enhanced by the mutual animosity of Cuzzoni and Faustina, which promised to develop into something very juicy. Matters were not helped by Senesino's continuing absence, on which John Rich, the buccaneering impresario of Lincoln's Inn Fields theatre, cashed in by staging a revival of *Camilla*, complete with Mrs Barbier and Richard Leveridge, veterans of the original run 20 years earlier:

> While Senesino you expect in vain,
> And see your Favours treated with Disdain:
> While, 'twixt his Rival Queens, such mutual Hate
> Threats hourly Ruin to your tuneful State,
> Permit your Country's Voices to repair,
> In some Degree, your Disappointments there,

said Mrs Younger in a specially written prologue. Meanwhile, Mrs Pendarves raved about Cuzzoni: 'Oh how charming! how did I wish for all I love and like to be with me at that instant of time! my senses were ravished with harmony. They say we shall have operas in a fortnight, but I think Madam Sandoni (Cuzzoni) and the Faustina are not perfectly agreed about their parts.'

Senesino at length returned and the season got going at last with Ariosti's *Lucio Vero*, but the *clou* was to be 'Mr Handel's opera performed by Faustina, Cuzzoni & Senesino', based on *L'Antigona delusa da Alceste*, a respectably antique Venetian libretto originally written by Aurelio Aureli for Marcantonio Ziani at the S. Zanipolo theatre in 1660. Handel and his librettist (probably Haym once more, given the alterations which took place) used another of Mauro's Hanover versions, and in its new form, as *Admeto*, the piece was premièred on 31 January. It was an immense success, with nineteen performances during the season, and remained popular during most of Handel's lifetime.

What its popularity had to do with the genuine artistic merits of the work is difficult to gauge. Though *Admeto* is better wrought than *Alessandro*, its libretto is almost as unsatisfactory, a mixture of classical tragedy with the footling intrigues of Spanish Baroque comedy. The usual accretions of divine and allegorical figures and *buffo* servants are cut away, but the central juxtaposition of the Alcestis legend with a romance for Admetus with a princess Antigona obviously has to remain, along with several other features such as portraits, disguises, outbursts of female jealousy and the employment of Antigona as a gardener (a convention which found its most successful treatment some 50 years afterwards in Mozart's *La Finta Giardiniera*), which distance the work from classical myth and give it an inalienably modern flavour. Haym, if it was he rather than Rolli, significantly altered the dénouement: the original has Admetus regaining Alcestis at the last minute ('Opportuno qui giungo', 'Not before time,' says Hercules) and thus having to hand Antigona (with whom, ironically, he has just sung the duet) to Prince Trasimede, the *secondo uomo*, but here Antigona simply cedes Admetus to Alcestis, who hails her as a *generoso rivale*, and Trasimede is left to comment vaguely that 'hope begins to revive within me'. Was this switch-round owing to Cuzzoni's need to preserve the dignity of her role?

For all its moments of elegant nonsense, *Admeto* remains the only opera of the Faustina years really worthy of being placed alongside the earlier masterpieces. Whereas in *Alessandro* there is the continual sense of subservience to the demands of the performers, its successor maintains a far greater cohesion, and the self-propelling energy created by the drama and its characters gives a terse, powerfully inevitable quality to the successive musical numbers. Handel was obviously inspired by the story's more authentic sections, at such moments as the opening *accompagnato* 'Orride Larve', in which Admeto rises from his sickbed tormented by Stygian shades with bleeding daggers, Alceste's subsequent lament in the composer's favourite pathetic F minor, punctuated by the sudden appearances of a single flute, and the exuberantly macabre second-act overture, whose spiky chromaticisms accompany Hercules's tour of Hades.

There is no evidence, however, that Handel knew Euripides any better than did his other lettered contemporaries. The Hellenic crazes of neo-classicism were far distant, and if the spirit of Greek tragedy does emerge in Handel's work it is in the oratorios rather than the operas, where the protagonists show a much more obvious debt to Racine and Corneille. Nor are his sympathies confined to Admetus and Alcestis. Antigona and Trasimede emerge so forcefully in their music as to seem redolent of characters from a Richardson novel in the ups and downs of their sentimental adventuring. Each is clearly and expertly defined within a distinctive musical context: Antigona is presented via a delectable rustic symphony over pastoral drones, leading, through a snatch of dialogue, to her ingratiating 'Spera allor che in mar turbato', and Trasimede has a wonderful entrance with hunting horns which are carried over into his spacious comparison of Antigona with the goddess Diana, 'Se l'arco avessi e i strali'.

The imaginative drive that shapes such personalities is an equally strong determining factor in Handel's treatment of the Senesino and Faustina roles. Admeto is no mere languishing lover or posturing paladin, but a fully-realized human figure caught in the toils of a dilemma for whose contrivance he is only partially responsible, as emphatically masculine a hero as Handel ever created for his temperamental *primo uomo*. The two women are differentiated not, as in the previous opera, by the quality of their music (Cuzzoni's numbers are pronouncedly modern in style, and it is Faustina who gets the melting siciliano normally associated with her rival) but by its subtlety of psychological insight. Nearly all Alceste's arias, for example, are vigorous outbursts resulting from the intolerable situations into which she is thrown: only at the close of the opera does the composer's sense of tender irony give her an affectionate minuet air, as she regains her husband, which sounds suspiciously like the sort of thing we have come to expect from Antigona. True, Cuzzoni has her siciliano in 'Da tanti affanni oppressa' and very good it is too, but everything else of hers has hoydenish gaiety about it which sets the young princess well apart from the loyal wife.

During the triumphant run of *Admeto*, during which, as Coleman noted in his register, 'the House filled every night fuller than ever was known at any Opera for so long together — 16 times', Handel had other business in hand besides superintending the Haymarket music. It is not yet clear why, after some sixteen years in England, he should suddenly have thought to become a naturalized subject of the monarch whose *Kapellmeister* he had once been. There is a suggestion that he may have been hoping to succeed Croft in his post as senior Chapel Royal composer, and since a sermon preached in Croft's presence in Hereford cathedral in September of the previous year implies that his health was failing, it is just possible that Handel, among others, may have expected that the older master would soon relinquish the job or that death would carry him off. Apart from this there is no substantial reason why Handel, unlike Pepusch, Galliard, Bononcini or Geminiani, all of them long-term foreign residents in Britain, should now decide to be an Englishman.

His petition to the House of Lords, filed on 13 February, stated that 'your petitioner was born at Hall in Saxony, out of his Majestie's Allegiance, but hath constantly professed the Protestant Religion, and hath given Testimony of his Loyalty and Fidelity to his Majesty and the good of this Kingdom', and asked that Handel's name should be added to the pending act 'for Naturalizing LOUIS SECHEHAYE'. Presumably, if proof of his fidelity were needed, they had only to look at the dedication of *Radamisto*. Was it, besides, mere coincidence that among members of the reviewing committee was Lord Waldegrave, an erstwhile Academy director? After the appropriate amendments and readings the bill was carried down to the Commons with the noteworthy adjunct, in an age when the upper chamber was still one to be reckoned with, that 'the Lords desire the Concurrence of this House'. Dutiful agreement from the members sent the bill back to the Lords, and the king pronounced his assent, using the words '*Soit fait comme il est désiré*'.

At 42 Handel was now an Englishman, and would pass most of his remaining years in the country of his adoption. His music lost nothing of its cosmopolitan flavour, and to the very last he showed himself capable of absorbing and transmuting a whole range of musical styles. The Englishness in works such as *L'Allegro, Il Penseroso ed Il Moderato* and *Susanna* is only a component element, never a dominant feature, and Hawkins's comment, already referred to, that it was necessary to know several languages in order to appreciate Handel's fund of good stories relates in a sense as much to the music as to the man. He never lost his German accent, though the German itself became distinctly vague, and he could write fluent, idiomatic English in his letters to friends. Anyone who has spent long periods abroad will know the social value of never quite mastering a foreign language and of the charm which a linguistic combination of eagerness, intelligence and inexactitude always conveys. Evidence abundantly suggests that Handel, nothing if not shrewd, understood this and exercised it to the full.

Admeto's success blinded nobody to the realities of the situation created by Faustina's presence. Cuzzoni, archetypally the Italian *prima donna* in her fretful, vulgar insecurity, resented the challenge from the outset, and Faustina, for all her common sense, was thoroughly conscious of her talents, requiring others to be so as well. Meanwhile, among the King's

Theatre patrons the battle lines began drawing up. The rage for opera had now turned into that favourite eighteenth-century aristocratic pastime, backing winners, and when one of Handel's most judicious admirers, the poet Henry Carey, published his *Discontented Virgin* in the *British Journal* of 25 March he expressed the situation neatly:

> At *Leicester Fields* I give my Vote
> For the fine-piped Cuzzoni;
> At *Burlington*'s I change my Note,
> *Faustina* for my Money.

> *Attilio*'s Musick I despise
> For none can please but *Handel*;
> But the Disputes that hence arise,
> I wish and hope may end well.

Pious but ineffectual. A collision course was inevitable, if only because the noble patrons so obviously flaunted their colours. Leader of the Cuzzoni faction was Mary, Countess of Pembroke, whose ardent partisanship was not of a type to cast lustre on her husband's position as a pillar of the Whig establishment. A letter to Charlotte Clayton, later Lady Sundon, favourite of the Princess of Wales, written towards the end of the 1727 season, indicates the extent to which Lady Pembroke and others were already committed. Cuzzoni had apparently received a warning that she was to be hissed off the stage at a forthcoming performance. 'She was in such concern at this,' says the Countess, 'that she had a great mind not to sing, but I . . . positively ordered her not to quit the stage, but let them do what they would: though not heard, to sing on, and not to go off till it was proper.' Backed by her patroness and the applause of her supporters Cuzzoni hung on, though one of her arias was drowned by catcalling from the Faustina claque. Matters were made worse by the appearance of the king's granddaughter Princess Amelia, an ardent Handelian but an embarrassing presence at such a time.

A further lack of respect towards royalty by the heavily engaged Haymarket audience was shown when the Directors presumed to dispute George's caution to them that if Cuzzoni were dismissed he would give up his attendance. Faustina, however, was a decided favourite, whose roster of distinguished backers included Burlington's wife Dorothy (Lord Hervey called her 'Dame Palladio'), Lady Cowper, who wrote opposite the siren's name in her *Admeto* word-book 'she is the devil of a singer' and

Catherine, Lady Walpole, who engineered a social *coup* by inviting both divas to her house for a concert 'at which were all the first people of the kingdom'. As neither of the two stars would deign to sing in the other's presence, the hostess, with admirable aplomb, had each of them taken to another part of the house 'under the pretence of shewing her some curious china' while her rival obliged with an aria or two.

Matters finally came to a head in a dramatic and, so far as can be known, unique fashion on the production of a new opera which had been coaxed from Bononcini for performance as the season's last novelty. Adapted by Haym from a Salvi text originally set by the composer's brother Marc' Antonio, *Astianatte* had a respectable pedigree in Racine's *Andromaque*, and was dedicated to Bononcini's lavish patroness Henrietta Marlborough. It was his last London opera, but was to be remembered for reasons which have little to do with music.

Patrons who attended the performance on 6 June 1727 can scarcely have been surprised by what took place, but the occasion was hot news for London journalists and pamphleteers. The *British Journal* noted gleefully: 'On Tuesday-night last, a great Disturbance happened at the Opera, occasioned by the Partisans of the Two Celebrated Rival Ladies, Cuzzoni and Faustina. The Contention at first was only carried on by Hissing on one Side, and Clapping on the other; but proceeded at length to Catcalls, and other great Indecencies: And notwithstanding the Princess Caroline was present, no Regards were of Force to restrain the Rudenesses of the Opponents.' The *London Journal*, in customary style, observed that the quarrel was sustained 'by the delightful Exercise of Catcalls, and other Decencies, which demonstrated the inimitable Zeal and Politeness of that Illustrious Assembly. . . . Neither her Royal Highness's presence, nor the laws of decorum, could restrain the glorious ardour of the combatants.' The central fact, however, was that Cuzzoni and Faustina had finally resorted to a scuffle, egged on by their partisans and perhaps even by their fellow performers.

The flavour of the event is admirably conveyed in a burlesque playlet, *The Contre Temps or Rival Queans, A Small Farce*, issued the following month. The epigraph, Virgil's '*Et cantare pares, et respondere paratae*', is slily rendered as 'Both young Italians, both alike inspir'd/To sing, or scold; just as the time requir'd. Modern Translation.' The cast, besides the three principal singers, includes Heidegger 'High-priest to the Academy of Discord', Handel himself, and the leaders of the respective claques.

Heidegger's opening speech effectively satirizes the public's preoccupation with opera in hinting at the comparative triviality of contemporary events such as the squabble over Minorca or the death of the Czarina Elizabeth. Faustina calls Cuzzoni 'that mushroom songstress of the other day', Cuzzoni tells her to 'resign the charge, you're past it now and old' and the sexual innuendo reaches a peak when the former advises:

> While you in rip'ning, like a medlar rot,
> At best a Gorgon's face, and Siren's throat,
> Help your decaying lungs, and chew *eringo*
>   [seaweed, a noted aphrodisiac]
> Thou little awkward creature! — can you *stringo*?

to which the latter ripostes:

> To do you justice tho; — I think — 'tis known
> That you to please, imploy more pipes than one.

The height of coarseness is reached in Faustina's reference to Sandoni's difficulty in making love to Cuzzoni owing to her excessively large vagina. The two women box and tear one another's headdresses, to an excited chorus of peers and tupees (beaux in smart wigs). 'The Queen and The Princess again engage; Both Factions play all their warlike Instruments; Cat-calls, Serpents and Cuckoos make a dreadful din; F-s-na lays flat C-z-ni's nose with a Sceptre; C-z-ni breaks her head with a gilt-leather crown: H-l, desirous to see an end of the battle, animates them with a kettle-drum; a globe thrown at random hits the high-priest in the temples, he staggers off the Stage. . . . '

While the state tottered at the Haymarket, England received the news of King George I's death at Osnabrück on 11 June, and four days later the Prince of Wales was proclaimed as George II. For the coronation of the new king and queen, arranged to take place in Westminster Abbey, Handel was commissioned to write four new anthems. As an official court composer, he was an obvious choice, the more so as he was personally known to George and Caroline, who remained unflinchingly loyal admirers of his music. They had besides already engaged him as music master to their daughters, a post in which documentary evidence confirms him from 1727 at a salary of £195. Some of his later harpsichord pieces were written as lessons for the youngest of the princesses, Louisa, while her sister Anne received a generous tribute from the master himself, when he told the organist Jacob Wilhelm Lustig that after he left Hamburg for Italy 'no power on earth could have moved me to take up teaching again — except Anne, the flower of Princesses.'

Parker's Penny Post told its readers a week before the ceremony, 'Mr Hendle has composed the Musick for the Abbey at the Coronation, and the Italian Voices, with above a Hundred of the best Musicians will perform; and the Whole is allowed by those Judges in Musick who have already heard it, to exceed any Thing heretofore of the same Kind: it will be rehearsed this Week, but the Time will be kept private, lest the Crowd of People should be an Obstruction to the Performers.' The secret, of course, got out and the rehearsal at the Abbey was attended by 'the greatest Concourse of People that has been known'. Forces included a choir of about 40 voices and an enormous band of 160 or so players. If the *Parker*'s correspondent is to be credited, the 36 Chapel Royal singers, including Handel's erstwhile soloists Gates, Hughes and Wheeley, were joined by singers from the opera. Perhaps this accounts for the manuscript fragment of *My heart is inditing* written out in phonetic spelling, now in the New York Lincoln Center Library, which reads 'Mai hart is indeitin, mai hart is indeitin of e gut matter ai Spick of di tinzs huic ai hef med end tu di Chink. Chinks Dators ouer hamanh Zij anorabel uijmin', though this may indeed belong to a later performance.

The success of the anthems was unconnected with their original performance at the Coronation Service, whose order, devised by Archbishop Wake, conflated Tenison's crowning of George I in 1714 and the ceremony used by Sancroft at the accession of James II in 1685. Forecast of a spring tide and dangers of flooding in Westminster Hall had put off the ceremony by a week, from the 4th to the 11th, but the extra time thus allowed for rehearsal did little to straighten out the confusions inevitable among the vast musical forces in the Abbey. Wake's notes in his copy of the service order tell the story succinctly enough. Against the first anthem, Purcell's *I was glad*, he writes: 'This was omitted and no Anthem at all Sung . . . by the Negligence of the Choir of Westminster.' At the Recognition the choir should have launched into *The King shall rejoice*, but according to another source they embarked on *Let thy hand be strengthened*. What probably happened was that the Chapel Royal singers got going in one gallery while the remaining voices set off on a different tack in the other. Wake laconically observes: 'The Anthems in Confusion: All irregular in the Music', and goes on to note that at the Anointing, through yet another blunder, *Zadok the Priest* knocked the hymn out of the way.

Despite this we can appreciate the evident enthusiasm of the performers. It was at least a decade since Handel had composed an anthem to English words, though why the *Coronation Anthems* should be so superior to almost everything in the *Chandos Anthems* it is hard to say.

Their absolute sureness of aim and perfectly calculated control of effect gave them an immediate popularity and they were given regularly in English choral concerts during Handel's lifetime. At least one, *Zadok the Priest*, that gloriously simple burst of D major acclamation, with a glance towards Italy in its opening allusion to the string arpeggiando in the 1707 *Nisi Dominus*, became an established element of the coronation ritual. Varying his choral and orchestral layers (no trumpets or drums in *Let thy hand be strengthened* and a scrupulous husbanding of these resources elsewhere) Handel is equally careful to shift the tonality so as to avoid too much D major tub-thumping. *Let thy hand*, for example, is in G, with a meditative E minor larghetto in 'Let justice and judgment', strangely mournful in its suggestion of the vanity of admonishing the king to 'let mercy and truth go before thy face'. Finest and most expansive of all four is the sumptuous *My heart is inditing*, into whose opening section the various components are worked one by one, the individual voices singing over a light *trommelbass* string accompaniment and the brass and timpani saved up for a thrilling arrival to round off the movement in grand style.

A Coronation opera was now in order and by a singular coincidence Handel had already composed just such a piece some six months earlier. The new season had opened with an *Admeto* revival and the last of Ariosti's London operas, *Teuzzone*, a Zeno drama set in 'Peckin, one of the Principal Cities of China'; the Handel novelty — ''tis delightful', exclaimed Mrs Pendarves — was *Riccardo Primo, Rè d'Inghilterra*, first performed on 11 November 1727.

Handel's reasons for withholding the piece are further complicated by the revisions made to the last two acts, which imply an attempt to adapt it to the new situation created by George I's death. The sensible suggestion has been made that the heroic figure of Richard the Lionheart was in any case supposed to represent George II as Prince of Wales and that the opera was originally intended for the previous season. Whatever the truth, the autograph (or, to use Burney's habitual expression, 'the foul score') is one of the most confusing ever left to us by Handel, and a fascinating display of the composer's working methods. The entire manuscript has passage after passage of text crossed out and new words substituted for no apparent reason. Cancelled music includes several arias, one of them an enchanting birdsong number with flauto piccolo, and a closing duet for Costanza and Riccardo, as well as scenes containing a character called Corrado who disappears in the final version.

The libretto, loosely linked with history (Richard's queen, Berengaria, here appears as Costanza) involves Coeur de Lion's exploits on Cyprus and derives, via a Rolli adaptation, from Francesco Briani's drama *Isacio Tiranno* set by Lotti for the S. Giovanni Grisostomo season of 1710 and perhaps passed on to Handel personally by the composer. Rolli's inexpert juggling with the text results in a notably uneasy relationship between recitatives and arias, clumsy and vague transitions in the actions and one or two downright unconvincing situations.

All this does much to spoil what is otherwise one of Handel's most appealing works. Burney's comment, that 'the last act of Richard is replete with beauties of every kind of composition', applies equally well to the other two. Throughout, the orchestration is supremely imaginative, its sensuous textures contrasting sharply with those of the 'basic band' in *Admeto*, two thirds of whose arias are supported by oboes and strings. This may well have been owing to Handel's awareness of the need for some additional means of persuasive advocacy for a work so much less obviously self-propelled than its predecessor. The overture, one of Handel's best, has independent oboe and bassoon parts, flutes, including a *traversa bassa*, characterize Costanza, already sharply defined by her identification with F minor, Riccardo directs the siege of Limassol to a background of paired trumpets (three are required in the ensuing chorus) and an alternative setting of Pulcheria's 'Quando non vedo', replaced before the first performance, exists for two chalumeaux, members of the clarinet family.

Despite its inconsistencies, the recitative is handled with typical sureness of touch. We have to wait until Gluck's *Iphigénie en Tauride* for anything as spirited as the opening scene, which replaces the last movement of the overture with a splendid tempest on Limassol beach, with a timpani part (given dynamic markings in English by the composer) and a dialogue between the shipwrecked Costanza and Berardo growing out of the subsiding storm. Two of the arias, at any rate, spring spontaneously from the recitative: Pulcheria's 'Bella, teco non ho' is a successful attempt to silence Costanza with the first words of the aria, and Costanza's 'Lascia la pace all'alma' is merely a natural consolidation of what she has just been saying to the evil Isacio.

The apportionment of roles to singers is an interesting reversal of what Handel had contrived for *Admeto*. Faustina as Pulcheria became the youthful '*vezzosa e vaga*' figure, and in Costanza Cuzzoni was given a character of genuine weight, almost another Rodelinda in the wifely loyalty suggested by her name. Boschi as Isacio had a far more important part to play in the drama than almost any he had been awarded earlier in the Academy operas, and two fine arias to prove it. As for Senesino, he was required to do little more than simper and bluster as the cardboard eponym, most conventional of the four protagonists.

After eleven performances *Riccardo Primo* was shelved, never to be revived until 1964. It was a respectable run, but it could not save the Academy. Mrs Pendarves told her sister: 'I doubt operas will not survive longer than this winter, they are now at their last gasp; the subscription is expired and nobody will renew it. The directors are always squabbling, and they have so many divisions among themselves that I wonder they have not broken up before; Senesino goes away next winter, and I believe Faustina, so you see harmony is almost out of fashion.' Around the time of the *Astianatte* fracas in June the Directors had made several rather querulous appeals to the subscribers, but we can scarcely blame the Academy's financial supporters for an increasing reluctance to lay out money on exorbitant stars. Opera was no longer a novelty, the wave of interest in the rival divas had broken, Bononcini had retired once again to his patroness, and the whole thing had become a deuced expense.

The success of John Gay's *The Beggar's Opera*, which played to packed houses during the early months of 1728, had little to do with the Academy's relapse, despite what has often been stated. As an associate and admirer of Handel's, Gay was not out deliberately to ruin his old acquaintance of Burlington days, and though his pioneering comic masterpiece pulled in a substantial proportion of Haymarket regulars, this was merely another large hole knocked in an already foundering ship. Much of the precision in Gay's parody is inevitably lost on those who appreciate the work simply for its 'popular' flavour: one wonders how much of the burlesque element Bertolt Brecht, for example, could relish. Hogarth's painting of the Gaol Scene effectively underlines the formal parallels, with Macheath as the Senesino figure between Polly and Lucy as Cuzzoni and Faustina (or vice versa) against a backdrop which could easily pass for one of the prison scenes in the King's Theatre stock.

Perhaps the most important contribution to the development of Handel's art made by *The Beggar's Opera* was its revelation of an English public which liked hearing English words to English tunes. Ballad opera was now set going as a genre, with countless variations on Gay's original. Via Charles Coffey's *The Beggar's Wedding* it established itself in Germany in the *Singspiel* format which would reach its apogee in *Die Entführung aus dem Serail* and *Die Zauberflöte*. In Samuel Johnson's *The Village Opera*, the simile aria, already parodied by Gay, gained a magnificent absurdity:

My Dolly was the Snow-drop fair,
   Curling Endive was her Hair;
The fragrant Jessamine her Breath;
   White Kidney-Beans, her even Teeth.

Two Daisies were her Eyes;
   Her Breasts in swelling Mushrooms rise;
Her Waist, the streight and upright Fir;
   But all her heart was Cucumber.

Colley Cibber wrote the attractive *Chuck or The Schoolboy's Opera*, in which Chuck, with his friends, mitches from school, but bribes the schoolmaster Dionysius to commute a threatened beating by offering him a 'new-mill'd Crown'.

   Handel pressed inexorably on with the new opera, less remarkable for its music than for its libretto. First produced on 17 February 1728, *Siroe* was only the second work by the greatest of the *opera seria* poets and one of comparatively few librettists who have had a decisive influence on the nature of operatic form. It is difficult to think of many other writers in the eighteenth century whose international reputation equalled that of Pietro Metastasio and whose fame declined so swiftly with the changes in taste brought about by the rise of Romanticism. Chilly and limited as we may find Metastasio's classicism (embodied at its most eloquently trivial in his surname, a Hellenizing of the workaday Italian Trapassi) there is no denying the profound impression made on contemporaries by his single-mindedness as a theatre poet determined to raise his professional role from that of a hack versifier to a dignified arbitrator preoccupied with artistic standards. His dramas, despite their mechanical solutions, at any rate codified *opera seria* conventions, cutting away trifling underplots, tightening up the story element and forging a much stronger link between character and moral decision. Their clean lines and scrupulous observance of the exit aria rule made them favourites with singers and composers alike, and it is no surprise to find that practically every operatic composer from Handel to Mozart (*La Clemenza di Tito* is rebuilt Metastasio) set these texts again and again.

   There is no space here to investigate the reasons why not a single one of all these settings should have achieved the classic status of, for instance, Gluck and Calzabigi's *Orfeo ed Euridice*. Sufficient to note that none of Handel's three such efforts is among his best work, though each is of course an efficient piece of craftsmanship. *Siroe*, a pseudo-historical

Persian tale, is the least successful of them. The score is strangely colourless, as though the lofty aridities of the poetry had somehow unmanned the composer. Once again, by simple contrast with the effects in *Riccardo Primo* and, in turn, with the sobrieties of *Admeto*, we can see how very far from stereotyped or haphazard is Handel's approach to the orchestra. Here there is nothing but oboes and strings, and in Act III the oboes do not play at all between the opening sinfonia and the final *coro*.

Though alert to the libretto's various dramatic challenges, Handel was evidently impatient of the restrictions imposed by the very long passages of recitative, already cut down by Haym. It is tempting to think that Siroe's 'Deh, voi mi dite, o Numi' at the beginning of Act II was broken off through sheer irritation at the rigidity of the textual structure. The text itself has in any case its full measure of Metastasian strengths and weaknesses: on the one hand, a tightly-knit intrigue, skilfully interlocked situations and strong characters, on the other the usual exit convention, huge swaths of dialogue unlikely to interest a London audience unless it was prepared to pore carefully over its word-books and a plot which, for all its nods in the direction of Aristotelian purity, conveys little of that element of chance which has played such a vital part in good drama from Aeschylus down to our own day.

Strongest of the protagonists is undoubtedly the scheming Medarse, sung by the 'second man' Baldi, to whom Handel gave three fine airs, culminating in the hugely ironic 'Benche tinta del sangue fraterno', in which pure black comedy clothes the villain's gloating. 'Even tinged with a brother's blood, the crown loses none of its splendour: a bold stroke for the throne, if it misfires, finds no mercy, but if it succeeds is always termed valour' — all this to a jaunty dotted F major tune with an accompaniment of dancing triplets and trills. 'Every family,' said an Italian critical commentator on Metastasio, 'has its Medarse', and this ultimate proof of the piquancy of Handelian wit helps us to credit it. Otherwise the best pieces are Laodice's 'Mi lagnero tacendo', where the simplest of orchestral lines (unison violins, no violas, rhythm bass) is touched with plangent chromaticisms, and Cosroe's 'Gelido in ogni vena', whose harmonic structure is founded on a creepy semiquaver ostinato allowing some free modulation (F sharp minor — E major — C sharp minor — B major) and reflecting a sort of shivering horror which Boschi had rarely before been asked to portray. Siroe himself emerges as a pallid, neurasthenic hero, allowed his moment in the excellent Act III *scena* 'Son stanco, ingiusti Numi', in the 'remote' key of B flat minor. The two ladies are both dull sticks.

The perfunctory quality of the seven-bar symphony evoking a civil broil in the square at Seleucia makes us realize how low the Academy was brought since the days of *Alessandro*, and it is noteworthy that everything about *Siroe*, perhaps even Handel's selection of it, suggests an urgent economy drive. Certain patrons, however, stayed loyal. George II, though scorned by historians, deserves a word of praise from musicians for his staunch and discerning championship of the composer. In any case, eighteen performances imply that things cannot have been altogether hopeless, though an anonymous attack on *The Beggar's Opera* in *The London Journal* for 23 March spoke of 'The Neglect into which the Italian Operas are at present fallen', and berated 'the fickle and inconstant Temper of the *English* Nation'.

In April the Directors made their last call on the subscribers, and on the last evening of the month Handel's last Academy opera, *Tolomeo, Rè d'Egitto*, was given the first of a run of seven performances. It was to be Handel's final collaboration with Nicola Haym, and it is tempting to suppose that the librettist's pastoral interpolations in his version of Capece's *Tolomeo ed Alessandro ovvero la Corona Disprezzata*, originally set by Domenico Scarlatti in Rome seventeen years earlier, were made with a genuine sense of the composer's fondness for country life. With the exception of one scene at the opening of Act III the entire opera takes place in the open air. Of the six scene changes two are duplicated and one other could quite easily be intended to appear later on as the *Campagna con villa deliziosa*. Evidently employing Goupy and Tillemans was out of the question, and the rest of the scenery was perhaps in too tatty a condition to be used.

Tolomeo's epigonic qualities are not simply owing to our hindsighted sense of its marking a terminal point in a remarkable episode in the history of English musical taste. There would be other operas, with Handel as their composer, as good as *Rodelinda* and *Radamisto*, and it was not as though his Muse was deserting him. Yet the cut-down nature of the drama, a series of attractive airs linked by sparse recitative, makes it difficult to conceive of *Tolomeo* in valid theatrical terms. Characters and motives in this vague 'tragical-historical-pastoral' mélange appear like the phantoms of their powerful forerunners in the brave old pre-Faustina days.

And very engaging these are, even if the temperature seldom rises higher than a kind of Bononcinian prettiness we last caught sight of in *Floridante*. The most famous of them, 'Non lo dirò col labbro', an artless little number like something from a Neapolitan intermezzo, became one of those Handel arias which survived the general neglect of his operas through having new words attached to it by the Victorians and may indeed still be known to some as 'Did you not hear my lady come down the garden singing?' Tolomeo himself, a more languishing and ineffectual figure than was usual even for Senesino, has a string of elegant mood pieces, including the by now almost obligatory F minor *siciliano* and the genuinely moving 'Stille amare', in which, after an accompanied recitative following his drinking poison, the effects of the bitter draught are portrayed in a B flat minor air, the rests in its string accompaniment creating the effect of a slow, gasping relapse — the vocal line, indeed, peters out on an unaccompanied E flat. It need hardly be added that Elisa (the Faustina role) has in fact saved his life by substituting '*un letargico umor*' for the poison. Alessandro, meanwhile, has rescued Seleuce from worse fates, she and Tolomeo launch into the second of their two duets (one of the few Handelian operatic couples to be so favoured) and the *coro*, in its customary wreaths of magnanimity and self-congratulation, returns us neatly to the horns and the F major of the opening.

Let us end with a view of the Academy in its last days by one of the audience. In April 1728 the French traveller Pierre Jacques Fougeroux, in the company of two friends, arrived in England for a prolonged tour of London, the Home Counties, East Anglia and the Midlands. His meticulous letters include, besides observations on country houses such as Blenheim and Wilton, Newmarket races, Stonehenge, football, prostitution, English cooking and the ubiquitous smell of coal in the capital, a detailed account of the King's Theatre music. He notes significantly the '*prix exorbitant*' of £1,600 exacted by Senesino for his salary and considers Faustina, despite her '*gosier charmant*' to have '*la voix assez grande mais un peu rude*'; he preferred the *douceur* of Cuzzoni.

The orchestra, he tells us, consisted of 24 violins (led by the Castrucci brothers), a lute, three cellos, two double basses, three bassoons 'and sometimes flutes and trumpets'. For the continuo there were two harpsichords, one of them played by '*Indel allemand grand joueur et grand compositeur*' and the lute, assisted by a cello in the recitative. Fougeroux noted, incidentally, what he considered the unpleasant manner of abruptly cutting off the recitative chords but praised the playing of the violinists in the airs. As a good Frenchman he deplored the absence in the operas (he saw *Admeto*, *Siroe* and *Tolomeo*) of ballet, machines and choruses, and equally appreciated their overtures, which must indeed have reminded him of home. As for the theatre itself, he found it small and badly decorated: there were the usual mirrors and candles for houselighting, but instead of a splendid confection of glass drops there were '*vilains chandeliers de bois*' on cords, reminding him of rope dancers. A footnote to his deprecating remarks on the scenery implies that a little bell rang whenever it had to be changed.

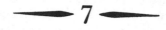

7

Airs of a Modern Cast

The years 1729 to 1741 form a crucial epoch in Handel's artistic career, and certain of the works composed during this period were never to be equalled, even in the last great oratorios, for their originalities of expression and form. Pieces such as *Israel in Eygpt*, *L'Allegro, Il Penseroso ed Il Moderato*, the two Dryden Odes and *Saul* achieve a lucidity of personal utterance to which *Messiah* offers the natural culmination, and the heart of Handel's unique achievement as a composer (an achievement whose sources continue to baffle those who look too narrowly in music for mainstreams and traditions) lies in these extraordinarily intense, crisis-ridden years of the 1730s. Pieces like *Semele*, *Theodora* and *Jephtha*, awing in their architectonic complexity, are not so much the destined perfecting of experimental attempts carried out during the previous decade, as consolidations upon ideas already fully developed by Handel. Had blindness not substantially stifled creativity, it is obvious that the composer, already responsible for putting his medium to imaginative uses without parallel in the music of the age, would have gone on to 'things unattempted yet' in the field of lyric drama.

His journey to Italy in search of singers for the new venture involved a tour of some five months (February to June 1729) and, in bringing him into direct contact with the newest kind of operatic writing, it inevitably marked his compositional style. Too much, however, has been made of the differences in manner between the Academy operas and the works of the 1730s, just as it has been asserted too often that Handel was a conservative in refusing to allow himself to become a carbon copy of Hasse, Leo, Vinci or any of the other masters now gaining popularity in European theatres. The truth is that Handel took what he wished to of the newer modes and retained, as he saw fit, elements of the other currents feeding his vast eclecticism. Thus an opera like *Orlando* (1733) can incorporate both an aria like Dorinda's 'Amor é qual vento', whose opening is resolutely new-fangled, and the triumphantly old-fashioned

'Gia lo stringo', with its ritornello blossoming exuberantly at the close like something from a Venetian opera of the previous century.

The 'new style' was, until recently, always termed Neapolitan, since many of its practitioners, such as Leo and Pergolesi, were born in the kingdom of Naples, but this is a gross misnomer. It was more likely to have been propagated in the lively operatic culture of Venice, whose greatest composer of the day, Antonio Vivaldi, had a powerful influence on the fundamental outlines. Calculated to flatter the talents of a rising generation of virtuoso singers, its textures were lightened, there was less obvious 'science' and counterpoint and a greater reliance on the type of repeated quaver bass lines which the Germans call *trommelbass* ('drum bass') to buoy up the syncopated rhythms in which the younger composers dealt. The orchestral continuo group of keyboard and bass instruments lost its independence and the nature of modulation grew more abrupt, something which in later years, so Hawkins tells us, Handel used to compare jokingly to a card game, crying 'Now A is trumps, now D!'. The character of the semiquaver divisions given to the singers for display also changed and new cadences clinched the melodies.

For the average concert-going, record-buying music lover, the one work in this style at all well known is Giovanni Pergolesi's *Stabat Mater*, in which many of its strongest mannerisms are exhibited. It is worth, for example, matching the 'Inflammatus et accensus', with its typical syncopated melody, against Handel arias such as 'My vengeance awakes me' in *Athalia*, 'Thy sentence, great king' in *Solomon*, or, more directly than either, 'Tiranna mia bella' in *Lotario*. Perhaps the ideal new-style piece, so much so that at certain moments it hardly sounds like Handel at all, is the delectable 'Voglio amare' from the second act of *Partenope*, an air which Burney, who knew about such things, called, in 1789, 'so smooth and free from wrinkles that it is difficult to imagine it to be near sixty years of age'. The germ of its melody may have originated in an idea for a sarabande, but Handel instead floats this gawky, rather childlike tune over a soft drum-bass to an *andante-allegro* marking.

'Airs of a modern cast' had in fact been part of Handel's stock-in-trade almost since *Rinaldo* days. He is unlikely to have been significantly affected by Vivaldi's manner while in Venice, for the simple reason that there was not much of the older man's music around for him to hear, but, if not Vivaldian, then there is something very Venetian about 'Non vo legarmi il cor' in *Il Pastor Fido*. Still more marked in this sense is a piece like 'La speranza è giunta in porto' in *Ottone*, or 'Da tempeste il legno infranto' in *Giulio Cesare*. After the production of the pasticcio *Elpidia* at the Haymarket in 1725 the impress becomes a direct one, pervading all the Faustina operas and at its most blatant in an air like Rossane's 'Lusinghe piu care' in *Alessandro*, where phrase after phrase might have come hot from a Venetian stage success of the current season.

The point has thus been well made that it was Handel and nobody else who familiarized London audiences with the latest operatic fashions, not merely through an assimilation into his own work, but through the seven pasticcios he presented during the 1730s. It may be that through these pasticcios, what is more, we can reconstruct his second Italian journey, since the original opera productions which gave him the librettos mostly took place during the spring and summer of 1729.

Handel set off for Italy on a note of mild optimism. Lord Percival (later Lord Egmont), a loyal Handelian, wrote in his diary for 18 January, 'I called Robin Moore and then went to a meeting of the members of the Royal Academy of Musick: where we agreed to prosecute the subscribers who have not yet paid: also to permit Hydeger and Hendle to carry on operas without disturbance for 5 years and to lend them for that time our scenes, machines, clothes, instruments, furniture etc. It all past off in a great hurry, and there was not above 20 there.' Heidegger had apparently already gone to Italy and returned, as Rolli hurried to tell Senesino, who was now in Venice but obviously interested in the possibility of a London come-back. The patrons of the new venture, headed by the virtuoso Lord Bingley, wanted Cuzzoni (currently delighting the imperial court) and Carlo Broschi, better known as Farinelli, rapidly fulfilling the promise as the greatest castrato of the age. Handel was to be paid a salary of £1,000, the annual subscription was set at £15, a total of £4,000 plus benefits was set aside for the singers, and the royal bounty was continued by the new king.

Poisonous as ever, Rolli detailed the various stages of the project to Senesino, in such a way as to imply that Handel was determined not to re-employ him and that, in line with the Directors' wishes, he would go all out for Farinelli instead. From the tone of his letters it is patent that Rolli knew the extent of his correspondent's typical castrato vanity, and that he was enjoying himself by playing on it to the full. A remark such as 'news has recently arrived from Venice . . . that all throng to the theatre at which Farinelli is singing, and that the theatre where you and Faustina are is nearly empty' speaks volumes for the degree of Rolli's integrity towards the man whose interests he claimed to be serving. Still worse is a further section of the same letter which appears directly calculated to set Faustina (then singing with Senesino at the San Cassiano theatre) against Handel.

Rolli concludes, licking his lips, 'I shall be curious to know how he will behave with you and with the celebrated prima donna; who, I fear, in her anger against the unfaithful man, may have him *thrown into the Canal.*'

The poet's fantasy was not gratified. If Senesino greeted Handel coldly enough at first on his arrival in Venice in March, the two were quickly reconciled, and it may well have been this gesture which paved the way for the castrato's successful return to the London stage the following autumn. At Venice Handel was given an introduction to Joseph Smith, English consul and Canaletto's patron, and must have met up once again with that engaging scapegrace Owen MacSwiney, who was to be a great help in finding and reporting on new singers for him. It was the carnival season and the opera companies were in full swing. At the San Giovanni Grisostomo they were giving Leonardo Leo's *Catone in Utica*, and at the San Cassiano Handel heard Faustina, Senesino and a young castrato, Domenico Annibali, whom he was to sign up seven years afterwards for London, in Orlandini's new opera *Adelaide*, to a libretto by Salvi, originally for the Bavarian Elector's marriage celebrations. Handel kept his word-book and used it for the first opera he composed on arriving home.

In the spring he left for Naples, possibly taking in Rome on his southward journey, since three of his later operas, *Arianna*, *Faramondo* and *Giustino*, all derive from Roman productions of the 1720s. Things were quieter in Italy since Handel's last visit, and Naples was full of excellent music. Here he could listen to and meet with several singers whose names later figured in his London casts, such as Anna Strada and the sopranos Antonio Bernacchi and Giovanni Carestini. These two and the alto Anna Merighi were the protagonists of the sort of partisan dispute Handel knew all too well. Count Francesco Zambeccari reported that 'the Viceroy, who likes Bernacchi well enough, told him that he was determined to have him remain for the coming year. Bernacchi replied that he would agree, on condition that all his stipulations should be fulfilled; among which were that the Merighi should stay, and that Carestini, his enemy of the rival party, should be dismissed. The Viceroy gave orders to the impresario (Carasale) that all this should be done, and that the contract should be signed. The ladies and gentlemen of Carestini's party at once made a fuss, and went in a body to the Viceroy, protesting that they should not be absolutely deprived of Carestini. The Viceroy now found himself in a difficult position, and ordered the impresario to set about settling the affair, saying that he wanted no part in it. . . . When Bernacchi heard about this, he went to the impresario saying that he was a man to make conditions and not one to accommodate himself to them; that he would not stay in a country where he was not liked, and that he would have no part in such foolishness. . . . '

If Handel wanted Bernacchi, difficult as he was, he would also have to settle for Merighi, rumoured, in whatever sense, to be the castrato's mistress; it was a good bargain, since she was a fine singing actress. Turning northwards with these two and Strada contracted, he may have stopped off at Bologna, home of Annibale 'Balino' Fabbri, a fine dramatic tenor in the Borosini mould, whom he now added to the company, and probably visited Parma, where he heard Geminiano Giacomelli's *Lucio Papirio Dittatore* in May and picked up the word-book of a recent carnival success by Farinelli's brother Riccardo Broschi, *Bradamante nell'isola d'Alcina*, to a libretto by Fanzaglia.

Crossing Germany he stopped at Halle to visit his family as he had promised Michaelsen in a letter written while he was at Venice. Once again the news of his arrival reached Johann Sebastian Bach — this time Wilhelm Friedemann was sent from Leipzig with an invitation — and once again Handel cheated future generations of music lovers by declining owing to lack of time, a fact which seems to have made no difference to Bach's continuing esteem.

He arrived in England on 29 June, but the singers were only gathered together in November. There was more vinegar from Rolli, who wrote to Riva in Vienna reporting the deaths of Haym and Ariosti, and added with evident sarcasm, 'Now learn that the famous Rossi, Italian author and poet, is Handel's bard.' Rossi it was who now tailored Salvi's *Adelaide*, which was retitled *Lotario*, finished on 16 November and given its first performance just over a fortnight later, though whether he was Giacomo Rossi, Handel's earliest librettist, we cannot be certain.

The *Norwich Gazette* reported: 'We hear the Operas will be brought on the Stage the Beginning of December, with great Magnificence, the Cloaths for the Singers, Attendants and Soldiers, being all imbroidered with Silver, and seven Sets of Scenes entirely new. And 'tis said that they will begin with a new Opera call'd Lotharius.' There are in fact ten scene changes in *Lotario*, but two of these, a prison and a throne room, could be furnished from the Academy stock leased to Heidegger. Among the others, suggestively ornate, are 'a square in Pavia with a triumphal arch' and 'the city walls of Pavia, with a drawbridge, towers and a rampart; afar off, military pavilions in Lotario's camp'. Despite this, the opera was a failure, as even Mrs Pendarves had to acknowledge. She supposed it might be because 'the opera really is not so meritorious as Mr Handel's generally are, but I never was so little pleased with one in my life'. Rolli and Bononcini took a more plainly sardonic view, but the former had to admit that, apart from Bernacchi who was not a favourite with the audience, the new Haymarket line-up was a considerable success.

The failure was ultimately Handel's own, and it is difficult to find much to say in *Lotario*'s favour. The fact that there is a more obvious element of melodrama in this opera than in several of its predecessors adds little interest to a work constructed along such traditional lines (usurping tyrants and distressed heroines in Lombard Italy) with fewer airs of real quality or interest than practically any work Handel had produced since *Il Pastor Fido*. Most of the good music went, not to Bernacchi or Strada as hero and heroine, but to Fabbri and Merighi as King Berengario and Queen Matilde, characters whose moral flaws had an obvious interest for Handel. Fabbri's arias, especially 'Vi sento, vi sento' in Act III, the fragmented quality of its rhythms mirroring Berengario's emotional collapse, all have a sturdy, muscular expressiveness lacking in the generally rather grey material given to Bernacchi. Excellent actress as she was, Merighi got the most rewarding role of all in the scheming, vengeful Matilde, first cousin to Gismonda in *Ottone*. Her richest dramatic moment comes not so much in any of her arias, or even in the magnificent accompanied recitative 'Furie del crudo Averno', as in a prison scene almost as complex in the nature of its action as the *locus classicus* in *Fidelio*. Having sent the captive Adelaide a choice of poison and a dagger if she refuses to marry the milksop Idelberto, or a crown and sceptre if she agrees, Matilde herself appears just as Adelaide, true to heroic form, is about to swallow the poison. Thereafter the scene runs as follows:

Matilde: So you still live, proud lady, despising both my gifts.
Adelaide: Ah, no, I cherish this one, which I raise to my lips.
Matilde: Drink then. Your survival offends me too deeply.

While she starts to drink, Idelberto enters with a naked sword, driving back the guards and threatening to kill himself if Adelaide takes the poison. Furious at such a check to her plans, Matilde hurls poison and sword to the ground as her henchman Clodomiro (sung by the Hamburg bass, Riemschneider, to whom Handel gave three fine arias) arrives with the bad news that Lotario's army has won the battle. In a brilliant flourish of savage sarcasm, whose opening phrases Handel was later to use for a poignant episode in *Jephtha*, Matilde tells Idelberto that he'd better stay behind to dart amorous glances at Adelaide, while the middle section is reserved for a fling at the heroine, still in chains and likely, if the frantic queen has her way, to stay there.

The new company was behaving no better than usually. Lord Hervey, Pope's 'Sporus', told his friend Stephen Fox of a quarrel between Strada and Merighi over whose name went foremost in the libretto: 'The latter, in the first flush of her resentment on the sight of this indignity, swore nothing but that Parliament should make her submit to it. You think this is perhaps a joke of mine; but 'tis literal truth, and I think too absurd to be imputed to anything but Nature, whose productions infinitely surpass all human invention, and whose characters have so indisputably the first place in comedy.' Both singers, however, were favourites with the audience, as even Rolli had to admit, though he was surprised at Fabbri's popularity. 'Would you have believed that a tenor could have such a triumph here in England?' There was a lesson for Handel in this, and the success of 'Balino' foreshadowed that of the great John Beard in the oratorios of the 1740s.

Bernacchi, Riemschneider and the pretty Roman mezzo Bertolli, who specialized in *travesti* roles, did not go down so well, and the two former, indeed, survived for a solitary season before leaving England for good. *Lotario* itself, 'poor dear swan', fell a victim to what Mrs Pendarves calls 'the ill-judging multitude', a decisive factor in Handel's shifts of direction throughout the decade, but his new operas for the next couple of seasons brought the public back again, typifying a pattern which was to become familiar in subsequent years. Again and again we hear the composer's admirers, as often as his enemies, wondering whether his skills are altogether used up, and as constantly Handel recovers himself to produce a masterpiece which astonishes with its liveliness of invention and resourcefulness.

Disappointing as *Lotario* is, its immediate successors, *Partenope*, *Poro*, *Ezio* and *Sosarme*, mark a brilliant revitalization of dramatic creativity. *Partenope*, produced with new scenery and costumes on 24 February 1730, is infinitely engaging, one of those pieces like *Acis and Galatea* or *Semele* which make us love the composer as much as the work. It is an anti-heroic comedy of the utmost refinement, which ought to be in the repertoire of any opera house which is ready to mount *Die Fledermaus*, *L'Elisir d'Amore* or *Die Entführung aus dem Serail*. The libretto, incorporating several new aria texts, adapts a popular drama by Silvio Stampiglia, which Handel may conceivably have come across in settings by Vinci, Porpora and others during his Italian travels. The legendary founding of Naples by Queen Parthenope is used as the martial background to an amorous intrigue of increasingly wonderful absurdity. Parthenope herself, wayward and imperious, is loved variously by the tenor Emilio, Prince of Cumae, whom she has also conquered in battle, Arsace, who has been followed to her court by his rejected sweetheart Rosmira disguised as the warrior Eurimene, and Armindo, Prince of Rhodes (sung by Bertolli, thus heightening the prevailing sense of comic ambiguity). Rosmira's sheer pluck and determination, summed up for us in the jaunty *aria da caccia*, its horns cantering along in 12/8, with which she finishes Act II, eventually win the day, but not before she is forced to reveal her identity when Arsace answers her challenge to a duel by making the condition that the pair of them fight stripped to the waist.

The masterly characterization and assured sense of pace and tone are sustained through a deliberate lightening of orchestral texture in the airs and an infusion of that Italianate sophistication which Handel could call up whenever it suited him. It is not only the enchanting 'Voglio amare' which bears the stamp of Venice and Naples. In the rhythms of Parthenope's 'Spera e godi', for example, Emilio's 'La speme ti consoli' or the triplets of Armindo's 'Nobil core' we catch at a kind of unquenchable optimism and high spirits which, like the melodies themselves, belong distinctively to that sunlit Parthenopean world, with its *lazzaroni*, its singers and comedians, at which Handel had taken his last look the previous summer. Was there perhaps some particular significance for him in the reverberations of the title and in the work as a whole? Certainly, like *Serse*, *Flavio* or *Ariodante*, *Partenope* is an opera which tells us more about its composer than others by Handel. Wit which is dry but never cynical, a readiness to appeal to our humane sympathies on behalf of their most unlikely recipients, an indulgent sense of the overriding effects of embarrassment, all these lend a subtler shading to figures like Arsace, pathetic in both ancient and contemporary senses, and the often infuriating Parthenope herself, and contribute to the splendid theatricality of the quartet at the opening of Act III or the trio 'Un cor infedele', where the unresolved amorous entanglement between the two, complicated as it is by the justifiable interference of Rosmira, forbids all three voices ever to blend together.

Poro and *Ezio* are Handel's second and last attempts on Metastasio texts, and his treatment of each is even more cavalier than his approach three years before to *Siroe*. *Poro* started life as *Alessandro nell' Indie*; its London title was obviously given so as to avoid confusion with the *Alessandro* of 1726, dramatizing earlier episodes in the conqueror's Indian campaign, and when given at Hamburg in 1732, a year after its English première, it was advertised as *Triumph der Grossmuth and Treue, oder Cleofida, Königin von Indien*, with recitatives in settings by Telemann.

The libretto is the usual Metastasian formula of heroism and gallantry among six characters distinguished by the polish of their poetic utterance, but the plot, turning on Queen Cleofide's exploitation of Alexander's love in order to further Porus's political cause, throws the opportunism and treachery of the central figures into unpleasant relief. Perhaps it was to modify this prevailing impression, and not simply because Riemschneider's replacement, Commano, was of little account, that Handel reduced the substantial role of the villainous Timagene to the only bass principal in any of the operas who is not awarded an aria. The text as it stood in any case disquieted the composer, and shows alterations were not limited to the customary excision and compression of recitative, but involved the cutting and the transplanting of arias in a revision which grew more radical as the drama progressed.

This does not, in fact, result in any startling improvement upon the original. Alessandro is an altogether feebler variation on his vigorous avatar of 1726 and the obligatory second pair of lovers, Erissena and Gandarte, become tiresome through superfluity. The interest of *Poro* is heavily weighted in favour of the music, and there is hardly a dull number in the piece. Handel's selective attitude towards the newer styles is shown by his readiness to accommodate them alongside fashions of a distinctly elderly cut without any obvious sense of incongruity. Cleofide, for instance, is introduced in a number decidedly reminiscent of Vinci and Leo, 'Se mai turbo il tuo riposo', especially in its continuing absorption of fresh material and plangent chromaticisms in the middle section: yet in the opera's penultimate scene, threatening suicide, she sings a tiny sixteen-bar aria making effective use of some hallowed Handelian clichés over a simple ground bass recalling Purcell to an English ear. Touches of Neapolitan intermezzo colour Erissena's 'Chi vive amante' just as surely as Alessandro's 'D'un barbaro scortese' sounds continually ready to turn into the most traditional Baroque fugato but never quite succeeds.

Such stylistic freedom carries over into the composer's handling of formal operatic conventions. The overture, focusing on widely-spaced intervals, ignores the usual concluding minuet and hurries us instead straight into the drama via a simple shift to the relative major, introducing an accompanied recitative as the defeated Porus rushes across the battlefield amid the scattered remnants of his army. Though several of the arias are extremely short and two at least are not cast in *da capo* form, Cleofide's 'Se troppo crede al ciglio' has a gigantic 36-bar middle section with divided strings. The most striking touch, however, was offered to Handel on a plate, as it were, by Metastasio. In Act I Poro and Cleofide have sworn a mutual fidelity in corresponding arias. A few scenes later, with the appearance of Alessandro, Cleofide, true to the spirit of the opera, flirts with the conqueror, well aware that she is making her lover jealous. Once Alexander has left, nobly implying that love is a passion unknown to him, the pair turn on each other and launch straight into a duet in which each ironically quotes the words and music of the earlier protestations of faith.

For this and much else *Poro* gained instant favour. 'Porus K of the Indies — New by Mr Hendel: it took much son confusa Pastorella &c', notes Colman's register, referring to the hit of the show, Erissena's Act III air with its pastoral drone. The last of Handel's Metastasio pieces, *Ezio*, produced the following year with a new tenor Pinacci in the cast and his wife Anna Bagnolesi in a *travesti* lead, was not nearly so successful, with only five performances and no subsequent revivals until modern times. This is a regrettable pointer to the importance of the external factors governing an opera's success, for the work is more consistent than *Poro* or *Siroe*, and Metastasio's libretto is generally superior.

The drama, nevertheless, in this late imperial story of Aetius, Honoria and the Emperor Valentinian, goes through the familiar motions of love, duty and deception, using embarrassment as its principal source of dramatic momentum (interesting to note how often Metastasio makes one character put another on the spot). Once again Handel was busy with the scissors, snipping away the recitative passages which London audiences must have found so tiresome and rearranging the order of the arias so as to reduce the emphasis on certain soloists and throw others into fuller relief. Bertolli, as the *seconda donna* Onoria had one of her numbers cut and another placed before instead of after an air for Varo the bass, presumably so as to ginger up the audience's expectations regarding an important new acquisition to the company, Antonio Montagnana, who had first appeared at the Haymarket in the *Tamerlano* revival which opened the 1731–2 season (though in fact his opening aria in *Ezio* is unremarkable).

Further re-ordering was made for Senesino's benefit as the hero, notably at the end of Act II. In the original Ezio's aria precedes one for Fulvia, his betrothed, followed in turn by arias for Valentiniano and the villainous Massimo. Probably as a sop to Senesino's vanity, since Strada had wound up the previous act with a fearsomely virtuoso piece full of modern triplet passages, Handel placed Strada first, dealt with Massimo and the Emperor in a little episode of recitative, and finished off with an affecting F minor *siciliano* for Senesino. It is hard, nevertheless, to imagine that either he or the audience was exactly satisfied with Handel's musical treatment of him, since the role, despite its traditionally heroic cast, is presented almost wholly without frills and flourishes. Of his seven arias the first is a tiny effusion without opening ritornello, the second, relying on a series of repeated sections, harks back to the Italian cantatas, and the third has the vocal line moving in unison with the orchestra for seventeen bars. It is only in the *siciliano* 'Ecco alle mie catene' that Ezio is allowed to dominate, and his penultimate air, 'Se la mia vita', a splendid compensation for earlier disappointments, is one of Handel's most ornately orchestrated vocal numbers, with paired horns, recorders and bassoons, and interjections from solo 'cello and violin (he had tried out a similar disposition in *Poro*).

Much of the best music in the work goes, not to Ezio or to the petulant, slightly ineffectual Valentiniano, or even to Fulvia, a virgin nightingale, but to Massimo, Onoria and Varo. Massimo's arias have a broad expressive range, from the foursquare simile piece with which he opens to his final remonstrance with his daughter, 'Tergi l'ingiuste lagrime', in which the orchestral accompaniment is reduced to a smattering of angular staccato punctuations, as though the composer were reluctant to allow such a thoroughpaced traitor to ingratiate himself with us. That Handel fully understood the type of political manipulator he represents is shown ideally in 'Se povero il ruscello', in which his sly comparisons of Ezio's growing popularity with the movements of a stream are complemented in the first section by an insinuating statement of a typically Handelian 'purling brooks' figure on the strings and in the second (describing the river in spate) by turbid flurries of descending scales. For her part Onoria gets one of the most attractive arias in all the operas, the radiantly pastoral 'Quanto voi felici siete', an enchanting rustic dance reminiscent of Telemann in one of his Polish or Moravian moods, an idea taken up later on with equal freshness by Varo, dilating on the ups and downs in the fortunes of shepherds and monarchs.

If the audience wanted a full display of Montagnana's enormous technical command, which brought him (little though he was later to deserve it) the finest of the composer's operatic bass roles, they got it here, in the amazing cadential leap of a twelfth to bottom F, and in the glorious 'Gia risonar', with its trumpet solo, the first bass number in any Handel opera since *Rinaldo* to exploit vocal agility and a wide tonal range, freeing the voice part from absolute dependence on the orchestral bass line. Yet *Ezio* flopped — 'Clothes & all ye Scenes New — but did not draw much

Company', and Handel quickly followed it with a freshly composed work which mercifully brought the public back again.

'I went to the Opera Sosarmis, made by Hendel, which takes with the town, and that justly, for it is one of the best I ever heard,' wrote Lord Percival in his diary. He was not, perhaps, to know that *Sosarme, rè di Media* had started its career in a more questionable guise as *Fernando, rè di Castiglia*, adapted from a libretto by Antonio Salvi for the Pratolino stage in 1707, and one which Handel had probably held in stock since the Italian trip. The story, turning on the uneasy relations between mediaeval Portugal and Spain, had suddenly been shifted, with corresponding name changes, to the remote Asia Minor of Herodotus and Xenophon, a fact unlikely to make much difference at the Haymarket but significant in view of England's political alignments. Portugal was not only a traditional ally but also riding on the crest of a boom in Brazilian mineral wealth which made her a valuable diplomatic support. King John V was noted for his lavish spending, examples of which can best be seen in the monstrous convent palace of Mafra, the exquisite gilt and lacquer library at Coimbra and the two extraordinary carriages, themselves like pieces of Baroque theatrical ornament, in which his ambassadors travelled to the Papal court. Since he himself had just married a Spanish princess there were likely to be diplomatic thunderings from the Portuguese embassy in Golden Square, Soho, at an opera based on the past conflicts of the two nations.

Sosarme has all the faults and virtues of *Poro* and *Ezio*, and shows yet again how much the composer relied on the stimulus of a really good libretto. As so often in Salvi's work, not enough attention is paid either to balance or motive, even though it is easy to see what attracted Handel in his lucid dramatic poetry, a powerful sense of situation and an ability matched by few other contemporary theatre poets to delineate credible human characters. As in *Ezio* the hero is folded rather too gently into the substance of the drama, in which his stance is that of an ardent romantic as opposed to a warrior hero. In the latter posture he only emerges halfway through the second act in 'Alle sfere della gloria', whose broad, leisurely musical paragraphs, sumptuously scored for oboes and strings with two horns, set up a heroic confidence echoed later on by the delightfully catchy 'M'opporrò da generoso', its distinctive colouring created by a rare use of *colla parte* oboes within bustling quaver patterns on the strings.

The women are treated with that utter certainty of aim and expression which Handel almost always brought to his heroines. In Erenice, Sosarme's prospective mother-in-law, Salvi had created a maternal figure somewhat more sympathetic than either the ambitious Gismonda or the tigress Matilde. Her wavering hopes and fears, embodied, for example, in the structure of her 'Vado al campo', its sense of urgent resolve underlined by the absence of ritornello and the pulse of the drumbeat bass, very quickly become our own. At moments like this, and in the anguished pathos of 'Cuor di madre', punctuated by violin solos, we can see just how unfair is the charge levelled at *opera seria* that it lacks an adequate sense of continuous drama.

Anna Strada as Elmira was rewarded with what is surely one of the strongest of Handel's later soprano roles. Like Durastanti before her and Susanna Cibber later on, she was evidently the kind of singer the composer liked best, not so much a flashy vocalist as an artist whose sensitivity and expressiveness suited themselves ideally to the full range of Handelian effects. We are told that he took such care in composing for her that 'from a coarse singer with a fine voice, he rendered her equal at least to the first performer in Europe'. How many other composers of the day would have dared to introduce a prima donna with an air on the scale of an exquisite miniature like 'Rendi'l sereno al ciglio,' a mere fifteen bars accompanied by strings alone, without continuo? He had done something of the sort before with Cuzzoni, and like her 'Falsa imagine' (though this was not Strada's first appearance) the little aria became an instant favourite. It is Elmira who begins and ends both Acts I and II, the latter counterbalancing A minor and A major in the plaintive opening arioso and simile aria in which she likens her errant brother to a bird returning finally to its nest, with the help of insinuating triple time string figures. Impossible to avoid feeling, whatever the librettist's contribution, that Handel must have appreciated a dramatic design which threw Strada, rather than Senesino, into such powerful relief though he flattered them both with the serene enchantments of 'Per le porte del tormento', perhaps his most attractive operatic duet.

Sosarme's success was more or less contemporary with events in the English musical world which may have given Handel a certain additional satisfaction. His old rival Giovanni Bononcini had remained in London after the break-up of the first Academy, as he was already under the protection of Henrietta, Duchess of Marlborough, 'with a salary of five hundred pounds a year, a sum no musician had before from any Prince, nor ought to have'. He had composed little following the notorious *Astianatte*, but at any rate found an appreciative patron in the duchess, at whose private concerts 'no other Music was performed to the first people in the kingdom than the compositions of her favourite master, executed by the principal singers of the opera'. Each was, however, proud and temperamental, and in 1731 they quarrelled irredeemably over the extras Bononcini added to his bills. He left her service for good, perhaps in a mood like that in which he had snubbed the Emperor Joseph I with the words: 'There are many sovereign princes and only one Bononcini.'

At the same period a scandal had broken which was to discredit him utterly in the eyes of many of his London admirers. The Academy of Ancient Music was a concert club, founded by some of Handel's friends and acquaintances, which met at the Crown and Anchor tavern in the Strand, and, besides giving excellent recitals, amassed an extensive music library from the members' donations. In 1728 Maurice Greene, newly appointed to the Chapel Royal post left vacant by the death of Croft, introduced a madrigal, 'In una siepe ombrosa', to one of the Crown and Anchor concerts as a work by Bononcini. Three years afterwards the club library acquired the newly-published *Duetti, Terzetti e Madrigali* by Handel's old Venetian associate Antonio Lotti, and what was everyone's surprise to find 'In una siepe ombrosa' included in the book.

Bononcini's initial response was an outraged denunciation of Lotti as a plagiarist, claiming that he himself had written the madrigal 30 years before for the Emperor Leopold. Application to Lotti himself by the club produced a declaration of authenticity which Bononcini declined to answer. A second letter to Venice elicited Lotti's affidavit, under seal of a public notary, with testimony from four witnesses who had either seen it in rough draft or sung it before it went to press, and from the author of the text, Paolo Pariati. As a venerable member of the Venetian musical establishment Lotti cannot have needed to pass off so unremarkable a piece as his own: Bononcini's reasons for doing so may have been connected with the sort of contemptuous arrogance for which he had become noted. Greene meanwhile stuck to his guns and on seeing his friend dishonoured withdrew to set up a rival society with the violinist Michael Festing at the Devil Tavern, further down the street, 'and the joke upon this occasion was that Dr Greene was gone to the Devil'. As for Bononcini, he became involved in the schemes of Eugenio Mecenati, a Parmesan intriguer and ex-friar masquerading as 'Count Ughi', but left London alone for Paris in October 1732, never to return.

Whatever his pleasure in seeing his rivals discomfited and his opera successful, Handel's triumphs were alloyed by a piece of musical piracy which was to have momentous consequences, not only for the direction ultimately taken by his own career, but for the concert life of eighteenth-century London as a whole. On 23 February 1732, eight days after the new opera's première, a private performance of the Cannons oratorio *Esther* (or *The History of Hester*, as Lord Percival calls it) took place at the Crown and Anchor in the composer's presence. This was undertaken by Bernard Gates, now Master of the Chapel Royal Children, who, according to the printed libretto, 'join'd in the Chorus's, after the Manner of the Ancients, being placed between the Stage and the Orchestra; and the Instrumental Parts (two or three particular Instruments, necessary on this Occasion, excepted) were performed by Members of the Philharmonick Society, consisting only of Gentlemen'. The all-male cast was drawn from among Gates's choristers and there were two further performances. It was a hit for all concerned, as Percival noted: 'This oratoria or religious opera is exceeding fine, and the company were highly pleased, some of the parts being well performed.' The evening was also Handel's birthday, and the Academy of Ancient Music adopted the pleasing habit of celebrating the occasion with *Esther* revivals in later years.

The novelty value of the whole venture as a likely commercial enterprise clearly appealed to somebody's entrepreneurial spirit, for around the middle of April advertisements began appearing for a pirate *Esther* at York Buildings in Villiers Street (where, years before, Haym, Clayton and Dieupart had tried their unsuccessful concert scheme). No legal sanctions protected Handel from such an act as this, and he needed to work quickly if he was to establish his authority in respect of the work itself. Accordingly he met competition head on with a revival of his own at the Haymarket, on 2 May, with additional music mostly adapted from earlier works, and a recast libretto by Samuel Humphreys. It was, moreover, a command performance at the request of the Princess Royal, George II's eldest daughter and Handel's former pupil. Her original notion had been of a staged version at the King's Theatre by Gates's team, but the advertisement in the *Daily Journal* made it clear that this was out of the question. 'N.B. There will be no Action on the Stage, but the House will be fitted up in a decent Manner for the Audience.'

It appears that a person of considerable force must have intervened to prevent a scriptural episode being given theatrical representation, and in so profane a setting as the opera house. Few public figures of the day wielded such influence as the Bishop of London, Edmund Gibson. A pillar of the Whig establishment and sterling in his efforts to unite the political interests of church and state, he was identified by Queen Caroline's favourite, Lady Sundon, as Walpole's Pope. 'Madam,' answered Walpole, 'he is my Pope and shall be my Pope. Everybody has some Pope or other. Don't you know that you are one? They call you Pope Joan.' Others were less admiring, including the Oxford antiquary Thomas Hearne (we shall meet him in the next chapter) who could never forgive the bishop for renouncing the orthodox non-juring line of Oxonian churchmen in favour of Revolution principles: 'a great Whig and sticks at nothing . . . a strange whiffler'. Yet in an age of prelates called Sprat and Herring and of famously apathetic clergy, Gibson was magnificently hardworking, scholarly, devout and well-intentioned, an exemplary figure who in many respects gave the established church a much-needed touch of dignity.

If he had a fault it was too ready a tendency to show his disapproval of the loose morals of the age. During his London episcopacy he operated, with varying success, against Heidegger's masquerades, 'houses which entertained Sodomitical Clubs', Sunday racing, prostitution and drunkenness. The staged production of a dramatic oratorio at the Haymarket was an ideal target for him, and his swift action in regulating the circumstances of the *Esther* performance meant that Gates's Chapel Royal singers were replaced by the Haymarket's operatic soloists. Probably for the first time at any great length Senesino, Montagnana, Strada and Bertolli all sang in English, with suitably bizarre results. An anonymous spectator noted that they 'made rare work with the *English* Tongue you would have sworn it had been *Welch*'. Some time afterwards James Bramston reflected a characteristic response in his Juvenalian satire *The Man of Taste*:

> I'm *English* born, and love a grumbling noise.
> The Stage should yield the Solemn Organ's note,
> And Scripture tremble in the Eunuch's throat.
> Let *Senesino* sing, what *David* writ,
> And *Hallelujahs* charm the pious pit.
> Eager in throngs the town to *Hester* came,
> And *Oratorio* was a lucky name.
> Thou, *Heeideggre*! the English taste has found,
> And rul'st the mob of quality with sound.

As if one piece of theatrical buccaneering was not enough, the *Daily Post* announced a forthcoming performance of 'a celebrated Pastoral Opera call'd Acis and Galatea' by the company currently engaged in presenting English operas at the New Theatre (formerly the Little Theatre) on the east side of the Haymarket. This enterprise was managed by Thomas Arne, father of the composer, assisted by the German bassoonist J. F. Lampe and the poet Henry Carey, an admirer of Handel. It was a thoroughly laudable scheme, though like so many others of its kind (Richard D'Oyly Carte's Royal English Opera of the 1890s, for example) it was destined to failure. What is interesting, however, is that both the piratical *Esther* and *Acis* were Cannons works — so was Thomas Arne responsible for the former as well, and if so, did he obtain the scores from one of the Cannons musicians? Pepusch, even if he must have taken part in the Crown and Anchor performances, seems as likely a source of supply as any, since, though he was always interested in what Handel was up to, his regard for him was distinctly grudging.

Whatever the truth of the matter Handel felt compelled to weigh in with a counter-attack, and on 5 June, an *Acis* revival was duly mounted at the King's Theatre, significantly without stage action 'but the Scene will represent, in a Picturesque Manner, a rural Prospect, with Rocks, Groves, Fountains and Grotto's; amongst which will be disposed a Chorus of Nymphs and Shepherds, Habits, and every other Decoration suited to the Subject'.

The end product was more grotesque than anything else. One of the least explicable aspects of Handel's creative outlook is his cavalier attitude towards his works after their initial run of performances. So far from being improved by his subsequent modifications, several of the oratorios and other English vocal works were seriously affected by his additions and subtractions on behalf of some sort of notional box-office appeal, or because he needed to adapt them to the accomplishments of a new cast. A phrase of the German critic Marpurg's sums up the 1732 *Acis* and needs no translation: *ein gar besonders mischmasch*, and so it was. For a start, the performances were bilingual (a lesson had been learnt from *Esther*) and sections of *Aci, Galatea e Polifemo*, on ice since 1708, were added to the Cannons *Acis and Galatea*. Airs from the early operas, the *Birthday Ode* and the *Brockes Passion* thickened the brew, and five new pastoral characters joined the dramatis personae. Nobody seemed quite certain what was actually being performed; Arne's pirates called it an opera and Lord Percival noted it as 'the fine masque of *Acis and Galatea* composed by Hendel'. It was unlikely, in its current form, to inspire a spate of English operas, but at least the composer himself renewed an interest in the work and revived it on several occasions during the next ten years.

The importance of the *Acis* and *Esther* revivals can be readily appreciated. Though neither was improved by the composer's additions and alterations, each was brought before a much wider public than the sort of select aristocratic audience for which it was originally devised. The novelty of the entertainment had been emphasized for Handel by Arne's performances, which pointed to a potentially responsive and enthusiastic audience for this kind of musical hybrid if only someone had the initiative to carry it further. As for Gibson's veto, that effectively put paid to the concept of staged oratorio and sowed the seeds of a controversy which looms large in modern Handel studies as to the validity and authenticity of these works in a fully theatrical context.

Since practically every Handel oratorio has now been given a staged revival, it may soon be possible to assess the whole issue more justly. His English librettos contain stage directions, several of which he transferred to his 'foul scores', but this does not mean that either the poet or the composer intended these to be executed literally. There is every difference between thinking dramatically, as Handel's long operatic experience had conditioned him to do, and creating a work that will function credibly on stage. Nor was it, surely, a question of his looking forward to an age when his oratorios *might* be given in the theatre, and composing with this in view. He remained a great dramatic composer to the end of his life; even in *Messiah*, perhaps, indeed, especially in *Messiah*, there is the sense of a highly visual imagination at work, and there is no reason to suppose that had the opportunity arisen, after his abandonment of opera in 1741, of re-entering the Italian lyric field, he would ever have rejected it. Yet the oratorios (we may except *Semele* and *Hercules*, English operas laid out in significantly theatrical terms) are unconvincing as theatre for the fairly obvious reason that none of them was intended for representation. This has not deterred the directors, however. Even *Judas Maccabaeus*, which is practically devoid of action, has been staged in recent years, while in 1833 at Düsseldorf, Mendelssohn, to whom in other respects Handelians owe a profound gratitude, undertook an *Israel in Egypt* performance assisted by *tableaux vivants* and preceded by choruses from Lotti and Weber, accompanying colour transparencies of Dürer and Raphael paintings.

Despite the evident popularity of the two revisions, a rumour seems to have got about during the early weeks of November 1732 that Handel's talent had somehow run dry. A production, in pasticcio form, of Leonardo Leo's *Catone in Utica* suggested, to those who imagined they were hearing Handel rather than Leo, that he was more or less finished. Among these was Lord Hervey, who wrote to Stephen Fox: 'I am just come from a long, dull and consequently tiresome Opera of Handel's, whose genius seems quite exhausted. The bride's recommendation of being the first night

could not make this supportable.' However, he liked the new mezzo-soprano Celeste Gismondi, 'Celestina': 'she seemed to take mightily, which I was glad of. I have a sort of friendship for her, without knowing why. *Toute chose que me fait resouvenir ce temps m'attendrit; et je suis sûr que ce soir à l'Opéra j'ai soupiré cent fois.*' Over at the New Theatre, Arne and Lampe's English opera *Britannia* and its star Cecilia Young, who was to sing for Handel two years later, evoked an anonymous eulogy in the *Daily Post* which began:

> No more shall Italy its Warblers send
> To charm our Ears with Handel's heav'nly Strains;
> For dumb his rapt'rous Lyre, their Fame must end.

They were but partially mistaken, for in truth Handel had nothing new prepared for the start of the season, which saw revivals of *Alessandro* and *Tolomeo*, and it was only on 20 November that he completed the score of *Orlando*, which did not in any case reach the stage until the end of the following January.

No more typical case of the composer's favourite device of *reculer pour mieux sauter*, something which seems continually to mark his career during the 1730s and 1740s, can be found than *Orlando*, a work which proved that so far from nearing exhaustion, his genius had undergone a startling renewal, resulting in a piece whose freshness and originality give it a high place not only in Handel's *oeuvre* but among eighteenth-century operas in general. That attentiveness to detail, exuberant variety of texture and warmly understanding treatment of character which show Handel at his incomparable best permeate the whole finished structure from first to last, and it is the harshest of ironies that, as we shall see, a work fashioned with such inspiration and care should have been designed for singers who were so far from appreciating it.

For his text Handel turned to the work of his former Roman associate Carlo Sigismondo Capece, librettist of *La Resurrezione*. His *L'Orlando ovvero la Gelosa Pazzia* had been written for Domenico Scarlatti in 1711, and was based on the materials of Ariosto's famous Renaissance epic *Orlando Furioso*, always a popular quarry for Baroque theatre poets. Two of the original characters in the drama were removed and Montagnana's magnificent bass voice was given more than adequate scope in the role of the magus Zoroastro who begins the opera. Apart from Claudio in *Agrippina* he is in fact the most influential character Handel ever allotted to an operatic bass. Where normally such figures on the Baroque stage were restricted to being either commentators, stooges or minor villains,

Zoroastro, as has been pointed out, bears a marked, though wholly coincidental, similarity to his near namesake, Sarastro, in *Die Zauberflöte*. His presence on the stage at the end of the sombre overture in the 'difficult' key of F sharp minor as the sage contemplator of eternal mysteries in the heavens in a solemn arioso establishes him at once as the moderating, visionary force in a drama which, as the printed libretto tells us, 'tends to demonstrate the Imperious Manner in which Love insinuates its Impressions into the Hearts of Persons of all Ranks, and likewise how a wise Man should be ever ready with his best Endeavours to re-conduct into the Right Way, those who have been misguided from it by the Illusion of their Passions'.

Zoroastro's four fine arias, marking crucial moments in his intervention during the opera's course, underline through their texts this paradoxically moral quality intrinsic to the work. In some respects its spirit seems closer to the gravity of Tasso than to the brilliant romancing of Ariosto, in that far from being a mere confection of magic and pastoral it celebrates the virtues of magnanimity and discriminating forbearance. The close of the drama, from both poetic and technical aspects one of the best Handel ever chose, lies not in the orthodox patterning of amorous couples but in the standing aside of Orlando and the shepherdess Dorinda to allow the love of Angelica and Medoro to prevail. Sublime renunciation underpins the joyful vaudeville finale, in which Orlando wishes the lovers happiness, they themselves look forward to peace and fidelity and Dorinda, casting sadness aside, charmingly sings 'I invite you all to my cottage for some further celebrations'. The story, incidentally, manages to retain its interest for us without the operation of malice or conspiracy as dramatic elements. It is the patient endurance of Angelica and Dorinda that is emphasized rather than the jealous machinations and sexual adventuring which so often motivate heroines in opera of this kind: the contrast between them is created by Handel himself.

Orlando's moral education through a fully staged psychological crisis forms the theme of the story. Zoroastro foresees glory for him, but first he must *learn* to be a hero — an arraignment, as it were, of the basic postures and premises of Baroque dramatic tradition. That he can strike these well enough emerges in his aria 'Non fu gia men forte Alcide', ironically martial in its scoring for horns since he is professedly forsaking arms for love, yet more ironically still the vicissitudes of the following scene force him to reassume this role in the stirring 'Fammi combattere'. Thereafter he descends into total and violent insanity, culminating in a mad scene closing Act II which even the most tepid of commentators can hardly fail to admire. The rhythms of the accompaniment gradually break down from dotted semiquavers to repeated quavers to long held notes, finally releasing the ultimate incoherence in passages of five beats to the bar; the skeleton of a rage aria ensues, quickly burning itself out in a vocal line punctuated by a single note, followed, with ghastly humour, by a parody gavotte and a pathetic larghetto; Orlando flares up again into the ultimate blaze of hysterical fury, only to be whisked away during the orchestral ritornello by the provident magus.

The hero's progress through the opera is anarchic and intrusive to the elegance and fluency with which Handel's score conveys the passions of Angelica, the amiable if somewhat absent-minded Medoro and the enchanting Dorinda, whose airs, such as 'O care parolette' and the nightingale arioso 'Quando spieghi i tuoi tormenti', are touched with a vernal innocence, even if the sophistication of her musical idiom in certain numbers makes her very much a modern girl. In the last analysis Handel's genius in *Orlando* transcends all the supposed limits of Baroque opera, turning it into a drama about young people confronting the challenge of their sincerest emotions, nowhere better expressed than in the trio 'Consolati o bella' which ends the first act, when Angelica and Medoro, secure in mutual love, can find time to comfort the grief-stricken Dorinda, who must now realize that she has lost Medoro for good.

Orlando, 'extraordinary fine & magnificent', was first produced at the King's Theatre on 27 January 1733, with a modest run of eleven performances. The figure of Orlando standing aside at its close for others to enjoy themselves vaguely and sinisterly foreshadowed events, for this was Senesino's last operatic engagement with Handel's company. Vanity rather than generosity was soon to carry him away.

And what of Handel's finances during these 'Second Academy' years? Little documentary evidence has survived to tell us how the company was run or to fill out the business aspects of the enterprise, but at least one manuscript has very recently come to light which summarizes the position during the 1732–3 season. It was probably designed as a calculation of total cash received and includes details of subscriptions, ticket sales, box rentals and money received from the royal family.

Subscribers paid fifteen guineas each, but could pay in instalments and drop out at any time. Those who did not pay up were generally too grand to be treated as anything but bad debts to be written off: thus Lady Anne Hamilton owed £52 and the Duchess of Newcastle, at 50 nights, a massive £105. The queen and Handel's pupils the princesses contributed £520 and the king kept up his £1,000 bounty. The only singer mentioned is Strada, paid £565 on account over a period from March to September (doubtless the classic history of debt).

The overall calculation of gross receipt has been estimated at £8,100. On top of the problem of unrecovered subscriptions and fluctuating ticket sales, there were immense outgoings, including a 1,400-guinea fee in 1730–1 to Senesino and payment for new scenery and costumes. Even if salaries to Handel and Heidegger are not taken into account, the total expense can hardly have been much less than £8,500. Ruin was often round the corner for Handel, but what invariably seems to have rescued him was a combination of sudden good luck with his own unquenchable spirit of venturesome initiative.

— 8 —

Music, Ladies and Learning

The professional lives of most eighteenth-century composers do not make for encouraging reading. Given the extremes of caprice in their employers to which they were constantly a prey, it is sometimes a wonder that they were able to write as they did or to get their music published and performed. Handel is a unique case, in that he was the victim not of princely vapours and megrims, but, ironically, of his own determination to freelance in the notoriously unpredictable world of musical London. Tied to no master, he was not bound to please an individual taste, yet his was the more difficult task of captivating an audience which often had no sense of his superior gifts, which fretted at what it considered his tyrannical attitude towards artistic standards, and which was unsophisticated enough still to be obsessed with the value of sheer novelty. By a cruel paradox, it often seems that it was only after he stopped composing that the London public began to realize Handel's genuine greatness, and revered as a grand old ruin what it had despised and rejected as a fully functional organism.

We have noted how much easier it was for Handel to countenance the activity of fellow composers from a distance than to endure it where he felt it threatened his own position. Thus, though he had been responsible for introducing the town to the work of younger masters such as Leo, Giacomelli and Orlandini, the recent Haymarket seasons had been dominated by his own operas to the extent that 1732–3 featured only one piece by another hand, the unsuccessful *Catone in Utica*. Who can blame the stars of the company, particularly those who, like Senesino and Montagnana, may have felt that they had an international reputation to maintain, for thinking, as they must have done, that the repertoire was rather too limited, and for wishing to spread their wings in other directions? Senesino, in any case, can hardly have needed much excuse to quit the preserve of a composer with whom he had never truly been in accord. As so often, Handel seems to foreshadow the attitudes of a far later generation of composers; his dedication to promoting his own work irresistibly recalls the superbly egocentric single-mindedness of a Wagner or a Berlioz.

The opportunity for open revolt arose from a scheme set afoot during the early weeks of 1733 and explained in a letter from the Earl of Delawarr to the Duke of Richmond. 'There is a Spirit got up against the Dominion of Mr Handel, a subscription carry'd on, and Directors chosen, who have contracted with Senesino. . . . The General Court gave power to contract with any Singer Except Strada, so that it is Thought Handel must fling up, which the poor Count [Heidegger] will not be sorry for, There being no one but what declares as much for him as against the Other, so that we have a Chance of seeing Operas once more on a good foot. . . . We doubt not but we shall have your Graces Name in our Subscription List. . . . There seems great Unanimity, and Resolution to carry on the Undertaking *comme il faut*.' So the Opera of the Nobility was born, as the most blatant and powerful gesture of inimical rivalry Handel had yet needed to contend with in his career as a composer.

Several of its directors were former Academy members and may have been genuinely motivated by a wish to bring the latest Italian successes to London, though Delawarr's 'Operas once more on a good foot' and 'the Undertaking *comme il faut*' hint at somewhat more characteristically snobbish reasons for the project. Other forces too were at work. A glance at the list of directors detailed in Delawarr's letter reveals a marked political bias towards the anti-Walpole parliamentary opposition, formed by the Tories and malcontent Whigs led by Pulteney, which was to become even more marked after the election of the coming year. Though, of the three dukes mentioned, Richmond and Rutland were government supporters, Bedford was an opposition Whig, as were the Earls of Stair and Cadogan (once inimitably described by Dr Atterbury as 'a bold, bad, blundering, blustering, bloody booby') and Lord Limerick. Lord Bathurst, one of the dedicatees of Pope's *Moral Essays*, was a noted Tory, member of the party traditionally supported by Delawarr's own family, while of Thomas Coke, Lord Lovel, the lampoon ran:

> To neither party is his heart inclined,
> Voted with Walpole, and with Pulteney dined.

They were joined by three opposition M.P.s, Henry Furnese, Sir Michael Newton and Sir John Buckworth (who seems to have been personally acquainted with Handel). The unkindest cut must have been the adherence of Lord Burlington, apparently prepared to sacrifice his enthusiasm for the composer to the trivialities of politics.

The patron of the enterprise was, of course, Frederick, Prince of Wales, by now deeply committed to that mutual detestation between parents and offspring which has recurred so frequently in the English royal family during the last three centuries, and childishly eager for any excuse to cock a snook at the King and Queen. He was a tolerable hand on the 'cello, as Mercier's charming group portrait emphasizes, and something of a composer, as well as a patron of English music at his country house at Cliveden, where 'Rule Britannia' was first heard as part of Arne and Thomson's *Alfred* in 1740. His presence was all that was needed to complete a picture of the whole scheme as a species of political rallying ground for the various elements opposed to George, Caroline and Walpole though there is evidence of an enduring loyalty to Handel.

Politics and royal partisanship aside, a share of the fault was Handel's own. Burney's implication that he saw in the oratorio performances a handy means of bailing out the opera seasons are borne out by manuscript comments on Mainwaring's published memoir, written around 1760 by the composer's friend Lord Shaftesbury. One of these tells us: 'In the Spring 1733, Mr Handell finding that the Oratorio of Esther had been well received, the Oratorio of Deborah, which he reckoned into the number of the 50 Opera's Subscribed for, and — as he had taken great Pains, and as this was a new kind of Musick attended with some Extraordinary Expence, and more over for his own Benefit, he took double Prices, vizt a Guinea for Pit & Box's. This Indiscreet Step disgusted the Town, and he had a very thin House.'

In justice to Handel it must be said that this is practically the only example of sharp practice in which we can find him engaged, but the town was indeed disgusted and ready to invoke comparisons with Walpole's unpopular and ultimately unsuccessful Excise Bill, brought in only three days before *Deborah*'s première. A few weeks later, on 7 April, there appeared a letter in the opposition journal *The Craftsman*, concurrently attacking both the minister and the musician, glancing at the conduct of the former while ostensibly pillorying the latter. Though this is of far more significance politically than musically the letter touches on some familiar traits: for instance, 'he had, for some Time, govern'd the *Opera's*, and modell'd the *Orchestre*, without the least Controul. No Voices, no *Instruments* were admitted, but such as flatter'd his Ears, though they shock'd those of the Audience. *Wretched Scrapers* were put above the *best Hands* in the *Orchestre*. No Musick but *his own* was to be allowed, though every Body was weary of it; and he had the Impudence to assert *that there was no Composer* in England *but himself*.' The author signed himself 'Your very humble Servant, P—LO R—LI' and, though it was for long doubted, Rolli's authorship has been supported by an Italian translation found among Senesino's papers now in the Biblioteca Communale at Siena. It is enough to add that Rolli became the official poet of the Opera of the Nobility.

Handel finished *Deborah* on 21 February and the first performance took place at the King's Theatre on Saturday 17 March, with 'the House . . . fitted up and illuminated in a new and particular Manner' and all the solo parts taken by Italians. The impressions of mass and weight created by the massed forces on the *Acis* and *Esther* evenings of the previous year had suggested new paths to the composer, and as we listen to *Deborah*, with its rich eight-part choral opening, we can readily appreciate the exciting experience it afforded of hearing what, apart from the 1727 coronation music, was perhaps the grandest noise so far known in eighteenth-century London of blended voices and instruments. No wonder Lady Lucy Wentworth could write four years later that 'last Sunday there was a vast deal of musick at Church, too much I think, for I doubt it spoilt everybody's devotion, for there was drums and Trumpits as loud as an Oritoria'. Lord Perceval noted of the piece that 'it was very magnificent, near a hundred performers, among whom about twenty-five singers', and Lady Anne Irwin told Lord Carlisle that ''tis excessive noisy, a vast number of instruments and voices, who all perform at a time, and is in music what I fancy a French ordinary in conversation'.

The work as a whole has generally been written off either as being a pasticcio, which to a large extent it is, and thus unworthy of comment, or simply as bad because its libretto is so heavy-handed. This is unfair, as anyone who has actually heard *Deborah* in performance will at once realize. True, Handel, eager to capitalize upon the novelty enthusiasm for oratorio and probably fired by Maurice Greene's *Song of Deborah and Barak* advertised the previous October, had hustled the piece into existence by redesigning large chunks of the *Chandos Anthems*, the *Brockes Passion*, the *Dixit Dominus* and three sections of *Il Trionfo del Tempo*, and had made use of Samuel Humphreys to carry out the Procrustean business of adapting to his music one of the most unattractive episodes in the Book of Judges, culminating in the spectacular betrayal of time-honoured Oriental traditions of hospitality whereby Jael, having lulled Sisera to sleep, nailed his head to the ground with a tent-peg. Yet the cumulative effect, enhanced for the seasoned Handelian by the sense of *déjà entendu* in the succession of favourite numbers, is undeniably fascinating.

It is, of course, the choruses which make the most telling impact and whose general predominance in the work anticipates *Israel in Egypt*, written some five years afterwards. Nearly every one contains some point of dramatic interest in its use of earlier material, as, for instance, in 'See, the proud chief', where the *cantus firmus* of the first number of the *Dixit Dominus* is used to create the impression of the Canaanite army's approach, and in 'Plead thy just cause', based on the same source but using it this time to express the Israelites' remonstration with God and introducing it with an astonishing fourteen-bar choral prelude designed to establish the mood in a few magisterial strokes — a field in which, as Mozart perceived, Handel has no rivals. Among the newly-composed numbers the best are the magnificent duet for Deborah and Barak 'Where do thy ardours raise me?' which, in terms of rhythm, harmony and texture, is quite unlike anything he had ever written before (it sounds more like Hasse or C. P. E. Bach than Handel) and the chorus 'Doleful tidings', in which the full significance of the closing words, 'despair and death are in that sound', is evoked by stripping away the orchestral accompaniment, leaving the vocal lines as a series of chromaticisms gasped out between rests, fading into four bars of concluding organ continuo. But even if the total effect of hearing such familiar pieces as 'O praise the Lord with one consent' recast in 24 vocal and instrumental parts as 'Eternal Lord of Earth and Sky' is like hearing new music, *Deborah* is without homogeneity either in intention or design, a *galimatias* of Italian, English and German idioms in which we can see Handelian eclecticism at its least disciplined.

The new oratorio enjoyed a run of six performances, for five of which Handel charged the ordinary prices, but the damage was now done, and on 13 June the Opera of the Nobility's subscribers were summoned to appear in person or by proxy at Hickford's Rooms in Panton Street, a dancing school famous for concerts featuring Geminiani, Veracini and other noted soloists of the day, 'in order to settle proper Methods for carrying on the Subscriptions'. The recipe was very much a case of 'the mixture as before' — a successful foreign composer, in this case Nicola Porpora, one year Handel's junior, a leading exponent of newer styles, but best known to us as the teacher of the young Joseph Haydn at Vienna, and a clutch of dazzling soloists, including, besides Senesino and Montagnana, the resurrected Cuzzoni and the most brilliant castrato star of the age, Porpora's own pupil, Carlo Broschi, nicknamed Farinelli, whose comparatively brief London career was a parade of meteoric triumphs culminating in the appropriate if blasphemous accolade given him when a fashionable spectator exclaimed: 'One God, one Farinelli!'

Handel's response was typical. At some stage during the spring of 1733, perhaps even earlier, Dr William Holmes, Vice-Chancellor of Oxford University, had invited him to a revival of the annual Encaenia ceremony, taking place immediately after the end of Trinity Term, to accept an honorary degree and to give a series of concerts with Strada, the sole remaining member of his Haymarket company, and other soloists, mainly English (exceptions were the bass Gustavus Waltz and the tenor Filippo Rocchetti). We still do not know why, if it really was offered to him, Handel declined the degree, but the Oxford jaunt was exactly the kind of boost to his morale which he most needed at this critical stage in his fortunes. That he took the experience to heart is proved by the fact that some eight years later he followed a similar course in retreating to Ireland in search of a justly appreciative audience.

Oxford had long been a notorious Adullam for Tory and Jacobite sympathizers, and it says a good deal for the success with which, by closely monitoring official appointments, Walpole and Bishop Gibson used their influence to neutralize the university that its members should so eagerly have welcomed the favoured musician of the Hanoverian monarch. Perhaps more remarkable still is the fact that the Vice-Chancellor himself was president of St John's, a college which even today perpetuates fervent Stuart loyalties. The Public Act, or Encaenia as it is now known, was scheduled to take place on Friday 6 July, and the Sheldonian Theatre had been specially fitted up for a Handelian musical fortnight. Two days before the festivities began, a correspondent to *Read's Weekly Journal* described the unprecedented enthusiasm which heralded the occasion: 'Almost all our Houses not only within the City, but without the Gates, are taken up for Nobility, Gentry and others: Many of the Heads of Houses and other Gentlemen of the University of Cambridge will be here on Wednesday Night; and we are so hurry'd about Lodging, that almost all the Villages within three or four Miles of this City, make a good Hand of disposing of their little neat Tenements on this great Occasion.'

Handel arrived probably on the Wednesday, and gave a performance of *Esther* 'to a very numerous Audience, at five Shillings a ticket' at five o'clock the following day. Amid the plaudits could be heard one remote but persistent grumbling voice. It was that of the diehard Jacobite antiquarian Thomas Hearne, whose diary records the archetypal observations of someone who did not approve and stayed away. That evening he wrote: 'One Handel, a forreigner (who, they say, was born in Hanover) being desired to come to Oxford, to perform in Musick this Act, in which he has great skill, is come down. . . . This is an innovation. The Players might as well be permitted to come and act. The Vice-Chancellor is much blamed for it.'

On Friday, at one in the afternoon, the degree ceremonies began, with the Sheldonian divided into special galleries for noblemen and doctors, inceptors in arts, strangers, ladies, gentlemen of the University of Cambridge and musicians. 'In the rest of the Area were the Batlers, Servitors &c.' After addresses by the Senior Proctor and the Vice-Professor of Poetry, there came a series of 'philological exercises' by undergraduates, including such topics as *Machina Orreriana*, *Vegetatio Halesiana*, *Morbus Anglicus*, *Carmine Heroico* and one by Bishop Gibson's son Edmund, of Christ Church, on the currently newsworthy *Colonia Georgiae deducta*. Of most interest to Handel would have been *Henricus Baynbrigg Buckeridge, e Coll. Div. Jo. Bapt. Sup. Ord. Comm.* on *Musica sacra Dramatica, sive Oratorium Carmine Lyrico*, a Horatian ode in elegant sapphics, apparently inspired by having heard a performance of *Deborah*. Through the mesh of rather awkward prosody in verses like:

> *Sed praeparatam iam ferit artifex*
> Handelus *aurem. Musa procax, tace.*
> *Victorias, pompas, triumphos*
> *Ille canet melior Poeta,*

we catch, as with Pamphilj years before, or with Revd Daniel Prat's 1722 effusion *To Mr Handel, On His Playing on The Organ*, a sense of the novelty and excitement of a first contact with the composer's music, enhanced, in the case of Buckeridge listening to *Deborah*, by an awareness of its rugged, monumental grandeur.

The next day, after a concert arranged by the professor of music, Richard Goodson, there were further Latin orations from the various schools, including *An Flatulentia a Concoctione laesa oriatur* and *An Emetica conveniant in Apoplexia*, after which Handel issued tickets for his evening benefit performance of *Esther*. 'Some of the Company, that had found themselves but very scamblingly entertained at our dry Disputations, took it into their Heads, to try how a little Fiddling would sit upon them. Such as cou'dn't attend before, squeezed in with as much Alacrity as others strove to get out; so that e're his Myrmidons cou'd gain their Posts, he found that he had little Likelihood to be at such a Loss for a House, as once upon a time, Folks say he was. . . . So that notwithstanding the barbarous and inhuman Combination of such a Parcel of unconscionable Chaps, he disposed, it seems, of most of his Tickets, and had, as you may guess, a pretty motley Appearance into the Bargain.' Hearne, still grutching into his journal about the whole business, noted of 'Handel and (his lousy Crew) a great number of foreign fidlers' that 'NB his book (not worth 1$^{\underline{d}}$.) he sells for 1$^{\underline{s}}$.'

Sunday brought performances of the *Utrecht Te Deum and Jubilate* and two Coronation Anthems and Monday featured further exercises and ceremonies, at which care was taken by the proctors to see that the newly-made doctors were wearing the proper kind of boots. But Handel himself, as a master showman, had reserved his biggest musical treat till last. On Tuesday 10 July, 'the Company in the Evening were entertained with a spick and span new Oratorio called *Athalia*. One of the Royal and Ample (i.e. a member of Christ Church) had been saying that truly, 'twas his Opinion, that the Theater was erected for other-guise Purposes, than to be prostituted to a Company of squeeking, bawling, out-landish Singsters, let the Agreement be what it wou'd'. Success was almost a foregone conclusion; *The Bee* reported that *Athalia* 'was performed with the utmost Applause, and is esteemed equal to the most celebrated of that Gentleman's Performances; there were 3,700 Persons present'.

It is always an exciting experience to examine Handel's manuscripts, so eloquent, in their blots and crossings-out, false starts and second thoughts, of the liveliness and spontaneity of the composer's creative processes. The foul score of *Athalia*, whose second page, for example, is so heavily marked by Handel's pen strokes that the paper has been almost furrowed through, is a wonderfully vivid testimony to the frenzied vigour with which his ideas poured on to the page. Few Handel premières can, in any case, have been so gratifying to audience and composer alike as this one, in its context of recent failures and frustrations. Oxford was honoured with the presentation of a work outstanding in its artistic consistency, one of those pieces which give point to the notion of the 1730s as the most fruitful decade in Handel's career.

Something had happened here which had not taken place since the second part of *Acis and Galatea* fifteen years before, and the two works draw upon similar resources for their respective strengths. There is the same sense of cleanness and clarity in the overall design, the same idea of formal elements, aria, chorus, recitative, serving one another instead of existing as mere independent shapes, and, most important, the same quality of a personal style which selects and concentrates on features drawn from a varied mass of musical traditions while ignoring others. As in *Acis* Handel is saying something new, and it is scarcely accidental that each is based on the inspiration of an English text. The quality of Samuel Humphreys' reliable adaptation of Racine's *Athalie*, whose irresistible sense of dramatic purposefulness and flawless plotting so appealed to Handel, is matched by the freedom and suppleness of English poetry. Emptier of Augustan cliché than the Morell librettos of the 1740s and superior to the banalities of Humphreys' *Deborah* text, *Athalia*, in the relationship between its verbal and musical languages, underlines Handel's stylistic sensitivity to the nature of the medium in which he found himself working.

This triumphant absence of pedantry in Handel, the ability to impress a personal homogeneity on a handful of intriguingly disparate elements, shows more clearly in *Athalia* than in many of his later oratorios perhaps because it was composed within the orbit of his last great operas. Thus an air like Athalia's 'My vengeance awakes me' has (as we noted in the previous chapter) the typical rhythmic bounce of a 'modern' aria in the Porpora style, yet its very sophistication of musical idiom, with suggestions of lethal elegance masking nervousness in the harmonies and accompaniment figures, is ideally suited to the Clytemnestra-like queen herself. No finer example of the composer's ideas of balance and definition is given us than the context of this flamboyant outburst, placed between the boy Joas's artless 'Will God whose mercies ever flow', scored for strings without continuo, and the duet 'My spirits fail', which carries us from Athalia's hectic B flat allegro straight into a slow F minor which in its turn becomes an andante solo for Josabeth over a wandering bass line.

Such a radiantly dramatic quality in the pacing and layout of the various numbers is emphasized by the choral element whose significance had been established by *Deborah*. The choruses in *Athalia* are the better for not being allowed to swamp the action and for being altogether more thoughtfully constructed. The idea of contrasted religious or ethnic groups, which was to reach its apogee eleven years later in the presentation of Jews, Persians and Babylonians in *Belshazzar*, is here developed amid the sensuous textures of the sequence following Athalia's magnificent arioso in Act I scene iii in which she recounts her dream (Racine's famous 'Songe d'Athalie') to Mathan, the priest of Baal, and his followers. As he was to do in 'Forever thus stands fix'd the doom', the uncannily similar chorus sung by the pagan Romans in *Theodora*, Handel gives the Baalites, in 'The gods who chosen blessings shed', a kind of jaunty winsomeness which is indefinably English in manner, its foreshadowings of Vauxhall or Ranelagh pastoral and the work of younger men like

Boyce and Stanley accentuated by a felicitous scoring for horns. Orchestration, indeed, does much of the necessary work of underlining traditionally 'pagan' associations: Mathan's 'Gentle airs, melodious strains' is accompanied by one of those 'cello solos which are such a trademark of 1730s Handel, and Athalia's 'Softest sounds no more can ease me' has an obbligato violin line (altered to solo flute before the first performance) serving to heighten our sense of the queen as having reached a point at which serenity will be impossible to regain.

The fullest weight and dignity in the music of *Athalia* is reserved for the Jewish choruses, in which the debt to classical drama demonstrated by Racine's play is magnificently acknowledged. The chorus is here both commentator and participant, punctuating Josabeth's 'Tyrants would in impious throngs' with its rhetorical outbursts, shaking a colossal fist at the court Baalites with a sturdy fugal Hallelujah and stirring the blood with their festal affirmations in 'The mighty power in whom we trust' which opens Act II. Here, as elsewhere in the work, Handel underlined the sense of confident determination on the part of the worshippers in the temple of the one God (there is later on a touch of loyal Whiggery in their 'bless the true church and save the king') by his spacious eight-part choral writing.

Handel concluded his Oxford series with a performance of *Deborah* on Thursday 12 July, and presumably returned to London immediately afterwards. The intended honour towards him of a doctorate of music was not accepted, but the university was no doubt pleased to see in *Athalia* a grateful tribute from the composer. So too thought the Abbé Prévost, anglophile author of *Manon Lescaut*, who issued, from London, a weekly review *Le Pour et Le Contre*, in which he noted that 'Mr Handel went to Oxford, but they were surprised to see him refuse the marks of distinction which were proposed for him. Such modesty alone could bear comparison with his talents. He did not fail to express his lively gratitude to the University, and to contribute to making the ceremony . . . more brilliant.' Prévost was intelligently appreciative of Handel's genius but others in Oxford looked back on the whole affair with misgivings. Hearne approvingly cited 'an old man of Oxford' who 'observed to me, that our late Oxford Act was the very worst that ever was', and the anonymous author of a ballad opera on the occasion portrayed undergraduates and dons who had 'squandered away all my ready Rhino . . . to make a gaudy Appearance for four or five Days this Publick Act' and wishing that 'I had been helping build the new town in *Georgia*, rather than in this cursed Place'.

In the end the students and their 'toasts' take precisely this way out to escape their creditors. No such expedient lay open to Handel. Instead a London bristling with professional challenges awaited him. His new company, chosen with typical regard for specific musical qualities, brought back Margherita Durastanti, seasoned Handelian campaigner that she was, to the English stage, and introduced two outstanding castrato singers, part of that distinguished series which Handel invited to London between 1719 and 1741. The Lombard soprano Carlo Scalzi, much admired by Metastasio, had enjoyed considerable success in Venice and Naples, but was destined to only a year in England, where nobody but Handel seems greatly to have esteemed him. A more interesting acquisition, in view of his reputation and subsequent career, was Giovanni Carestini, a *marchigiano* from the Ancona district, that rich breeding ground of fine voices. He made his first stage appearance at the age of sixteen (Farinelli, his exact contemporary, began a year earlier) and was later to star in the historic performances of Johann Josef Fux's coronation opera *Costanza e Fortezza* at Prague in 1723. Burney describes him as 'tall, beautiful and majestic. He was a very animated and intelligent actor; and having a considerable portion of enthusiasm in his composition, with a lively and inventive imagination, he rendered everything he sung interesting by good taste, energy and judicious embellishments. He manifested great agility in the execution of difficult divisions from the chest in a most articulate and admirable manner.' An imaginative artist with a good stage presence and a considerable vocal range, he was just the sort of performer calculated to interest Handel, though the details of his subsequent career, with its flourishes of boastfulness and 'insolence', suggest that he was as temperamentally difficult as Senesino.

'It's not just a story,' wrote Rolli in one of his epigrams, 'that those two champions Scalzi and Carestini have come over for Handel, for that great man never sits down to table without a dish of two fat capons. But to send away this capon Senesino is a mistake liable to ruin Handel, for my Senesino is reckoned the cock of all the British hens.' Part of the castrato's continuing allure was indeed a certain dubious sexual attraction, but whatever Carestini's ability to match Senesino's success with *le Britanniche Galline*, the disingenuous Lady Bristol's judgment of the new Haymarket company was probably shared by a good many aristocratic opera-goers that season. 'I am just come home,' she told her husband 'from a dull empty opera, tho' the second time; the first was full to hear the new man, who I can find out to be an extream good singer; the rest are all scrubbs except old Durastanti, that sings as well as ever she did.'

Armed with all Handel's former line-up except Strada (it has been suggested that her loyalty to the composer was due simply to the fact that she was not wanted at Lincoln's Inn Fields) the Opera of the Nobility opened its first season in splendid style with a new piece by the prestigious Porpora, *Arianna in Nasso*, on 29 December 1733. Its popularity, registered in a run of thirteen performances, established Porpora as a rival on the scale of Bononcini and demanded a return broadside from Handel. It was a simple enough matter for him to prepare his own *Arianna in Creta*, based on a libretto by Pietro Pariati originally set by Leonardo Leo for the Rome carnival five years previously, with interpolated aria texts from an earlier Leo piece on the same subject.

None of Handel's dramatic works is so bad that we would rather not hear it performed again. *Arianna* is to him what *Alzira* and *Il Corsaro* are to Verdi, stilted and mechanical when viewed as a configuration of notes and staves, but full of crude, resistant life when heard in performance. There are a few notable set pieces: the fine overture follows the same pattern as *Ezio*'s in introducing Act I with an instrumental item following the raising of the curtain (in this case the much-admired 'Minuet in Ariadne'); there is also a splendid fight with the Minotaur which grows directly from the ritornello material of Teseo's 'Qui ti sfido, o mostro infame'. A musical and dramatic peak is gained at the beginning of Act II in the hero's dream scene, where five pages of the score show Handel abandoning formal considerations for the sake of pace and authenticity. A few of the arias have genuine distinction. Arianna's 'So che non e piu mio' in Act II shows Handel's interest temporarily reviving in the evident care he has taken over the accompaniments, and this impetus is continued in the following aria, 'Qual Leon, che fere irato', with its virtuoso bassoon and viola parts and paired horns adding a gloss to the texture. There is a great deal of rather flashy coloratura, especially for Strada and Carestini in the Ariadne and Theseus roles.

Hawkins's verdict as to 'the Ariadne of Handel, in which, excepting the minuet at the end of the overture, there is scarce a good air' seems more or less correct, particularly when we remember that the previous year had produced *Orlando* and that *Ariodante* and *Alcina* were soon to follow. Brooding over the score is the spectre of Handel's wish to beat Porpora at his own game, something he had tried earlier with Bononcini in *Floridante*, and which consistently clogs his style, so though the music is new, we seem to have heard most of it somewhere before. It might pass muster as the worthy offering of an Italian composer in the later Venetian manner of Lotti and Gasparini, but as a piece by the creator of the

Academy masterpieces or even of the flawed brilliance of *Poro* and *Sosarme*, it demonstrates the overpowering waywardness of Handel's talent.

None of *Arianna*'s shortcomings had the least effect on its popularity, enhanced by the novelty of Carestini. *Colman's Opera Register* mentions it as 'a new Opera & very good & perform'd very often — Sigr Carestino sung surprisingly well: a new Eunuch — many times perform'd' — seventeen times during this season, with revivals the following November and December. We cannot discount an element of *succès de scandale* either at the Haymarket or at Lincoln's Inn Fields, since the whole issue of competition was focused so strongly on the ever-widening rift between the Prince of Wales and his parents. Lord Hervey summed up the matter in his memoirs: 'The King and Queen . . . were both Handelists, and sat freezing constantly at his empty Haymarket Opera, whilst the Prince with all the chief of the nobility went as constantly to that of Lincoln's Inn Fields. The affair grew as serious as that of the Greens and the Blues under Justinian at Constantinople. An anti-Handelist was looked upon as an anti-courtier, and voting against the Court in Parliament was hardly a less remissible or venial sin than speaking against Handel or going to Lincoln's Inn Fields Opera. The Princess Royal said she expected in a little while to see half the House of Lords playing in the orchestra in their robes and coronets; and the king (though he declared he took no other part in this affair than subscribing £1,000 a year to Handel) often added at the same time he did not think setting oneself at the head of a faction of fiddlers a very honourable occupation for people of quality.'

Handel had of course been music master to Anne, the Princess Royal, and her loyalty to him was one of the causes of Prince Frederick's patronage of the Opera of the Nobility. The prince's animus against his sister was increased by her impending marriage to the Prince of Orange, Stadholder of the Netherlands. 'A miserable match, both in point of man and fortune, his figure being deformed and his estate not clear £12,000 a year', says Lord Hervey, adding that 'Her Royal Highness's opinion was . . . whether she would go to bed to this piece of deformity in Holland, or die an ancient maid immured in her royal convent at St James's.' The Stadholder was hunchbacked and halitotic and the Princess was fat and pockmarked, but their innate common sense and a Civil List jointure of £80,000, financed by the recent sale of crown lands in St Kitts and Nevis, made it a mutually acceptable match. The attendant rejoicings were shared in by everyone except Frederick, incensed at his sister's marrying before him.

The behaviour of the engaged couple retained a dignity made the more touching by the king's arrogant treatment of the bridegroom, who fell ill on the morning before the proposed wedding ceremony and had to remove, first to Kensington and thence to Bath. In March 1734 preparations originally scheduled for the previous November got under way once more, and the *Daily Journal* advertised 'amongst other publick Diversions that are prepared for the Solemnity of the approaching Nuptials . . . a Serenata, call'd, Parnasso in Festa . . . some what in the Style of Oratorio's. People have been waiting with Impatience for this Piece, the celebrated Mr Handel having exerted his utmost Skill in it.'

On the evening of 13 March the entire royal family, including the Prince of Wales, who had been studiously polite to the Stadholder so as to annoy the king and queen, attended the first of Handel's two nuptial offerings, *Il Parnasso in Festa*, performed at the Haymarket by the opera soloists. A *festa teatrale* of the sort later exemplified by such occasional pieces as Gluck's *Le nozze di Ercole ed Ebe* and Mozart's *Ascanio in Alba*, the work has suffered much the same species of oblivion as *Deborah* and for substantially similar reasons, since most of the music is recycled *Athalia*. Neglect has been comparably undeserved. Though the sketchy plot, an omnium gatherum of classical deities and demiurges celebrating the nuptials of Peleus and Thetis, is unlikely to interest us, the chance to hear again *Athalia*'s stirring, ample choruses is surely not to be rejected, and the freshly composed items, including a finale alternating a solo for Carestini as Apollo with choral interjections, are wholly delightful.

At seven o'clock the following night came the wedding itself, in the Inigo Jones chapel at St James's, approached through an enormous covered gallery leading from the palace. Fond of making a splash, the king had laid on a splendid occasion, heightened by the magnificence of the Prince of Orange's retinue and of his gift of a necklace worn by the Princess 'which was so large that 22 diamonds made the whole round of her neck'. George behaved very well, but Queen Caroline and the other princesses made the procession to the chapel, according to Hervey, 'put one rather in mind of an Iphigenia leading to the altar than of a bride'. After the vows (the ceremony was conducted by none other than Dr Edmund Gibson) 'a fine anthem compos'd by Mr Handell, was perform'd by a great number of voices and instruments'.

To students of Handel, the anthem, a re-run of movements from *Il Parnasso in Festa* in whose use we can detect either an unmitigated cynicism or else a wish that the old *Athalia* numbers should not be forgotten, is altogether less interesting than the circumstances attached to its commission. For it seems that this had originally, during preparations the previous October, been given to his old rival Maurice Greene, 'the humpback organist of St Paul's and the King's Chapel, the chief undoubtedly of our English composers now living', as Lord Egmont calls him. Evidently Handel secured the commission because of the royal family's general penchant for his work, but at a time when he was in need of friends the fact is likely to have cost him a useful ally or two in the musical world.

Yet, as we might expect, his sociable nature and somewhat eccentric charm, as well as, presumably, the possibility that he might be ready to sit down to an extempore performance, was collecting a circle of devoted and emphatically partisan acquaintance. Further down Brook Street lived Mrs Pendarves, soon to marry a music-loving Irish clergyman and become Mrs Delany. From her letters during this period we catch a charming glimpse of the unbuttoned composer relaxing among friends. 'I must tell you of a little entertainment of music I had last week,' she writes to her sister, ' . . . I never was so *well* entertained at *an opera*! Mr Handel was in the best humour in the world, and played lessons and accompanied Strada and all the ladies that sang from seven o'clock till eleven. I gave them tea and coffee, and about half an hour after nine had a salver brought in of chocolate, mulled white wine and biscuits. Everybody was easy and seemed pleased, Bunny staid with me after the company was gone, eat a cold chick with me, and we chatted till one o' the clock.' Among the guests were Lord Egmont's son and daughter-in-law, and their relative Anne Donellan, to whom Handel was to bequeath 50 guineas. Biography is best confined to facts but there is something irresistible to the imagination in the idea of Mrs Pendarves and her brother Bernard 'Bunny' Granville sitting down to pick at their 'cold chick' after the guests' departure, and indulging in a pleasurable post-mortem on the evening.

Handel needed and valued their loyalty, as much as he depended on the professional skills of performers and publishers. As regards the latter, his connexions with the firm of John Walsh were strengthened throughout the decade. Most of the first Academy operas had been issued (with the customary absence of recitatives) by the firm of Cluer, but it was perhaps owing to a reorganization in the house of John Walsh during the early 1730s, as also to Walsh's piratical forays, that Handel was drawn to publish with this firm instead.

The mainstay of music publishing in eighteenth-century London was instrumental compositions, sets of sonatas and concertos issued mostly in dozens or half dozens. Between 1730 and 1734 Walsh issued three such collections under Handel's name, but only recently have the first two, twelve sonatas for a solo instrument with bass and the six trios of Opus 2, been identified as belonging to this period. Their title pages bear a forged imprint of the Amsterdam firm of Roger, and they have traditionally been assigned to the 1720s: nobody, however, seems to know the exact reason for Walsh's imposture.

The brevity and simplicity of the solo sonatas scarcely places them among the classics of the genre, but the limpid progress of their melodic lines at once evokes that world of song in which Handel was paramount. The trios, on the other hand, typify this favourite contemporary form at its best, and the presence of a third voice in the dialogue gave some happy inspirations to the composer, who made effective use of material from the Chandos Anthems, *Esther* and *Acis and Galatea*.

Custom dictated the application of opus numbers to instrumental pieces rather than the large-scale vocal works for which Handel is most famous. Opus 3, published in 1734, was a set of six concertos, several of which, as their earliest title page tells us, 'were perform'd on the marriage of the Prince of Orange with the Princess Royal of Great Britain in the Royal Chappel of St James's.' The publication as a whole was probably not overseen by Handel himself, though he presumably allowed Walsh to go through with it: some share in the proceedings, however, is indicated by the substitution, in later printings, of one of the concertos with that now known as no. 4 in F.

Whatever their history, the concertos are scarcely the most orthodox of their kind and look forward, in their wholehearted freedom of approach, to the organ concertos Handel was to write for his oratorio evenings during the 1740s. Several individual movements are derived from the Chandos Anthems, others relate to specific opera performances and one uses material familiar from the 1713 *Birthday Ode*, the *Brockes Passion* and *Deborah*. The use of oboes in five of them (no. 3 is for solo flute or oboe) led to their early labelling as 'Hautboy Concertos', but prominent parts are variously given also to recorders, bassoons and solo violins, while the last of the set contains a reworked version for organ of a movement from the D minor keyboard suite of 1720.

Each concerto is thus stamped, as one would expect, with an individuality which makes nonsense of any attempt to generalize on Handel's attitude to the form, except to say that he seems to have regarded it as a springboard for any and every change of mood and manner. From this aspect it is instructive to listen to these pieces at one sitting, and to relish their singular mixture of wit, grace, power and deftness. We cannot

Frederick, Prince of Wales, and his sisters, 1733, by P. Mercier

Vauxhall Gardens. The Grand Walk, with the orchestra playing

Berenstadt, Cuzzoni and Senesino performing in *Flavio*

Green Park, April 1749. The 'magnificent structure' erected for the fireworks

know exactly how the composer put them together or what his intentions were, but their expressive resonance and suppleness are genuinely Handelian.

The Haymarket season concluded, after three *Sosarme* performances to nearly empty houses, with a revised version of *Il Pastor Fido*, not heard since 1712 and rather more successful, judging by its fourteen-night run. It was the end, for the time being, of any further arrangement with Heidegger, who was no doubt glad to see the contract terminated and to welcome in the smart Nobility outfit, complete with Rolli, Porpora and the immortal Farinelli. In *Le Pour et Le Contre* Prévost reported that Handel, ruined by the loss, was about to leave England. If that was true, he only got as far as Tunbridge Wells, where he began work on a new opera, presumably enjoying the select company at the spa among its rocky outcrops and taking the cold iron-flavoured waters. He was not, in any case, a ruined man, since the king, who must have realized what the enterprise had cost him and was still costing him with a company of singers to maintain, had directed that the customary royal bounty to the opera management should go, not to Heidegger, but directly to Handel himself.

Awaiting the distinguished exiles was a splendid new theatre at the top of Bow Street, Covent Garden, the first on a site now occupied by the Royal Opera House. Well designed, with decorations by the Venetian painter Amigoni, it had opened in December 1732, with a performance of Congreve's *The Way of The World* by John Rich's company, who had moved from Lincoln's Inn Fields fresh, as it were, from their triumph in *The Beggar's Opera*. And by way of an additional draw, Rich had engaged for a fifth London season one of the most talented ballet stars of the day, the Parisian *danseuse* Marie Sallé.

Sallé is often referred to as 'notorious', though in fact she was a good deal less so than her celebrated rival La Camargo, and possibly no more than any other ballerina before or since. More important than her notoriety was the degree of her artistry, which had already been appreciated by Pope and Gay, who paraphrased Virgil in her honour:

> I know her now, the syylvan goddess cries,
> Aeneas saw her once in such disguise,
> Delusion vain! her grace, her easy mien,
> Her every step discloses beauty's queen.
> But soon the laughing nymphs the fraud confess'd,
> For they to grace her feast had Sallé dress'd.

During her previous London season she had had to combat the coarseness of the footmen's gallery and the malice of her female audience, who found her conceited and affecting '*la milady*', but by sheer tenacity she had established herself as a creative dancer of the first rank, laying on for Rich the sort of spectacle which the rigidly conservative Opéra had hitherto scorned. If there was any notoriety, it came not from her conduct (she refused, according to Prévost, to part with her virtue for 2,000 guineas) but from the daring muslin draperies she wore '*sur le modèle d'une statue grecque*' in her ballet *Pigmalion*. Her 1733 benefit, to a packed house, remained fresh in the memory of the seventeen-year-old David Garrick, who told the great dancer Noverre years afterwards of latecomers hammering on the theatre doors: if it went on like this, thought Prévost, she would need a lot more than 2,000 guineas.

As a prelude to the revised *Pastor Fido* with which Handel's company opened at Covent Garden on 9 November 1734, he prepared a *divertissement* for Sallé based on one of her previous successes, Colin de Blamont's *Caractères d'amour* and entitled *Terpsichore*. The piece was also designed to mark the arrival of the new company. Apollo, sung by Carestini, arrives from Parnassus to discover whether his new 'Academy' (Covent Garden) is worthy of him, and asks Erato (Strada) what has become of Terpsichore. On she bounces, to perform various dances illustrative of passions described by the singers. So that the audience could have their fill of *la ravissante Sallé* Handel interpolated ballet numbers into *Il Pastor Fido* itself and into all that season's subsequent operas, doubtless as part of his contract with Rich. With a star ballerina and a spanking new theatre, this might have been enough: Handel, however, was a giant refreshed and ready with two of his greatest operatic masterpieces, to confound his doubters and delight the Covent Garden public.

Apart from the pasticcio *Oreste* there were no novelties introduced until the following January, when the piece on which Handel had worked at Tunbridge Wells, and in whose perfections it is not hard to see the benevolent influence of a country holiday, was finally brought on. *Ariodante* enjoyed a modest run of nine performances, with the customary revival the following year. As with a good many genuine Handelian masterpieces, recognition has arrived two centuries too late for the composer to enjoy it, and the work is nowadays justly ranked beside *Rodelinda*, *Tamerlano* and *Orlando* as among the great creations of early eighteenth-century opera.

For his text Handel turned once more to Antonio Salvi, and to one of his best librettos. *Ginevra, Principessa di Scozia* had been originally prepared for production at Pratolino in 1708, Salvi having adapted it from episodes in the fourth and fifth books of Ariosto's *Orlando Furioso*. The scene is set in Scotland, though, as elsewhere in the poem, there is no attempt at local colour, since one of the poem's essential factors is a complete geographical topsy-turveydom. Polinesso, jealous of Ariodante's love for Ginevra, uses Dalinda to engineer a situation whereby the princess will be dishonoured and condemned to death (Shakespeare used this episode as a source for the plot of *Much Ado About Nothing*). Salvi, as he admits, made some alterations to both Polinesso and Dalinda. 'I have emphasized Polinesso's criminal character, making him operate more through interest and ambition than through love, so that the audience feels less horror at his death and to make the virtue of the other characters stand out the more.' As for Dalinda, who in Ariosto becomes a nun in Romania, Salvi says that he has made her somewhat more decent in manner, 'since in our century she would not have appeared without blame upon the stage'.

This sort of blackening and whitening makes little real difference to the nature of Handel's music, designed to create an ideal balance in the story between love, treachery and the thoughtlessness which allows Dalinda to be tempted into deceiving Ariodante. Balance, indeed, is of paramount importance here, and the opera is one which does not cut at all easily. The first act, with its emphasis on the festivities surrounding the engagement of Ariodante and Ginevra, has the kind of jubilant atmosphere which is so often a prelude to disaster. Ariodante's Pergolesian 'Con l'ali di costanza', Ginevra's 'Volate, amori' and the song and dance finale to the act, taking place in a '*valle deliziosa*', are simply the elements of doomed celebration, an interrupted *festa teatrale*. We should in any case guess that all will go wrong by the appearance of Polinesso like Carabosse at the christening: his music throughout the work has a compelling awkwardness about it, as if Handel were deliberately trying not to engage our sympathy while at the same time making us appreciate his motives.

The little ten-bar sinfonia introducing the moonlit second act over a falling ground bass throws the first real shadows, leading to the doughty Lurcanio, a figure of true old-fangled probity, accusing Ginevra of causing Ariodante's death. Only when she is vindicated, after the false championship of Polinesso has led to Lurcanio killing him and Ariodante returns to defend her honour in the field, can the raptures and rejoicings resume. Thus, when Ginevra and Ariodante are given their second duet,

'Bramo aver mille vite', it is not, like their first, allowed to be broken off.

Ginevra's father, the king, is the original intruder, cutting benevolently into the middle section with the words 'Do not be alarmed, fair loved ones'. His prevailing paternal gentleness and anxiety give him a dignified pathos transcending anything among Handel's earlier bass roles and deepen the drama's credibility. Every response is naturally evoked, there are no preposterous displays of heroism or fustian conflicts of love and duty, and Ariodante himself, youthful, ardent and vulnerable, is so believable a figure that he seems to earn his final *aria di bravura*, the unforgettable 'Dopo notte', with its immense virtuoso divisions for Carestini, simply through having endured.

If *Ariodante* aroused only modified rapture, the second new opera of the season, *Alcina*, was a runaway success. Mrs Pendarves, hearing it for the first time at Handel's domestic rehearsal in Brook Street, thought it 'the best he ever made . . . 'tis so fine I have not words to describe it. . . . While Mr Handel was playing his part, I could not help thinking him a necromancer in the midst of his own enchantments.' The composer, thus happily transmogrified, became Ariosto's sorceress, the Circe of a magic realm, who, in Fanzaglia's libretto *L'isola di Alcina*, enthralls the lovelorn Ruggiero and turns the father of young Oronte into a lion, but is finally defeated by the steadfastness and courage of Ruggiero's sweetheart disguised as the warrior Bradamante, aided by the wise Melisso. At least one member of the audience, an anonymous writer to the *Universal Spectator*, saw the moral point of it all, finding 'a beautiful and instructive Allegory' designed to prove that 'neither the Council of Friends, nor the Example of others . . . can stop the giddy head-strong Youth from the Chase of imaginary or fleeting Pleasures'.

Such an interpretation is wholly acceptable in the context of a work which so genuinely absorbs that quality of shape-changing magic which forms its theme. The opera's enduring strength is that *Alcina* becomes what we choose to make it, a delightful confection of wizardry and dalliance, a Baroque entertainment, or something a little more profound, a story in which the artist Alcina, confronting the strength of her own passions, is finally crushed by them. The emotional pitch is established in the swift strokes of the orchestral introduction and carried on through the airs of the soubrette Morgana, incapable of taking love seriously, and Oronte, desperately searching for his lost father, to reach a peak in Alcina's threats of revenge in 'Ma quando tornerai' and the defiant resolve of Bradamante and Ruggiero, fused in the magnificently vigorous ensemble, 'Non e amor ne gelosia'. Ruggiero breaks the magic urn, and in so doing destroys Alcina and Morgana to liberate those they have transformed.

Yet, as Handel understands, the loss of Alcina means a finish to the opera. Like Agrippina or Rodelinda, she makes her eponymous drama. Her varying moods, whether expressed in the sinking phrases of 'Di cor mio' or the quaver sighs of 'Ah mio cor' (her heart is of the essence here) or in the nervous string counterpoint of 'Ombre pallide', all focus on the dedication to love which undermines her power. Each of the other figures, the vacillating Ruggiero, the fearless Bradamante, even Morgana, who is only extinguished because of her complicity with the sorceress, is of slightly lessened substance in comparison. She, however, stands alone, almost a tragic figure in her musical voyage towards the nemesis of a single bar of simple recitative.

The opera's triumph was partially alloyed by the reception given to the unfortunate Marie Sallé, who appeared in the ballets as Cupid and was whistled at for her pains. The Abbé Prévost thought it was all owing to an anti-Handel claque among the audience: whatever the cause she hastened back to Paris, where her art would be appreciated as something higher than mere 'notoriety'. Carestini, too, left England shortly afterwards. As Ruggiero he had been awarded a string of airs devised to flatter his virtuosity to its uttermost, yet the simplest and most striking of them all, 'Verdi prati', had offended him by its sheer artlessness. Giving it back to Handel he was met with the magisterial rebuke 'You dog! don't I know better as yourself what is best for you to sing? If you will not sing all the song what I give you, I will not pay you one stiver!' Carestini sang, was admired, was paid, and took ship for the continent when the season finished.

Alcina has had the singular fortune in our own day of being the one work of Handel's which has gained popularity among that canary-fancying section of opera-goers who know every detail of a diva's private life and collect every note ever emitted on record by Maria Callas. Thanks to the enterprise of Joan Sutherland and Richard Bonynge on their historic recording, the opera established Handel's claim to attention as one of the great writers for the voice, in a performance which, littered as it is with elements both uncanonical and inauthentic, has a verve and brilliance which bring the arias glowingly to life. Perhaps this is not the way to perform Handel, but it has given the opera a fame which bears out the convictions of its first London audience — right, for once.

— 9 —

The Fate of Harmony

The picture of Handel which emerges during the late 1730s has the curiously haunting air of solitude about it which we are much more accustomed to associate with artists of the Romantic era and after. One of the most intriguing aspects of his life is provided by the fact that we possess more details of audience reaction to his music than exist for any other Baroque composer, and it would be easy enough to write a whole monograph on the responses of eighteenth-century listeners from Cardinal Pamphilj to Mrs Pendarves. From the remarks of his acquaintance, the endless series of laudatory verses inspired by his compositions and performances, and the comments of musical Londoners, partisan or otherwise, we can discern an attitude towards him which combines an awed respect with a sense of remoteness and mystification. People watched him with an interest which was or was not sympathetic, and reported to each other on what his intentions might be: he was both the Orpheus of his age and an eccentric, volatile bachelor who, in spite of English naturalization, would remain a lonely foreigner among his adopted countrymen until the day of his death.

Two reactions from among his 1735 audiences offer typical examples of the way in which London looked at him. An anonymous 'Philharmonick' in Henry Fielding's *Grub Street Journal* described the effect of *Alcina* as a synthesis between her magic and Handel's art:

> Or she improves his wondrous lay;
> Or he by a superior spell
> Does greater melody convey,
> That she may her bright self excel. . . .

> When Handel deigns to strike the sense,
> 'Tis as when heaven, with hands divine,
> Struck out the globe (a work immense!)
> Where harmony meets with design.

Towards the end of the year Lord Hervey, in waiting to the king, attended Veracini's *Adriano in Siria* at the Haymarket. Returning bored and angry at 'yawning four hours at the longest and dullest Opera that ever the ennobled ignorance of our present musical Governors ever inflicted on . . . an English audience', he sat down at once to describe the occasion to his cousin Charlotte Digby. Besides the ineptitude of Veracini's music and the vocal inadequacies of Senesino (Farinelli and Cuzzoni were also starring) Hervey noted the presence of Handel, who 'sat in great eminence and great pride in the middle of the pit, and seemed in silent triumph to insult this dying Opera in its agonies, without finding out that he was as great a fool for refusing to compose, as Veracini had shown himself by composing . . . (Handel) having more sense, more skill, more judgement, and more expression in music than anybody. . . . What his understanding must be, you may easily imagine, to be undone by a profession of which he is certainly the ablest professor. . . . His fortune in music is not unlike my Lord Bolingbroke's in politics. The one has tried both theatres as the other has tried both Courts. They have shone in both, and been ruined in both; whilst everyone owns their genius and sees their faults, though nobody either pities their fortunes or takes their parts.'

There is something touching in Hervey's generous fury at what he considered the perversity of Handel's genius. He was correct in saying that Handel gained little public sympathy during these years. Though, as we have already seen, a group of loyal and admiring Handelians was beginning to assemble around him, they were not enough to provide the sort of audience he deserved, an audience which could confront and appreciate the singular individuality of most of the works created in these years of sudden triumph and gloomy disaster, between the move to Covent Garden in 1735 and the journey to Dublin in 1742.

We can go some way towards reconstructing a Handelian public through examining the lists of names published at the front of the subscription editions of various of his works (there were thirteen of these in all). Many of the subscribers were fellow musicians, not always professed admirers of Handel but doubtless privately eager to see what the man was up to. Thus, among familiar figures such as John Stanley, Bernard Gates, John Travers, organist of St Paul's Covent Garden, and Thomas Chilcott, doyen of musicians at Bath, we also find the names of Pepusch, Greene and Festing, along with leading instrumentalists who played for Handel such as the violinist Carbonelli and the flautist Weidemann. Musical societies, in which eighteenth-century England abounded, were quick to subscribe, and orders came in from Oxford and Exeter, the Windsor Apollo Society, the Dublin 'Accademy for Vocal Musick' and the 'Musical Society on Wednesday at the Crown and Anchor'.

Besides the imposing rosters of royalty and aristocracy (more obvious in the later publications) the names of several significant figures connected with various aspects of Handel's life appear. There are Charles Jennens, collator of the *Messiah* text, Theodore Jacobsen, one of the benefactors of the Foundling Hospital, Handel's favourite charity, and John Christopher Smith, the composer's chief musical assistant. Interesting also is the appearance of members of London's Sephardic Jewish community, such as Isaac Nunes and Moses Mendez da Costa, who were to form a mainstay of Handel's oratorio audiences during the 1740s. And this being the eighteenth century, some of the names have a distinctly bizarre, exotic or fanciful ring to them. Who were Leake Okeover and Fitzherbert Plumbtree, Henry van Couwenhovengz or Obstrapus Danby, and what did David Boswillibald, a musical diplomat in the King of Prussia's service, make of the *Admeto* to which he subscribed?

Hervey was wrong in thinking that Handel was simply refusing to compose. In fact he was about to embark on a spate of composition which would have killed anyone less stalwart and which forms one of the most remarkable (we might almost say grotesque) episodes in his life. By the middle of January, 1736, he had finished his setting of Dryden's St Cecilia ode *Alexander's Feast or The Power of Music*. Dryden's poem, originally set by Jeremiah Clarke, takes the form of a series of vivid Baroque narrative pictures, such as might have been painted by Guercino or Solimena, based on the destruction of Persepolis by Alexander, fired by the songs of Timotheus and the beauty of the courtesan Thais. The work presents a combination of imaginative grandeur, lyrical tenderness and a characteristic Augustan wit, upon which, in addition to the poem's deliberate changes of mood, Handel's genius readily seized.

His sensitivity to the superior quality of the text before him irradiates this stirring and brilliantly conceived piece, one of the noblest examples of English Baroque art and the finest setting of a vernacular text since Purcell. What had been started in *Athalia*, the authentic sound of Handel's English voice, not heard since *Acis and Galatea* and even there pronouncedly Italianate, was here given its fullest articulation. The choral writing breaks new ground in its dramatic outbursts, most notably in the passacaglia 'The many rend the skies with loud applause', in the threnody for the dead Persian king, where a deliberate monotony in the accompaniment underscores the prevailing gloom, and in 'Break his bands of sleep asunder', whose farouche, cacophonous screams over an ostinato figure imitating the sound of timpani create a type of music without obvious parallel until the infernal choruses of Gluck's *Orfeo ed Euridice*.

The solo numbers, by turns elegant, rousing and meditative, show the warmest of responses to the nature of Dryden's original concept, an ode which would adequately reflect the varying moods and powers of music. Several, such as 'Bacchus ever fair and young', with its agreeably vulgar horns sustaining a tune which shows that Handel seldom lost the common touch, and 'Thais led the way', a piece of bland and sinister loveliness, perfectly suited to its theme, are linked with choral treatments of their material. Others feature instrumental obbligato: we must remember that in the midst of his difficulties Handel never allowed performance standards to decline, and his orchestra throughout the 1730s was of the very best, including the virtuoso oboist Giuseppe Sammartini, the Castrucci brothers Pietro and Prospero, both violinists (the latter traditionally Hogarth's 'Enraged Musician'), and Valentine Snow, sergeant-trumpeter to the king. Snow was presumably the trumpeter in 'Revenge, Timotheus cries', the most grandly-conceived of all Handel's bass arias, an intensely dramatic *scena* whose clangorous outer sections frame a vision of the Grecian ghosts made the eerier by its dotted accompaniment figures on a trio of bassoons. Beside 'Softly sweet in Lydian measure' Handel wrote in the foul score the name of Andrea Caporale, the great 'cellist, who, with Pasqualino, another of the original performers in the ode, brought the instrument into solo prominence in the London concert world.

Alexander's Feast was prepared for Handel's setting by Newburgh Hamilton, who wrote in his preface: 'I confess my principal View was, not to lose this favourable Opportunity of its being set to Musick by that great Master, who has with Pleasure undertaken the Task, and who only is capable of doing it Justice; whose Compositions have long shewn, that they can conquer even the most obstinate Partiality, and inspire Life into the most senseless Words.' Hamilton, a devoted Handelian and author of the librettos to *Samson* and *The Occasional Oratorio*, was gentleman house-steward to the Earl of Strafford, mingling a love of music and a taste for poetry (he addressed some verses to the countess herself) with the humdrum business of paying off servants, chivvying tradesmen, looking after the horses and handling the accounts. To the earl's children, the young Wentworths, he was more of a friend than a servitor, and he seems to have taken good care to foster a firm Handelian partisanship in the family.

As well as dividing Dryden's Ode into formal aria, recitative and choral sections, Hamilton added a conclusion designed to emphasize the celebration of St Cecilia, to whom the original poem merely alludes in the closing lines. Judging by this and other features of the first performance it seems probable that what we are now accustomed to hearing, the Dryden poem without Hamilton's final section, is only about two thirds of Handel's initial concept, which was clearly designed as a kind of musical festival to which *Alexander's Feast* itself formed the containing framework (he may also have been concerned that the audience should feel it was getting its money's worth). Magnificent as they must already have appeared in the ode, the band were given further chances for display in the performance of three concertos. One of these was for lute and harp, later published as the sixth of the Opus 4 Organ Concertos, played, as the autograph indicates, before the accompanied recitative 'The song began from Jove'. Between the end of the poem and Hamilton's 'Additional Chorus' 'Your voices tune', came the Organ Concerto in G minor (Opus 4 no. 1), probably written for the *Athalia* revival at Covent Garden in the April of 1735, and at the opening of Act II, already enriched by the Italian cantata *Cecilia, volgi uno sguardo*, sung by the lutenist Carlo Arrigoni, appeared the C major *Alexander's Feast Concerto*.

A word needs to be said about the tenor soloist John Beard, whom Handel had thrown into such sharp relief in the piece through a succession of fine arias and recitatives. Born around 1717 Beard had been trained by Bernard Gates in the Chapel Royal choir and took part as a soloist in the 1732 *Esther* performances at the Crown & Anchor. As a tenor lead he made his debut in 1734 as Silvio in *Il pastor fido*, rapidly earning praise thereafter for his dignified stage presence and for great professional integrity in a field where such a quality is not always at a premium. 'He let his own discretion be the tutor', said a contemporary, 'and held the mirror up to nature.' Handel certainly admired him, more, perhaps, than any other singer for whom he composed, if the number of major roles created expressly for him is anything to go by. Jupiter in *Semele* and the title roles of *Samson*, *Belshazzar*, *Judas Maccabaeus* and *Jephtha* show how much importance the composer attached to a singer in whom virtuosity was always tempered with sensitive intelligence.

Alexander's Feast had the success it deserved. The première took place on 19 February, and on the following night, with members of the royal family present, the *London Daily Post* observed that 'never was upon the like Occasion so numerous and splendid an Audience at any Theatre in London, there being at least 1300 Persons present; and it is judg'd that the Receipt of the House could not amount to less than 450 l.'. Some found the remoteness of the performers rather inconvenient, and one disgruntled auditor pencilled in his libretto the words 'O for Senesino!'. It was two years, however, before John Walsh the younger published his splendid subscription issue of the Ode, costing two guineas, with a separately released portrait, of an exceptional standard, drawn and engraved by Jacob Houbraken, surmounting a Gravelot design of Alexander, Thais and Timotheus in the palace of Persepolis.

To the end of his career as a working musician Handel was unable to count on anything consistent in the patterns made by triumph and catastrophe. It might have been supposed that nothing could endear him, as the king and queen's favourite master, to the pathetic figure of the Prince of Wales, desperately courting popular sympathy in his role of unwanted child, yet Frederick's residual loyalty finally drew him to Handel's cause during the early summer of 1736. George and Caroline had settled on a bride for their son in the person of the seventeen-year-old Princess Augusta of Saxe-Gotha, and the wedding and its preliminaries were hustled along with the indecorous haste which marked so many of the ceremonial occasions in George II's bizarre family life. Eager to get off to his mistress in Hanover, George bullied his ambassadors into hurrying home with the Princess tucked, as it were, into their luggage, and she and Frederick were married on 27 April, two days after her landing at Greenwich.

In a characteristic atmosphere of bickering among the prince, his parents and his sisters, the wedding took place at nine in the evening in the chapel at St James's, handsomely adorned for the event. Lord Egmont was among 'a prodigious crowd' present and noted that 'Over the altar was placed the organ, and a gallery made for the musicians. An anthem composed by Handel for the occasion was wretchedly sung by Abbot, Gates, Lee, Bird and a boy.' The speed with which the wedding had been set on had clearly not left enough time for rehearsal of *Sing unto God*, an altogether more inspired offering from the composer than his earlier effort for the Princess of Orange.

What seems to have charmed Frederick most, however, was the royal wedding opera *Atalanta*, brought on at Covent Garden on 12 May. Handel had in fact completed the score some three weeks earlier, but so as to bring it into line with the general air of expedition dictated by the king's notorious impatience it was rushed into rehearsal at once, while 'great Numbers of Artificers, as Carpenters, Painters, Engineers, &c.' busied themselves with the specialized scenic arrangements of the last act, and the singers went through their paces in a revival of *Ariodante*.

Good fortune for *Atalanta* was, as usual, underwritten by spectacular visual effects and the presence of a new castrato. 'The Fore-part of the Scene represented an Avenue to the Temple of *Hymen*, adorn'd with Figures of several Heathen Deities. Next was a Triumphal Arch on the Top of which were the Arms of their Royal Highnesses, over which was a Princely Coronet. Under the Arch was the Figure of *Fame*, on a Cloud, sounding the Praise of this Happy Pair. The Names *Fredericus* and *Augusta* appear'd above in transparent Characters.' Further elements of the confection included embracing Cupids supporting the princely arms and 'Loves and Graces bearing Hymeneal Torches, and putting Fire to Incense in Urns, to be offer'd up upon this joyful Union'. In addition there was the risky but exciting bonus of a firework display in the last scene, managed by a Mr Worman, who had devised a contraption for producing a fiery fountain which he showed off again five years later at Cupers Gardens on the South Bank, using the *Atalanta* music.

'The new man' was the celebrated Gioacchino Conti, nicknamed Gizziello (from his Neapolitan teacher Domenico Gizzi) and perhaps, in terms of sheer vocal artistry, the most effective rival to Farinelli Handel had yet been able to produce. It was indeed Farinelli who had encouraged Gizziello to persevere with his London engagement after his own singing had apparently caused the younger eunuch to burst into tears and eventually to faint away in despair. Just as well, for of all Handelian castrati (Guadagni possibly excepted) he seems to have been the most refined in manner and execution. 'Handel never till now,' says Burney, 'had a first man to write for with so high a soprano voice. Nicolini, Senesino and Carestini were all *contraltos*. There was often dignity and spirit in their style; but Conti had delicacy and tenderness, with the accumulated refinements of near thirty years, from the time of Handel's first tour to Italy. I think it is not difficult to discover, particularly in the first act, that in composing Conti's part in this opera, he modelled his melody to the school of his new singer. Indeed, Handel was always remarkably judicious in writing to the taste and talents of his performers; in displaying excellence and covering imperfections.'

Such features are more obviously marked in *Atalanta* than in several of the operas surrounding it, though the Covent Garden company remained fundamentally the same (apart from the substitution of Conti for Carestini) from 1734 until 1737. Based on Belisario Valeriani's libretto *La caccia in Etolia*, originally set by Fortunato Chelleri for the Ferrara opera, the story is a lighthearted treatment of the spirited courtship of Atalanta and Meleager, and the format owes much to the type of comedy cliché reflected on a rather less sophisticated level in *Il Pastor Fido*, making use of contrasted couples in a pastoral setting and rounded off with ceremonial festivity. Beard and Negri, as Aminta and Irene, the secondary pair, were given altogether more superficial material than in *Ariodante*, where they sang Lurcanio and Polinesso, and this is typical of the work as a whole, in which the studied contrast of various elements creates the ideal *divertissement* for bored and fractious royalty.

Slight though *Atalanta* is, each of its three acts contains arresting features. Both Conti and Strada, as the protagonists, were given spectacular entrances, the former at the very beginning of the opera in the arietta 'Care selve', designed to exhibit his 'new, graceful and pathetic style of singing', and the latter halfway through Act I, as Atalanta leading the shepherds in pursuit of the wild boar which she slays in Meleagro's presence. Rather like Norma, Atalanta is hardly ever off the stage from the moment she first appears, and the brilliance of her arias, culminating in 'Bench'io non sappia ancor', with its play upon rhythmic alternations, shows how carefully Handel had nurtured Strada's talent so as to project it to maximum advantage. As Meleagro Conti was allowed to display more than a mere soulful elegance: both in 'Non saria poco', which ends Act I, and in 'Tu solcasti il mare infido', just before the concluding jubilations, his virtuosity, evidently based on his agility in negotiating divisions, with the assistance of an impressive upper register (he is the only castrato for whom Handel wrote a top C) glitters through the light-textured orchestration.

As a pair, the two characters inhabit the opera more fully than many another Baroque couple. Their encounter in Act II, growing out of a rustic chorus of Atalanta's followers accompanied by antiphonal oboes and horns over the strings, forms a continuous movement, with Atalanta's 'Lassa! ch'io t'ho perduta' springing directly from her last words in recitative and a superb duet, starting in arioso style without ritornello and only gradually turning into a fully organized piece as embarrassment develops and Atalanta mocks Meleagro's desperation.

The audience were probably much less excited by this than by the rousing trumpet overture, featuring the talents of Valentine Snow, with its Telemannesque allegro and extended gavotte. The poet Thomas Gray was present on at least one *Atalanta* night and described the firework effects to Horace Walpole. 'Conti,' he adds, 'I like excessively in everything but his mouth which is thus, ⊜ ; but this is hardly minded when Strada stands by him.'

It was not as if all this enthusiasm were going to save Handel. The violinist Matthew Dubourg at Dublin was told by a friend that ' . . . the two opera houses are, neither of them, in a successful way; and it is the confirmed opinion that this winter will compleat your friend *Handel's* destruction, as far as the loss of his money can destroy him. . . . On Tuesday last, we had a new opera of Handel's; and at the appearance of that great prince of harmony in the orchestre, there was so universal a clap from the audience that many were surprized, and some offended at it. As to the opera, the critics say, it is too like his former compositions and wants variety — I heard his singer that night, and think him near equal in merit to the late *Carestini*, with this advantage, that he has acquired the happy knack of throwing out a sound, now and then, very like what we hear from a distressed young calf. . . . As to the Operas, they must tumble, for the King's presence could hardly hold them up, and even that prop is denied them, for his majesty will not admit his royal ears to be tickled this season. As to music, it flourishes in this place more than ever, in subscription concerts and private parties, which must prejudice all operas and public entertainments.'

If he and the Nobility managers were facing the realities of economic disaster in the phenomenon of two opera companies trying to survive on the patronage of a small public in a city where opera-going was still identified with foreignness, decadence and Popery, Handel nevertheless found several things to cheer him during the summer. Allusion to a country retreat in a letter to his friend Lord Shaftesbury at the end of June suggests another visit to Tunbridge Wells, and in August he wrote to his brother-in-law Michaelsen with congratulations on his niece Johanna Friederika's marriage to Dr Flörcke, professor of law at Halle University, sending a gold watch, a chain and two seals as '*un petit présent de Nopces*' for the bridegroom, and a solitaire diamond ring '*de la première Eau et de tout Perfection*' for the bride. In September he was confirmed as music master to the Princesses Amelia and Caroline at £200 per annum, and the following month an outstanding new castrato joined the Covent Garden company in the person of Domenico Annibali, star of the Dresden court opera.

The season, which was to prove, in most other respects, so markedly disappointing, began in festoons of royal patronage. The Prince and

Princess of Wales appeared at an *Alcina* revival, seated in a box adorned with white satin and 'a flaming heart between two Hymenaeal Torches, whose different Flames terminated in one Point, and were surmounted with a Label, on which were wrote, in Letters of Gold, these Words, MUTUUS ARDOR'. *Atalanta* was revived on the prince's birthday, and Annibali's debut was planned with *Poro*, always a favourite with the royal family.

Mrs Pendarves rightly praised the strengths of the company — 'Strada, that sings better than ever she did; Gizziello, who is much improved since last year, and Annibali, who has the best part of Senesino's voice and Caristini's, with a prodigious fine taste and good action' — and looked forward to Handel's two new operas. 'He was here two or three mornings ago and *played me both the overtures*, which are charming.' The first of the pair, *Arminio*, though finished on 14 October 1736, was not brought on until 12 January 1737, perhaps because the *Poro* revival had had to be postponed as Strada had gone down with influenza. Despite the admiration of Handel's friends and unflagging support from royalty, the new piece was not popular and sustained only five performances.

Few have ever cared, or are likely to care, for *Arminio*. The libretto, by Antonio Salvi, originally for Pratolino performances in 1703, based on the story of the German hero Arminius — Hermann — as treated by Tacitus, is adequate, though it never grabs the imagination with quite the force of the same author's *Rodelinda* or *Ariodante*. The characterization is patchy, failing to offer Handel an opportunity to explore a really wide range of emotions. Arminio, his wife Tusnelda, and Sigismondo (the Conti role) are each very strongly drawn, and receive a musical treatment that goes beyond a mere display of agility. Varo, the Roman general, and the German prince Segeste are allowed too easily to fade into insignificance, while Tullio, sung originally by the contralto Maria Caterina Negri, has the kind of commentator's role more usually given to a bass.

Handel was not sufficiently concerned to give the drama real momentum. The most arresting sequence occurs during the early scenes of the last act, where the absence of a middle section and *da capo* in two of the numbers and a sense, in Sigismondo's 'Il sangue al cor favella', of the action being pushed along by musical means, indicate the composer's close involvement with the text. The structure of this aria is brilliantly unconventional: no introduction, five bars of the voice moving in unison with the first violins, unsupported by any bass, a further six bars during which the word *favella* — 'speaks' — is appropriately extended, and only in bar twelve the appearance of the continuo line. Even then the character is almost allowed to break down on the words *salvarlo* and *svenarlo* as he contemplates the choice between betraying Roman trust and killing Arminio. Thence the accompaniment lines fragment into a series of agonized semiquaver gasps as Sigismondo's dilemma increases.

There is little enough of such originality elsewhere. Apart from the 24-bar oboe solo for Sammartini introducing Sigismondo's 'Quella fiamma', most of the instrumental colour is saved for Act III, where two horns and flutes are featured, and the strings play mostly in separate parts. But *Arminio*'s main shortcoming is its lack of those good tunes we have a right to expect from Handel, whose gift for melody matches that of a Mozart, a Schubert or a Bellini. The opera is otherwise notable for containing no simile arias, for being the only Handelian drama to open with a duet, and for containing the most fatuous of those portmanteau lines for which Salvi had such a dire penchant:

> *oh padre! o amore! oh sangue! o Arminio! oh sorte!*
> *oh Ramise! oh sorella! oh affetti! oh morte!*

The second of Handel's new operas was doomed to a failure which seems to have had little connexion with the suffrage of the audience. *Giustino* was scheduled for performance on 16 February, and a run at Covent Garden was presumed to carry over into Lent, when performances were advertised on Wednesdays and Fridays. Somebody, Burney suggests the Lord Chamberlain but it seems more likely to have been Bishop Gibson, piously interfered and a ban was placed on all Lenten opera at Covent Garden — an obstacle the composer had never had to face during the Academy seasons. Handel was thus forced to cobble together a programme of non-dramatic works to fill the theatre until Easter. *Parnasso in Festa*, *Alexander's Feast* and *Esther* were all revived, and *Il Trionfo del Tempo* was dusted down and given several additional numbers.

As on other occasions in Handel's career, accident dictated precedent and the Lenten oratorio season established itself as a major element in his professional calendar. This was, as Burney says, 'not merely on account of their gravity and fitness for that holy time, but to avail himself of the suspension of all other public amusements which were likely to divide the public attention and favour'. (Charles Jennens made a similar point in 1744.) Like Mozart, Handel was a working entertainer and had long ago realized that 'we that live to please must please to live'. The improvised season, what is more, had its successful peaks, especially during the *Alexander's Feast* performances, at one of which 'the Prince and Princess of Wales were present, and seem'd to be highly entertain'd, insomuch that his Royal Highness commanded Mr Handel's Concerto on the Organ to be repeated, and intends to Honour the same with his Presence once again. . . . '

Yet the loyal Handelians were distinctly perturbed by what they saw as the composer's gradual collapse under the strain of hard work and fluctuating popularity. Mrs Pendarves's niece wrote despondently to her mother on 8 March: 'Music is certainly a pleasure that may be reckoned intellectual, and we shall *never again* have it in the perfection it is this year, because Mr Handel will *not compose any more*!' There seems to have been a prevailing notion among friends and admirers that he was ready to relinquish creative endeavour for good, since, some eight weeks after this letter, another anxious voice signalled alarm. The *savant* James Harris, brother-in-law of Handel's friend Sir Wyndham Knatchbull, wrote to his cousin Lord Shaftesbury in a valedictory strain: 'If Mr Handel gives off his Opera, it will be the only Pleasure I shall have left in ye musicall way, to look over his Scores, and recollect past Events — Here Strada used to shine — there Annibale — This was an Excell^t Chorus, and that a Charming peice of Recitative — In that I shall amuse my Self much in the Same manner as Virgil tells of ye Trojans . . . the war yr Lordp knows was renewed with double Earnestness & Vigour. May my Pleasure find ye Same Fate, & be lost by ye Return of that Harmony wch I have given over, Supported & carried on by ye Same Spirit & Resolution.'

After six performances before the Lenten interdict *Giustino* was brought back for three more, two in May and one, as a species of last bid, almost a month later. Thereafter, save for the shadows of its melody which appear in *L'Allegro and Il Penseroso*, it sank without trace. It is impossible to guess what special possibilities Handel could have seen in Nicola Beregan's libretto, originally written in 1683 for Giovanni Legrenzi and later revised by Paolo Pariati (Handel used a version made for Vivaldi in 1729). The plot, based vestigially on events in Byzantine history and tracing the rise to glory of the humble ploughboy Giustino, ultimately bidden to share the imperial dominion, is typical of seventeenth-century Venetian opera in its frantic efforts to alleviate the boredom of the spectators by incessant twists in the story, and, as such, offers an interesting contrast with the simplified narrative outlines of Metastasian drama. Focal interest is by no means concentrated on Giustino, and practically everybody has their moment; one heroine enters 'pursued by a bear', another is saved from a sea monster, the emperor Anastasio indulges in a burst of jealousy, the empress Arianna is followed by a hopeless lover, the brigand Vitaliano, who makes one of his appearances on a rope suspended from a tower and is identified (by means of a strawberry mark and the operation of a divine voice) as Giustino's long-lost brother.

Perhaps it was this very diversity which most appealed to the composer. Few of his operas display such a remarkable catholicity of style, and the various troughs of doodling and banality typical of an overburdened invention such as Handel's during this period are counterbalanced by the untiring range of his resources. We can scarcely ignore the signs of exhaustion — his obsessive reliance, for example, on descending scales as a sort of binding agent in the statement of themes — but at the same time the opera's diffuseness allows us to appreciate the wealth of its allusions. The polyglot Handel, who spoke, wrote and thought in a sophisticated babel of tongues, exercises a similar freedom in his music and an appreciation of this is central to our understanding of his work during the late 1730s, when, besides showing himself to be an accomplished practitioner of modern styles, he worked back towards the origins of his own in the choral and operatic traditions of the previous century.

Thus in *Giustino* we find recollections of his more orthodox Academy manner in the smooth siciliano measures of Anastasio's 'O fiero e rio sospetto' and in the majestic tread of Giustino's 'Sull'altar di questo nume', whose dotted quavers *larghetto e staccato* and firm melodic line provide the definitive Handelian touch. Cheek by jowl with these lie such successful essays in the style of Porpora as the simile arias 'Zefiretto, che scorre nel prato' and 'Quel torrente che s'innalza'. Beside these in their turn Handel includes one of those little French sinfonias to which he remained loyal from *Rinaldo* to *The Choice of Hercules*, and at least one scene which, in structure and tone, recalls the Venetian operatic world from which its text ultimately derived. This is the moment at which Fortune, seated on her wheel and surrounded by genii, appears to Giustino asleep beside his plough. Fortune's aria, with its contrapuntal imitations, its motto figure in the accompaniment, and its welding, via a recitative, with the subsequent chorus (based on the same material) recalls the style of Legrenzi's own works with which Handel was fully familiar.

The opera reflects his apparently unquenchable enthusiasm for romantic narrative, seldom without a hint or two of picaresque adventure and comedy, but handled far more primitively here than in *Orlando* or *Alcina*. Finished at almost the same time as *Giustino*, *Berenice*, brought on at Covent Garden in May 1737, returns us immediately to the universe of strangled emotions among monarchs and courtiers which provides the most familiar territory of Baroque lyric drama. Salvi was once again the author, subtitling his libretto 'The Contests of Love and Politics', a phrase neatly included in the work's closing *coro*, and mirrored in the amatory dilemmas faced by the Egyptian Queen Berenice, her sister Selene and their various lovers as a result of diplomatic bullying from Rome.

Salvi's plot has much to commend it, and the story opens with sensational abruptness as the heroine's public and private lives clash head on. Two of the characters, Princess Selene and her clandestine admirer Demetrio, are presented sympathetically enough for the drama to be really theirs. The dénouement, however, is more than usually artificial: some six or seven bars before the *coro* the villainous Arsace, responsible for most of the misery and deception in the story, having exulted at the thought of possessing Selene, suddenly experiences a twinge of pity for her and Demetrio and is rapidly turned into the generous rival who cedes all his sentimental advantages. Salvi, as we saw in *Rodelinda*, could make an expert job of last-moment remorse, but Grimoaldo's guilty change of heart is rather different from Arsace's preposterous heroic flourish. Perhaps the greatest flaw lies in Berenice herself, who, far from engaging our compassion, seems motivated by self-will, sexual greed and peevishness, as she attempts to manipulate political realities by trampling on the emotions of those closest to her.

This was surely not what Handel or Salvi intended. The interest of *Berenice* lies in the distinction with which it so consistently fails to transcend these limitations and in its various attempts to do so. Amid the music's platitudes, shown at their worst in Arsace's 'Amore contro amor', whose vacuous gesticulations bring it close to the realm of parody, we can sense the flickers of a response to a fast-moving and generally cohesive libretto, which, ten years earlier, would have evoked a genuine quickening in the composer. Interestingly, it is the numbers most unabashedly recalling the idiom of earlier operas which breathe real life into the work, pieces such as Demetrio's 'No, soffrir non puo il mio amore', an exquisite elaboration of the materials of Teofane's 'Falsa immagine' in *Ottone*, and his vigorous, elegant duet with Berenice, 'Se il mio amor fu il tuo delitto', with its reminiscences of the lighter moments of *Partenope* or *Alcina*, which closes Act I. Nothing in the work, however, quite lives up to the promise of the masterly overture, a worthy rival to that in *Alexander's Feast* and featuring one of those gently-paced triple-time airs whose delicate simplicity makes them uniquely Handel's.

As in *Siroe*, the orchestra for *Berenice* is simply the basic band of strings, oboes, bassoons and continuo, with the oboes only heard in three numbers and a solo for Sammartini. Handel is so obviously one of the great masters of orchestral sound, gifted with a rarefied sense of timbre, balance and colour, that it would be absurd to suggest that this limited palette was among the work's shortcomings, yet, given the financial state of the Covent Garden enterprise, we might suppose that the composer was making a desperate retrenchment. If so, it was useless. *Berenice* enjoyed a miserable four performances and the season concluded with revivals of *Alcina, Giustino* and the pasticcio *Didone abbandonata*, which had first been brought on in April.

Handel might have been consoled by witnessing the almost simultaneous collapse of his Nobility rivals at the King's Theatre, Haymarket, as audiences, by now bored and satiated with novelty fare and the erstwhile amusement of pitting one company against another, fell rapidly away. Porpora had left London the previous year after the failure of his royal wedding offering *La Festa d'Imeneo*, and Farinelli now slipped out of England as well, soon to begin the most bizarre adventure in his extraordinary career, as a sort of music therapist to the psychologically disturbed King Philip V of Spain, whom he soothed with the same four songs nightly for nine years. Several of Handel's own singers returned to Italy, including Conti and Annibali, while Strada, though remaining in London until the summer of 1738, never sang again for the composer who had done so much towards making a distinguished career for her.

'Great fatigue and disappointment,' says Lord Shaftesbury, 'affected him so much, that he was this Spring [1737] struck with the Palsy, which took entirely away the use of 4 fingers of his right hand; and totally disabled him from Playing: And when the heats of the Summer . . . came on, the Disorder seemed at times to affect his Understanding. . . . ' He had witnessed the onset of Handel's illness early in May and written apprehensively to James Harris, the tone of whose reply indicates the intense respect in which the composer was now held by discerning English music lovers. ' . . . When ye Fate of Harmony depends upon a Single Life, the Lovers of Harmony may be well allowed to be Sollicitous. I heartily regrett ye thought of losing any of ye executive part of his meritt, but this I can gladly compound for, when we are assured of the Inventive, for tis this which properly constitutes ye Artist, & Separates Him from ye Multitude.' Shaftesbury must have thought that Handel was on the way to recovery, for Harris adds: 'It is certainly an Evidence of great Strength of Constitution to be so soon getting rid of So great a Shock. A weaker Body would perhaps have hardly born ye Violence of Medicines, wch operate So quickly.'

A measure of Handel's significance in Augustan cultural life is offered by the fact that his paralysis made news in the papers. The *London Daily Post* reported a likely recovery on 30 April, but a fortnight later the *London Evening Post* noted that 'the ingenious Mr Handell is very much indispos'd, and it's thought with a Paraletick Disorder, he having at present no Use of his Right Hand, which, if he don't regain, the Publick will be depriv'd of his fine Compositions'. The journeys to Tunbridge Wells in previous years must have been connected with this, but an altogether more serious form of treatment was now required for what has since been convincingly diagnosed as recurrent muscular rheumatism exacerbated by sheer physical exhaustion. Who suggested the baths of Aachen to Handel we do not know — possibly his former pupil the Princess of Orange, whose husband had taken a successful cure there in 1730 — but the prescription was perfect almost to a miracle.

Handel was the latest in the long series of illustrious patients at Aachen which had included Charlemagne (who fixed his imperial court there), Petrarch, Dürer, Peter the Great, four popes and, more recently, several leading Jacobites. Scattered about the city were the 20 or so thermal springs, the hottest in Europe and giving off an overpowering sulphurous stench. Their specific application had long been celebrated in cases of rheumatic paralysis and, used as sweat baths, in the treatment of venereal disease. The company was thus, as in so many other spas, distinctly mixed, and part of the pleasure (and sometimes the risk) of visiting Aachen lay in the astonishingly diverse clientele.

Thanks to Count Carl Ludwig von Poellnitz, who visited the city two years before Handel himself, we know a great deal about both the atmosphere of the place and the nature of the cure. As at Bath and Tunbridge there was a prevailing air of pleasant holiday trifling, enhanced by gambling and gallantry, whether at the four o'clock balls at Baugy's rooms or at the Café du Gascon near the principal springs. Those who drank the waters were recommended to alternate each draught with mouthfuls of orange or lemon peel, caraway comfits or ginger roots to take away the taste or to eat a special pap known as *manillette*, made of thin, dry aniseed biscuits soaked in white wine and water. The recommended diet (of which Handel would certainly have taken note) permitted roast meats, game and fish, but no garlic, lard or salt, carp, tench, eels or lampreys. Rhenish, Moselle, watered Burgundy and light beers were the only alcoholic drinks allowed. The waters themselves, though 'mortal to infancy or old age', if taken internally, were good for practically everything else, including barrenness, nosebleeds, piles, scurvy, colic and 'for moderating a canine appetite'.

It was typical of Handel, strong-willed, impatient and, as Harris had noted, physically very resilient, that he should have chosen bathing rather than drinking and have submitted himself to the kind of regime known in German spas as a 'horse cure'. The baths themselves were undoubtedly pleasurable, and the bathers, dressed in 'a grotesque bonnet in the shape of a woman's cap' and loose linen drawers, were regaled with titbits from little floating trays. 'The water,' says Poellnitz, 'which is fat and unctuous to the touch, gently softens the skin, and by the help of the salts with which it is impregnated, opens the pores, restores the nerves to their natural tone, and enlivens the body in so sensible a manner that, however well a man be at entering the bath, he always comes out of it more healthy and cheerful.' Handel certainly did so, as Mainwaring tells us: 'Whoever knows any thing of the nature of those baths, will, from this instance, form some idea of his surprising constitution. His sweats were profuse beyond what can well be imagined. His cure, from the manner, as well as from the quickness with which it was wrought, passed with the Nuns for a miracle. When, but a few hours from the time of his quitting the bath, they heard him at the organ in the principal church . . . playing in a manner so much beyond any they had ever been used to, such a conclusion in such persons was natural enough.'*

All seemed set for a triumphal return to the operatic stage. A fresh agreement had been reached whereby Handel would join forces once more with Heidegger at the Haymarket and take on several members of the Nobility company, including the renegades Montagnana and Merighi and the new castrato hired to replace Farinelli. Soon after his return he began a fresh opera for the forthcoming season, but only four days later, on 20 November 1737, London received the news that Queen Caroline was dead.

It had been a slow and agonizing decline, the result of an untreated rupture, which the queen had borne with stubborn fortitude. The shock caused not only to her family but to the court and city as a whole was immense. From contemporary accounts it is immediately obvious that she was the kind of woman who was either fervently admired or else deeply loathed, and her influence on the king and his ministers was never taken

*According to a letter purportedly written by Johann Christoph Schmidt to Matthew Dubourg and first published by Joseph Müller Blattau, Handel is supposed to have visited the Pomeranian city of Elbing at this time to provide music for its quincentenary celebrations. Modern scholarship has failed to discover the original of this letter and the entire episode seems doubtful.

lightly. The range of her interests and sympathies was enormous, and to this day she has never really been given the appreciation due to her vibrant, forceful personality by a nation which, even in her own epoch, mistrusted her foreign sophistications.

Reaction to her death varied between nostalgic regret and opprobrious scorn. To the anonymous hack who bewailed 'Carolina waiting for the tomb' as 'An Hypocrite in nought but *hiding Pain*', an unsigned lampoon (perhaps by Swift, who had never forgiven her for neglecting him) angrily rejoined:

> An Hypocrite in all but disbelief in God.
> Promoted Luxury, encourag'd Vice,
> Her self a sordid slave to Avarice . . .
> To her own offspring mercy she deny'd,
> And unforgiving, unforgiven dy'd.

Attributed to Pope was the memorably unpardonable:

> Here lies, wrapp'd up in forty thousand towels,
> The only proof that Caroline had bowels.

Others, recipients of her kindness and appreciation, offered significant tributes. Down at Kew, the curate of the parish, preaching to her servants, including 'the Thresher Poet' Stephen Duck, praised the discrimination, constancy and charity of a woman who was 'discreetly generous and elegantly frugal'; he himself was the 28-year-old Thomas Morell, who was to be one of Handel's principal librettists during the 1740s. Perhaps the most touching tribute came from none other than Paolo Antonio Rolli, who rightly saw Caroline's death as marking the end of an epoch. Soon after his return to Italy, addressing the Marchese Teodoli in a rhythmically spirited ode, he wrote: 'From the warlike Thames, never before noted for sweetness, a gentle harmony arose while the Royal Lady lived to delight in it . . . but then she paid to nature the due of all living things: an immense horror filled those shores and the Muse dwelt there no longer. Civil war threatened, the Spaniards infested the seas, defiant trumpets echoed from the distant frontiers. My sweet lyre, said I, it is time to retire to the forsaken haunts of Peace: come back to Umbria's fruitful hills, where Ceres and Bacchus reside.'

Handel's veneration of the woman for whom he had written duets when she was a princess in Hanover, who sang snatches of his opera airs to tease her husband, and who had never wavered in her advocacy of his music, found utterance in one of the most deeply-layered of all his works, a piece which openly displays his own sense of personal loss, and stands beside *Alexander's Feast* and *Israel in Egypt* as a product of that single-minded originality of concept and design which sets these compositions of the 1730s apart from the orthodox modes of opera and dramatic oratorio and lays the ground for *Messiah*.

The Ways of Zion Do Mourn, the great elegy for Queen Caroline, formed part of the long funeral service taking place in King Henry VII's Chapel at Westminster Abbey on the evening of 17 December. The procession of mourners and attendants, a tremendous affair involving the entire royal household, the Earl Marshal, the Archbishop of Canterbury, heralds and pursuivants and 'the Royal Body' carried by yeomen of the guard and followed by sixteen duchesses, went from the Prince of Wales's lodgings to the Abbey along a route spread with black baize. Among those present was the Earl of Carnarvon, now Duke of Chandos, who wrote to his nephew, Dr Theophilus Leigh, 'The Solemnity of the Queen's Funeral was very decent, and performed in more order than any thing I have seen of the like kind. . . . It began about a quarter before 7, & was over a little aften ten; the Anthem took up three quarters of an hour of the time, of which the composition was exceeding fine, and adapted very properly to the melancholly occasion of it; but I can't say so much of the performance.'

With 'near 80 vocal performers, and 100 instruments from his Majesty's band, and from the Opera, &c', as well as 'several musical Gentlemen of distinction' who 'attended in surplices, and sang in the burial service', the anthem must have needed more rehearsal than was possible in the five days between its completion and the actual ceremony. It made, nevertheless, a telling impression on those present at the occasion and was performed in various guises until well into the nineteenth century, after which (despite the Novello score remaining in print) it promptly disappeared from public notice. Nor is there much likelihood that it will ever regain popularity; an extended meditation, uncompromisingly austere even in its gentler moments, it reveals Handel thoroughly at home with the styles and forms of German and Italian church music of the Renaissance and Baroque, as 'profound' or 'scientific' as the demurest, most pious music lover could require.

The words were compiled from Scripture with great skill by Edward Willes, sub-dean of Westminster, dovetailing passages from the Psalms, Lamentations, Job, the Apocrypha and St Paul into a coherent sequence, and moving, in a way typical of the age, from misery to confidence, from a particularized vision of the queen herself to a general prospect of reward for virtue. Handel unites the whole through emphasis on the home key, G minor, and by recalling the words 'How are the mighty fall'n! She that was great among the nations, and princess of the provinces!' as agonized outbursts introducing two subsequent choruses (the phrase lengths and note values are identical, but the modulation is subtly altered).

Though the anthem, at its rare modern performances, is sometimes given with solo episodes, its original disposition is exclusively choral, and one of its many claims to consideration is the sheer ingenuity and suppleness with which he handles his chosen medium. The solemnity here is neither pompous nor heavy-footed; in the tender E flat andante larghetto of 'When the ear heard her' and the energetic pulses of 'She delivered the poor that cried' there is reflective contrast with the long elegiac paragraphs of the surrounding movements. Yet here also the outlines enclose that intense intellectual sophistication which typifies Handel's approach to the work in general. Far from forgetting the world of the opera house and the court to which Caroline belonged, he embraces it by constructing 'When the ear heard her' and 'The righteous shall be had in everlasting remembrance' in the manner of those chamber duets he had composed for the queen nearly 30 years before, with answering pairs of vocal lines clinched by the full chorus and by the use of recitative-type passages in 'How are the mighty fall'n' and 'The people will tell'.

The most interesting aspect of the Funeral Anthem lies in its conscious return to Handel's German roots. It is hard to believe that his recent Aachen visit cannot have been connected with this, and difficult also to reject the idea that he was celebrating Caroline's memory in an idiom they both understood, a kind of private language. The opening chorus, for example, features part of the Lutheran chorale 'Herr Jesu Christ, du höchstes Gut', and its final section reproduces (in a significantly improved form) an organ fugue by Johann Philip Krieger. 'She delivered the poor that cried' is spanned by the cantus firmus of the chorale melody 'Du Friedefürst Herr Jesus Christ' and 'Their bodies are buried in peace' quotes from 'Ecce quomodo moritur' by Jacob Handl.

It is an enduring reproach to our limited modern sensibilities that this magnificent piece should nowadays be almost totally ignored, even among those conversant with the operas and oratorios. Its significance in Handel's development as a composer cannot be too highly emphasized, and the variety of its choral writing makes it a kind of pendant to *Israel in Egypt* and *Messiah*. The experience of creating it was surely decisive in edging Handel ever closer towards a type of musical work in which the chorus could occupy a major role.

All for War and Admiral Haddock

The reason most frequently given in the past for Handel's renunciation of opera in favour of oratorio has always been based on the belief that he had somehow managed to grow out of writing operas and that the greater formal elasticity of oratorio allowed him a freedom he would not thereafter give up for the sake of a return to the stage. To this the Victorians added a cherished conception of their beloved choral composer as one who looked forward to Tennyson's 'We needs must love the highest when we see it' and who, like Chaucer and Botticelli, exercised repentance for earlier profanities in the devotion of his art to God's service. Writing in the *Musical Times* of March 1869, Sir George Macfarren, in an essay significantly entitled 'The Italian Language: its evil influence upon music', described the operas as 'cast in a form that limited the workings of the mighty genius of the master, and allowed no play to its higher attributes'. They afforded 'the rarest opportunity for characterization' and were in any case 'obsolete and lost to the world for ever'. 'Based upon subjects that are entirely unsympathetic to our times, and constructed upon principles that are totally uncongenial to our stage, his operas will never, and can never, be performed again.'

It would be wrong, however, to assume that Londoners were growing tired of current operatic forms. Opera on the London stage did not die out after Handel stopped composing for it, neither was there any sign of a waning enthusiasm for the most sophisticated types of Metastasian melodrama which were to predominate in the musical theatre almost until the end of the century. Great days were in any case to come, with the triumph of outstanding composers like Galuppi, Johann Christian Bach and Sacchini, and fine castrati such as Monticelli, Rauzzini and Pacchierotti. As for Handelian oratorio, whatever the incidental breaks with tradition, its outlines are resolutely operatic and show few signs of moving significantly in any other direction. Many of Handel's leading oratorio singers, what is more, had had valuable operatic experience, and some, such as Giulia Frasi, maintained a career in both fields during the 1740s.

There is little enough evidence to support the view that Handel gave up opera because he was dissatisfied with its artistic limitations. His German excursion in 1737 must have fuelled his interest in sacred dramatic works, and he no doubt chafed at opera's formal restrictions, at the financial exigencies of theatrical production and at the dictatorial habits of singers. But his remark, recorded by Hawkins, that oratorio composition was 'better suited . . . to the circumstances of a man advancing in years, than that of adapting music to such vain and trivial poetry as the musical drama is generally made to consist of' may well be simply wisdom after the event, on the part of a seasoned old entertainer making his peace with the shifts of taste and circumstance. Perhaps there really was a crisis of faith during this physically and mentally taxing period at the close of the decade, but the production of such secular works as *Semele* and *The Choice of Hercules* in the ten years which followed suggests that it cannot have had lasting effects. The most likely cause of his defection to oratorio lies in the economic realities of the situation. The close of the 1730s saw the collapse of both the Haymarket and the Covent Garden companies and the dissolution of the Opera of the Nobility. Subsequent efforts during the early 1740s to recover the prestige and box office credibility of opera were spasmodic and variably successful, and it was perhaps not until 1754, with the arrival of the soprano Mingotti, that a really consistent initiative was taken in promoting Italian lyric drama once more.

The successive failure of Handel's last four operas was thus due, not to a lack of faith in the validity of the genre as a whole, either from the public or from the composer, but to an overall disillusionment as to what the Haymarket and Lincoln's Inn Fields had to offer in the way of spectacle, stars and novelties. Unlike Bach or Telemann, Handel, during his London years, could never be wholly confident of his audience, and the move to oratorio, like the journey to Ireland which clinched it, was dictated by the medium's apparent potential drawing power. Only later did Handel have to cope once more with the caprice of musical Londoners, when works such as *Hercules*, *Belshazzar* and *Theodora* foundered, and there is nothing to prove that he would not, guaranteed materially and artistically favourable conditions, have returned to the operatic stage.

He and Heidegger between them had collected a dependable cast for the new season, most of them singers for whom Handel had never written before. Besides Montagnana and Merighi, there was Maria Antonia

Marchesini, '*La Lucchesina*', a mezzo, and Elizabeth Duparc, known as La Francesina, whose 'natural warble, and agility of voice' clearly pleased the composer and who was destined to take Strada's place as his prima donna in the coming decade. The finest acquisition was another of those superb castrato stars whom Handel, presumably with the aid of local Italian contacts, was always able to select as the focus of his company. This season it was the great Gaetano Majorano *detto il Caffarelli*, vain and quarrelsome both in his professional and his private life, but a performer who made an unforgettable impression upon all who heard him and a worthy rival to Farinelli.

The season opened at the King's Theatre, Haymarket, on Tuesday, 3 January 1738, with the première of *Faramondo*, whose composition had originally been broken off for writing the Funeral Anthem the previous year. The new piece was a *succès d'estime*: eight performances was a modest run, but the first night played 'to a splendid Audience, and met with general Applause. It being the first Time of Mr Handel's Appearance this Season, he was honour'd with extraordinary and repeated Signs of Approbation.' Newburgh Hamilton and the Wentworth children were loyally admiring. 'Every body seems to like Pharamond the new opera vastly & they say Caffrielli is a much better person than Farinelli; but I do not hear any body likes his voice near so well . . .' wrote Lady Lucy to the earl her father, ' . . . tis mightily liked, twas so applauded that Mr Hamilton who would not doe less than another body, when Mr Handel was in ye Case, clap'd till his arms aked.'

So he should have done, for if *Faramondo* is scarcely a well-knit dramatic masterpiece, it has a forcefulness of concept and expression which is lacking in the operas of the preceding season, and certainly deserved to fare better. The libretto is a ruthlessly truncated version of a drama by the prolific Habsburg *poeta cesareo* Apostolo Zeno, originally set by Carlo Pollarolo for Venice in 1699. Reflecting Zeno's typical penchant for recherché barbarian backgrounds (witness, for example, *Ambleto*, his treatment of the Hamlet story, *Gianguir*, set in the India of the Moghul emperor Jehangir, or the Chinese *Teuzzone*) the story, shot through with passion and violence, concerns the fortunes of Faramondo, King of the Franks (the historical Pharamond) confronted with the implacable vindictiveness of Gustavo, ruler of the Cimbri, sworn to avenge his dead son Sveno. However ineptly reduced, such a drama, with its constant plot twists and powerfully sketched characters, is bound to have appealed to Handel, and his response was suitably enthusiastic.

The overture, managing to make the traditional Lullian opening sound distinctly unorthodox and to carry this individuality over into the superbly wrought concerto movement which follows, is one of the best from these years and sets the tone of solid craftsmanship that prevails throughout the entire work. The six principals (there are two additional comprimario parts) share in a series of splendidly imaginative arias, often drawing upon the striking array of chromatic effects which forms such a marked feature of Handel's style in this opera. Caffarelli's music, as Faramondo, represents some of the most opulently expressive the composer ever produced for a castrato (his range appears to have been c to g') and such dramatic predominance identifies him as the star performer in a way denied to either of the female leads, Clotilde and Rosimonda. The variety among his airs, from 'Si, tornero a morir' and 'Poi che pria di morire', in which Handel squeezes pathos from gently flowing rhythms and major tonalities, to the bouncing insouciance of 'Se ben mi lusinga' and the nervous chromatic steps forming the centrepiece of 'Voglio che sia l'indegno', enhances his right to round off the work with an extended festive *envoi*, coloured by a brace of horns, which leads directly to the ornate reprise making up the closing *coro*.

Nothing, however, can quite rescue the drama from the weakness of its text as set by Handel. Admirable in themselves as are numbers like Clotilde's 'Combattuta da due venti', where the composer's piquant sense of humour uses the modulations of the vocal line to portray a ship tacking between the contrary winds described in the counterpoint of the string accompaniment, or 'Caro, cara, tu mi accendi', her Act III duet with her ever-loyal swain Adolfo, their perfections of design overburden the superficiality of the libretto, and that ideal balance which in the best *opera seria* is achieved between the recitative and the arias is here never reached.

Faramondo is thus a highly distinguished casualty among Handel's operas, transfused as it is with his customary alert, comprehensive intelligence. Such a quality is emphasized rather than diminished by the knowledge that the work is an elaboration of musical shapes and ideas found in an opera of the same name written for the Roman carnival season of 1720 by Francesco Gasparini. Handel's close attention to Gasparini's handling of rhythms had shown itself years before in *Tamerlano*, certain of whose airs use the earlier composer's work as a springboard, and in *Faramondo* the allusion is strengthened by similarities in the choice of various keys. He probably borrowed the Gasparini score from Charles Jennens, with whom he was then on good terms and who was being supplied with contemporary Italian music by his friend Edward Holdsworth, 'bear-leader' to young noblemen on the Grand Tour.

The essentially organic nature of Handel's art nullifies the idea that he remained a stolid musical conservative. The facts of the case seem more complex. That he was continually interested in newer trends is shown not solely by the incessant flourishes of modernism in the later operas, but by the use made during the 1740s of material by Telemann, Clari, Muffat and Habermann. His own work provided an unending source of ideas which could be re-stated in differing forms and contexts. Nothing he ever composed was truly finished in the sense that he left it alone for good. His sharply honed memory fixed continually upon opportunities for using themes and entire numbers again where the occasion arose, and he was always ready to change the layout of any work according to the resources at his disposal. Thus in the majority of cases to speak of a definitive text beyond the initial autograph, itself always so eloquent of the care taken over even the most ephemeral touches of art, is impossible.

A return to the fountainhead of his vocal style colours not only *Faramondo* but also its successor, *Serse*. For this Handel turned to a setting by his old Academy associate and rival Giovanni Bononcini, using both the text and whole sections of the music from his 1694 Roman version. The borrowings, as so often with Handel, are no mere plagiarisms, but inspired transformations and elaborations of the original. The libretto is a systematic revision by Silvio Stampiglia (Handel used a shortened version) of a typical Venetian romantic mischmasch, loosely alluding to events in the life of King Xerxes (we get both the famous bridge of boats across the Hellespont and his 'strange Lydian love, the platane tree') by Niccolo Minato for Cavalli in 1654.

Stampiglia, whose work Handel had already used in *Partenope* (they may actually have come across one another in Italy), was an important link between the looser type of seventeenth-century lyric drama and the marmoreal austerities of Metastasio. In a brilliant contemporary survey of the whole genre, *Le Rivoluzioni del Teatro Musicale Italiano*, the Jesuit critic Stefano Arteaga says of him 'he deserves some distinction . . . for having been among the first to purge *melodrama* of the ridiculous mixture of seriousness and buffoonery, of too many plot complications and too heavy an accretion of machinery. Otherwise his style is dry and lacks warmth. He cannot make harmonious recitative or arias fit for musical setting.'

Whatever his shortcomings he made an excellent job of adapting Minato's libretto to the altered conditions of eighteenth-century opera while retaining its fundamental buoyancy and wit. The characterization is of the very firmest, with a strong contrast offered from the outset between the tenderness and sensitivity of Romilda, pining for love of Serse's brother Arsamene, and the sexual ruthlessness of her sister Atalanta, calculating to the very last. In addition to Serse's rejected sweetheart Amastre, *en travesti* as a warrior, Stampiglia retains another Venetian stock figure, the comic servant Elviro, who acts as go-between and commentator in the comedy. As for Serse himself, he is throughout presented as a heroic blunderer, flamboyant and preposterous in his passionate gesticulations and only brought to his senses by threats of suicide from the long-suffering Amastre.

It was by no means a conventional drama, but Handel's eclecticism made him able to contrive splendidly appropriate solutions for its more recherché moments. In outline, structure and scoring it is the most unusual of all his operas and its blithe disregard of the rigid *da capo* and exit conventions observed elsewhere may have helped to win for it that acclaim which has made it the most often performed of all his operas in our own day.

Several numbers recur either in the form of ironic quotations or else as repetitions for dramatic effect, and the *coro* employs the formula devised in *Faramondo* by resuming the serenities of Romilda's 'Caro voi siete all'alma'. That delicacy of touch which evokes Mozartian associations whenever the opera is discussed gets to work from the start in the arresting opening to Act I. Alone in his Persian garden Serse apostrophizes the plane tree in the gentle larghetto 'Ombra mai fu', better known to Victorian organists as 'Handel's Largo': Arsamene appears, on the other side of the garden, with Elviro, and they listen enraptured to the music for recorders, muted strings and pizzicato bass which so memorably introduces Romilda, singing, like Wagner's Brangäne, from a belvedere. Snatches of her song and its ritornello are interrupted by the comments of the listeners, joined by Serse himself, who realizes that the singer is distantly mocking his 'vegetable love', and the scene closes with a lighthearted cabaletta for Romilda.

Ultimately *Serse*'s strength lies in the remarkable consistency of its aims. The balance between banter and seriousness is maintained through an insistence on the validity of human emotions, no matter how absurd the circumstances which give rise to them. Thus Serse's 'Piu che penso', springing though it does from erotic obsessions which are more than a little ridiculous, dignifies the release of feeling in one of Handel's most majestic outpourings, yet the very stateliness of its dotted rhythms and demisemiquaver flourishes hints at an ambiguous pomposity typical of Serse himself.

What audiences made of all this we do not know. It was not, as has sometimes been stated, Handel's only comic opera, but it was the first since *Atalanta* to lay so strong an emphasis on lighthearted amorous intrigue. It was also his only opera after *Almira* to feature an old-fashioned Spanish-style comedy servant, and Elviro's street-cries, in his disguise as a flower-seller in Act II, may have raised an eyebrow or two. Handel's sketchbooks contain a notation of at least one among London's innumerable cries, from a man selling matches in Tyburn Road (now Oxford Street) and his friend Lady Luxborough later told the poet William Shenstone that he 'has told me that the hints of his very best songs have several of them been owing to the sounds in his ears of cries in the street', but the Haymarket audience, even if inured by now to ballad opera, can hardly have expected this sort of thing in a full-length Italian lyric drama.

Serse flopped after only five performances and was never revived in Handel's lifetime. Not, in any case, that the season was a success. The biggest draws were Giovanni Battista Pescetti's *La Conquista del Vello d'Oro* and Veracini's *Partenio*, on eight and nine nights respectively. *Alessandro Severo*, a Handelian pasticcio with a new overture and five fresh arias, only had six performances and we can appreciate the spirit in which Heidegger, on 24 May, slipped into his notice to potential subscribers for next season the caveats 'in case the Opera should not go on . . . provided I can agree with the Performers . . . in case the Money is not paid.' As it happened, none of the Haymarket soloists except Francesina and perhaps Lucchesina stayed on, since the impresario could not gather enough subscriptions to pay them. His ominous announcement to that effect in the *London Daily Post* of 26 July stated that 'I could not agree with the singers, though I offered ONE THOUSAND GUINEAS to *one* of them.' Caffarelli maybe?

As though this were not enough, Handel, so Newburgh Hamilton told Lord Strafford, had been caught in the continuing crossfire between George II and the Prince of Wales. 'The P— design'd to have a concert every friday night & desir'd Mr Handel to make one, which he readily agreed to; but it came to the K—'s ears, & he sent Mr Handel an order, not to go near the P: I did not believe it, till I had it this morning from his own mouth.' Dependent on the continuance of long-standing royal favour, he can honestly have had no choice. His sole practical consolation lay in the benefit concert given at the Haymarket on 28 March, featuring *As pants the hart*, selections from *Deborah* and *My heart is inditing*, and at which Lord Egmont, counting 'near 1,300 persons besides the gallery and upper gallery', estimated that 'I suppose he got this night 1,000 l.'.

Almost opposite his house in Brook Street, however, was an alley whose name, Poverty Lane, may currently have held a certain menacing significance. He was never actually insolvent, but the realities of being a poor musician in a city already bursting with musical life were seldom far away. Early in 1738 the flautist Carl Friedrich Weidemann, Richard Vincent, Covent Garden's principal oboist, and Michael Festing, leader of the Vauxhall band and noted for 'good sense, probity, prudent conduct, and a gentleman-like behaviour', standing together at the door of the Orange coffee-house in the Haymarket, noticed two boys leading milch-asses up the street and recognized them as the children of the oboe virtuoso Johann Christian Kytsch, who had recently died in poverty in nearby St James's Market. It was this sight which prompted the three instrumentalists to conceive of a fund 'for the support of decayed musicians and their families', raised from among a society whose first meetings were at the Crown and Anchor tavern during the spring of that year. Early subscribers included Arne, Boyce, Greene, Roseingrave and Stanley, and of course Handel himself, and the scheme gave birth to what eventually became the Royal Society of Musicians.

Even if London was niggard of material benefits to Handel, it was ready to pay him honours of a more grandly abstract kind. Vauxhall Gardens, in Upper Kennington, had now been opened for six years, under the discriminating ownership and management of Jonathan Tyers and offering the kind of masked summer entertainment known as a *ridotto al fresco*. The silver season tickets were designed by Hogarth, and the smart company, often led by the Prince and Princess of Wales, walked among the lantern-decked groves, took refreshments (including the famous wafer-thin slices of ham, through which it was reputedly possible to read a newspaper) in the pavilions and grottoes hung with special paintings by Francis Hayman (one of which represented 'Two Mahometans gazing in wonder at the beauties of the place') and listened to the band in the New Music Room, later known as the Rotunda, its interior design clearly influenced by the type of theatrical scene painting familiar to Handel's opera audiences.

With their dark walks and wildernesses and triumphal arches framing a painting of the Ruins of Palmyra, the twelve acres of Vauxhall, stretching from the river into the Kennington hayfields, and coyly blending London artifice and rural nature, became the classic embodiment of Georgian pleasure-seeking, and figure largely in the novels, letters and diaries of the period. They also reflected significant trends in contemporary English taste, since the artists whose work adorned the gardens in the early years were nearly all members of a group, centred upon Hogarth, which gathered at Slaughter's coffee house in St Martin's Lane. Patronized by the Prince of Wales and identified with the anti-Walpole opposition of the 1730s, the Slaughter's set included such pioneers of English rococo as the engraver Hubert Gravelot, the plasterer William Collins and the sculptors Henry Cheere and Louis-François Roubiliac.

The initial idea for a statue of Handel among the Vauxhall groves was perhaps Tyers's own, and it seems reasonable to assume that either he or Gravelot, whose engraved decorations for the *Alexander's Feast* portrait had recently appeared, or maybe even the Prince himself, brought Handel and Roubiliac together. The result, in any case, was spectacular, not merely because this was the first such tribute to a living man in the annals of contemporary sculpture but because Roubiliac, whose three other Handel portraits include the superb Windsor bust of 1739 and the Westminster Abbey monument so admired for its fidelity by Hawkins, is arguably the only artist to have caught something of that mixture of ease and alertness so essentially the composer's. Of the paintings, only Philip Mercier's vision of him, shiny-nosed, unshaven, turban rakishly pushed back over his cropped head as he sits with his oblong manuscript sheets before him, gives us a human glimpse. Otherwise he is the bob-wigged porker of Balthasar Denner, the obese pudding-face of Bartholomew Dandridge, or the elegant bourgeois of the likeness commissioned by Jennens from Thomas Hudson in 1756.

Besides its extraordinary precision of detail, in the wide-nostrilled *retroussé* nose, the slightly protruding underlip, the baggy eyes and that most emphatic Handelian facial feature, the bushy black eyebrows, Roubiliac's portrait, in its sinuous rococo compositional lines, captures with an engaging sense of humour those qualities of mingled grandeur and intimacy reflected in the music. The composer is presented as Apollo plucking a lyre, while a putto, leaning on a viola da gamba at his feet, notes down what he plays. Yet this is an Apollo in the crumpled informality of Georgian undress, with a floppy turban, loose dressing gown, breeches unbuttoned at the knee, and one slipper off. The statue is both the ultimate expression of nonchalant genius and of what Handel's presence in England really meant to contemporaries who liked music enough to understand him.

Carved in Roubiliac's workshop in St Martin's Lane 'out of one entire Block of white Marble', it was given a place of honour 'in a grand Nich erected on Purpose', where it was 'set finely off by various Greens, which form, in Miniature, a sort of woody theatre'. Ferried over the river on 27 April, it encouraged the inevitable crop of magazine verse, such as that of 'a Gentleman of Oxford' who wrote:

See *Handel*, careless of a foreign fame,
Fix on our shore, and boast a Briton's name:
While, plac'd marmoric in the vocal grove,
He guides the measures listening throngs approve.

Listening throngs in the capricious Vauxhall weather were always able to hear his concertos, which formed a staple of the band's repertoire, though he never wrote any of them specifically for the gardens themselves. As we have already noted, the recent oratorio performances often featured organ concertos in which Handel himself was the soloist, and Walsh now published, in October 1738, the set of six works for harpsichord or organ subsequently labelled the Opus 4 Organ Concertos. The second of these had already appeared the previous month in Walsh's anthology *The Lady's Entertainment*, and he warned the public that 'a mangled Edition' of the concertos was in the press. All six had, of course, already been heard before, but the issue of Opus 4 is something of a landmark in English musical history, introducing to a wider public a form which Handel, so far as is known, had invented.

His keyboard virtuosity had been celebrated since his Roman contests with Domenico Scarlatti, but we must not imagine him playing in London the sort of massive German instruments for which Bach was currently writing. Pedal boards on English organs were comparatively rare, and the many sets of lessons and voluntaries published by eighteenth-century organists in London and the provinces assume the use of the manuals alone. The instrument Handel used at Covent Garden had one manual and seven stops, and he was to recommend an almost exactly similar instrument to Charles Jennens in 1749 as 'every thing that is necessary for a good and grand Organ'. The two-manual instrument he presented to the Foundling Hospital chapel had, of course, more stops but still no pedals.

Hawkins, who had heard him play at oratorio performances, praises his 'amazing command of the instrument, the fullness of his harmony, the grandeur and dignity of his style, the copiousness of his imagination, and the fertility of his invention'. His custom was apparently to introduce each concerto with a voluntary, 'the harmony close wrought, and as full as could possibly be expressed; the passages concatenated with stupendous art', and this improvisatory element was carried over into the concerto itself. The result is inevitably that what has come down to us is, in several cases, not the entire work as originally given, and one of the features of Handel's art most admired by his contemporaries is now lost to us more or less irrevocably. Burney tells us that, after his blindness came on, he played several of his old concertos from memory, giving the ritornellos to the band, who waited for the shake at the end of his improvisations 'before they played such fragments of symphony as they found in their books'.

As we have already noted in the case of Opus 3, Handel never regarded the concerto form as rigidly sacrosanct. Where he was concerned, it was an opportunity for the band to show its qualities of well-drilled virtuosity, and in his organ concertos this extreme freedom in the disposition of movements, which makes many of his instrumental works closer to dance suites than to the orthodox models of Vivaldi, Telemann and Bach, relates perfectly to the 'ad libitum' spontaneity of the solo line. Each concerto, each movement indeed, holds its surprises, reworking material from earlier pieces and moulding conventional forms to offer new solutions. No. I in G minor, for instance, begins in traditional *larghetto e staccato* overture style, but soon breaks up into a species of commentary by the soloist against a background of orchestral interjections recalling the original opening, to be followed by the dazzling brilliance of Handel's longest concerto movement, a 158-bar *allegro*. No. IV in F cradles, between its extrovert outer movements, the delightfully suave andante (the composer specifies 'Open Diapason, stopt Diapason & Flute' with strings alone) in which the organ and the band sport with each other, though seldom actually interchanging material.

Another instrumental collection, seven sonatas registered in Walsh's cash book on 7 October 1738 and published the following year, was partly based on Handel's felicitous arrangements of music from the Chandos Anthems, whose autographs show absorbing evidence of the work thus carried out. These Opus 5 trios, incorporating a certain amount of new music and making use of some of the dance movements composed for Sallé and her company in 1734–5, are lighter in mood than their Opus 2 forerunners, perhaps reflecting a specific request from Walsh himself.

During the summer Handel had been at work on a new oratorio, to a text by Charles Jennens, probably the work referred to in a letter sent three years previously from composer to librettist, thanking him for 'the inclosed Oratorio', and continuing: 'I am just going to Tunbridge, yet what I could read of it in haste, gave me a great deal of Satisfaction. I shall have more leisure time there to read it with all the Attention it deserves.' The subject chosen was the story of David, Saul and Jonathan, beginning with an 'Epinicion, or Song of Triumph for the Victory over Goliath and the Philistines' and ending with a paraphrase of David's lament over the dead king and his son which opens the second book of Samuel. It had provided themes for several seventeenth-century Italian oratorios, for one of Johann Kuhnau's biblical keyboard sonatas, for Purcell's dramatic *scena In Guilty Night*, focusing upon Saul's visit to the Witch of Endor, and for Charpentier's magnificent sacred opera *David et Jonathas*, written in 1688 for the students of the College Louis le Grand and featuring several fascinating though entirely coincidental parallels with Handel's treatment of the same material. Interestingly, Porpora had created a work using a related biblical story in his *Davide e Bersabea*, produced by the Opera of the Nobility in 1734, and it was perhaps this which prompted Jennens to turn to a similar subject for Handel.

A wealthy nonjuror who derived his income from the Birmingham iron foundries established by his grandfather, Charles Jennens lived partly at Gopsal, near Market Bosworth in Leicestershire, and in London, where his princely lifestyle was the theme of interested gossip. The Shakespearian scholar George Steevens, with whom Jennens later crossed swords, recalled that 'in his youth he was so remarkable for the number of his servants, the splendour of his equipages, and the profusion of his table, that from this excess of pomp he acquired the title of *Solyman the Magnificent* . . . so enamoured . . . was our *Magnifico* of pomp, that if this transit were only from Great Ormond-street, Bloomsbury, where he resided, to Mr Bowyer's, in Red Lion-passage, Fleet-street, he always travelled with four horses, and sometimes with as many servants behind his carriage. In his progress up the paved court, a footman usually preceded him, to kick oyster shells and other impediments out of his way.'

This aside, Jennens was a discerning and benevolent patron, whether in aiding his fellow nonjurors or in encouraging his friend Edward Holdsworth to send him the latest music from Italy, some of which, during the early years of their association, he lent to Handel. As the librettist of *Saul* and *Belshazzar* and the skilful compiler of *Messiah*, he contributed significantly to the superlative quality of all three works and we must certainly not dismiss his texts as being the mere hackwork characteristic of certain other poets upon whom Handel relied.

Saul remains without equal among the oratorios for the colour and variety of its incidents. As well as the king's jealous harrying of David, the narrative encompasses the romantic interest of the hero's relationships with Saul's daughters Merab and Michal, his friendship with Jonathan, the Macbeth-like consultation with the Witch of Endor, and the warfare between Israelites and Philistines. Yet Jennens prevents the drama from degenerating into a mere succession of crowded tableaux by using the dispassionate reflections of the chorus to offset the key moments of the story and by throwing the character of Saul himself into appropriate relief. It is emphatically his story rather than David's, even if his share in it is couched predominantly in recitative and arioso forms, as opposed to full-scale aria. This last feature relates directly to an understanding of the essentially incomplete nature of Saul's personal achievement, originally determined at the moment when he faltered at killing King Agag of the Amalekites and Samuel declared that 'the Lord hath rent the kingdom of Israel from thee this day, and hath given it to a neighbour of thine that is better than thou'.

Jennens and Handel seem to have appreciated the tragic flaws of envy and self-loathing intrinsic to such a character, though, as with all early eighteenth-century forays into the territory of classical drama, the atmosphere of *Saul* as a whole owes less to Euripides than to Racine. The king's *hamartia* is pointedly contrasted throughout with the unsullied excellence of David, who, though his relationship with Michal purges him of absolute priggishness, cannot be allowed to usurp Saul's dramatic prominence by being made the centre of too much sympathetic interest. This is further underlined by the vocal allocations: Saul is a darkly brooding bass of Verdian intensity, while David's countertenor reflects Handel's enduring associations of the timbre with youthful dignity, grace and kingly virtues.

It was a more stirring and colourful libretto than any he had ever set before or was to set again, and he matched it with music of extraordinary conviction and authority, whose abundance is overwhelming in a way unmatched by any other dramatic work in the European music of the period, with the same inclusive grandeur and assurance of gesture as are found in *Die Zauberflöte*, *Aida* and *Die Meistersinger*. Yet it is almost impossible to write calmly of so monumental an achievement. The scale of the overture alone, an expansive four-movement symphony based on a trio sonata, is enough to indicate the overall generosity of concept in the oratorio, and the choruses, whether in the glitter and revelry of the opening Epinicion, the relentlessly probing 'Envy, eldest born of Hell', ruminating fretfully above its ground bass, or the extended elegy over the dead of Mount Gilboa which crowns the work, consolidate upon what had been brought about in *Athalia* and prefigure the expressive sublimities of *Israel in Egypt*. Hardly a single one of the airs is without some individuality of design or instrumentation; they veer from the simple purity of David's 'Oh Lord, whose mercies numberless' or Jonathan's 'Sin not, oh King' to Merab's Pergolesian 'My soul rejects the thought' and the spectacularly mangled middle section of Saul's 'A Serpent in my bosom warm'd', where, after a mere three bars, the aria suddenly breaks off in a descending double octave as the king hurls his spear at his erstwhile protégé.

The work's most memorable moment constitutes a sequence which ought to be basic material in any study of dramatic music and which is without rivals or precedents in Baroque lyric drama. Saul's desperate recourse to the Witch of Endor and the ghost of Samuel caught at Handel's compassionate imagination to produce a scene which, as well as being eerie and baleful, reaches out to invoke our pity for the king in the agonized *accompagnato* recitative 'Wretch that I am', his aching loneliness best summarized in the heart-stabbing trill on the dotted quaver F for the violins in Saul's first address to Samuel. The Witch summons the dead prophet in a weird invocation whose grotesquerie is effected by laying a four-beat string figure across an irregular bass, interleaved with sustained oboe and bassoon chords, the whole piece measured in 3/4. These grisly bassoons, the Grecian ghosts from *Alexander's Feast*, introduce Samuel himself, a *basso profondo* inexorable and remote, with whom Saul is destined to plead in vain, and whose final pronouncement, closing all with shattering abruptness, is:

> Thou and thy sons shall be with me tomorrow,
> And Israel by Philistine arms shall fall.
> The Lord hath spoken; he will make it good.

Jennens, whose admiration for Handel's genius was tempered with a nagging desire to offer his own suggestions for its artistic refinement, criticized his use of a carillon for the Israelite rejoicings over Saul's thousands and David's ten thousands and his purchase of 'an organ of £500 price . . . he has bespoke of one Moss of Barnet. This organ, he says, is so constructed that as he sits at it he has a better command of his performers than he used to have, and he is highly delighted to think with what exactness his Oratorio will be performed by the help of this organ; so that for the future instead of beating time at his oratorios, he is to sit at the organ all the time with his back to the Audience.' Jennens dismissed both instruments as Handel's 'maggots' but each contributed to that opulence of orchestration which the composer lavished upon the work. To show off the organ he threw in a concertante movement in the middle of Act II, while the carillon, flourishing a little tune of marvellous banality for the Israelite women, enhances our sense of embarrassment as the enraged Saul writhes at the gleeful plaudits for David. Elsewhere in the score there are parts for two flutes, a harp, two trumpets, three trombones in both choral and instrumental numbers, besides the basic orchestra of oboes, bassoons and strings. At certain points, notably during the final chorus, the noise must have been even louder than that produced in the *Deborah* performances.

Saul, aided by 'general Applause by a numerous and splendid Audience' when the royal family attended the second night, met with a modest success and went on to become an established favourite among the dramatic oratorios, given six subsequent revivals by Handel himself. Lord Wentworth, pondering the composer's bold instrumental effects and the indifferent quality of the cast, was sceptical of its fate: 'I hear Mr Handell has borrow'd of the Duke of Argylle a pair of the largest kettledrums in the Tower, so to be sure it will be most excessive noisy with a bad set of singers; I doubt it will not retrieve his former losses.'

It did not, neither did a solitary revival of *Il Trionfo del Tempo* nor a proposal by Walsh to publish the Opus 5 trios by subscription, which met with no takers. 'Nothing shews the Worth of a People more, than their Taste for Publick Diversions', observed one member of 'a crowded Audience of the first Quality of a Nation', signing himself 'R.W.', at the third performance of the new oratorio *Israel in Egypt*. But he grossly over-estimated the enthusiasm: more to the point was Lord Shaftesbury's comment, made many years later, that Handel's season failed owing to 'his Singers in general not being Capital, nor the Town come into a relies of this Species of Musick'.

The first night audience for *Israel in Egypt*, on 4 April 1739, must indeed have been baffled by the overall character of the work presented to them. In its original form the oratorio consisted of three sections, beginning with the Funeral Anthem, adapted by the thrifty Handel as *Lamentations of the Israelites for the death of Joseph*, continuing with the sequence of plague choruses and ending with the Song of Moses from Exodus 15. The words of the second and third parts, making up the piece as we know it today, may have been selected by Jennens, but it is as likely that Handel, who piqued himself on his knowledge of scripture, prepared his own text and that the genesis of the work, as Dean and Streatfeild suggest, was probably an anthem, from which the composer developed the notion of a full-scale oratorio.

In any event the piece was choral to the almost total exclusion of solo numbers. There are four airs, two duets and some patches of recitative for tenor, whose relationship to the work was obviously based on that of a narrating Evangelist in a German passion. This last point is as significant as the inclusion of the Funeral Anthem, for what 'the Town' was actually hearing and noticeably failing to relish was a consolidation upon the achievement of the earlier work in exploiting the dramatic and evocative potential of the chorus, and a strengthening of those links with European sacred music renewed in *The Ways of Zion Do Mourn*.

However much he may have misread the audience's interest in the piece, 'R.W.' was intelligent enough to appreciate its singular nature, encapsulated in 'the Sublimity of the great Musical Poet's Imagination', and sensitive also to the special problems presented by *Israel in Egypt* to Georgian Protestant theatregoers. Admittedly success was hardly guaranteed by the apparent inadequacy of the choir, 'the many of his *Vocal Instruments*, which fall so vastly short in being able to do due Justice to what they are to perform', and the enormous length of the original work (Handel tried it with a couple of new organ concertos on 7 April and in a cut-down version on the 10th with Italian airs for Francesina) probably discouraged several listeners. But the main difficulty was one which, in various forms, has bedevilled Handel oratorio ever since, namely that singularly deep-rooted reaction against the use of the Bible for entertainment purposes.

He had come across it first in Italy, when Pope Clement had censured Prince Ruspoli for allowing Durastanti to take part in the première of *La Resurrezione*, and later in London, when Bishop Gibson had discouraged staged oratorio, and though he was never confronted with an absolute hostility from the public *en masse* there was a continuing barrage of criticism, often from the most unexpected sources, some of which must have reached his ears. We shall take note of these audience reactions in their proper place, but it is worth noting here that disapproval had already started building up during the *Esther* and *Athalia* performances in 1733. James Bramston's satire *The Man of Taste* cynically decreed that:

> The Stage should yield the Solemn Organ's note,
> And Scripture tremble in the Eunuch's throat.
> Let *Senesino* sing, what *David* writ,
> And *Hallelujahs* charm the pious pit

while Thomas Newcomb's Juvenalian *The Manners of the Age* asked:

> If sacred operas shall instruct us still,
> And churches empty, as ridotto's fill;
> The *Hebrew*, or the *German* leave the field,
> And *David*'s lyre to *Handel*'s spinnet yield.

Thus we can detect a defensive note in 'R.W.'s' claim that 'the Theatre on this occasion, ought to be enter'd with more Solemnity than a Church; inasmuch, as the Entertainment you go to is really in itself the noblest Adoration and Homage paid to the Deity that ever was in one. So sublime an Act of Devotion as this *Representation* carries in it . . . would consecrate even Hell itself.' An anonymous correspondent in the *London Evening Post* suggested that the fate of *Israel in Egypt* was in question from the start, owing merely to its title, let alone to the text itself.

Nothing rescued the oratorio from oblivion during Handel's lifetime. He seldom revived it, and its popularity only began with the mushroom growth of choral societies during the Victorian era. Since then the work has become an established Handelian favourite, one of the handful of his vocal works which gets a frequent hearing. As performed today, it is given without the Funeral Anthem, and those shifts in taste and practice which have contributed so much to our appreciation of Handel since the turn of the century have never sought to restore this original beginning. The public has, as it were, decided on the composer's behalf, a decision, unlike that which for so long deprived us of the closing numbers of *Alexander's Feast*, justifiable in the light of the oratorio's unique design.

Choral writing in any age has rarely achieved such a pitch of expressive intensity. So dedicated was Handel to the fullest possible exploitation of his medium that he cast the majority of choruses in eight parts, thereby heightening effects of mass and contrast. The ten plagues of Egypt were scarcely promising material for him (potentially the most bathetic moment in his entire *oeuvre* is afforded by an alto aria complete with hopping violins, which deals with the frogs and the cattle murrain and requires the soloist to repeat the words 'blotches and blains') yet out of these he fashioned an audacious sequence of descriptive choruses, imposing a tonal unity by a predominance of flat keys (G minor, B flat, E flat) and a return at the close of Part I to the C minor of the opening. A gawky, stooping chromatic fugue subject, rather like the 'royal theme' of Bach's *Musical Offering*, conveys the Egyptians' disgust at drinking the blood-laced Nile water, shimmering demisemiquavers portray the buzz-ing flies, the storms of hail and fire begin with the first pattering drops as the downpour gets underway, the darkness fragments the vocal lines in spectral semibreves before they bind once again in the slashing, percussive 'He smote all the first-born of Egypt' and the Israelites are 'led forth like sheep' in radiant pastoral complete with drones and pipes.

A comparable firmness of design controls Part II, framing its paeans of triumph between the two colossal C major outbursts of Moses and

Miriam, scored for double choir, three trombones, two trumpets, wind, strings and timpani. Monotony in the praise of God, of a sort which all too easily clouds works like *Joshua* and *The Occasional Oratorio*, is avoided here by the continuing flexibility with which Handel manipulates his forces. Nowhere is this better shown than in the sequence dovetailing the serene 'The depths have covered them' with 'Thy right hand, o Lord, is become glorious', a farouche war-dance, blending in its turn with the ascetic fugato of 'Thou sentest forth thy wrath' and the whirling rhythms of 'And with the blast of thy nostrils'. The key, however, to the significance of the whole work, as an essay in interpreting the relationship between man and God, comes not at moments like these, but in 'The people shall hear'. This is arguably the finest chorus he ever wrote, its sombre evocations of fear ushered in by those dotted quaver patterns forming one of his favourite rhythmic foundations, and sweeping us into a series of amply-developed episodes, as the dark mass of jagged chords dissolves on the words 'all the inhabitants of Canaan shall melt away' and the three *a capella* bars 'they shall be as still as a stone' introduce the sinewy harmonies illustrating the Israelites' wanderings through their regained land.

Israel in Egypt is in every sense Handel's most allusive work, a piece in which he takes stock of an entire musical heritage and at several points consciously recalls the voices and idioms of the past. As in *Saul* the feeling of archaic grandeur is emphasized by the use, in various numbers, of three trombones, whose timbre immediately recalls the musical world of Schütz and Monteverdi, and fugues like 'And I will exalt him' and 'And the earth swallowed them', each with a heavy chordal introduction, carry us back even further, towards Hassler and the Gabrielis. The thematically independent orchestral ritornellos ending 'And with the blast' and the Plague of Flies are a device more familiar in the context of early Venetian opera.

Not all of this is simply respectful imitation, for the work is famous for containing more borrowings from other composers than practically anything else in the Handel canon. Why did Handel, here and elsewhere, borrow and adapt? He was not the only Baroque composer to do so — an entire book has been devoted to Bach's forays of this kind — and the practice has certainly not been limited to that period alone. Yet since the intense nineteenth-century interest in Handel was concurrent with the growth of musicological study of manuscript holdings in the libraries of Europe, it was inevitable that he should be among the first to be tarred with the brush and that the notoriety should well and truly stick to him.

The post-romantic concept of the importance of total originality in an artist's work was not something which plagued Baroque composers. Like the improvements made by Tate and Garrick to Shakespeare, Bentley to Milton or Hawksmoor to Westminster Abbey, the liberty to alter and adjust a piece of music was taken for granted, to the extent that works such as Durante's chamber duets, which are free paraphrases of extracts from recitatives by Alessandro Scarlatti, were justly admired in their own right. In the theatre it was common practice until well into the following century to transplant arias from other operas, whether acknowledged or otherwise, to meet the particular demands of an individual performance. An age which extolled imitation could permit and encourage adaptation, unless, like Bononcini with Lotti's 'In una siepe ombrosa', the musician actually attempted to pass off the piece as his own.

There is no evidence that Handel ever did this, or, on the other hand, that he was forced to. His borrowing habit was certainly known: Mattheson had drawn attention to it in respect of his work as early as 1722 and some two decades later Johann Adolph Scheibe was to describe the composer as 'many times developing not his own thoughts but those of others'. Perhaps the most exasperated comment came from Jennens in 1743, who wrote to Holdsworth acknowledging a fresh parcel of music and telling him that 'Handel has borrowed a dozen of the Pieces & I dare say I shall catch him stealing from them; as I have formerly, both from Scarlatti & Vinci. . .'. If Jennens's tone suggests some expectation of guilt on the composer's part when caught red-handed lifting airs and recitatives, it also reveals the gulf between a professional musician, using every means at his disposal to make a living, and a dilettante amateur with the leisure in which to be scrupulous.

So far from being embarrassed in his thefts, Handel could have drawn Jennens's attention to innumerable other examples of the practice, many of them by composers the squire of Gopsal most admired. Holdsworth, what is more, could have told him that it was a commonplace in the Venetian operatic world: five years before the letter just quoted, for instance, Vivaldi's *Rosmira* had featured an aria drawn from Handel's *Ezio*. Fresh evidence continues to emerge of Bach's indulgence in the habit, a fact which, given the uncritical piety which continues to surround our appreciation of him, ought to go far towards vindicating Handel. The whole issue is one of 'Let him who is without sin among you cast the first stone', and underlines the need for a radical reappraisal of the nature of the European musical community during the period.

In Handel's case what must be emphasized is that in practically every instance so far noted the borrowing is either a free paraphrase or the germ of a musical idea and invariably an improvement on its original. He is seldom if ever content to leave the existing construction as it stands without amplifying its melodic and harmonic outlines and using these as a launching pad for his own invention. Certain examples have become famous among Handelians: the six masses in František Habermann's *Philomela Pia* collection of 1747 provided source material for some of the best numbers in *Jephtha* and *Theodora*, while Telemann's *Tafelmusik* (1733, with Handel among the subscribers) was another useful mine. Elsewhere he made use of works by Stradella, Kerll and Krieger and of the chamber duets of Giovanni Maria Clari, whose neutral orthodoxies of design made them perfect raw material for experiment. In one or two cases over-zealous allusion-hunting has produced sources of which Handel was probably unaware. The suggestion of a theme from a canzona in Kerll's *Toccates & Suites Pour le Clavessin* as the basis of 'Let all the angels of God' in *Messiah* overlooks the essential ordinariness of the fugue subject, a Baroque commonplace which might as easily have been one of Handel's juvenile exercises and whose similarity to Kerll's is surely coincidental.

Naturally the biggest quarry for Handel's musical ideas lies in his own work: material was there to be re-used, fresh solutions were to be found by employing old formulas, and his continuously lively, forceful imagination reached back into the resources of a rich experience. This is nothing unusual. What in the end surprises is his constant reliance on other composers' works, something which research goes on disclosing as an essential element of his creativity.

Yet interestingly the volume of borrowing is at its fullest during these years of failure immediately preceding Handel's departure for Ireland in 1741. We can discount the implication that this was due to a nervous breakdown: there is no substantial evidence for it. What seems much more likely is that at this time a gruelling programme of compositional work (a far cry from the two operas a year of the old Academy days) was taking place concurrently with a major stylistic reappraisal, in which he was busy surveying an extensive range of music both past and present. Thus a work fraught with antique gravity and 'science' like *Israel in Egypt* can exist side by side with the resonantly modern *Imeneo*. At any rate, we cannot examine the works of 1738–41 without feeling that something wholly enthralling is going on within the context of their relationship to one another.

Recourse to a pasticcio *Giove in Argo*, using a text from one of Lotti's

Dresden operas, did nothing to recapture the public which had spurned *Israel*, and Handel's King's Theatre season closed prematurely in the first week of May 1739. We know little or nothing of his activities during the summer, though there was no doubt a visit or two paid to country friends like Sir Wyndham Knatchbull, James Harris or Lord Shaftesbury and perhaps a trip to Bath or Tunbridge. By late September he was back at work, fortified the following month by canny John Walsh's new royal copyright. 'Whereas *George Frederick Handel*, of the Parish of *St George the Martyr Hanover Square*, in our County of *Middlesex*, Esq; hath humbly represented unto Us, that he hath with great Labour and Expence composed several Works consisting of Vocal and Instrumental Musick, and hath authorised and appointed *John Walsh* of the Parish of *St Mary le Strand*, in our said County of Middlesex, to print and publish the same; and hath therefore humbly besought us to grant Our Royal Privilege and Licence to the said *John Walsh* for the sole Engraving, Printing and Publishing the said Works for the Term of Fourteen Years; We being willing to give all due Encouragement to Works of this Nature, are graciously pleased to condescend to his Request. . . . '

November ushered in the hardest winter England had known for a decade, the worst, some claimed, in living memory. The Thames, above and below London Bridge, became choked with pack-ice and the river was full of stranded ships, wrecked lighters and wherries and the sinister flotsam of corpses of those who had drowned while trying to save cargoes or guide their vessels through the floes. The ducks left St James's Park and people dropped dead of cold in the streets. In the new year the river froze over entirely and during the ensuing frost fair a Mr Cunningham of Fulham galloped a horse along the ice to Hammersmith and back again in three quarters of an hour for a 20 guinea wager. But of course all this can have been nothing new for the Princess Sherbatoff, 'Spouse to the *Russian* Minister Plenipotentiary', who 'appears at Court in a *Russian* Habit, *viz.* a Robe of Ermine and Furr, with a Sable Tippet, being the *Winter* Dress of that Country'.

Advertisements for Handel's new season included the assurance that 'Particular Preparations are making to keep the House warm; and the Passage from the Fields to the House will be cover'd for better Conveniency'. He had left the Haymarket, or had not been asked to return owing to his recent box office failures, and now hired Lincoln's Inn Fields Theatre from John Rich. Rich managed it in tandem with his newer enterprise at Covent Garden and the actors and dancers in his company were sometimes expected to take part in performances at both theatres on the same night. Handsomely restored in 1714, its stage lighting enhanced by the use of looking glasses and with a *trompe-l'oeil* design over the pit showing 'Shakespeare, Johnson, & c. . . . in conference with Betterton', its seating capacity of approximately 1,400 was more or less equivalent to Covent Garden's.

The opening concert, featuring *Alexander's Feast* and two of Handel's new string concertos, took place on 22 November, St Cecilia's Day, and began appropriately with a freshly-composed setting of Dryden's *A Song for St Cecilia's Day*, intended, no doubt, as a kind of illustrative pendant similar to those created for the longer work at its first performance by *Cecilia, volgi uno aguardo* and the *Alexander's Feast Concerto*. In attempting Dryden's poem Handel must have been aware, as with *Alexander's Feast*, that he was tackling a modern classic, accorded the highest contemporary regard as a formative influence upon the writers of the age. The interest of each composition would have lain less obviously in his music alone than in the marriage of his talents to Dryden's admired achievement. Not for nothing would Charles Avison, one of his sterner critics, later compare the two. 'Mr Handel is in Music,' he wrote 'what his own Dryden was in Poetry; nervous, exalted and harmonious; but voluminous, and, consequently, not always correct. Their Abilities equal to every Thing; their Execution frequently inferior. Born with Genius capable of soaring the boldest Flights; they have sometimes, to suit the vitiated Taste of the Age they lived in, descended to the lowest. . . . '

The poem is a gift to the imaginative composer, and Handel ignores none of its hints or nuances. Apart from the more obvious illustrations, the soft complaining flute, the trumpet's loud clangour, the sacred organ, solo 'cello divisions for Jubal striking the corded shell, and strings in A major for 'sharp violins', he is at pains to bring out in subtler ways the all-pervading, god-given power of music which the ode asserts. The structure of the opening recitative and chorus imitates Dryden's vision of harmony resolving chaos and finding its ultimate fulfilment in the image of man himself. In the closing 'Grand Chorus' Handel includes, as a kind of professional signature, a striking harmonic flourish in which modulation becomes a positive *coup de théâtre*. To heighten the dramatic element even further, the soloists (in the first performance those redoubtable Handelians Beard and Francesina) take on the role of evangelist narrator and angelic visionary, the soprano tessitura kept ethereally high, perhaps taking its cue from 'Sing ye to the Lord' in *Israel in Egypt*.

War-fever, quite as strong as the cold weather, gripped London and must have diverted much popular attention from Lincoln's Inn Fields concerts. Fury at Spain's failure to honour the financial terms of the Treaty of Madrid, made some eighteen years previously, was incensed still further by her high-handed behaviour towards the English merchants and their ships, and vulgar patriotic sabre-rattling was stirred up by Lord Gage's angry remonstrance to the House of Lords in July and by Captain Jenkins's production of a shrivelled human ear, said to be his own, as a proof of Spanish atrocity. The War of Jenkins's Ear began in earnest during the autumn, and the dashing exploits of the aptly-named Nicholas Haddock, commanding the Mediterranean fleet, monopolized everybody's interest. A disgusted Richard West wrote to Horace Walpole: 'Plays we have none, or damned ones. Handel has had a concerto this winter. No opera, no nothing. All for war and Admiral Haddock'.

A British Sixpence

During that troubled autumn of 1739 Handel had been at work on a series of twelve string *concerti grossi*, his Opus 6, ten of which were to be given their premières during the forthcoming season. With typically feverish energy he completed the entire set in the space of one month, beginning number 1 in G on 29 September and dating the last, subsequently issued as number 11, 30 October, Walsh having already proposed a subscription for '*Twelve Grand Concerto's*, in Seven Parts, for four Violins, a Tenor, a Violoncello, with a Thorough-Bass for the Harpsichord. Compos'd by Mr Handel.' Publication was held over, for obvious reasons, until near the season's close, and 100 subscribers, including most of the royal family (King George and the Waleses were significantly absent), Jennens, Tyers, Rich and a host of country music societies, among them the 'Ladies Concert in Lincoln', took 122 copies.

It was no more than a respectable subscription list — there were fewer takers than for *Arminio* or *Giustino* two years earlier, for instance — and any hopes on Handel's part for a spectacular commercial success must inevitably have been disappointed. Yet the concertos made their mark, appealing as they must to the already well-established English taste for the sort of music which emphasized ensemble playing and orchestral groups rather than exhibition solo performance.

Unlike the organ concertos, the *concerti grossi* were heirs to a solid tradition, but it would be wrong to suppose that there is anything especially traditional in Handel's approach to composing them or that they mark a *terminus ad quem* in the history of English instrumental music. Though it is true that the framework of these pieces is on the lines provided earlier in the century by Giuseppe Torelli and Arcangelo Corelli as 'the model of grand concertos for a numerous band' and sedulously followed by writers for the English market, they are far less specifically Corellian than those of the popular London concert violinists such as Geminiani, Castrucci and Festing, at whose recently published sets

Handel seems to have had a glance before embarking on his own. Nor did Opus 6 stop this particular style dead in its tracks. Far from doing so, it inspired a crop of respectable imitations among English masters, Stanley, Avison, Alcock and others, as well as being followed up in the succeeding years of the decade by collections from Locatelli, Geminiani and Sammartini.

Handel would have been well aware of the continental penchant for the newer three-movement Venetian layout so brilliantly developed by Vivaldi, yet something more than a mere wish to please the Lincoln ladies or the 'Monday Night Musical Society at ye Globe Tavern' must have inspired his choice of the Corellian model, in which a variety of movements in differing tempi and styles, mingling the idioms of church and stage, allowed him the free exercise of his mercurial genius. For the success of Opus 6, which stands beside Bach's Brandenburgs and Vivaldi's great string sets at the summit of all achievement in the genre, lies in the remarkable consistency of its refusal to compromise with received ideas of 'correctness' and 'kinds' in musical form. Both the consistency and the refusal are fundamentally Handelian. Rather than imitate Corelli, Albinoni, Georg Muffat or Telemann, he absorbs the characteristic manner of each, mixing it with his own virtuoso treatment of the various forms and styles.

None of the twelve repeats the pattern of another or seeks, in refurbishing ideas from the operas, oratorios and keyboard pieces, merely to capitalize on the success of an already valid formula. Number 5, for example, bases three of its six movements on the overture to the *Ode for St Cecilia's Day*, but here Handel, seldom content to let his concepts gather moss, tacks on a theatrical two-and-a-half-bar flourish to the opening and makes certain other small but subtle alterations to the plan of the other two, almost as if to say 'you only *thought* you had heard these before'. He uses them, what is more, as a frame within which to present three fresh pieces, a delightful *presto*, like a little air in a Neapolitan *opera buffa*, a B minor *largo*, a sobering hand upon earlier jauntiness, with interlocking voices hankering for a resolution, and a robust Vivaldian *allegro* poised upon a vigorous bass line.

The entire set is permeated by that tender lyricism which never deserted Handel. We are unlikely to reject its appeal to us in the stately tread of number 4's opening *larghetto* or in the justly famous E major air with variation in number 12, but the eighth concerto, which few would claim as a masterpiece, wins with the listener precisely through this gentle intimacy, permeating the wistful melodies of the *allemande* and the romantic *siciliano*, its textures thickened by rapturous contrapuntal embellishment on first and second violins.

The essential Handelian wit, which renders him a true contemporary of Pope and Swift and which made Wagner, after playing through *Alexander's Feast*, describe him, with grudging admiration, as 'the Rossini of his day', is always present. There is something positively roguish, for example, about the opening of the fugue subject in the *allegro* of number 7 or the incongruous irruption of birdsong into the sedate dotted beginning of number II. Related to this is the airy, protean sleight-of-hand with which he switches from one idiom to another, indulging in that favourite Baroque musical pastime of contrasting national styles. The Englishness of the gigue in the ninth concerto spills over into the bluff little 20-bar movement of the tenth. The passagework of the first *allegro* in number 12 is authentically Italian, while the edgy, dotted zigzags of its closing fugue take us back to the organ loft of the Liebfrauenkirche at Halle. Wilder shores are visited in the peasant *musette* of number 6, and the third concerto's boisterous polonaise (a rhythm Handel explored again in the English hornpipe 'Now love, that everlasting boy' in *Semele*) shows a touch or two of his friend Telemann's penchant for Polish and Moravian dance measures.

The significance of Opus 6 in relation to the rest of Handel's work as one of the most easily accessible means of examining his interests and methods as a composer cannot be too highly estimated. There is a wealth of tuneful and accomplished English instrumental music of this period, much of it lying all too easily neglected in the long Handelian shadow, but none of it matches these concertos in their encyclopaedic inventiveness, that sense of spontaneous, improvisatory compilation with which Handel so loves to astound us. The noblest of all tributes to the work, that by Arthur Hutchings in *The Baroque Concerto*, is worth reproducing here:

Those who know it by heart carry with them a perennial source of joy and wonder — joy because no scores of the period, not even Rameau's, are so exquisitely sensuous within the bounds of strength and sanity, and wonder because organic form, the fulfilment of great ideas in great style, is the most wonderful phenomenon both of the natural order and also of that order in which a divine hand is withdrawn so that the creature may share the experience of creation. How lavish a bounty is showered on the few from whom not even the perfection of form is withheld! — How much is denied to an artist who received a second share of endowments! A hundred years of orchestras, fifty years of concertos, the pains of living and working to perform and compose them well — all would have been justified if every one were lost, provided that we still had the Great Twelve. 'There is the truth.'

Two at least of the concertos were featured in the new vocal work Handel brought on at the end of February 1740. It was a setting of cleverly alternated extracts from Milton's *L'Allegro and Il Penseroso*, the text prepared by Jennens, who, apparently at the composer's request, added a third part extolling the virtues of a temperate mean between mirth and melancholy, entitled *Il Moderato*. As an educated man, with a good reading knowledge of five languages, Handel may have known both poems already, but the impulse to set them to music was no doubt prompted by the success of Thomas Arne's *Comus*, given at Drury Lane in 1738. The fresh, unaffected Englishness of Arne's adaptation, which quickly became one of the most successful works of its age, made due impact on Handel, and Burney was later to point out its significance for our national music as a whole. 'In this masque [Arne] introduced a light, airy, original, and pleasing melody, wholly different from that of Purcell or Handel, whom all English composers had hitherto pillaged or imitated. Indeed, the melody of Arne at this time, and of his Vauxhall songs afterwards, forms an aera in English music; it was so easy, natural and agreeable to the whole kingdom, that it had an effect upon our national taste . . . it was the standard of all perfection at our theatres and public gardens.'

L'Allegro is Handel's most fundamentally English creation, a companion piece to Gainsborough's rustic scenes, to Kent's incomparable garden at Rousham, to the landscape poetry of Cowper and Thomson, distilling the rural moment in a series of intensely observed vignettes and matching better-known musical instances like Haydn's *Seasons* and Beethoven's 6th Symphony. The pastoral vision is no longer that of the decorative nymphs and swains in the first part of *Acis and Galatea* but a far more localized world created initially by the wealth of detail in Milton's two poems and carried over into Handel's own experience of the countryside as a man whose imagination was fully attuned to the romantic sensibilities of the age. It is still an idealized picture, yet neither its sincerity nor its authenticity are ever in doubt. Within its lyrical, rapturous perspectives lies the consummation of that love of nature which permeates the operas — at the beginning of *Serse*, for instance, in the garden scenes of *Ariodante* or in the delicious peasant strains introducing Antigona in *Admeto* — and breaks into *Acis* with the appearance of that genuine hobbinoll Polyphemus.

233

The English sound reverberates throughout the score. We hear it in 'Mirth, admit me of thy Crew', the bass hunting song with horn obbligato, the little air with carillon 'Or let the merry bells ring round' which develops into a lively jig, and in the accompanied recitative 'Mountains on whose barren breast'. It tinges the nightingale aria 'Sweet bird' (well known to opera addicts as a Melba lollipop) and characterizes with pointed artlessness the tenor's 'Haste thee, nymph', of which the singer Michael Kelly wrote: 'I laughed all through it, as I conceived it ought to be sung, and as must have been the intentions of the composer: the infection ran; and their Majesties (George III and Queen Charlotte) and the whole audience, as well as the orchestra, were in a roar of laughter. . . '.

Yet, graphically pictorial as the whole piece is, from the bellman's 'Past ten o'clock' on the strings in 'Far from all resort of mirth' to the distant curfew chime in 'Oft on a plat of rising ground', it is never banal. Recent performance has tended to obscure the complexity of Handel's viewpoint by ignoring the crucial contrast created so skilfully for him by Jennens's alternation of merriment and pensiveness, preferring to detach *Allegro* from *Penseroso* completely. In some sense they have compensated by reviving the *Moderato* numbers which the mistaken good taste of hyper-literate England has suppressed. Without *Moderato*, whose text, though hardly Milton, is decent enough, we cannot fully appreciate the design and intention of the work in its eighteenth-century context. We lose in any case some fine music, including a single number which bids fair to be considered the most beautiful thing Handel ever composed, the duet 'As steals the morn upon the night'. Of its oboe and bassoon dialogue, the fluid vocal lines and the sinewy grace with which the harmonies evoke the dawning light of reason it is needless to write in praise.

Some years after the first performance, however, Henry Fielding noted in the *Covent Garden Journal* that 'when Mr Handel first exhibited his Allegro and Penseroso, there were two ingenious Gentlemen who had bought a Book of the Words, and thought to divert themselves by reading it before the Performance began. *Zounds* (cried one of them) *what damn'd Stuff this is!* — *Damn'd Stuff indeed*, replied his Friend. *God so*! (replied the other, who then first cast his Eyes on the Title-Page) *the Words are Milton's.*' Perhaps they were looking at *Il Moderato*, of which Jennens later wrote to Holdsworth that 'I overheard one in the Theatre saying it was Moderato indeed, & the Wits at Tom's Coffee House honour'd it with the name of Moderatissimo'.

Though this offending third part was soon to be dropped, the work kept its place throughout the century as a popular favourite during oratorio seasons, and the critic Joseph Warton even went so far as to suggest that it was thanks to Handel that the Milton poems had reached a wider public. William Hayes, that doughty Oxford champion of the composer, put it best when he wrote: 'For is there not a Scene which MILTON describes, were CLAUDE LORRAIN or POUSSIN to paint, could possibly appear in more lively Colours, or give a truer Idea of it, than our GREAT MUSICIAN has by his *pictoresque* Arrangement of musical Sounds; with this Advantage, that his Pictures *speak*.'

That first Lincoln's Inn Fields season revived *Saul*, *Acis* and *Esther*, but the unknown 'G.O.'s verses in the *Gentleman's Magazine*, describing Handel filling 'a thousand tubes with voice' and featuring the apposite line

> To form thee, talent, travel, art, combine

also asked why British audiences paid more attention to inferior musicians. Johann Mattheson, publishing his *Grundlage Einer Ehren-Pforte* that year, implied that Handel was currently suffering neglect at a time 'when the Court and Nobility, indeed the whole nation, have been more intent on the harmful war than on plays and entertainments' and querulously berated the composer for forgetting their ancient friendship so far as not to send him an autobiographical sketch for inclusion in the book.

The first of the new operas, brought on in November 1740, was begun two years earlier but only prepared for performance the previous month. *Imeneo*, one of the shortest of Handel's stage works, was set to a libretto by Stampiglia originally designed (hence the allusion of the hero's name) for a wedding opera, composed by Porpora in Naples. The cast of this had included Annibale Fabbri in the role of Argenio (a bass in Handel's version) so perhaps this was how he came to know the text.

Like Stampiglia's *Partenope*, and no doubt interesting to him for similar reasons, the story is a romantic comedy in a classical setting. The plot is of the simplest, concerning the love of Tirinto and Imeneo for Rosmene. She eventually chooses Imeneo, but the triumph of duty is somewhat muted and her closing duet with Tirinto in the 1742 Dublin revival ('Per le porte del tormento', no less) with its reminder that 'there is no rose without a thorn', seems to imply that though she really loves him they had better make the best of it.

The score has a lightness and certainty of handling which show the composer developing that vein of sophisticated wit which sends such a powerful undercurrent through the operas from *Agrippina* onwards. Like those of *Serse*, its airs demand the appreciation of a livelier audience than London could then offer, and Rosmene's 'In mezzo a voi due' or her sister Clomiri's 'E si vaga del tuo bene' show us that Handel, even if he had paid a last visit to Italy a decade before, had never lost touch with its spirit. Tirinto's 'Sorge nell'alma mia' has the same self-mocking heroic loftiness as Serse's 'Piu che penso', but the ultimate proof of Handel's control of his resources, that synthesis of music and drama which guarantees his operatic mastery, lies in the trio which closes Act II. Rosmene's wavering between her suitors is answered by their heartfelt pleas, and the varying dialogue is mirrored in the continuing shifts of orchestra balance in the accompaniment. The force of such artistry has made itself felt in our own day, even if eighteenth-century London failed to appreciate 'the operetta of Hymen', as an early advertisement appropriately called it.

Imeneo failed, as Handel must have guessed it might. The presence of a new castrato, Andreoni, and of the English soprano, Miss Edwards, was no sort of a draw, and the single repeat performance following the première on 22 November had to be postponed because Francesina was ill. Nothing daunted, Handel pressed ahead with a new opera, *Deidamia*, finished in November and brought on in the new year of 1741. Given only three performances this too was a flop, and with it the composer took his leave of the stage for good.

Ironically the work reunited him with Paolo Antonio Rolli, presumably willing to bury his dislike of '*l'Uomo*' and to make an honest penny by turning out a passable *melodrama* with comically equivocal overtones from the story of the youthful Achilles concealed on Scyros in female disguise by his anxious mother, Thetis. The element of sexual ambiguity in the tale, with the fledgling hero's masculinity declaring itself *malgré tout* when shown some weapons by the wily Ulysses, made it a favourite with Baroque painters and poets. Several librettists, including Metastasio, had already produced versions of the Grecian legend by the time Rolli set his hand to it, but the text of *Deidamia* is more pointedly witty than any of these and seems to catch fire from Stampiglia. Perhaps this is how Handel wanted it: at any rate it is interesting that his last three operas all show a trend towards a lighter manner, and that *Deidamia* sometimes seems like an amused rejection of the grandiose postures of the Senesino and Cuzzoni era.

The plot and characters, among them a wonderfully brash and innocent Achilles (sung, it should be noted, by a woman), a contrasted pair of heroines, the *ingénue* Deidamia and a soubrette part for Nerea, and the skilfully drawn castrato role of Ulysses, ought to have made this one of

Handel's liveliest dramatic works. Yet a glance at the score suggests that *Deidamia* is not an especially notable farewell to the lyric theatre and that the public verdict on it, whatever the causes, may for once have been justified. Much of the writing is jejune and indicative of hurry and fatigue. What are we to make, for instance, of an air like Ulisse's 'No, quella belta non amo', which might decently pass muster in any jobbing Italian opera of the day, but will scarcely answer our expectations of the mature Handel in its mechanical semiquaver sequences? In certain numbers he seems almost to be guying the modern style by underlining its direst trivialities, while others, like Deidamia's 'Se il timore', are a case of the-mixture-as-before, shamelessly dusting down well-tried clichés. No wonder Burney thought the whole thing 'languid and antique'.

Perhaps Handel, returning after so momentous a break, was browned off with opera, but the sparkle of *Imeneo* gives the lie to that. We can never know precisely why he abandoned the struggle for good, though there were plenty of contributory reasons. It is easy to imagine his exasperation at the public's indifference, during what was probably the least successful season of his entire London career. Had there, perhaps, been a fresh Senesino or Caffarelli or a young Faustina in the offing, had Sallé danced or Mr Worman contrived a few special firework effects, the takings might have kept *Deidamia* in being. As it was, the new soprano, Monza, failed to please even the charitable Mrs Delany: 'Her voice is between Cuzzoni's and Strada's — strong, but not harsh, her person *miserably bad*, being very low, and *excessively crooked*.'

There were always enemies to bring him down. Ever since his Haymarket ascendancy in the 1720s he had known opposition, and his famously short temper and peremptory manner with singers and instrumentalists cannot have endeared him to those who preferred wheedling and flattery to an insistence on solid musical standards. Unfortunately, despite the various examples of his having given offence during his London career, we know practically nothing of the actual nature of the quarrel. Who, for example, were the writer and the objects of the unsigned letter to Catherine Collingwood, dated 27 December 1734, among the Throckmorton papers, which says: 'I don't pity Handell in the least, for I hope this mortification will make him a human creature; for I am sure before he was no better than a brute, when he could treat civilized people with so much brutality as I know he has done'? And what was the mysterious 'single Disgust . . . a *faux Pas* made, but not meant', referred to by 'J.B.' in the *London Daily Post* for 4 April 1741? This extended defence of Handel constitutes a magnificent appeal to our sense of national honour in according better treatment to the great man in our midst. 'If we are not careful for him,' says J.B., 'let us be for our own long-possessed Credit and Character in the polite World . . . if even such a Pride has offended, let us take it as the natural Foible of the great Genius, and let us overlook them like Spots upon the Sun. . . . ' Those who had taken umbrage apparently sought to sabotage his concert nights even by ripping his advertisements off the walls. The letter closes with a heartfelt plea to Londoners not to turn their backs on him, and voices the fear that he was preparing to leave England for good.

No one seemed to know exactly what he planned to do. Lord Egmont, who went to *Allegro and Penseroso* on the last night of the season, thought he was 'intending to go to Spa in Germany', but in July Dr Dampier, bear-leader to milords on the continent and an acquaintance of Handel's, wrote to friends in Geneva, not long after returning to England, indicating that the composer was still in London. In the summer Handel had taken up writing Italian duets, as in Hanover days, though it is not clear whether these were merely musical exercises or written for some specific singers and occasions. But Dampier's letter also implies that he had refused offers of participation in Lord Middlesex's new opera venture, set on foot at the King's Theatre during the autumn and clearly, to Handel's practised eye, destined to the kind of expensive disaster recipe familiar from the 1730s: 'the men of penetration give hints that his Lordship's sole aim is to make his mistress, the Muscovita, appear to great advantage on the stage'. Horace Walpole was an interested party, through his amorous penchant for Henry Seymour Conway, one of the directors, and wrote anxiously to Sir Horace Mann about 'the improbability of eight young thoughtless men of fashion understanding economy'. Handel went to the opening night on 31 October, a pasticcio *Alessandro in Persia*, arranged from the latest Italian successes by Hasse, Pescetti, Lampugnani and others, which, as he afterwards told Jennens, 'made me very merry all along my journey'. A few days later he set off for Ireland.

His invitation to Dublin came from William, third Duke of Devonshire, who had succeeded Lord Middlesex's father, the Duke of Dorset, as Lord Lieutenant of Ireland in 1737. Horace Walpole described him and his son the Marquis of Hartington as 'the fashionable models of goodness, though if it were necessary for the good man to be perfect like the Stoic's wise man, their want of sense and generosity would have rendered their titles disputable . . . The Duke's outside was unpolished, his inside unpolishable. He loved gaming, drinking, and the ugliest woman in England, his Duchess. . . . ' Seeing him taking office under Sir

Robert Walpole in 1731, Lord Egmont was reminded of Caligula's horse being made a consul. But his viceroyalty, continuing Dorset's benign and sensitive administration of the kingdom, showed him to be far from coarse or stupid. One historian called him 'the most magnificent of the viceroys of this kingdom since the time of the great Ormond; for he expended his private revenue not only in a splendid stile of living, but also in works of public utility'. The request made to Handel, whom he may have met at Aachen or Tunbridge as a fellow spa-fancier, touched on both aspects. It was a feather in Dublin's cap to acquire one of the leading masters of the age and it was a distinct asset to the wealth of charitable enterprises which characterized the life of the city.

Handel's route to the coast took him through Cheshire, where he may have visited his friend Charles Legh at Adlington, whose splendid timber-framed mansion between Wilmslow and Prestbury still contains the organ in the gallery on which the composer is said to have played. Legh, an ardent Handelian, later published a hunting song 'The morning is charming' in the *Gentleman's Magazine* which included the lines:

> See, see where she goes, and the hounds have a view,
> Such harmony *Handel* himself never knew

originally set by Ridley, the Prestbury organist. Handel presented his own setting to Legh in 1751 and it was subsequently incorporated in Stanley's dramatic pastoral *Arcadia*. Did Handel recall that other occasion, 40 years before at Rome, when he had put his own name to music in the 'old fool' Cardinal Pamphilj's cantata?

It was customary to board the Irish packet boats at Parkgate on the Dee, then still navigable though silting up apace. A new quay allowed ships of up to 350 tons to anchor alongside and the place was developing as a fashionable seaside resort. Dr and Mrs Delany, taking ship in 1754, found it so crowded that they only just managed to get the last bed, but they, like everyone else, had to await a favourable wind. So, of course, did Handel, who now found himself delayed for several days and spent them profitably at Chester, where he stayed at the Falcon in Northgate Street. Someone who saw him for the first time here was the young Charles Burney. 'I was at the Public-school,' he later recalled ' . . . and very well remember seeing him smoke a pipe, over a dish of coffee, at the Exchange-Coffee-house; for being extremely curious to see so extraordinary a man, I watched him narrowly as long as he remained in Chester. . . . ' Burney's music master Edmund Baker, the cathedral organist, rustled up a scratch choir to try out some of Handel's new choruses for him, but one of them, a printer named Janson, proved sadly inadequate to the task. 'Handel let loose his great bear upon him; and after swearing in four or five languages, cried out in broken English: "You shcauntrel! Tit you not dell me dat you could sing at soite?" "Yes, sir," says the printer, "and so I can, but not at *first sight*."'

The Parkgate to Dublin crossing, taking fourteen hours with a fair wind, was notoriously perilous, and the four weekly packets were manned by an exiguous crew of a master, three sailors and a boy. Handel reached Ireland safely, however, on 18 November 1741, the event being duly chronicled in the *Dublin Journal*. The paper pointed out that he was 'known . . . particularly for his *Te Deum, Jubilate, Anthems*, and other Compositions in Church Musick of which for some years past have principally consisted the Entertainments in the Round Church'. This was St Andrew's, scene of the annual concerts in aid of Mercer's Hospital, who announced in the same issue that divine service would be performed at the church on 10 December, with Handel's music and a sermon by Dr Delany. Minutes of a meeting by the hospital governors on the same day noted that 'Mr Putland, Dean Owen, & Docr Wynne be & are hereby desir'd to wait on Mr Handel & ask the favour of him to play on the Organ at the Musical Performance. . . .'

There were several charitable societies in the city and their concerts formed part of a lively and sophisticated musical scene, supported by an aristocracy many of whom were enthusiastic amateur performers. Master of the State Music in Ireland until 1727 had been Johann Sigismund Kusser, whom Handel had known both in Hamburg and in London, and he was followed by that fine violinist Matthew Dubourg. It was Dubourg's job to provide the royal birthday ode for the Lord Lieutenant at the Castle, but he was generally better known as a soloist than a composer. Once he visited an Irish country fair at Dunboyne, disguised as a wandering fiddler, but all his attempts at rough playing could not conceal his sweetness of tone 'and the audience crowded so about him, that he was glad to make his escape'. Geminiani too, though ultimately passed over as Kusser's successor on the grounds that he was a Catholic, visited Dublin in 1737 and later returned to spend the last years of his life there.

From his lodgings in Abbey Street Handel now took subscriptions for six concerts to be given 'in the New Musick-Hall in Fishamble street' first opened two months earlier. *Allegro e Penseroso* was given with three concertos on 23 December, and the *Dublin Journal* reported 'a more numerous and polite Audience than ever was seen upon the like Occasion. The Performance was superior to any Thing of the Kind in this

Kingdom before; and our Nobility and Gentry to show their Taste for all Kinds of Genius, expressed their great Satisfaction, and have already given all imaginable Encouragement to this grand Musick.'

The season had begun auspiciously, and Handel was able to write exultantly to Jennens that the subscription scheme was a triumph 'so that I needed not sell one single Ticket at the Door . . . the Musick sound delightfully in this charming Room, which puts me in such Spirits (and my Health being so good) that I exert my self on my Organ with more than usual Success. . . . I cannot sufficiently express the kind treatment I receive here, but the Politeness of this generous Nation cannot be unknown to You, so I let You judge of the satisfaction I enjoy, passing my time with Honour, profit, and pleasure.' The Duke of Devonshire attended all the performances with his family and was prepared to ask the King to extend the royal permission apparently necessary for Handel's stay in Ireland so that more concerts could be given.

No sooner was the first series, including *Acis*, the *Cecilia Ode* and *Esther*, finished than 'the Desire of several Persons of Quality and Distinction' thus brought about a second. Patrons had been asked to bring their coaches and sedan chairs down the street to avoid crowding and were assured that 'as there is a good convenient Room hired as an addition to a former Place for the Footmen, it is hoped that Ladies will order them to attend there till called for'. Advertisements for the printed word-books were tagged with 'Price a British Six-pence', reflecting the ever-sensitive issue of the Irish coinage.

Alexander's Feast and *Imeneo*, presented in concert performance as 'a new Serenata called HYMEN', were offered in March and everything seemed to run smoothly, though a solitary fly in the ointment had presented itself early in the new year of 1742 in the form of an extraordinary injunction from the dean of St Patrick's Cathedral, Dr Jonathan Swift, to his sub-dean and chapter. The great satirist was now verging upon insanity, and in the first version of his order (later much toned down) we can sense the famous *saeva indignatio* beginning almost to overpower his reason. 'And whereas it hath been reported,' he thunders, 'that I gave a licence to certain vicars to assist at a club of fiddlers in Fishamble Street, I do hereby declare that I remember no such licence to have been ever signed or sealed by me . . . intreating my said Sub-Dean and Chapter to punish such vicars as shall ever appear there, as songsters, fiddlers, pipers, trumpeters, drummers, drum-majors, or in any sonal quality, according to the flagitious aggravations of their respective disobedience, rebellion, perfidy and ingratitude. . . . ' He had in fact granted his licence the day before, and the matter was further complicated by the fact that certain of the St Patrick's vicars choral also sang at the rival establishment of Christ Church, whose dean, Charles Cobbe, had made no objection.

All was smoothed over, however, by 27 March, when the *Dublin Journal* featured what must be one of the most famous of all musical advertisements. 'For Relief of the Prisoners in the several Gaols, and for the Support of Mercer's Hospital in Stephen's Street, and of the Charitable Infirmary on the Inns Quay, on Monday the 12th of April, will be performed at the Musick Hall in Fishamble Street, *Mr Handel's new Grand Oratorio call'd the* MESSIAH, in which the Gentlemen of the Choirs of both Cathedrals will assist, with some Concertoes on the Organ, by Mr Handell.' Tickets cost half a guinea each, with the bonus of a free rehearsal ticket. The paper reported the rehearsal on the 9th, 'to a most Grand, Polite and crouded Audience' and noted a request for ladies to come to the first night 'without Hoops, as it will greatly encrease the Charity, by making Room for more company'. Gentlemen were subsequently asked to appear without swords.

The first night of Handel's *Messiah* took place on Tuesday 13 April 1742, and it need hardly be said that the work was an unqualified success. The newspapers rose to superior heights of Hibernian eloquence: 'Words are wanting to express the exquisite Delight it afforded to the admiring crouded Audience. The Sublime, the Grand, and the Tender, adapted to the most elevated, majestick and moving Words, conspired to transport and charm the ravished Heart and Ear.' With his usual generosity Handel allotted his share of the proceeds (£400 from an audience of about 700) to be divided equally between the society 'for the benefit and enlargement of poor distressed prisoners for debt in the several Marshalseas of the City of Dublin', the Charitable Infirmary and Mercer's Hospital, and all the other performers followed suit.

The singers at the first *Messiah* included Christina Maria Avoglio and Mrs Maclaine, wife of an organist assistant, all of whom the composer had brought with him to Dublin, and a group of male soloists from the two cathedral choirs. Perhaps the most interesting member of the line-up was the contralto Susanna Maria Cibber, sister of Thomas Arne and shortly to become one of the greatest tragic actresses on the London stage. For her the visit to Ireland was a sort of artistic convalescence from a grotesque adultery case in which her husband, Theophilus Cibber, attempted to sue the man with whom he had hitherto complaisantly tolerated her affair. Her engagement with James Quin to act in Dublin in the same season as

Handel's concerts must have created an atmosphere akin to that of a modern civic festival, later enhanced by the arrival of Arne himself and his wife, and of the young David Garrick, whose performance of Hamlet at the Smock Alley theatre Handel is said to have witnessed.

Susanna was now 28 and Handel was 57. His great personal fondness for her was no doubt paternal rather than romantic, but its practical effects are shown in the way he carefully shaped certain roles to suit her gifts as a musical actress. Burney tells us that 'her voice was a thread, and her knowledge of Music very inconsiderable', but praises 'her intelligence of the words and native feeling', while Thomas Sheridan, the Irish actor-manager, wrote ' . . . it was not to any extraordinary powers of voice (whereof she has but a very moderate share) nor to a greater degree of skill in musick (wherein many of the Italians must be allowed to exceed her) that she owed her excellencies, but to expression only; her acknowledged superiority in which could proceed from nothing but skill in her profession'. No wonder that at the première of *Messiah* Dr Delany was so moved by her singing of 'He was despised' that he rose from his seat among the audience crying, 'Woman, for this be all thy sins forgiven thee!'

The Dublin choir probably featured sixteen men and as many boys (no women) and the orchestra, led by Dubourg, consisted of a string band reinforced at certain points by oboes and bassoons and additional parts for trumpets and drums. Apart from the leader, the players' names are unknown to us, but Handel himself was of course at the keyboard to direct the performance. He was presumably the soloist in the organ concertos included in the second *Messiah* evening on 3 June, when 'in order to keep the Room as cool as possible, a Pane of Glass will be removed from the Top of each of the Windows — N.B. This will be the last Performance of Mr Handel's during his Stay in this Kingdom.'

Handel had written *Messiah* in less than a month, starting work on 22 August 1741, completing the outline score on 12 September and rounding off the achievement two days later. The text was prepared for him by Charles Jennens who wrote that July to Edward Holdsworth: 'Handel says he will do nothing next Winter, but I hope I shall perswade him to set another Scripture Collection I have made for him, & perform it for his own Benefit in Passion week. I hope he will lay out his whole Genius & Skill upon it, that the Composition may excell all his former Compositions, as the Subject excells every other Subject. The Subject is Messiah. . . . ' However shortsighted and ungenerous Jennens may often have appeared in his judgment of the composer, we cannot undervalue his qualities as a librettist or deny that one of the reasons for *Messiah*'s universal appeal is a genuine artistry in the selection and arrangement of the scriptural texts. They are more than simply a set of pious extracts: taken from a wide variety of Old and New Testament sources ('I know that my Redeemer liveth', for example, is a conflation of Job and Corinthians I) they are here and there discreetly rewritten by Jennens and laid out in such a way as to form continuous sequences grouped around three central themes, illustrated by the quotations prefixed to the complete text. Part I deals with the prophecy of Christ's coming and the nativity, Part 2 with Jesus's sacrifice for mankind and Part 3 with the Christian soul's victory over death.

This scheme, with its careful balance of openings and conclusions and the interlocking subjects of its airs and choruses, gave Handel the perfect basis on which to construct a work whose powerful architecture gives its utterances indestructible authority. The manuscript is, as ever, vividly evocative of the actual processes of composition, blots, thumb-marks, scratchings, second thoughts and all, but though three and a half weeks is a rapid enough gestation period, it is unremarkable by Handelian standards — *Solomon*, even grander in scale, took 20 days and the first draft of *Theodora* was finished in nineteen — and etherealized visions of the elderly master refusing food, weeping into the semiquavers and having angelic hallucinations are mostly moonshine. Ferocious concentration and excitement there undoubtedly were, however, side by side with an unshakeable faith and an evident concept of the work in its entirety, illustrated for us by the tonal unities governing the piece.

A further consistency is afforded by the dramatic approach Handel adopts towards his material. The three parts of *Messiah* recall the three acts of an Italian opera and to see the work only as a series of disjointed meditations is to ignore its nature as a piece designed, in the best sense of the term, to entertain listeners in a concert room, and written by an operatic professional. Beyond the more obviously theatrical moments, such as the angel's appearance to the shepherds, the intense visual allusions in 'The people that walked in darkness' and 'Thou shalt break them', or the shattering bar's silence in the cadence of the *Amen*, there are innumerable reminiscences of the Haymarket and Covent Garden, in the bass rage aria 'Why do the nations?' with its shades of Boschi and Montagnana, in the *siciliana* 'How beautiful are the feet', which in another context might have been designed for Strada or Cuzzoni, or in 'Oh death, where is thy sting?' whose duet form surely surely owes something to recollections of similar penultimate duets celebrating achieved felicity in *Giulio Cesare*, *Admeto* and other operas.

This all-embracing quality is typical of Handel, and *Messiah* represents to perfection that stylistic synthesis of which much has been said earlier in this book. For example other Italian strains than those of opera are recalled in the symphony (originally 21 bars which Handel subsequently shortened to eleven) introducing the shepherds and in 'He shall feed his flock': both consciously allude to the music of the *pifferari* (the symphony is entitled *Pifa*), country bagpipers who to this day in Italy come down from the mountains during the Christmas season and play in the streets of towns and villages. 'He shall feed his flock' has indeed some curious melodic parallels with that best-known of Italian Christmas songs 'Tu scendi dalle stelle', traditionally a *pifferaro* signature tune, but we are reminded in any case of the composer's abiding fondness for this popular music by countless pastoral references in his other works. Elsewhere in *Messiah* we hear echoes of German chorale in the Hallelujah chorus, where snatches of 'Wachet auf' seem to be quoted in 'The kingdom of this world' and 'And he shall reign for ever and ever'.

What has always ensured the work's unchallenged supremacy in the English choral repertoire is a certain not always easily definable Englishness in the character of Handel's melody and word setting. Two of the most famous airs, 'He was despised' and 'The trumpet shall sound', follow the approved *da capo* model to which the audience would have been accustomed but from which he himself was starting very gradually to draw away, yet even here the rhythms of the language and the flexible quality of the text decree a greater lucidity and directness than he had ever contrived to produce before, even in the Funeral Anthem or *Israel in Egypt*. The best illustration of this is surely the sublime 'I know that my Redeemer liveth', whose power defies analysis because its music is in a sense invisible, a clear current of unforced expressiveness supported on the sketchiest of basses. 'Its effect,' as one writer on *Messiah* remarks, 'rests primarily on Handel's particular speech, the fusion in his arias of the almost instrumental melody of classical Italian bel canto with a speaking declamatory style bred up in England.'

This is the kind of transcendent immediacy which not even the dreariest performance of *Messiah* can kill, yet, as Handel's sketchbooks show, these 'great effects by simple means' were often arrived at through a series of calculated experiments. Nor was he satisfied with the work as it stood: fresh performers during successive London seasons meant serious modifications to several numbers. 'But who may abide', for instance, has no fewer than six versions, the original short form for bass, with no change of tempo at 'for he is like a refiner's fire', the same a tone higher for the tenor Thomas Lowe, three forms of the version written for the castrato Gaetano Guadagni, and as a recitative used in the first Dublin performance.

The fact is that no definitive text of *Messiah* exists, though a close study of Handel's original manuscript, of his conducting score with its various revisions, insertions and alterations, and of the Foundling Hospital copy, is able to give us a clearer outline of what the composer himself would have expected to hear than is offered by traditional modes of performance dating from the vast Handel Commemoration festivals at the close of the eighteenth century. It is difficult to imagine a general return to this elephantine manner, with its massed choirs, orchestration thickened with flutes, clarinets and additional brass, and its inordinately slow tempi; the contemporary practice, favouring small forces, crisp rhythms and a respect of what is taken to have been an authentic performing style, will now, perhaps, be with us forever.

Yet *Messiah*'s resilience is such that, like Shakespeare's plays, it has taken a place among those works which every epoch moulds to its own fancies and desires. Too much has sometimes been made of Handel the populist, the poor man's Bach, the glib melody-maker for the vulgar enthusiast, but there is no denying that it was precisely this factor, of the art which conceals art, of the spontaneity which encloses an inexhaustible musical intelligence, which has guaranteed *Messiah*'s survival as one of the most popular pieces of music ever created. Ironically, as we shall see, it has been this same quality which has made the composer the victim of that cultural snobbery which so often surrounds the appreciation of art. *Messiah* gave Handel to the world: whether the world has treated either the master or his work very well in recompense is a questionable point.

Brave Hallelujahs

Handel left Ireland on 13 August 1742, and though he planned a further Dublin concert season, it was destined never to take place. Nevertheless he was grateful to 'that generous and polite Nation' and on several occasions in subsequent years must have looked back nostalgically to the enthusiastic welcome which the Irish had given him. In a letter to Jennens he enclosed some critical remarks on *Messiah* by Dr Edward Synge, Bishop of Elphin, who noted justly that 'it seems to be a Species of Musick different from any other, and this is particularly remarkable of it. That tho' the Composition is very Masterly & artificial, yet the Harmony is So great and open, as to please all who have Ears & will hear, learned & unlearn'd . . . ' as well as emphasizing the supposed advantages of there being no dramatic dialogue in the text.

No doubt Jennens was pleased with this, but the idea, suggested by later remarks in letters to Holdsworth, of himself as a sort of artistic mentor to the composer was discouraged through Handel's independence of spirit. As the latter had said, 'the report that the Direction of the Opera next winter is committed to my Care, is groundless. The gentlemen who have undertaken to middle with Harmony can not agree, and are quite in a Confusion,' though when he added: 'Whether I shall do some thing in the Oratorio way (as several of my friends desire) I can not determine as yet,' he was perhaps trying to throw Jennens off the scent, for a new and hitherto unperformed oratorio had already been written over a year before and in early January 1743, Handel and John Rich of Covent Garden were applying to William Chetwynd, inspector of stage plays, for licence to present it.

A month later, *Samson* was advertised as the opening novelty of a Covent Garden subscription season. Tickets were to be issued from Handel's house in Brook Street at six guineas each, entitling subscribers to three box places at the first six performances. There was to be a new organ concerto (Opus 7 no. 2 in A) played by the master himself, and at the fourth performance Dubourg, who had returned to London for the concerts, played a violin solo. The first cast included Beard as Samson, Mrs Cibber as Micah, Signora Avolio as the Israelitish Woman, and the Irish comedienne Kitty Clive as Dalila. The most important addition to the little nucleus of musicians loyal to Handel and rewarded by him with a succession of outstanding vocal numbers in later works was the German bass Henry Theodore Reinhold, reputed to be a natural son of the Archbishop of Dresden, and who had already sung in *Acis* and *Esther* performances.

The new oratorio was an overwhelming success and remained among the composer's most popular works for the next two centuries. Horace Walpole, still biting his nails over the fate of Lord Middlesex's operas, wrote to Horace Mann: 'Handel has set up an Oratorio against the Operas, and succeeds. He has hired all the goddesses from farces and the singers of *Roast Beef* from between the acts at both theatres, with a man with one note in his voice, and a girl without ever an one; and so they sing, and make brave hallelujahs; and the good company encore the recitative, if it happens to have any cadence like what they call a tune.' Lady Hertford told her son that the audience was 'filled with all the people of quality in town; and they say Handel has exerted himself to make it the finest piece of music he ever composed, and say he has not failed in his attempt'. An anonymous correspondent to the *Dublin Journal* hinted that the enormous run on tickets, with crowds being turned away at the doors each night, was owing to a general disillusion with the way things were going over at the Haymarket. Jennens, however, was rather more tepid and selective: though he thought *Samson* was 'a most exquisite Entertainment . . . yet it increas'd my resentment for his neglect of the Messiah. You do him too much Honour to call him a Jew! a Jew would have paid more respect to the Prophets. The Name of Heathen will suit him better, yet a sensible Heathen would not have prefer'd the Nonsense foisted by one Hamilton into Milton's Samson Agonistes, to the sublime Sentiments & expressions of Isaiah & David, of the Apostles & Evangelists, & of Jesus Christ.'

Jennens's carping is understandable. He had not been asked to write the libretto, was probably not aware that *Messiah* was to receive its first London performance a few days later, and may have been somewhat irritated at not having known about *Samson*'s composition. Actually Newburgh Hamilton's text is an extremely competent adaptation of *Samson Agonistes*, with generally discriminating additions in the airs and choruses from Milton's shorter poems like 'At a Solemn Music' and 'On Time' to create a blend of varied material ideal for Handel's setting. So as to heighten contrast and narrative continuity Hamilton introduced a Philistine chorus and a confidant role, Micah (possibly also motivated by the composer's consideration for Mrs Cibber). Whatever faults the libretto has are owing in part to Samson's essentially passive role as a series of temptations are flung at him by his father Manoa, his ex-wife Dalila and Harapha, the Philistine *miles gloriosus*, and in part to Hamilton's over-eagerness to deliver the goods.

Most of Handel's more extended works justify their length (it is instructive to hear the operas in their all-too-rarely-performed entirety) but is it blasphemy to suggest that *Samson* loses little by occasional cuts? Handel revised the piece in preparation for the Covent Garden season, adding, among other numbers, the jubilant 'To song and dance' and the magnificent mutual taunting between Israelites and Philistines 'Great Dagon has subdued our foe', as well as a new finale, which, in approved eighteenth-century fashion, redeemed the reflective Miltonic ending with a brightly-toned soprano solo and chorus, the well-loved 'Let the bright seraphim'. The result of all this is something distinctly top heavy, if not a 'loose, baggy monster' then a work whose stateliness of pace is easily confused with loftiness and solemnity — the sort of work, indeed, which Handel's public in its more self-critical moods felt that it ought to be enjoying as an antidote to the frivolity of balls, masquerades and ridottos. This is not to say that any of the musical conceptions which go to make up *Samson* are in any sense pompous or flatulent. The choruses, tautly and economically constructed, occupy a significant place within the drama as a whole. Airs like 'Thus when the sun' and 'Total eclipse' are as attractive as anything else in the oratorios, and even the pallid Micah is rewarded with the stark grandeur of 'Return, o God of Hosts'. Yet at times the effect is that of being asked to pause and admire something for its own sake, rather than as a component of some broader scheme.

To a large extent this is compensated for by Handel's innate dramatic alertness to every possibility afforded by the text. The jejune qualities of Act I are amply made up for by the oratorio's excellent closing scenes, which so successfully encapsulate the essence of the story as a whole that the work might almost begin here. The braggart Harapha hurls his final threats at Samson, and the chorus, with terrifying suddenness, breaks into 'With thunder arm'd', a piece couched in that musical language which Handel had perfected in the choruses of *Israel in Egypt*, set off to greater advantage by the delicacy of Samson's ensuing 'Thus when the sun'. The note of calm resignation to the divine will is retained in the airs for Micah and Manoa which follow, but no amount of foreknowledge either of the biblical history or of Milton's play is likely to have prepared us for the ultimate catastrophe, superbly illustrated by the 'symphony . . . of horror and confusion' which interrupts Manoa's recitative and through which we hear the despairing cries of the Philistines as the hero pulls down Dagon's temple on top of them. Samson himself is commemorated in a series of elegiac movements obviously suggested to librettist and composer by similar features in *Saul* but altogether more flexibly handled, and the work as nowadays performed closes with the brilliant affirmations of 'Let the bright seraphim', and its pendant chorus.

The individual characters make their impact. In casting Samson as a tenor Handel may have recalled the suffering Bajazet in *Tamerlano*, but was able here to project a figure of more obviously heroic proportions and in so doing show his confidence in John Beard, who, whatever his limitations, 'constantly possessed the favour of the public by his superior conduct, knowledge of Music, and intelligence as an actor'. Dalila is the perfect foil, charming in 'With plaintive notes' but stung to a comprehensible fury in 'Traitor to love': Handel's selection of a popular comedy actress, Kitty Clive, to create the role tells us something as to the theatrical terms on which he conceived his protagonists. The two bass parts of Harapha and Manoa offer a piquant contrast between the older type of raging operatic thunderer and the benign priests and fathers to be found in later oratorios.

Samson's enormous popularity guaranteed several revivals during Handel's lifetime and made it a favourite with English provincial music societies. Its triumph in 1743, however, was compounded for Handel himself by what Mainwaring calls 'some return of his paralytic disorder'. Horace Walpole, too, told Mann that 'Handel has had a palsy, and can't compose'. The onset of the attack seems to have been during April, immediately following the close of the Covent Garden season, and was exacerbated by Jennens's nagging intransigence in insisting that *Messiah* should be retouched. 'I have not done with him yet . . . ' he gleefully told Holdsworth, who answered from Florence with commendable humanity: 'You have contributed by yr. own confession, to give poor Handel a fever, and now He is well recover'd, you seem resolv'd to attack him again. . . . This is really ungenerous, & not like Mr Jennens. Pray be merciful: and don't you turn Samson, & use him like a Philistine. . . . '

During the summer the Middlesex opera project finally crashed, a victim of ruinous overspending by aristocratic virtuosos eager to prove the true extent of their Italianized taste. Subscribers were asked to defray the £1,600 debt incurred by the directors, one of whom absconded, another discreetly retiring into the country and a third becoming 'as pale as death and trembles for his money'. Apart from a November revival of Handel's own *Alessandro* as *Rossane* (annotations on the conducting score suggest that the composer had some connexion with this) Haymarket presented no more opera until 1746. When Middlesex became engaged to the heiress Grace Boyle Walpole wrote: 'She proves an immense fortune; they pretend a hundred and thirty thousand pounds — what a fund for making operas!'

In the summer of that year the European war to which England was committed took a more decisive turn with the sweeping victory gained at Dettingen, near Frankfurt, by combined British and German forces against the French army led by the Dukes of Grammont and Noailles. An action of great rashness and heroism lasting from daybreak until ten at night, the battle was distinguished by the bravery of King George himself. Forsaking a restive horse, he had personally led the infantry, crying 'Now boys, now for the honour of England; fire and behave bravely, and the French will soon run', as indeed, for all Grammont's vigorous leadership, they did.

Handel was the natural choice to provide a festive Te Deum and anthem to celebrate the victory. Given in the Chapel Royal on 27 November 1743, the *Dettingen Te Deum* gained rapid popularity and as a neat fit on a disc it has been more often recorded than many of his other works, yet of them all it is surely the most overrated. Relying heavily on a Te Deum by the seventeenth-century Milanese composer Francesco Urio, it pushes home its illusions of splendour with an almost cynical blatancy of effect. Handel is famous for his economy and straightforwardness of expression, but the coarseness of grain in the style of this piece makes it strangely inauthentic, and we turn with relief to the more discriminating language of the anthem *The king shall rejoice.*

Handel's recovery had taken a more positive form in the composition of two new pieces for the coming season. Nothing more perfectly illustrates the way in which his imagination depended upon the powerful inspiration of a strong dramatic text than the fact that the first of these, *Semele*, is nowadays acknowledged as among the finest creations of his mature years and that the second, *Joseph*, written only a month or so afterwards, is perhaps the least satisfying of all his dramatic works.

Semele is an English opera, using a libretto originally written by William Congreve, with music by John Eccles, and published by the poet in 1710. We know nothing as to who prepared the drama for Handel or made the effective additions from other sources, including the score's most famous number, 'Where'er you walk', whose words are taken from one of Pope's pastorals, but the cumulative result is a text of admirable conciseness and variety, the lively pulse of whose action is not seriously slowed down even by the obligatory romantic subplot. The charm of the piece lies in the extraordinary sophistication of its comedy: the story of Jupiter's love for Semele and Juno's vengeful jealousy is treated by Congreve with just the degree of delicate wit we might expect from the author of *The Way of the World* and *The Double Dealer*, but his abundant sense of irony probes beneath the comic surface, exposing veins of tenderness and melancholy, and allowing Handel a relaxed freedom of mood. Thus the underplot, describing the apparently hopeless passion of Semele's sister Ino for Prince Athamas, can be seen as a conventional commentary on the wilder, more frankly erotic behaviour of Jupiter and Semele. In essence, however, the drama belongs to two women, Semele herself, the heedless mortal compromising all her finer qualities in the fulfilment of vain dreams of immortality, and the implacable goddess Juno, wholly unmoved by her rival's plight as, by means of disguise and temptation, she drives her towards self-destruction.

The spirit in which Handel rises to the challenge of all this confounds any idea that abandoning the operatic stage involved a renunciation of worldliness. It also underlines his sensitivity to dramatic nuance, to the way in which a scene ought to go, to the fluctuations of feeling within an individual character. To type *Semele* as a comedy in the modern sense is too severely limiting: it is more obviously a musical blend of *opera seria*'s most attractive elements, emphasizing amorous intrigue, and those of oratorio, where the chorus plays its classic role as commentator on the action. When we laugh it is with a rueful sense of the inevitable. Most of Handel's audience would have known the story, and an awareness that the uproariously funny exchange between Juno and Somnus, god of sleep, is meant ultimately to hasten the catastrophe lends additional spice to an already potent brew.

Limiting his instrumental palette to a series of finely wrought string accompaniments (oboes are used for choral reinforcement and a brace of horns lends colour to the first act) the composer produced a work of marvellous inventiveness, which deserves a permanent place in the modern operatic repertoire. We feel the driving enthusiasm carried over from the opening surges of the dark-hued overture into the unconventional patterns of the first act, with its abundance of accompanied recitative, its quartet, foreshadowing an even greater ensemble in *Jephtha*, and the urgent participations of the chorus, defining, describing, but never destroying the central intimacy.

Congreve's professionalism ensures that dramatic interest is kept alive by tautly constructed incidents and a continuous novelty element. From the first stages of Semele's hubris, marked by the joyousness of 'Endless pleasure', we shift abruptly to her irate rival Juno, bursting on to the scene with Iris in tow in one of those passages of passionate declamation in which the score is so rich. This in its turn gives way to the first of Semele's scenes with Jupiter, where Handel's true gift for sensuous evocation is allowed full play in 'O sleep, why dost thou leave me', whose languorous melismas perfectly catch the sense of lazily awakening beauty, and in the lilting choral dances for her attendant cupids and zephyrs. Ino's arrival, however, leads to a duet and chorus whose reflective abstractions create a meditative interlude similar to 'Wretched lovers' in *Acis and Galatea*, if less obviously menacing. Act III, beginning with Juno's appearance in the Cave of Sleep (Dean calls it 'the licensed rudeness of a matron entering a school dormitory') hurries inexorably towards Semele's death in a blaze of lightning, the rash consequence of her determination to see Jupiter in his full godlike splendour. The chorus, here as elsewhere fully committed, breaks into music whose expression of poleaxed disbelief succeeded by an awed recognition of the moral truth makes us aware of how well Gluck must have known and appreciated the work, and that *Semele* is surely a lineal ancestor of *Iphigénie en Tauride*, *Alceste* and *Orfeo ed Euridice*.

The classicism of 'O terror and astonishment' is as essentially eighteenth-century as the work's conclusion: wonderfully Euripidean as Congreve's 'And all our boasted fire is lost in smoke' may have been, the age demanded a serene close. Apollo promptly descends, in a majestic sinfonia, and promises the infant Bacchus as the pledge of Jupiter and Semele's amours. Juno's triumph is ephemeral, and the spirit of hedonistic delight with which Semele has from the outset been identified now reigns supreme.

Opera or oratorio? The Handelians knew it for the former. Lord Shaftesbury calls it 'a Dramatic Piece of Mr Congreve's', Mainwaring refers to it as 'an English opera, but called an Oratorio', while Jennens dismisses it as 'a bawdy opera' and later quotes a friend as having dubbed it 'Bawdatorio'. The first-night audience on 10 February 1744 may have been pardonably confused by an offering less Lenten than carnival, and Mrs Delany noted 'the house full, though not crowded'. Beard, Reinhold and Avoglio were among the soloists, and Arne's sister-in-law Esther Young doubled as Juno and Ino. Francesina excelled herself in the title role: 'her notes are more distinct, and there is something in her running divisions that is quite surprizing'. Handel apparently thought so too, for Semele's airs are distinguished by a wealth of florid roulades, but no amount of versatility or inventiveness could create a loyal following for the work or establish it with the public in the same way as *Saul* or *Samson*. A solitary revival that December made no impact and, apart from 'Where'er you walk', the first of Handel's two English operas went to ground, to be rediscovered only during the present century, and only recently accepted for what it is, a mature music drama, vividly expressive and consummately theatrical.

From a sublime pagan tragicomedy to a sacred oratorio whose more mediocre levels even the most devoted Handelian can hardly deny. *Joseph and his Brethren* was the second new work in the 1744 Covent Garden programme. A bitter paradox, which Handel himself must have appreciated, since he revived it in four later seasons and made plans for a fifth, decreed that it would be remembered when *Semele* had been long ignored. The librettist, Joseph Miller, vicar of Upcerne, Dorset, was already known to the composer, who had written a song for Kitty Clive in his Drury Lane comedy *The Universal Passion* seven years earlier. Described as 'firm and stedfast in his Principles, ardent in his Friendships, and somewhat precipitate in his Resentments', he was an enthusiastic scribbler, so enthusiastic, indeed, that his dedication of *Joseph* to John, Duke of Montague, deplored the restricting nature of oratorio, which prevented adequate time being allowed for development of the hero's character. Nowadays we may tend to feel that it has all been too much rather than too little.

Everything possible is wrong with the libretto. Its handling of the bible story concentrates most of the action within the last of its three parts, discards any awareness of dramatic motive or human interest, reduces the soprano heroine Asenath to a superfluity and writes off the principal bass role of Pharaoh altogether after Act I. Miller's poetry is often so excruciating as to be truly hilarious, invoking shades of *The Critic* or *The Rehearsal*. Choruses like

> Swift our numbers, swiftly roll,
>> Waft the news from pole to pole;
> Asenath with Zaphnath's join'd,
>> Joy and Peace to all mankind!

we might overlook, but the world of fustian, as Pope's *Dunciad* had reminded Miller and his contemporaries, was a large one, and the vicar of

Upcerne explores it to the full. Lines such as 'Treasure for the public hoarding' and 'Ah Jealousy, thou pelican' are grim harbingers of the matchless exchange between Joseph and Simeon:

JOS: How died he?
SIM: A wild beast, my Lord, devour'd him.
JOS: Devour'd by a wild beast? Have, have a care!
    Didst thou then see his bleeding arteries?
    His mangled limbs?

and the gem which occurs when Joseph answers Asenath's anxious enquiries as to what is the matter with him in the words: 'A slight disorder — public cares . . . '.

Handel did what he could with all this: often it was not very much. The first act holds practically nothing to detain the listener between the excellent overture and prison scene which open it and the rousing bass aria 'Since the race of time begun' with obbligato trumpet which initiates its finale. A second prison episode in Act II, for Simeon, leading to a turbulent G minor air, has greater harmonic interest and dramatic force, and its impetus spills over into Joseph's expression of longing for his homeland through an extended accompanied recitative and a dulcet pastorale over a drone bass. The whole matter of Joseph and the brethren, indeed, seems to have fired Handel's flagging inspiration, and such moments as Simeon's 'Imposter! Ah! my foul offence', where his feelings of remorse dictate the shape of the aria, or the fascinatingly fluid encounter between the hero and his brothers in Act III, where arioso and varied recitative are continually blending, recall far finer points elsewhere in the oratorios.

Why did the composer settle for such a farrago? As the best-known figure in the London musical world he must have received a good many efforts at oratorio writing, whether from dilettante squires, parsons interested in eking out their stipends, or even true Grub Street hacks. Mrs Delany herself, in March of that year, was passing her time in hammering a drama 'to give Mr Handel to compose to' out of *Paradise Lost*, though its subsequent fate is unknown. Good-natured as he always was to the needy, he perhaps wanted to do Miller a good turn. In any event, though the *Joseph* rehearsals were unpromising (the alto Sullivan, in the name part, was described as '*a block* with a very fine voice' and he and Beard between them put Handel in a bad temper), the piece had a respectable success, and at dinner at Mrs Delany's in Clarges Street in April, soon after the season ended, Handel entertained the company by playing over the new oratorio at the keyboard.

Some indication that the concerts had been fairly lucrative is given by the record of Handel's purchase, on 10 April, of £1,300 worth of three per cent annuities. Any momentary complacency, however, must have been alloyed by yet another of those cabals which sprang up against the wretched composer throughout his London career. It might have been thought that at 59, an international celebrity with a devoted English following, he could have been left alone to enjoy a discreet triumph or two. After all, he had earned it. The 1743–44 season had nevertheless brought in its wake a quarrel with the Prince of Wales (its details are obscure) and implacable hostility from Margaret, Lady Brown, wife of the Paymaster of the King's Works, and a well-known concert hostess and patroness of 'foreign musicians in general, of the new Italian style'. Burney tells us that she was in danger of having her windows broken for holding her music parties on Sundays. We know nothing of the causes of her anti-Handel campaign, though the fact that the Browns had formerly lived in Venice suggests a possible connexion with Italian singers who had quarrelled with the composer (Senesino perhaps?). When Mrs Delany wrote that 'Semele has a strong party against it, viz. the fine ladies, petit maitres and *ignoramus's*', and added that 'all the opera people are enraged at Handel' she was pointing the way towards an unexpected opposition which gathered ground throughout the year.

The storm broke in the early days of 1745, when Handel had already opened his new season. This time the oratorios were given not at Covent Garden but on his old battleground at the King's Theatre in the Haymarket, whose management was presumably encouraged by a decent box office at the rival establishment the previous spring. Twenty-four concerts were planned, starting with *Deborah* and *Semele* as runners-up to the first new work, *Hercules*, premièred on 5 January. Few first nights can have been more disastrous, if we are to judge from the nobly pathetic letter Handel sent to the *Daily Advertiser* twelve days later. 'As I perceived that joining good Sense and significant Words to Musick', he wrote, 'was the best Method of recommending this to an English Audience; I have directed my Studies that way, and endeavour'd to shew, that the English Language, which is so expressive of the sublimest Sentiments is the best adapted of any to the full and solemn Kind of Musick. . . . I am assur'd that a Nation, whose Characteristick is Good Nature, would be affected with the Ruin of any Man, which was owing to his Endeavours to entertain them. I am likewise persuaded, that I shall have the Forgiveness of those noble Persons, who have honour'd me with their Patronage, and their Subscription this Winter, if I beg their Permission to stop short, before my Losses are too great to support . . . and I intreat them to withdraw three Fourths of their Subscription, one Fourth Part only of my Proposal having been perform'd.'

From its style the letter was presumably drafted by one of Handel's friends, with his signature appended, but the effect was a wave of sympathy towards him which did honour to his subscribers. The very next day an anonymous declaration of loyalty from some of them was published in the *Daily Advertiser*, touchingly rounded off with the words: 'I would lament the Loss of the Publick in Mr Handel, in Strains equal to his if I was able, but our Concern will be best express'd by our Generosity. . . . Your obedient Servants, Subscribers.' On the 21st, the *Advertiser* issued an admiring address to the composer by an unnamed but tolerably competent satirist, comparing him to Orpheus savaged by the Thracian maenads, and making explicit reference to Lady Brown:

> But chiefly ONE, of envious Kind,
> With Skin of Tyger *capuchin'd*,
> Was more implacable than all,
> And strait resolv'd poor Orpheus' Fall,

but promising that national honour would ultimately be vindicated in the favours yet to be shown the composer. The gratifying upshot of such reactions was a general refusal to withdraw subscription money, for which Handel thanked his patrons in a further letter to the paper on the 25th, adding that he would 'in some Time proceed with the Oratorios, let the *Risque* which I may run be what it will'.

The 'Risque' was not sufficient to ensure the success of *Hercules*, aptly described in the advertisements as 'a new Musical Drama' and as such never destined to capture public favour during Handel's lifetime. To be fair to Lady Brown and the 'fine ladies, petit maitres and ignoramus's' it was not only they who kept away the audiences. Mrs Cibber, in the newly expanded role of Lichas, fell ill on the first night, and those bemused by *Semele*, angry at what may have seemed like yet another attempt to steal a march on the opera managers or disgusted by the presentation of such blatantly secular fare amid musical treatments of holy scripture, were no doubt unwilling to be persuaded.

It was their loss, for *Hercules*, though its libretto lacks the panache of *Semele*, stands beside it as one of the peaks of Handel's dramatic achievement, among those very few operatic works in the half-century before Gluck and Mozart which, by overwhelming the limitations of a traditional style, create a discourse of their own. Fusing several of Handel's favourite plot interests, the violence of wifely jealousy, the relationships of parents and children, the collapse of the individual beneath a weight of personal folly and obsession, and the tension between private agony and public performance, its classical world mingles nervous radiance and anguished darkness like some canvas of the Italian Baroque. The union of Hyllus and Iole, the young prince and princess, which concludes the piece possesses a sort of exhausted determination to retain whatever order is left after the tragedy of their doomed elders, Hercules and Dejanira, has hewn out its course. The effect recalls *Tamerlano* and *Alcina*: we are less interested in those who survive than those who have departed from view.

Based on Sophocles's *Trachiniae*, with touches from Ovid, the drama, most capably managed by Thomas Broughton, a Salisbury clergyman, tells the story of Hercules's return from war in Oechalia with the captive Iole and the groundless suspicions of Dejanira, whose use of the poisoned shirt of Nessus in a misguided effort at winning back the love she believes lost leads to the hero's death and her own insanity. The recipe, as far as Handel was concerned, was the one perfected in *Semele*, a concentration not simply upon exhibiting voices and characters, but on a clear relationship between musical form and dramatic episode, on the validity of aria and recitative as vehicles of expression, and, most interesting of all, on the essential function of the chorus.

The musical language of *Hercules* is, quite deliberately, more restrained, less elastic than we mostly find in the oratorios. Yet this only strengthens the work. Hyllus's 'Where congeal'd the northern streams' or Dejanira's 'The world, when day's career is run', both in Act I, ideally fulfil the terms of Baroque aria in expanding thoughts and desires which the formalities of recitative have kept constricted. Too heavily conditioned by the type of opera which celebrates complete emotional indulgence, we easily forget that much of the real power of *opera seria* at its best (and *Hercules* is a sophisticated variant on the form) lies in what its characters are forced to suppress and in the struggle between anarchic personal conflict and a dignified orthodoxy in outward behaviour. Iole's grief-stricken re-enactment of her father's death becomes, by the very nature of its tortured harmonic structure, a protest against the complacency of her captors and a harbinger of the ensuing débâcle. By the close of the drama the ceremonious declamatory frameworks of the eighteenth-century lyric stage have dissolved into the dying gasps of the ravaged Hercules and for Dejanira a mad scene without parallel in the music of the age.

'It seems to me that he is a little mad,' said Count Flemming years before; now Handel's eccentricities were distinctly pronounced, and friends occasionally feared for his reason. Lunacy was more immediate and accessible a phenomenon to his period than to ours, as Hogarth's *Rake's Progress* cycle famously demonstrates, and like many an imaginative genius Handel may now and then have contemplated the thin defences of his own sanity. His handling of Dejanira's madness, with its alternations of snarling rage and delusively wistful calm, buoyed up by a free manipulation of tempo and key, has an eerie authenticity about it which makes the episode more deeply disturbing than the mad scenes of Italian opera, such as that of his own Orlando.

The chorus lend weight and solemnity to the piece, as well as a note of rejoicing to lighten the gathering gloom. In the tremendous rhythmic swirl of 'Crown with festal pomp the day', with its trumpets and drums and Slavonic hints from Telemann's *Musique de Table*, Handel gave them one of his most infectiously breezy numbers. He also rewarded them with the piece which, more than any other, encapsulates the essence of the tragedy. Like its counterpart 'Envy, eldest born of hell' in *Saul*, 'Jealousy, infernal pest' occupies a focal point in the drama, casting a prophetic shadow over events to come. In order to focus concentration, Handel paid special attention to the form of the piece, casting it as a rondo introduced by a series of unison string figures climbing down through the bass in diminished sevenths and thence battered into nothingness by the savagely discordant entry of the voices.

Once again it is tempting to suppose that a score of *Hercules* may ultimately have found its way to Vienna, for there are premonitory echoes of late Mozart and Beethoven in this chorus. However much informed musical opinion may have admired the work, it was another in the array of brilliant commercial failures which punctuated Handel's 1744 and 1745 seasons. His London audience, still fairly unsophisticated and conventional in its musical tastes, was simply not prepared to accept an English opera without the bonus of star singers and the usual trimmings of handsome sets and costumes, as Jennens sensibly pointed out to Holdsworth. Renting the opera house at £400 and buying a new organ for the concerts must have set Handel back, but to give 'an English Opera call'd Hercules . . . on Saturdays, during the run of Plays, Concerts, Assemblys, Drums, Routs, Hurricanes, & all the madness of Town

Diversions' was to court disaster. He would have done better, said Jennens, to stick to his Covent Garden Wednesday and Friday series, where a mere dozen evenings in each case had brought him in £2,100 and £1,600 respectively.

Handel and Jennens had been in collaboration again, despite their differences over *Messiah*, during the summer and autumn of 1744, and the composer's letters to his librettist are precious to us not only because so little of his correspondence, private or professional, actually survives, but because they give us an invaluable insight into his working methods and prove, if proof is needed, how seriously he took the whole business of setting words to music.

The last of Jennens's three fine 'scripture collections' for Handel was a dramatic oratorio on the story of Belshazzar's feast, the prophecies of Daniel and the siege of Babylon by King Cyrus of Persia. It shares with *Saul* and *Messiah* an overall sense of a refined literary taste at work, allied to an intelligent awareness of Handel's own priorities as a musical dramatist. However meanly Jennens may sometimes have felt towards Handel, he was never lacking in appreciation of his true gifts, and in *Belshazzar* he furnished precisely the sort of stirring and colourful narrative line which the composer's fancy most readily seized upon.

Though his English summers by now often included visits to country friends and admiring aristocratic amateurs, Handel was still in London when, on 9 June 1744, he wrote to Jennens saying that he should be 'extreamly glad to receive the first Act, or what is ready of the new Oratorio with which you intend to favour me.' Ten days later he was eagerly reading the first instalment: 'Your reasons for the Length of the first act are intirely Satisfactory to me, and it is likewise my Opinion to have the following Act short.' He settled down in the meantime to composing *Hercules*, and Jennens's second act had arrived by 21 August. *Belshazzar* itself was started two days afterwards and on 13 September he was writing: 'Your most excellent Oratorio has given me great Delight in setting it to Musick and still engages me warmly. It is indeed a Noble Piece, very grand and uncommon; it has furnished me with Expressions, and has given me Opportunity to some particular Ideas, besides so many great Choru's.' By 2 October the last act was ready, but Handel was having doubts about the oratorio's length: ' . . . if I should extend the Musick, it would last 4 hours and more,' he wrote, 'I retrench'd already a great deal of the musick, that I might preserve the Poetry as much as I could, yet still it may be shortened,' subsequently going into detail as to the layout of the final movement.

This last letter offers valuable supporting evidence to that presented by the manuscripts that Handel nearly always composed with a specific group of singers in mind. The parts in *Belshazzar* were cast long before the work's first performance, on 27 March 1745. Under the circumstances it is needless to add that it was a total failure. The loyalty of Handel's partisans had not helped to fill the King's Theatre, and one of his most impressive artistic achievements was favoured with a beggarly three performances. 'This proved a very bad season, and he performed with considerable loss,' noted Lord Shaftesbury. The bluestocking Elizabeth Carter wrote at greater length to her friend Catherine Talbot, with some meaningful italics: 'Handel, once so crowded, plays to empty walls in that opera house, where there used to be a constant *audience* as long as there were any dancers to be *seen*. Unfashionable as I am, I was I own highly delighted the other night at his last oratorio. 'Tis called Belshazzar, the story the taking of Babylon by Cyrus; and the music, in spite of all that very bad performers could do to spoil it, equal to any thing I ever heard. There is a chorus of Babylonians deriding Cyrus from their walls, that has the best expression of scornful laughter imaginable.'

The presence in the story of three national groups, the Babylonians, their Jewish captives and the attacking Persians, gave Handel the chance to develop a type of contrast he had already illustrated in *Athalia* and *Samson*, where worshippers of the true God and pagan idolaters receive distinctive musical treatments. In *Belshazzar* each nation is clearly identifiable. With its fierce, foot-stamping rhythms, the Babylonian music reaches a pitch of primitive exultation in the drunken orgy, 'Ye tutelar gods of our empire look down', which sets the scene for the Writing on the Wall. Who else but Handel could have achieved such an effect with so confident a simplicity of means? The Persians, on the other hand, give utterance with a sturdiness and lucidity which emphasize their uncompromising resolve. In the limpid fluency of 'See, from his post Euphrates flies' (later effectively transformed into a movement for the first of three double wind band concertos written for the 1747–8 season), we can hear a gleeful rejoinder to the facile laughter of the Babylonians 'deriding Cyrus as engag'd in an impracticable Undertaking'. For the Jews, grave, patient and dignified, an altogether more thoughtful vein is exercised, and both *Israel in Egypt* and the Funeral Anthem are recalled in their hieratic solemnities.

Belshazzar deals as cogently with individuals as with abstracts. The opening soliloquy, in which the king's mother Queen Nitocris (pertinently borrowed from Herodotus) contemplates the 'vain, fluctuating state of human empire' in an accompanied recitative of profound gloom, sums up the entire nature of the work in the tension sprung between the realities of power and destiny on the one hand and the human beings who confront them on the other. There is no romantic interest, nor do we feel a need of it, but the characters' emotions and motives are varied and convincing throughout. Nitocris, a matriarch of truly Racinian grandeur, ultimately finds her peace in the counsels of Daniel, an eloquent alto role, and in the heroic magnanimity of Cyrus, the 'new man' in the imperial struggle, who is given appropriately modern-sounding airs ('Destructive war' might easily have been composed by Hasse or Graun). Belshazzar himself is an insouciant bon viveur, a noisily drunken aristocrat of apparently imperishable breed.

The great scene of the Writing on the Wall, the drama's pivotal episode, offers a check to the king's arrogance which, though only temporary, is yet severe. In the midst of his defiance of Jehovah's power, the music crumbles into recitative and the astonished chorus of feasting nobles loses all tonal foundation as the horrified king watches the spectral hand spelling out the doom of his realm. The authentic quality of sheer terror must have been enhanced here by recollection of the Bible's vivid 'his thoughts troubled him, so that the joints of his loins were loosed, and his knees smote one against another'. In come the hastily summoned Chaldean soothsayers, to an *Allegro Postillions* borrowed from Telemann's *Musique de Table* to evoke their fussy inconsequence. Only Daniel can resolve the enigma, which he does with awesome, almost contemptuous remoteness, after which the scene closes abruptly with Nitocris's sombre 'Regard, O son, my flowing tears', a *largo siciliano* charged with all the pathos at Handel's command.

If this number brings back reminiscences of Cuzzoni and Faustina, the association is scarcely accidental, for *Belshazzar* is among the most markedly dramatic of the oratorios. It was not written for stage performance, but that did not prevent composer and librettist from conceiving it in histrionic terms, with detailed stage directions to help the audience with word-books in hand, and the airs, choruses and recitatives are often thrillingly theatrical. The debate endures as to whether or not the oratorios may be adequately staged, but the directions in *Belshazzar* frequently seem less like real indications for performance than hints to the audience as to how Handel and Jennens wanted them to imagine the various scenes. In fairness, however, to advocates of fully dramatic presentation, it must be said that the piece undoubtedly works in the theatre and holds out splendid opportunities to the imaginative director.

All three of Handel's new works written for the 1744 and 1745 seasons had been rejected by his London public, and his subsequent attempts to rehabilitate them by carefully adapted revivals were wholly unsuccessful. Each was a creation of bold originality in design and intention, displaying its composer's authoritative grasp of musical idiom as something from which he had fashioned his own markedly personal, rich and cosmopolitan language, to make each piece into something unique in the dramatic music of the day. It has taken over 200 years for *Semele, Hercules* and *Belshazzar* to gain their due of admiration from those less hidebound either by conventional genres or by notions of sacred choral proprieties. An indication that Handel realized that he may have gone too fast for the taste of his audiences to catch up with him is given by the fact that each of his next four oratorios represents an effort to regain popularity by appealing to the simpler, louder, less intellectual elements among the concert-going English. For a time he would give the people what they wanted.

13

Next to the Hooting of Owls

Handel was now 60 years old, and despite the bewildering uncertainties of his professional career, the malice of his enemies and the incalculable fluctuations of popular favour, he had established himself as the doyen of London's musical life. More significantly, from a personal aspect, he had surrounded himself with a select circle of loyal and trusted friends, able to appreciate his stature as an artist as well as valuing his cheerful presence as a dinner guest, a travelling companion or a country visitor. Younger musicians and amateur performers, playing at his concerts or meeting him socially, noted their impressions, and gradually a wealth of anecdote and reminiscence began to surround him. He was, in short, becoming the great man.

Portraits tell us something of what he looked like, but the comments of Burney and Hawkins are far more eloquent of the deep impression he made upon his contemporaries. Burney, who, as a schoolboy, had seen him at Chester, later joined his orchestra and formed a lifelong admiration for him. 'Handel's general look,' he recalls, 'was somewhat heavy and sour; but when he did smile, it was his sire the sun, bursting out of a black cloud. There was a sudden flash of intelligence, wit and good humour, beaming in his countenance, which I hardly ever saw in any other.' Sir John Hawkins, who came to know him during his final years, tells us that 'he was in his person a large made and very portly man. His gait, which was ever sauntering, was rather ungraceful, as it had in it somewhat of rocking motion, which distinguishes those whose legs are bowed. His features were finely marked, and the general cast of his countenance placid, bespeaking dignity attempered with benevolence, and every quality of the heart that has a tendency to beget confidence and insure esteem.'

Evidence, however, tends to contradict Hawkins's notion of Handel as a demure hermit, with 'no impertinent visits, no idle engagements to card parties, or other expedients to kill time'. We can readily accept his impression of a composer perpetually brimming over with ideas and always eager to be composing, so much so that the keys of his 'favourite Ruckers harpsichord . . . were hollowed like the bowl of a spoon', but those suppers at Mrs Delany's, Mainwaring's comment apropos of Handel and food that 'he paid more attention to it than is becoming to any man' and the eloquent jotting by the composer himself in one of his sketchbooks '12 Gallons Port 12 Gallons French Duke Street Meels', besides the attribution to him of the dictum that 'the goose is a most inconvenient bird, too much for one and not enough for two', rule out any idea of a recluse whose 'social affections were not very strong'. A satire published in 1750, *The Scandalizade*, has Heidegger describing Handel thus:

How amply your corpulence fills up the chair —
Like mine host at an inn, or a London Lord Mayor!
Three yards at the least round about in the waist;
In dimensions your face like the sun in the west.
But a chine of good pork, and a brace of good fowls,
A dozen-pound turbot, and two pair of soles,
With bread in proportion, devour'd at a meal,
How incredibly strange, and how monstrous to tell!
Needs must that your gains and your income be large,
To support such a vast, *unsupportable* charge!
Retrench, or ere long you may set your own dirge.

As if these testimonies were not enough, his friend the scene painter Joseph Goupy published a caricature of him, entitled *The Charming Brute* in which a monkey and a racehorse listen to a pig playing the organ (decorated with hams and dead fowl) among a litter of musical instruments and oyster barrels. The cause of Goupy's attack, for which Handel quite naturally expunged the artist's name from his will, was a dinner in Brook Street at which the composer had apologized for the frugal fare, promising Goupy that he would treat him with a better meal when he had more money to hand. After dinner Handel excused himself from the table and was so long away that Goupy, bored with waiting, wandered into the next room, from which a window giving on to the adjacent parlour showed him Handel guzzling off 'claret and French dishes'.

The style of living at Brook Street was plain but not mean. Judging by the details of the inventory made at his death, the furniture had got a trifle shabby, and his 'family' of servants seems only to have consisted of two men, whose names, Peter Le Blond and John Duburk, suggest that they were probably Huguenots. Hawkins praises him for not having kept a carriage — he used to hire 'a chariot and horses' when he went into the city to see his broker Gael Morris at Garraway's or Batson's coffee house, or to bank his takings — but how many London musicians, we may wonder, had their own equipages?

His stormy temper remained a force to be reckoned with. Burney recalls that 'at the close of an air, the voice with which he used to cry out, "Chorus!" was very formidable indeed; and at the rehearsals of his Oratorios, at Carlton House, if the Prince and Princess of Wales were not exact in coming to the Music-room he used to be very violent . . . if the maids of honour, or any other female attendant talked during the performance, I fear that our modern Timotheus not only swore, but called names; yet at such times, the Princess of Wales, with her accustomed mildness and benignity, used to say, "Hush! hush! Handel is in a passion".'

They relished his wit as much as his passion. Once, auditioning an ambitious chorister, he asked him 'This is the way you praise God at Worcester?'. 'Yes,' replied the unsuspecting victim. 'God is very good,' the answer came back, 'and will no doubt hear your praises at Worcester, but no man will hear them at London.' In Dublin no less a master than his friend Matthew Dubourg was teased, as Burney tells us: 'having a solo part in a song, and a close to make, *ad libitum*, he wandered about in different keys a great while, and seemed indeed a little bewildered, and uncertain of his original key . . . but, at length, coming to the shake, which was to terminate this long close, Handel, to the great delight of the audience, and augmentation of applause, cried out loud enough to be heard in the most remote parts of the theatre: 'You are welcome home, Mr Dubourg!'

'Social affections' had brought him friends among the nobility as well as 'within the pale of his own profession', and his summers seem by now to have established a fairly regular pattern in alternating visits to the country estates of his aristocratic acquaintance with trips to the watering places in search of elusive cures for his recurrent rheumatic ailments. In Kent he could journey over from Tunbridge to stay with Sir Wyndham Knatchbull, in Dorset he might be the guest of Lord Shaftesbury at St Giles before going on to Salisbury to call on James 'Hermes' Harris, and in the north midlands he was a welcome visitor at Calwich Abbey, Staffordshire, home of Mrs Delany's brother Bernard Granville, at Gopsal with Jennens, at Teddesley Hall, where, according to uncorroborated tradition, he used to play at Fisher Littleton's amateur concerts and at Exton in Rutland, where we catch a glimpse of him during June 1745, on his way to Scarborough.

Exton belonged to Lord Gainsborough, whose sister was Shaftesbury's wife and whose brother James Noel wrote describing a performance of *Comus* got up to celebrate a family anniversary while Handel was a house-guest. The Noels opted for Milton's original masque, with one or two modifications, rather than the recent theatrical version by Arne and Dalton; their favourite composer's presence was a stroke of great good luck. 'As Handel came to this place for Quiet and Retirement we were very loath to lay any task of Composition upon him. Selfishness however prevailed; but we were determined at the same time to be very moderate in our requests. His readiness to oblidge soon took off all our apprehensions upon that account. A hint of what we wanted was sufficient, and what should have been act of Compliance he made a voluntary Deed.'

Their reluctance to put upon Handel says much, both for the intelligent kindliness of the Noels towards someone they might well have been disposed to patronize as a mere musician, and for the esteem in which he was now held. *Comus* was put together by the enthusiastic summer house party in the space of five days, but rain forced them to perform indoors, though 'we contrived however to entertain the Company there afterwards with an imitation of Vaux Hall: and in the style of a newspaper, the whole concluded with what variety of fireworks we could possibly get'. It must all have been tremendous fun, and Handel's three agreeably lightweight pieces, only discovered in 1969, conjure up a delicious atmosphere of festive conviviality.

Scarborough, fashionable as it was fast becoming as a bathing resort, did little for Handel's health. James Harris's brother William, meeting him in the street soon after his return to London in August, noted his anxiety in this respect, and two months later Jennens told Holdsworth that he thought Handel was going mad, an opinion shared by some of his rural hosts. By the end of October Shaftesbury was writing to Harris that 'poor Handel looks something better. I hope he will entirely recover in due time, though he has been a good deal disordered in his head'.

Disorders of a more general kind had come upon England with the hoisting, in July, of a rebel standard at Moidart in the Highlands of Scotland by Charles Edward Stuart, the Young Pretender. Initial panic gave way to a suspended apprehensiveness mingled with bulldog pugnacity and despite the Pretender's advance (through the largely Catholic preserves of the north-west) as far as Derby, nobody in the south seems seriously to have considered the likelihood of a wholesale Stuart restoration. Hogarth painted the guards marching to Finchley, and Handel wrote 'A Chorus Song . . . for the *Gentlemen Volunteers* of the CITY OF LONDON', 'Stand round, my brave boys' to words by John Lockman, first sung at Drury Lane on 14 November after a performance of Vanbrugh's *The Relapse* and repeated the next night 'by particular desire'.

A bellicose patriotism, of a sort the nation had not properly known since the days of Purcell's 'Britons, strike home' and the wars of King William and the Duke of Marlborough, was the mood of the hour, and London's musicians were quick to sense it. The spirit of Jenkins's Ear and Dettingen, the realization that England's future lay in the prosaic expediencies of Hanover rather than in a dubious Popish nostalgia for exiled Stuarts, had already begun to be heard in works such as Arne's *Alfred*, with its showstopping 'Rule, Britannia', and in the gradual appearance, at theatres and concerts during the early 1740s, of the tune which eventually became the National Anthem. A letter published in *Common Sense* during 1738 had suggested that 'the learned Doctor Greene' compose a nationally inspiring tune, adding that 'it is not from the least Distrust of Mr Handel's ability that I address myself preferably to Doctor Greene; but Mr Handel having the Advantage to be by Birth a German, might probably, even without intending it, mix some Modulations in his Composition, which might give a German tendency to the Mind, and therefore greatly lessen the National Benefit'.

It has been suggested that Greene really was the creator of 'God save the king' and that 'Stand round, my brave boys' was Handel's rival riposte to it. Someone else who showed that a foreigner could seize the moment was the composer of *La Caduta dei Giganti*, the opera chosen to open the King's Theatre in the Haymarket on 7 January 1746 (it had earlier been closed 'on account of the rebellion and popular prejudice against the performers, who being foreigners, were chiefly Roman Catholics'). Christoph Willibald von Gluck had newly arrived in London in the suite of the Austrian nobleman Prince Lobkowitz, scion of a family well known in Viennese musical annals. *La Caduta* was the first of two operas he gave at the Haymarket and was intended as a direct compliment to William Augustus, Duke of Cumberland, now in command in Scotland.

Gluck stayed in London until the spring of the next year, and though Handel was unimpressed by *La Caduta dei Giganti* (he told Mrs Cibber that Gluck knew no more about counterpoint than his cook) the two performed together at a benefit concert for the Decayed Musicians at the King's Theatre and became acquainted. Handel advised the young master not to take so much trouble over operas for the English. 'Here in England,' he said, 'that is mere waste of time. What the English like is something they can beat time to, something that hits them straight on the drum of the ear.' Burney rightly detected a Handelian influence on the style of the later and more famous operas, and the tenor Michael Kelly recorded a tribute which, allowing for a little Hibernian embroidery, reflects an obvious debt: Gluck showed him Handel's portrait, saying: 'There, Sir, is the portrait of the inspired master of our art; when I open my eyes in the morning, I look upon him with reverential awe, and acknowledge him as such. . . . ' Handel need not have worried about the approach of a potential rival; neither of Gluck's two London operas (the second, *Artamene*, was given on 4 March) made much of an impression on audiences or musicians.

Handel himself had prepared a topical confection to suit the mood of the times, in a new piece to be given at Covent Garden, the theatre which now became his permanent London auditorium. There was no attempt at an oratorio season during the winter and spring of 1745–6, presumably because of the national emergency, but it was precisely these special circumstances which called the *New Occasional Oratorio* into being. The disappointed subscribers from last season could take up their unused tickets for these performances (on 14, 19 and 26 February) — an honourable concession of Handel's, amply compensating for the sharp practice over *Deborah* ten years before, supposing anyone remembered that.

William Harris went along to hear a rehearsal at Brook Street and told his sister-in-law, diplomatically, that the oratorio was 'extremely worthy of him, which you will allow to be saying all one can in praise of it. He has but three voices for his songs — Francesina, Reinholt and Beard; his band of music is not very extraordinary — Du Feche is his first fiddle, and for the rest I really could not find out who they were, and I doubt his failure will be in this article. The words of his Oratorio are scriptural, but taken from various parts, and are expressive of the rebels' flight and our pursuit of them. Had not the Duke carried his point triumphantly, this Oratorio could not have been brought on.'

A calculated risk, therefore, based on hopes of a speedy victory for the Hanoverian forces led by Cumberland and Wade. *The Occasional Oratorio* was put together in something of a hurry, with a text based on Milton's psalm paraphrases and passages from Spenser by Newburgh Hamilton, and music relying heavily on borrowings from Handel's earlier works and such former quarries as Stradella's serenata *Qual prodigio* and

269

Telemann's *Musique de Table*. Part 3 of the piece was originally introduced by the opening movement of the first of the Grand Concertos and contained three choruses and an aria from *Israel in Egypt*. Handel could have flung anything into the brew, 'Son confusa pastorella', 'The flocks shall leave the mountains', 'Honour and arms', without it really making very much difference to the overall quality and nature of the work.

In recent years the undervaluing of *Deborah* has been commensurate with overestimations of *The Occasional Oratorio*. The sum total of the piece, a tissue of ripe Handelian cliché, adds scant lustre to the composer's name. Jehovah, invoked by Hamilton and Handel, turns into a mitred pluralist in lawn sleeves being plied for patronage over the port by a brace of sycophantic prebendaries. A great deal of trumpeting (ten numbers — the heaviest use of the instrument in any Handel work) creates a certain sameness of mood, limiting harmonic interest in several of the choruses, though Handel pulls himself sufficiently together in the bass air 'To God our strength sing loud and clear' leading to the chorus 'Prepare the hymn, prepare the song' to produce a single movement of brilliant colour and suppleness, in which solo trumpet and oboe converse over arpeggiando string accompaniment during the aria, whose sprightly middle section ushers in the choral entries. Otherwise triteness and prolixity, in the featureless attitudinizing of 'Jehovah is my shield, my glory' or the note-spinning passagework of 'Prophetic visions', all too easily invade the oratorio.

A redeeming moment or two occurs. This is, after all, Handel and nobody worse. The best number in the whole work is the soprano's glittering 'When warlike ensigns wave on high' from Part 3, a happy reminiscence, in its first section, of the mood of 'Let the bright seraphim', and containing what is perhaps the longest and most carefully worked second part (there is no *da capo* indication) in any of the composer's airs. The structure in this unusually interesting piece is thus wholly episodic. A G major evocation of battle (mercifully, in this context, without real trumpets) is followed by nine bars of modulation through E minor and B minor as the words describe 'the frighted peasant' who 'sees his field for corn an iron harvest yield', to a delightfully witty ebullition of country dance by the strings, subsequently woven above one of those bagpipe drones Handel could never resist. Echoes of these last ideas (the main melody, used again in *Theodora*, is borrowed from *Musique de Table* and made almost unrecognizable by what Handel does with it) are developed in the final section, where by breaking them up against the words 'Be calm and Heaven will soon dispose to future good our present woes' and leaving the vocal line resting on mere fragments of the original bass, he is able to suggest the clangour of war dying away, only to resume everything in the air within the eighteen-bar orchestral ritornello which concludes it.

In purely formal terms 'When warlike ensigns' is one of the most absorbing proofs of Handel's mastery of design, just as *The Occasional Oratorio* offers some of the most blatant evidence of his faith in expediency and rapid results when he felt the occasion called for them. The oratorio was not, as it turned out, more than a mere *succès d'estime*, though the splendid march in the overture became a deserved favourite. Cumberland, in the wake, as it were, of London's musical and theatrical plaudits, trounced the contumacious Highlanders at Culloden on 16 April, and in July another of Handel and Lockman's patriotic ballads, 'A Song on the Victory over the Rebels . . . Sung by Mr Lowe in Vauxhall Gardens', appeared, beginning

> From Scourging Rebellion, and baffling proud France;
> Crown'd with Lawrels, behold British WILLIAM advance

and urging us

> Commanded by WILLIAM, strike next at the Gaul,
> And fix those in Chains who would Britons enthrall,

set to a tune recalling 'Volate amori' in Act I of *Ariodante*.

Lady Brown and her satellites had also been routed, and Handel had little to fear from the Haymarket operas, now carried on via a subscription scheme undertaken by Lord Middlesex and his noble syndicate. Shaftesbury told James Harris, on 20 January 1747, that 'Mr Handel called on me tother day. He is now in perfect health and I really think grown young again. There is a most absurd and ridiculous opera going forward at present and as it is not likely to meet with success he is delighted.' This was *Fetonte* by Domenico Paradies, better known as a keyboard master, on which Burney drily comments: 'Unluckily, neither the composition, nor performance of Phaeton had the Siren power of enchanting men so much as to stimulate attention at the expence of reason.' The Directors had also got hold of a far abler hand in the person of the Catalan composer Domenico Terradellas, one of the finest of Durante's pupils at Naples and a sensitive writer for the voice. The following year, what is more, London was to be visited by its first Italian *buffo* troupe, giving performances of the comic operas which were becoming so important a feature of Neapolitan theatrical life. Though these made no obvious impression on Handel, he had the opportunity of hearing the young Gaetano Guadagni, later to be the last of his great castrato stars and, as creator of the title role in Gluck's *Orfeo*, linking one composer to the other through the medium of a vocal style owing much to the English love of dramatic directness and simplicity.

A slightly shaky start was given to the 1747 oratorio season by the magnetic fascination of the trial of the obese turncoat Lord Lovat, with whom even the most mawkishly sentimental Jacobites found it hard to sympathize. Revivals of *The Occasional Oratorio* and *Joseph and His Brethren* gingered up the excited Handelians for the new work on which the composer had been engaged during the previous summer and which William Harris and Shaftesbury, who expected that it would 'both give delight to the lovers of harmony and profits to the fountain whence it flows', had presumably heard in rehearsal.

Judas Maccabaeus, with *Messiah* and *Samson* the most consistently successful of all Handel's vocal works, had its première on 1 April. Beard and Reinhold figured, as usual, in the principal tenor and bass parts, Judas and Simon, and the soprano was the accomplished Elisabetta de'Gambar-ini, herself a composer, to whose collection of keyboard lessons and songs Handel subscribed the following year. The mezzo, Caterina Galli, was already an established singer of male roles at the King's Theatre, though it was Handel's oratorio which was to bring her genuine celebrity. 'There was something spirited and interesting in her manner', says Burney, 'however, she was little noticed by the public till she sung in Handel's oratorio of *Judas Maccabaeus*, when she acquired such favour in the air "Tis liberty alone" that she was not only encored in it every night, but became an important personage, among singers for a considerable time afterwards.' Her reputation may later have suffered from her role as go-between in the sensational affair between Lord Sandwich's mistress Martha Ray and Captain Hackman, which ended with the former being murdered by the latter as she left the theatre, but Galli soldiered on in increasing poverty, with concert engagements as late as 1797 and dying in 1804 — 'the last of Handel's scholars' as the *Gentleman's Magazine* puts it.

The libretto of *Judas* was the first of five written for the composer by the Reverend Thomas Morell, a fellow of King's College, Cambridge, rector of Buckland, Hertfordshire, and as perpetual curate of Kew a member of the circle surrounding Queen Caroline, on whose Richmond Grotto he wrote a poem and of whose memorial sermon to her household we have noted him as the preacher. He was an accomplished classical scholar, an experienced if not inspired translator, and the friend of Garrick and Hogarth. 'He was warm in his attachments,' says John Nicholls in his

Anecdotes, 'and was a cheerful and entertaining companion. He loved a jest, told a good story, was fond of musick, and would occasionally indulge his friends with a song. In his exterior appearance, however, he never condescended to study the Graces; and, unfortunately for himself, he was a total stranger to economy.'

He and Handel seem to have got along very well together. For the composer the working relationship was probably easier than his rather more deferential collaborations with Jennens. Morell, more relaxed, more compliant, less self-regarding than his predecessor, and Handel, impatient, peremptory and exacting, are not unlike another celebrated pairing of librettist and composer, Francesco Maria Piave and Giuseppe Verdi. Morell was to recall their partnership somewhat wrily in later years, when he wrote of the difficulties of supplying oratorio text, 'especially if it be considered, what alterations he must submit to, if the Composer be of an haughty disposition, and has but an imperfect acquaintance with the English language'.

'Mr Handell,' he goes on, 'applied to me, when at Kew . . . in 1746 [*sic*] and added to his request the honour of a recommendation from Prince Frederic. Upon this I thought I could do as well as some that had gone before me, and within 2 or 3 days carried him the first Act of *Judas Maccabaeus*, which he approved of. "Well," says he, "and how are you to go on?" "Why, we are to suppose an engagement, and that the Israelites have conquered, and so begin with a chorus as

Fallen is the Foe

or, something like it." "No, I will have this", and began working it, as it is, upon the Harpsichord. "Well, go on." "I will bring you more tomorrow." "No, something now,

So fall thy Foes, O Lord

that will do", and immediately carried on the composition as we have it in that admirable chorus. . . . '

This episode probably took place before the production of *The Occasional Oratorio* since the appearance in that work of the air 'O Liberty, thou choicest treasure' was subsequently remarked on by the librettist in a footnote to the *Judas* word-book: 'the following Air was design'd, and wrote for this Place, but it got I know not how, into the *Occasional Oratorio*, and was there incomparably Set, and as finely executed.' What may have happened was that *Judas* was originally projected without any obvious reference to current events, but was shelved in favour of the other work, and only given its pronounced air of national triumph and popular rejoicing when the victorious outcome of Cumberland's Scotch campaign became apparent during the spring and summer of 1746.

Judas Maccabaeus is the least dramatic of Handel's narrative oratorios. There are no characters (Judas, Simon and Eupolemus are the only named figures) and the chorus is a pious mouthpiece for a range of collective emotions — sadness, reverence, festal joy, martial resolve, steadfast faith. The military actions which form the work's historical background, based on passages in the first book of Maccabees and Flavius Josephus describing the Jewish struggle against Antiochus Epiphanes of Syria and ultimate acceptance of Roman protection, are all reported by messengers, and the significant absence of personal relationships is enhanced by the abstract nature of the female roles, essentially disembodied voices. Morell's verse is not particularly distinguished, sometimes ungainly, and there are signs in the music, especially in the uncharacteristically rebarbative rhythms and textures of 'O never, never bow we down' in Act II, that Handel was losing interest in, and patience with, the mood of the text. It is significant that his later additions of 'Sion now her head shall raise', 'Wise men flatt'ring' and 'See the conq'ring hero' have all kept their place in the work, where so many of his other inserted pieces for oratorio revivals have since been cast aside.

Yet why, if *Judas* really is the 'decline into claptrap' that modern commentators seem to think it, has its popularity so powerfully endured? The answer surely lies in its very absence of local, individualized drama, a weakness according to some, but the inevitable spring of its occasionally rather coarse appeal to communal sentiment. The serene, unyielding beauty of 'From mighty kings he took the spoil' and 'O lovely Peace', reflecting that English melodic temper of which Handel was now the nonchalant master, and the classic sublimity of 'Father of Heaven' opening the Chanukah celebrations in Act III, win us over paradoxically because they do *not* belong to anybody in particular, because they are the universal expressions of happiness, freedom and religious devotion. From a purely artistic aspect, few of the choruses bid fair to rival those in many of the other oratorios. But *Judas* succeeds through this very simplicity. Its ambition is that not unworthy one of distilling those general feelings which bind us all together.

The oratorio, revived, with one exception, each succeeding season until Handel's death, sent its reverberations through his bank accounts (the second of two performances in 1752 brought him the staggering total of £640) and became a dependable moneyspinner. Everyone, from

Shaftesbury, who noted that it 'went off with very great Applause' to Lady Luxborough's steward Mr Outing, who 'speaks with such ecstasy of the music, as I confess I cannot conceive anyone can feel who understands no more of music than myself', was enraptured and Catherine Talbot memorably told Miss Carter: 'Those oratorios of Handel's are certainly (next to the *hooting of owls*) the most solemnly striking music one can hear.'

Cashing in upon the wave of Handelian enthusiasm the Haymarket opera directors, anxious to curb rising debts, announced a pasticcio *Lucio Vero* based on 'Airs, borrow'd entirely from Mr Handel's favourite Operas. . . . The Lovers of Musick among us, whose Ears have been charm'd with Farinello, Faustina, Senesino, Cuzzoni, and other great Performers will now have an Opportunity of Reviving their former Delight. . . . Mr Handel is acknowledged (universally) so great a Master of the Lyre; that nothing urg'd in Favour of his Capital Performances, can reasonably be considered as a Puff.' Handel himself seems to have made no objection to such an act of homage from his former rivals and Walsh, a publisher to the bone, issued the favourite songs using his stock of old plates from *Admeto*, *Siroe* and other pieces. Comment is superfluous on the fact that *Lucio Vero* was given every Saturday during the season from 14 November to 26 December, and revived the following January and March. As if this were not enough, *Alessandro* was once more brought on at the opera as *Rossane* during February. Everyone, it seemed, suddenly wanted to hear nothing but Handel.

His 1748 Lenten programme at Covent Garden began fittingly with *Judas Maccabaeus*. Beard had quitted the company, not to return for four years, and was replaced by Thomas Lowe, a popular singer at pleasure gardens, but according to Burney 'with the finest tenor voice I ever heard in my life, for want of diligence and cultivation, he never could be safely trusted with anything better than a ballad, which he constantly learned by his ear' — shortcomings which made little difference to the sort of music Handel was prepared to give him. Francesina's place as 'the first woman' (she had not sung in the *Judas* première) was taken more or less permanently by the Haymarket soprano Giulia Frasi, whose clear and agile voice was assisted by a good English accent. She was a flighty and indolent creature: Horace Walpole notes her as the mistress of the M.P. Sir Thomas Winnington, and Handel was greatly tickled when Burney, briefly her music master, told him of her intention to study thorough-bass. The composer, who knew her all too well, simply remarked with his inimitable dryness, 'What may we not expect?'

She did not, as it turned out, sing in the new oratorio of *Joshua*, given its first performance on 9 March, where the soprano role of Achsah was taken by her fellow King's Theatre star Casarini. Like its predecessor, which in certain points it was obviously intended to follow up, *Joshua* was an instant and continuing success. A typical audience reaction came from the romance-writer and *feuilletoniste* Eliza Heywood, who wrote: 'I closed my Eyes, and imagined myself amidst the angelic Choir in the bright Regions of everlasting Day, chanting the Praises of my great Creator, and his ineffable *Messiah*. I seemed, methought, to have nothing of this gross Earth about me, but was all Soul! — all Spirit!' She was moved enough to suggest that free oratorio performances be given 'in every City and great Town throughout the Kingdom' with the object of arresting the depravity and irreverence of the age.

Mrs Heywood, however, was unimpressed with Morell's libretto, which she thought 'not quite so elegant, nor so well as I could have wished adapted to the Music'. Warfare, liberty and patriotism once more play their part, in this story of Joshua's victories over the Canaanites, among them the siege of Jericho, assisted by divine intervention, but Morell also introduces a love interest between the warrior Othniel and Achsah, daughter of grizzled old Caleb. The pair, foreshadowing the more strongly characterized Hamor and Iphis in *Jephtha*, are little better, in words and music, than some simpering Colin and Kitty from bourgeois Vauxhall pastoral. Othniel is treated to two of Morell's most bathetic lines when in Act I he has to confront an angel with the words 'Awful, pleasing being, say', and in Act III, volunteering to take the city of Debir in exchange for Achsah's hand he exclaims: 'Transporting thought! Caleb, the town's thy own.' Achsah herself gets by far the worst of it in an air to the quatrain:

> Oh! who can tell, oh! who can hear
> Of Egypt, and not shed a tear?
> Or, who will not on Jordan smile
> Releas'd from bondage on the Nile?

Handel's impatience with all this makes itself clear. Whatever his anxieties as to the state of his bank account or the need to replenish his cellar, he could scarcely do without the inspiration of powerful character and vicissitude upon which to build artistic concepts which would be more than mere sops to the bourgeois piety of his audience. The third act, for instance, illustrates with grim clarity the composer's loss of interest in his material. The choruses, mere noisy flourishes, culminate in 34 bars of

D major rejoicing, as perfunctory an ending as he had ever composed to any of his works (even the final ensembles of the most routine operas, *Lotario*, say, or *Arianna*, have greater power to engage us). Of the four airs Caleb's 'Shall I in Mamre's fertile plain' alone has real distinction. Achsah's 'O had I Jubal's lyre' loses little as a concert piece, and, indeed, it has proved popular as a show-piece for warbling divas.

Joshua himself, a cardboard captain along the lines of Judas Maccabaeus, comes into his own in the two truly compelling moments of the work, in which Handel awakes from torpor to produce music whose graphic immediacy in its dramatic use of the chorus looks across the centuries to the ambience of *Boris Godunov* or *Aleksandr Nevsky* (and Handel was well enough regarded in nineteenth- and early twentieth-century Russian musical circles for a direct link to be not unimaginable). In Act I the hero ushers in a choral picture of the crossing of the Jordan whose declamatory opening, stressing Joshua's role as intermediary with God, contrasts with rich Baroque description of the river standing 'in wat'ry heaps affrighted' and turning itself backwards. Still better is 'Glory to God', at the beginning of Act II, whose overwhelming blaze of sound we might well believe to have brought down Jericho's walls. Its deceptively simple start dovetails into the vivid dotted quaver passages portraying the fall of the city, leading in turn to the shatteringly original 'The nations tremble', with its unforgettable sonorities created by demisemiquaver rushes on the strings and menacing timpani tremolandi, with trumpets and horns rallying urgently across the B minor war clouds, far distant from their traditional celebratory roles.

It was this chorus which made Haydn tell the English composer William Shield that he 'never knew half its powers before he heard it, and he was perfectly certain that only one inspired author ever did, or ever could, pen so sublime a composition'. He must also have been stirred by the act's uniquely spectacular finale, in which the famous staying in their courses of the sun and moon is re-enacted in music whose effectiveness is created as much by orchestral as by choral means. Joshua, as earlier, sets everything going as the sun climbs to a high A on the first and second violins, reinforced by the moon on third violins and violas and by the entrance of a solo trumpet, and held as a pedal point for 24 bars while the chorus, against bustling string patterns, describes the scattered nations flying before it. The accumulated volume of sound dies away as the accompaniment is fragmented with rests and the oboes and brass, marked pianissimo, fall out, leaving the bare strings to articulate a solitary final D.

Handel had begun *Joshua* on 19 July and completed it exactly a month later. Some six weeks before this he had started another piece to a Morell text, the oratorio *Alexander Balus*, but with some shrewdness he had chosen to make this the second of his Covent Garden novelties for 1748, since he must have foreseen that the title, even to those who knew their Apocrypha especially well, was hardly likely to draw as powerfully as that of its companion work. There is little evidence, even from that bible-reading age, that many people were acquainted with the eponymous hero, for whom Morell had had to quarry deep into the well-excavated *Maccabees* to produce the story of the usurping Syrian king, Alexander, whose love for Cleopatra is thwarted by the wicked designs of her father, Ptolemy of Egypt, and whose alliance with the warlike Jews ends in his death.

Neither the story nor the libretto itself promised much to Handel. Morell, who does not really seem to have known exactly what he was doing with his sketchy materials, was at any rate a compliant collaborator. 'As to the last Air' (Cleopatra's 'Convey me to some peaceful shore') he wrote to a friend: 'I cannot help telling you, that when Mr Handell first read it, he cried out *D — m* your Iambics. "Don't put yourself in a passion, they are easily Trochees." "*Trochees, what are Trochees?*" "Why, the very reverse of Iambics, by leaving out a syllable in every line, as insted of

> *Convey me to some peaceful shore,*
> *Lead me to some peaceful shore.*"

"That is what I want." "I will step into the parlour, and alter them immediately." I went down and returned with them altered in about 3 minutes; when he would have them as they were, and set them most delightfully accompanied with only a quaver, and a rest of 3 quavers.' Before we dismiss so apparently cavalier an attitude towards the text, it is worth recalling once again the Verdi–Piave parallel, where the exchange of letters between composer and poet bears witness to the latter's need to keep his verses flexible in the face of the streamrollings of the martinet musician. *Prima la musica, poi le parole* indeed.

Even with its iambics reversed, the stark beauty of 'Convey me to some peaceful shore', its skeletal accompaniment (merely punctuating the rests) eloquent of the heroine's emotional exhaustion, can scarcely save *Alexander Balus* from oblivion. It was given only three performances in 1748 and one subsequent revival during Handel's lifetime (plans for another had to be scrapped because of the Prince of Wales's sudden death). Nor has the gradual Handelian re-emergence in modern times brought about much of a reappraisal. The first act is manifestly top-heavy and the second does little to advance the story, which only gets properly going in Act III, when Cleopatra makes the work her own in a succession of potently effective arias and accompanied recitatives. The protagonists are otherwise pallid and conventional, in the case of Alexander and Ptolemy respectively, though the latter's unregenerate villainy at least gave Reinhold a chance for stronger vocal acting than was required of him in *Judas* and *Joshua*. The tenor role of Jonathan, priggish and detached, is perhaps the most antipathetic Handel and his librettists ever created.

A sense of confusion and irritation, stronger here even than in *Joshua*, irradiates the composer's autograph score. That his mind was not wholly on the job is indicated by such telling details as 'Judah' for 'Jonathan' against the vocal stave of 'Great God from whom all blessings spring': 'Judah' is referred to in the air itself and in the preceding recitative, but it was clearly all one to Handel. The manuscript is in any case fuller than ever of second thoughts, erasures and wholesale transferences of verse lines from one place to another, suggesting that several pieces may have been composed in anticipation of their texts. Yet the old dramatic flair leaps out at us in a handful of irresistible moments, as when Cleopatra's liquid *siciliano* 'Here amid the shady woods' is broken in upon by the entry of Ptolemy's gang of ruffians, who haul her off like the *Rigoletto* courtiers abducting Gilda, or in the unaccompanied opening to her 'O take me from this hateful light'. Perhaps what Handel really wanted to do here was to write opera rather than oratorio. The very title *Alexander Balus* recalls Italian double-barrels like *Lucio Papirio* or *Caio Fabrizio*, and the sensuality of a score enriched with brass, flutes, a harp and a mandoline seems to hint at a world to which sententious monotheism is alien and disagreeable. Failure here is understandable: in Handel's last works, four oratorios of incalculable brilliance, public caprice alone determined the measure of success.

Overplied in Music's Cause

The last and greatest phase of Handel's career as a composer saw him the approved master of a form for which his imagination had devised new dimensions. The term 'oratorio' seems altogether too limiting to apply to the type of work which he had developed during the course of the 1740s. Though *Semele* and *Hercules* are not oratorios they represent a crucial stage in this process, for without them *Belshazzar* and *Judas Maccabaeus* are inconceivable, just as none of these works is imaginable without the experience of *Messiah*, a piece which appears like a sublime exercise in the reduction of Handel's genius to its essential components. Nor does any of the oratorios aim merely at formulaic repetition of another. Like the plays of Shakespeare or the operas of Verdi, each, despite external pressures from the entertainment world, creates its own individual terms, and though, like the English playwright and the Italian composer, Handel had occasional recourse to quickfire solutions and half-hearted fudging, the particular quality of his absorption in the work gave each a unique character. Thus when we speak vaguely of 'Handel oratorio' we mean something whose connexion with the form as then accepted in Italy and Germany is only a general one. Yet the more closely we look at pieces like *Susanna* and *Theodora*, works imparting an intimacy comparable to the novels of Richardson or the comedies of Goldoni being written in the same epoch, the more necessary it becomes to discard our English notions of oratorio as something involving hippopotamus contraltos shaking the dome off the Albert Hall, and to relate such compositions more nearly to the seventeenth-century religious mixture of introspection and sensuality in which the form itself is rooted.

To carry his special kind of elastic expressiveness in the mature oratorios Handel significantly altered his approach to orchestration. He had never relinquished the very highest standards in his demands on all his performers. Burney recalled that 'Handel wore an enormous white wig and, when things went well at the Oratorio, it had a certain nod, or vibration, which manifested his pleasure and satisfaction. Without it, nice observers were certain that he was out of humour.' He could command some of the best musical hands in a city whose expectations went increasingly higher as each new continental virtuoso arrived, and players such as the violinist Matthew Dubourg evidently found working with him a stimulating experience. But, unlike Bach or Vivaldi, he consistently refrained from treating his medium as a platform for instrumental display. After Sammartini's oboe pyrotechnics had graced the operas of the late 1730s Handel never again sought to throw an orchestral soloist into such bold relief. Though his sense of instrumental colour in terms of appropriate shading is subtler than that of any other contemporary master, he created a deliberate and momentous area of difference between his opera and oratorio scorings in his resolute restriction of the oboes, in the latter, to the choral numbers. Not, of course, exclusively or dogmatically, but enough, in a piece like *Solomon*, where they do not participate in a single air, for their former function of giving bite to the string tone in the ritornelli of opera arias to be substantially abrogated.

It is not clear why he should have done this, unless he saw the oratorios as demanding a distinctive orchestral sound or was beginning to view the oboes in terms closer to those of his younger German and Italian contemporaries, anticipating the symphonists of the mid-century. Brass instruments are treated in similar fashion. The trumpet is still given an occasional solo outing, most notably in 'With honour let desert be crown'd' from *Judas Maccabaeus*, where the striking use of it in an unaccustomed A minor effectively pinpoints the moral underlay of the hero's aria, but otherwise its use is to brighten moments of victorious festivity and religious assertiveness. Horns, as we have noted earlier in *Athalia*, could be used to conjure up the world of pagan revelry or to lend a dignified amplitude to pieces like 'See, the conqu'ring hero comes', (originally in *Joshua* and transferred to *Judas* around 1750) or the overture in *Samson*. The flute (recorders do not figure in any of the mature oratorios) has a special function in enhancing erotic tenderness, as in the nightingale chorus of *Solomon*, or in deepening an atmosphere of solemn sadness like that which broods over the prison scene in *Theodora*. Yet, like the other instruments of Handel's oratorio orchestra, it is simply an artistic component of the score, never an obbligato in the full sense of the label.

His setting of English texts had grown correspondingly more sensitive. He was never quite to rival Purcell in demonstrating the language's full validity as a medium for song, and his own grasp of it led him now and then to some odd stresses — 'extravagántly' in *Hercules*, for instance, 'to réceive' and 'incórruptíble' in *Messiah* (though the Germanic 'Philístine' in Samuel's prophecy to Saul is wholly owing to Jennens) — but his understanding of the colour and nuance of English words is comparable in its awareness to that of another great foreign Englishman over a century later, the novelist Joseph Conrad.

Certainly Handel's turn from Italian to English not only gave an immense fillip to the growth of a native tradition of solo singing in its introduction of talents like those of John Beard and the Young sisters, Cecilia and Esther, but encouraged other composers to follow his example in the field of oratorio and its kindred forms. Younger masters, William Boyce, Thomas Augustine Arne and John Stanley among them, looked towards newer styles in their music yet simultaneously reflected the powerful impress of his manner, whether in form or idiom. When the progress of the blindness which began its serious onset in 1751 put an end, despite flickering hopes of a recovery, to full-scale composition, there was the gratification for Handel of feeling that he had ended, not in stale repetition of trusted formulas, but at the height of his powers, extending even further the scope of the oratorio as a dramatic medium. *Jephtha*, his last original work, makes a memorable and impressive conclusion to half a century of unyielding dedication to his art.

Rivals were in any case now less likely to trouble him, the more so since foreign composers visiting London tended to concentrate upon opera, and none of them seriously set up to dare him on his own ground. Some time in 1747 the news may have reached him of the death in Vienna, at the age of 76, of his old challenger Giovanni Bononcini. Almost forgotten in circles where he had formerly reigned supreme, the Modenese composer lived in squalid desolation on the pension of 50 florins granted him by Maria Theresa in consideration of services to the imperial household. A pathetic list of his effects, made on the day after he died, includes, among such items as a mouse-coloured coat, an old hat, two wigs with a block, a spinet and a fiddle bow, a night commode and two tin lamps, the tantalizing mention of two travelling trunks 'wherein various musical concertos'. But it was not much for the man whose pride had rebuked emperors and duchesses.

The contrast with Handel as he found himself at the opening of the 1749 season can scarcely have been more marked. Lady Shaftesbury went to the new oratorio of *Susanna* 'in the light operatic style' and told James Harris 'I think I never saw a fuller house. Rich told me that he believed he would receive near 400 l.' Sir Edward Turner urged his friend the talented amateur architect Sanderson Miller to come at once to London: 'Will not the sedate Raptures of Oratorical Harmony attract hither an Admirer of the sublime in music? . . . Glorious Entertainment! Divine Efficacy of Music!' and glorious entertainment the new piece indeed was, Handel depositing some £550 in his bank account after three performances.

He had begun work on *Susanna* the previous July, completing it within seven weeks, on 24 August. Morell, for the time being, stepped aside as his librettist. Since there seem to have been no hard feelings over the issue on either part, some practical consideration doubtless forced Handel to turn elsewhere and choose an anonymous poet who supplied him with the texts of *Susanna* and *Solomon*. We know that both had a common source simply through the widespread and recurrent parallels in the poetry of each. The writer may have been Newburgh Hamilton, though only the vaguest evidence supports his candidature. For the time being these capably handled and often felicitous librettos retain their secret.

The story of Susanna, with its inbuilt paradox of senile lust opposed to wounded innocence and wifely fidelity, had always been popular in Baroque art, but its most outstanding expression in music before Handel was in Alessandro Stradella's vividly conceived oratorio of 1666, written for Queen Christina of Sweden, a score of which the younger composer may have seen in Italy. The elements in each, Susanna, the two Elders, the Prophet Daniel and a chorus, are more or less the same, with the addition in Handel's setting of Susanna's father Chelsias and her husband Joachim. Each, too, fully partakes of that essentially secular narrative quality which has placed the tale alongside those of Tobit and Judith in the Apocrypha. As material for a sacred oratorio the little Book of Susanna is justified only by its Jewish background and the presence of the boy Daniel. Otherwise its atmosphere is that of a rustic folktale, and it was in this vein that Handel and his librettist chose to treat it.

We return at once to the countryside of *Allegro, Penseroso and Moderato*, and while Susanna and Joachim don the straw hat and leather gaiters of figures of a Gainsborough landscape, the two elders, unforgettably preposterous in their panting adoration, seem to have wandered in from the pages of *Joseph Andrews*. The quintessential Englishness of everything is brought home to us from almost the very beginning in the sophisticated naïveté with which Handel treats the married idyll of husband and wife in the duet 'When thou art nigh', whose very rhythms and harmonic simplicity relate it to the world of ballad opera, brought even nearer in the two little songs for Susanna's companion early in Act II, the first of which,

'Ask if yon damask rose', is the most winsomely simple thing Handel ever composed.

Such a spirit becomes still more marked in the characterization of the two elders, differentiated with all the shrewdness at Handel's command. The First Elder's music, in his introductory recitative and air 'When the trumpet sounds to arms', leaves us in no doubt as to how much the composer understood the subliminal eroticism of his text. In the agonized accompagnato shudders of the former and in the latter's mocking glissandos and roulades we hear not so much a parody of nobler heroic passions as a grotesque attack of satyriasis matching the bawdy *double-entendre* of the words. The bass Second Elder, on the other hand, has all the impatient bluster of Polyphemus, a genuine *buffo* figure embarrassed by his desires, at once fatuous and menacing.

Susanna herself gathers depth and dignity as the work progresses. From its very outset her airs communicate and retain a uniquely exalted beauty, linked on the one hand with graces which, as Handel implies in the limpid semiquaver accompaniment of her bathing song, must surely tempt a saint, let alone an elder, and on the other with the unassuming virtue in which she is finally to triumph. Such unadorned excellence is expressed in the vein of antique solemnity, already established in the overture's quotation from a piece by John Blow, which animates the structure of 'Bending to the throne of glory', almost like a seventeenth-century instrumental canzona, and the grave wretchedness of 'If guiltless blood', where the central section, a hymn of serene resignation, is brusquely interrupted by the Second Elder. Similar qualities colour the longer of the two numbers given to the youthful prophet Daniel: the lines and textures of 'Chastity, thou cherub bright', using tied crotchets as *points d'appui*, are a study in luminous, unruffled calm anticipating 'As with rosy steps the morn' in *Theodora* the following year.

If *Susanna* has any flaw it is in the anonymous librettist's approach to the chorus. They inhabit the first two acts solely as a guarantee that what we are hearing is an oratorio in the approved manner. The fact that their opening outburst, a lament of the captive Jews over a Purcellian ground-bass, is as fine a piece as anything elsewhere in these late works does little to annul its monumental irrelevance to what follows. Sophistry alone can establish connexions between the central story and an utterance more appropriate to the world of *Judas Maccabaeus* or *Israel in Egypt*. This dichotomy between overall function and individual quality in the choruses is upheld until the close of Act II, when the massed voices are at last drawn into the drama as witnesses of Susanna's supposed apprehension *in flagrante delicto*. Otherwise the magnificent architecture of 'Righteous heaven', with its four contrasted sections, seems, however excellent in itself, to lay a wholly disproportionate emphasis on the moral implications of the story. The work cannot effectively carry a chorus of such Michaelangelesque stature, whereas the primitive rhythmic bite of 'The cause is decided' at the beginning of Act III is wholly apposite to the air of tension in the court scene.

So awkward a juxtaposition was easily avoided in *Solomon*, written before *Susanna* but brought on after it. Here the chorus is more of a participant than in any of the other dramatic oratorios, and thus, though it is not an obvious link in the chain of historical influences through which musicology traces the progress of the art, the work can be said to occupy a singular position in the development of non-liturgical choral writing. From the very beginning, in the eight-part 'Your harps and cymbals sound', whose meticulous layout, with concertino and ripieno groupings, typifies one of Handel's richest and most imaginative scores, the chorus establishes its primacy. It is, in a sense, the presenter of the vivid and contrasting tableaux of the piece, inset like brilliant fresco panels into the sturdy musculature of a Baroque ceiling. Its responses firmly govern the succeeding moods: it can take on the guise of a solemn assembly of temple priests, as in the opening modulations of 'With pious heart and holy tongue', or assume the role, closer to the *Song of Solomon*, of a wedding party hastening bride and bridegroom to bed in the ineffable beauties of 'May no rash intruder', in which a pair of flutes over whispering strings become the nightingales who 'lull them to sleep with their song'. In the final act it provides, using the king himself as a master of ceremonies, an entertainment which is in effect a Cecilian ode celebrating the varying charms of music, from serene harmonies through martial clangour and the anarchies of passion to an emotional calm in the closing analogy to the passing of a storm at sea.

Not that *Solomon* is by any means the type of static chorus and aria sequence represented by a piece such as *Judas Maccabaeus*. The anonymous librettist cleverly shaped his drama around four different aspects of Solomon's kingship, all of them appropriate within the eighteenth-century context. First we see the king as, by inference, head of the church, in his newly built temple, then as the ardent lover of his Egyptian queen, then as the wise judge in the famous incident of the two harlots wrangling over the child, and finally as the welcoming host to his illustrious foreign guest the Queen of Sheba 'from Arabia's spicy shores, bounded by the hoary main'. Fittingly the title role is given to a mezzo-soprano, embodying those qualities of youthful positiveness and optimism which emerge in similar castings for high voice elsewhere in the oratorios (Cyrus in *Belshazzar*, for example). Yet Solomon's own music is less memorable than the exuberant numbers given to the tenor Zadok (the priest, indeed) especially the whirring instrumental catherine-wheels of 'Sacred raptures', the Egyptian queen's 'With thee the unshelter'd moor', which has the same graceful cleanness of line as 'I know that my Redeemer liveth', or the exalted radiance of the Queen of Sheba's 'Will the sun forget to streak', another of Handel's inimitable evocations of dawning light, worthy to set beside 'As steals the morn' in *Il Moderato*.

For vigour and pathos, however, it is the two harlots who steal the show, and their judgment scene is a perfect example of Handel's accomplished dramaturgy. The child's real mother wins our sympathy at once in her initial F sharp minor plea at the opening of the extraordinary trio 'Words are weak to paint my fears', couched in rhythms and harmonies reminiscent of the more poignant moments of the *Brockes Passion*; the false claimant bursts in with skipping A major quavers, 'False is all her melting tale', and the king himself establishes an E major balance through Handel's punning treatment of 'Justice holds the lifted scale', before the pair fall away to leave the first voice in its plaintive solitude. Restlessly, in suitably meretricious modern vein, the second harlot flatters the monarch's wisdom, but her rival, by piercing to the heart of true parental anguish in the despairing phrases of 'Can I see my infant gored', whose eleven-bar closing adagio reduces her to a figure of noble abjection, conquers and earns her right to join Solomon in a final duet.

Both trio and duet bear witness to Handel's interest in the potential of ensemble, something which Baroque lyric drama, with its focus on solistic glamour, tended understandably to shy away from, but which he had already begun to develop in middle-period operas such as *Partenope* and *Orlando*. The mature oratorios feature several outstanding examples, such as *Semele*'s quartet in Act I, and the confrontation between Susanna and the two Elders, in which, as with the *Solomon* trio, the rhythmic patterns of the several lines are carefully adjusted to the character and intentions of the protagonists.

Susanna enjoyed a modest success at its first performances, and several individual numbers in *Solomon*, such as 'With thee the unshelter'd moor', became popular favourites. At the season's close, with a *Messiah* performance (the first since 1743) on 23 March, Handel turned to an altogether different project in the composition of what has since become one of his best-known works, the *Music for the Royal Fireworks*, designed to be given as 'a grand Overture of Warlike Instruments' to the opulent pyrotechnical display in the Green Park to celebrate the Peace of Aix-la-Chapelle, signed with France the previous October.

The war of the Austrian Succession had degenerated into aimless attrition, with neither side seeing much more advantage in sustaining an expensive and desultory international conflict. If victory festivities were not in order, and if George II's motives as Elector of Hanover in pursuing the war to preserve his German domains were all too readily appreciated, he could at least now be hailed as the bringer of harmony. As such, in effigy at least, he formed the centrepiece of the amazing confection specially constructed for the open-air spectacle on 27 April 1749.

Its architect was the Florentine Servandoni, scenic artist to the French court (his services were perhaps a generous gesture by Louis XV) and best known today as the creator of the grandiose church of St Sulpice in Paris. The 'Machine', as it was called, stood at the bottom of the park and represented 'a magnificent *Doric* Temple, from which extend two Wings terminated by Pavillons . . . adorned with Frets, Gilding, Lustres, Artificial Flowers, Inscriptions, Statues, Allegorical Pictures & c.' together with Latin inscriptions and 23 figures by Andrea Casali, an Italian statuary and painter much in favour with young English patrons of the Rococo style. The descriptions only make its essentially ephemeral nature more regrettable, particularly when we read that Servandoni and his Bolognese assistants Gaetano Ruggieri and Giuseppe Sarti had devised a special firework trick whereby eighteen pictures suddenly appeared as 'Marble Basso Relievos' then changed colour by means of 'a great Number of Lampions' to culminate in the image of the king giving peace to Britannia, Neptune and Mars.

Handel's instrumental suite of overture and dances was to open the programme, but its rehearsals were not without their difficulties. The whole show was managed by Charles Frederick, 'Comptroller of his Majesty's Fireworks as well for War as for Triumph', and Captain Thomas Desaguliers, Chief Fire Master of the Royal Laboratory, and to the former the Duke of Montague, Master of the Ordnance, wrote anxiously discussing the composer's orchestral forces. Uncharacteristically the king had jibbed at there being any music, but 'when I told him the quantity and nomber of martial musick . . . he was better satisfied, and said he hoped there would be no fidles'. Handel, however, had suddenly decided to cut down the number of trumpets and horns from sixteen to twelve apiece and to introduce 'violeens', something which Montague was sure would put George out of humour. 'I am shure it behoves Hendel to have as many trumpets, and other martial instruments as possible, tho he dont retrench the violins, which I think he shoud, tho I beleeve he will never be persuaded to do so.' We can sympathize with the Duke in having to act as intermediary between two such intransigent characters as the sovereign and the composer.

Further problems were being created by Handel's unwillingness to release the music for a public rehearsal at Vauxhall Gardens, where Jonathan Tyers had offered to lend his illuminations and servants to manage them for the Green Park *fête*. Montague, exasperated at Handel's apparently 'absolute determination' on the point, told Frederick: 'If he wont let us have his overture we must get an other, and I think it would be proper to inclose my letter to you in your letter to him, that he may know my centiments; but don't say I bid you send it to him.' This was a covering note to a longer letter written on the same day, in which the Duke artfully stressed the king's interest in the whole matter, implying that Handel's consent would best show his duty to his sovereign. The ruse was successful, and after a shuffling of rehearsal dates owing to wet weather and a desire to accommodate the Duke of Cumberland, the music was played to 'the brightest and most numerous Assembly', though the *General Advertiser* noted that 'several Footmen who attended their Masters, &c thither, behaved very sausily, and were justly corrected by the Gentlemen for their Insolence'.

Five days later off it all went at the showery close of a hot April day, the salute of 101 brass ordnance, the Girandole and Caduceus rockets, the mortars with 'Air Ballons', the 'Magnificent *Jet de Feu* of forty Feet High', the 141 large fountains, the explosions of serpents, rain and stars, the Tourbillons, Pots de Brins and 'Marrons in Battery'. John Byrom, witty bard of 'Tweedledum and Tweedledee' Handel versus Bononcini, sat down under a tree stump to write a line to his wife. 'It has been a very hot day, but there is a dark overcast of cloudiness which may possibly turn to rain, which occasions some of better habits to think of retiring; and while I am now writing it spits a little. . . . 11 o'clock: all over, and somewhat in a hurry, by an accidental fire at one of the ends of the building, which, whether it be extinguished I know not, for I left it in an ambiguous condition that I might finish my letter, which otherwise I could not have done.' He was better off, he considered, in the park with 'the mobility' than in the official stands, where privy councillors had been issued with twelve seats and peers got four. During the fire Servandoni quarrelled with Charles Frederick and drew his sword on him, and was only released from custody the following day after he had asked pardon in the Duke of Cumberland's presence.

The titles of two of Handel's pieces in the *Fireworks Music* suite, 'La Paix' and 'La Réjouissance', suggest that they may have been intended to accompany the display itself, though there is no evidence that this was finally the case. The programme described the six movements as an overture, and such, apparently, they were, cast by the composer in the grandest French manner familiar to us in other Baroque dance sets such as Bach's first orchestral suite. Reworking earlier sketches he devised a grandiose opening in the traditional mode of dotted slow section followed by fugal allegro, an ideal amalgam of simple basic ideas with a confidence in their maximum effectiveness which can only belong to Handel. A gentle, almost sly contrast is offered by the succeeding bourrée, and still more by the warm serenities of 'La Paix', in that lilting triple time he had already so memorably linked with 'lovely Peace' in *Judas Maccabaeus*. 'La Réjouissance' is what its title implies, a jubilant rejoicing played three times over by varying instrumental groups, and the work ends with a brace of minuets.

Far from losing interest in orchestral music, as has been suggested, Handel seems, during this period, to have tackled it with renewed originality. Few of his instrumental pieces outside the Opus 6 concertos can quite rival the imaginative power in remodelling earlier material which irradiates the three concertos for double wind and strings written presumably for the 1747–8 oratorio performances — 'Jehovah crown'd' from *Esther*, 'Io seguo sol fiero' from *Partenope* and 'See, from his banks' from *Belshazzar* are electrifying in their new guises — but the clutch of organ concertos published by Walsh in 1761 as Opus 7 shows a continuing readiness to treat the form with as much freedom as it would allow.

Like the Opus 4 concertos, these relate directly to individual performances, exhibiting Handel's talents as a keyboard virtuoso, but linked with the world of the oratorios by an increased grandeur and boldness of design. The fourth, for instance, starts with a darkly coloured D minor adagio, with divided 'cellos augmented by bassoons, culminating in a cadenza which perhaps reflects only part of what the composer gave his audience. The clouds are packed away, however, with the sprightly second movement, based on a piece from Telemann's *Musique de Table* and a textbook example of Handel the borrower at work on tightening up the musical structure throughout. The B flat concerto which begins the set opens, on the other hand, with two magisterial elaborations, strongly contrasted in treatment, on ground basses, recalling similar pieces among his solo keyboard works, but given greater amplitude by the participation of the orchestra. The whole set represents a fascinating glimpse of Handel's consistently untrammelled attitude to instrumental forms as an adjunct to his vocal works.

The *Fireworks Music* was brought out again on 27 May as part of 'a Grand Performance of Vocal and Instrumental MUSICK' under the composer's direction in the chapel of the newly-built Foundling Hospital in Lamb's Conduit Fields (now Coram's Fields). The royal charter for the hospital's foundation was granted in 1739 to Captain Thomas Coram, whose dogged determination to better the lot of London's pauper children by setting up a charitable institution, where they could be fed, clothed and educated, had succeeded in getting a large orphanage built for the purpose on land to the north of Gray's Inn on the fringes of Bloomsbury. Georgian England was always a curious mixture of cynical coarseness on the one hand and profoundly, often romantically humanitarian sentiments on the other, but though the latter were now deeply engaged in the scheme, the foundation still desperately needed funds. It is no surprise to find the painter William Hogarth among the hospital's patrons, and only natural that Handel, with typical liberality, should now follow suit in helping the work along. On 7 May he was present at a Governors' Meeting, which enthusiastically accepted his offer of a charitable concert and elected him to the board. It was to be a lasting and fruitful association, even though Handel at first declined the governorship 'for that he should serve the Charity with more Pleasure in his Way, than being a Member of the Corporation'.

The concert featured selections from *Solomon* and a special anthem skilfully compiled from items in the 1737 Funeral Anthem and *Susanna* (a chorus cut before the first performance) and ending with the Hallelujah Chorus. This is particularly significant as the harbinger of those *Messiah* performances at the Hospital from 1750 onwards which, every year until Handel's death, brought increased popularity to the oratorio and may be said to have established its primacy with English audiences. So conscious indeed were the Governors of the work's drawing power that they tried to secure exclusive rights to it by a petition to Parliament. Handel's fury, expressed in his outburst: 'For what shall the Foundling put mine oratorio in the Parliament! The Devil! mine musič shall not go to the Parliament!' is meekly rendered in the committee minutes as 'the same did not seem agreeable to Mr Handel for the present', though he did leave a score and parts to the hospital in his will and obviously meant well by Coram's foundation from first to last.

In September 1749, Heidegger died, aged 85, at his house in Richmond. His 'well-known Character', said the *General Advertiser*, 'wants no Encomium; of him, it may be truly said, what one Hand received from the Rich, the other gave to the Poor.' Handel, linked in perpetuity to Covent Garden, had had no connexion with his old impresario and business partner for several years, but the death of the man who had helped to present his earliest London successes must have made him feel his age. Earlier in the year Lord Shaftesbury had written of him as 'the old Buck . . . excessively healthy and full of spirits', and his indefatigable resource now addressed itself to the novel exercise of writing incidental music for a play by the young novelist Tobias Smollett. 'I have wrote a sort of Tragedy on the story of Alceste, which will (without fail) be acted at Covent Garden next Season,' Smollett told a friend, 'and appear with such magnificence of Scenery as was never exhibited in Britain before.' If it had ever got off the ground, the project, including Handel's sumptuous symphonies, airs and choruses, and sets by Servandoni himself, must indeed have marked an epoch in English theatrical production, but alas, nothing came of it, and though the music and scenes survived, the play disappeared altogether. The cause, according to Sir Walter Scott in his *Lives of the Novelists*, was a quarrel between Smollett and Rich, whom the irascible doctor-turned-writer had already satirized in his poem *Reproof*.

Handel solaced himself for these reverses by attending picture auctions and making several purchases, including the large landscape of the Rhine attributed to Rembrandt but probably by his pupil Philips van Koninck, which he subsequently left to Bernard Granville. The oratorio season was in any case about to start, with revivals of *Saul* and *Judas Maccabaeus* and an entirely new piece written during the previous July to a text by Thomas Morell and premièred on 16 March 1750.

Morell himself recalled that 'the next I wrote was *Theodora* . . . which Mr Handell himself valued more than any Performance of the kind; and when I once ask'd him, whether he did not look upon the Grand Chorus in the Messiah as his Master Piece? "*No*," says he, "*I think the Chorus at the end of the 2d part in Theodora far beyond it*. He saw the lovely youth &c."' The work took its place immediately among the roster of his distinguished box office failures. Beyond a solitary revival in 1755 it received only four performances in Handel's lifetime and he himself was inimitably dry in his resignation to the débâcle. 'The 2d night of *Theodora* was very thin indeed,' says Morell, 'tho' the Princess Amelia was there. I guessed it a losing night, so did not go to Mr Handell as usual; but seeing him smile, I ventured, when "Will you be there next Friday night," says he "and I will play it to you?" I told him I had just seen Sir T. Hankey, "and he desired me to tell you that if you would have it again, he would engage for all the Boxes." "He is a fool," answered Handel, "the Jews will not come to it (as to *Judas*) because it is a Christian story; and the Ladies will not come, because it is a virtuous one."' To the requests for free tickets for a *Messiah* performance later in the year he exclaimed: 'Oh your servant, *mein herren!* you are damnable dainty! you would not go to *Theodora* — there was room enough to dance there, when that was perform.'

That small circle who really appreciated what the composer was attempting to do saw the point of the oratorio at once and took it to their hearts. Shaftesbury told James Harris: 'I can't conclude a letter and forget *Theodora*, I have heard it three times and will venture to pronounce it, as finished, beautifull and labour'd a composition as ever Handel made. To my knowledge, this took him up a great while in composing. The Town don't like it at all, but Mr Kelloway and several excellent Musicians think as I do.' Joseph Kelway was Mrs Delany's music teacher, and she herself adored the piece. 'Don't you remember our snug enjoyment of *Theodora*?' she wrote to her sister Ann, who herself declared: 'Surely *Theodora* will have justice at last, if it was to be again performed, but the generality of the world have ears and *hear not.*'

Too true, alas. But why did it fail? Not solely because of the Jews staying away, or because of the current earthquake scares in England, reaching their peak in the hysteria caused by the Lisbon disaster of 1755 but already having an effect on wayward London audiences. Handel may have been right in attributing his setback to the nature of the story, for among his religious English vocal works it is the only one not related to a biblical source and the only one dealing with virgin martyrdom in a way more obviously related than anything else he ever wrote to the specifically Catholic world in which the oratorio form had been nurtured. Contemporary Protestantism had little truck with the world of persecuted saints, while feeling naturally at home with the warriors, prophets and kings of the Old Testament. In some ways *Theodora* is the most un-English of Handel's late works: in every way it is a creation of unquestionable sublimity.

It is emphatically not devoted, however, to extolling frigid female virtue in a fashion calculated to deter the *beau monde* of mid-eighteenth-century London. Its point of departure was in fact one of those Restoration essays in prurient titillation which, like Dryden's play on a similar theme, *Tyrannick Love*, were designed to tickle jaded palates by lacing religion with sex. Morell based his libretto on *The Martyrdom of Theodora and Didymus* by Robert Boyle, author of *The Sceptical Chymist* and formulator of the celebrated physical law, who had written his sententious little novel as a neurotic reaction to his disturbed private life. The historical Theodora, better known as St Dorothy, was a victim of Diocletian's persecution of the Christians in the early fourth century. In Handel's oratorio Valens, the Roman governor of Antioch, condemns her to serve as a prostitute in the temple of Venus, but she seeks imprisonment and death instead, and after a temporary rescue by her lover Didymus, he and she go towards a glorious martyrdom.

Boyle's novelette is reminiscent of the Edwardian hostess whom one of her guests described as 'stumbling upwards into fatuity', and Morell was inevitably hampered by its more rambling excursions into moralizing. The composer evidently found the business of transmuting his text into a workable and convincing artistic whole an increasingly fascinating exercise, and the autograph manuscript of *Theodora* is one of the most absorbing in the entire British Library Handel collection. A mass of coffee-coloured blots, pencilled cuts and sealing wax marks bears witness to his preoccupation, both before and after the first performance, with getting the work across in a way which should not obscure his essential concept of it.

What this was emerges irresistibly from the score, whose character dwells, not on simpering religious kitsch, but on the enduring human values which invigorate martyrdom and suffering in any great cause. It is not that Handel explicitly plays down the Christian element but that he emphasizes the universality of his theme by giving music of immense verve and charm to his pagan Romans, in much the same spirit as animates the Baalites in *Athalia* or the Philistines in *Samson*. The protagonists here, Theodora herself, Irene her fellow Christian, Didymus and his noble comrade in arms Septimius, impress by their mingled toughness and tenderness, by their imagination and enthusiasm. The Christians, above all, are treated quite unsentimentally, and their choruses have the lambent intensity of a conviction which needs no priggishness or dogma to sustain it. Whereas the Romans, in 'Forever thus stands fix'd the doom' and 'Venus laughing from the skies', bounce along in insouciant dance rhythms, Theodora's friends follow more complex musical paths in Handel's loftiest choral tradition, capturing the spirit of the entire work — and perhaps the composer's own philosophy — in 'He saw the lovely youth', Handel's own favourite among all his choruses. A tightly-knit dramatic description, the piece, portraying Christ's raising of the widow's dead son in Luke VII.xi., begins with slow, lugubrious chromaticisms against a fragmented accompaniment, abruptly changes minor to major as the youth revives, and closes with a jubilant evocation of the mother's pleasure at her child's recall to life.

The shift of mood here is significant. Areas of darkness and light are contrasted throughout the work, nowhere better than in the Act II prison scene, one of the most compelling examples of Handel's control of structure. Minor keys prevail, as they do throughout the oratorio, and the gloom is intensified by the ghostly interjections of two flutes, like water dripping into a vault, yet against this Theodora's supreme courage increasingly prevails. From the seeming hopelessness of 'With darkness deep as is my woe', an invocation to death, she turns to the bright promises of her faith, in a florid E minor andante, 'O that I on wings could rise', its radiant middle section ushered in with a Handelian cliché used in *Esther* and the third sonata of Opus 2. The cavatina-cabaletta principle, as in *Rodelinda*, effectively operates here years before its general adoption in opera.

Yet, glorious as is the apotheosis achieved by Theodora and her Didymus in the glowing climax to the oratorio formed by the duet 'Streams of pleasure' and the gentle G minor valediction of the closing chorus, it is to Irene, associated elsewhere with the theme of changing light, that Handel awards his most melting air. From its very outset 'As with rosy steps the morn' shows the range and depth of his artistry, as the strings softly, stealthily climb upwards over the discreetest of bass lines which gradually amplifies to introduce a vocal line which itself billows and expands in the 'hopes of endless light' sealed in the eight-bar middle section welded to the first section by the gentle persistence of the bass figure.

Introspective without coldness, awing both in its plainness and complexity, eschewing the mawkish or the vulgar yet always proclaiming its creator's wonderfully human spirituality, *Theodora* has still to join those works of his that have recently begun to return him to our notice. Certainly the London public of his day disdained it, though 'Angels ever bright and fair', probably because of its unadorned vocal line, only once straying below the octave compass and lacking difficult divisions, quickly entered the 'concert favourites' repertoire.

The cast, besides such stalwarts as Frasi, Galli and Reinhold (in the rewardingly vigorous role of Valens) included, as Didymus, the exciting new addition of the Lombard castrato Gaetano Guadagni, one of the most arresting vocal artists of his day. He had first appeared in an Italian company at the Haymarket and showed an uncommon interest in acting, in which he was encouraged by Garrick. England, for which he retained a lifelong fondness even after quitting London angrily and for ever in 1770, seems to have influenced his general approach to his art, an approach which favoured simplicity and dramatic truth as opposed to bravura display and which took its most notable effect in the first performances of Gluck's *Orfeo ed Euridice* in Vienna in 1762, with Guadagni in the title role. Burney praised his nobility and elegance of manner, noting that 'his attitudes and gesture were so full of grace and propriety, that they would have been excellent studies for a statuary', and tracing the power of his singular style to 'his artful manner of diminishing the tones of his voice like the dying notes of an Aeolian harp'. Handel was enthralled enough by this to compose two new versions of 'But who may abide' and 'Thou art gone up on high' for him to sing in the Covent Garden *Messiah* performances of 12 April. In subsequent years Guadagni virtually took over the alto numbers in the oratorio, being given besides a C minor version of 'How beautiful are the feet'.

That spring the master sat for his portrait to Thomas Hudson, who had already painted him two years before and was to do so again for Jennens in 1756. The Foundling *Messiah* on 1 May, to celebrate the laying of the chapel's foundation stone, went off with immense success (the antiquary William Stukely noted 'an infinite croud of coaches at our end of the town to hear Handel's music') and the run on tickets required a repeat a fortnight later. 'I am sure it pleased our friend Handel, and I love to have him pleased,' Mrs Delany wrote with endearing loyalty. Plainly in fine form he set out during the summer on what was to be his last visit to Germany, but we know nothing of where he went or whom he met until a brief notice in the *General Advertiser* in late August tells us that 'between the Hague and Haarlem' he 'had the Misfortune to be overturned, by which he was terribly hurt' but 'is now out of Danger'. He probably remained convalescent in Holland during the autumn, since he tells Telemann, in a letter written in December, that he was 'on the point of leaving the Hague for London when your most agreeable letter reached me'.

Telemann had recommended the soprano Christina Passerini to his friend's notice (she was later to play a significant part in English provincial oratorio performances of the 1750s) and the tone of Handel's reply suggests that the two had maintained a warm regard for each other over the half-century which had passed since their youthful first meeting at Halle. Though there were only four years between them, Handel congratulates Telemann on 'the perfect health that you are enjoying at your somewhat advanced age' and adds that he is hoping to send him a box of exotic plants as a gift. We know that the plants were actually sent off, via the Hamburg skipper Johann Carsten, but not until four years later, after a false rumour of Telemann's death had reached Handel and been happily contradicted by the arrival of a list of the older composer's horticultural requisites which Handel busied himself in obtaining.

The Dutch carriage accident may have contributed in some way to his increasing eye trouble, which began seriously plaguing him during the composition of *Jephtha*, the season's new oratorio, started in January, 1751. Handel's normal practice was to compose during the long, clear days of July and August, and writing during the candlelit gloom of a London winter can hardly have helped matters. On 13 February we find him noting in German, on his score 'got as far as this on Wednesday . . . unable to go on owing to weakening of the sight of my left eye'. Ten days later he tells us he is 'a little better, started work again', but the oratorio was not completed until 30 August that year. In the meantime sight had gone from the one eye altogether.

A connexion between his blindness and any other disorder, rheumatic or digestive, which in the past may have sent him to spas and watering places for relief, has never properly been established. By the middle of March this condition was being discussed anxiously by the Handelians, and Sir Edward Turner told Sanderson Miller that 'noble Handel hath lost an eye, but I have the Rapture to say that St Cecilia makes no complaint of any Defect in his Fingers'. It was not quite the end, rather, on the other hand, the beginning of a bizarre and unexpected final phase in a great career.

15

Great and Good

A gloomy picture of the blind Handel being led towards the keyboard may be all too easily acceptable, but even total blindness need not necessarily have meant an end to composition. There was the example before him of John Stanley, organist of the Temple Church and sightless from the age of two, a composer of sterling gifts whose playing drew admiration from Handel himself. Yet after 1752 Handel was never to produce another entirely original work: whatever the special pleading on behalf of the 1757 version of *Il Trionfo del Tempo* in its English dress as *The Triumph of Time and Truth*, we have only to listen to it to appreciate its essentially garbled and inauthentic character. His use of a musical assistant, in the shape of John Christopher Smith, son of his business manager Johann Christoph Schmidt, was nearly always as arranger and interpolator rather than as the transcriber of freshly conceived ideas.

So far, however, only one eye had given up, and Handel's health was otherwise excellent. Shaftesbury wrote on 16 February that 'Belshazar is now advertized and Smith tells me the parts will go off excellently. Handel himself is actually better in health and in a higher flow of genius than he has been for several years past. His late journey has help'd his constitution vastly.' At the end of the season he noted that 'the Buck', as he affectionately called him, was 'now so well that I much hope [harmony] will flourish yet another year in renewed vigour'.

Jephtha was not yet finished by the time the 1751 concert series opened, and thus the performances of *Belshazzar*, *Judas Maccabaeus* and *Esther* framed only one new work, the little nonesuch worked up through the marriage of an already existing text to the music for Smollett's *Alceste* and entitled *The Choice of Hercules*, produced on 1 March as 'an Additional New Act' to *Alexander's Feast*, given on the same evening. No doubt the composer felt that something was needed to offer the public their money's worth, since even with extra concertos Dryden's ode was hardly as long as any of the full-scale dramatic oratorios. The new act, based, like the story of Alexander at Persepolis, upon a classical hero's obligation to make a moral choice, would come in opportunely as a conclusion to the evening, though on subsequent occasions when Handel revived the two works together he chose unaccountably to use *The Choice* as an interlude between the acts of *Alexander's Feast*.

The text had been adapted, probably by Thomas Morell, from a poem originally published in Glasgow in 1743 and based on an allegory by the Greek poet Prodicus, whose fundamental concept became the 'Hercules at the Crossroads' emblem so beloved of Renaissance moral philosophy. The young champion, faced with the challenge of Virtue and the blandishments of Pleasure, of course opts ultimately for the former — regardless, it would seem, of mythology's evidence that Hercules's noble acts were performed in the interstices of a life of unbridled and wholly unexemplary self-indulgence, with whose last moments Handelians were already familiar. Musicians were also drawn to the story. Maurice Greene wrote a *Judgment of Hercules* in 1740, and John Stanley's *Choice of Hercules*, though using a different libretto to Handel's, follows similar outlines. J. S. Bach, meanwhile, had composed a *Hercules am Scheideweg* as a homage to an infant Saxon prince, reworking much of its music into the Nativity sections of the *Christmas Oratorio*.

The author of Handel's *Choice* was Dr Robert Lowth, bishop of St David's, a witty and talented Wykehamist, author of elegant if sometimes rather risqué verse and a distinguished Hebrew scholar, noteworthy, later in his career, for having nearly become Archbishop of Canterbury, finally rejecting the appointment on grounds of illness. Morell, if he was the actual adaptor, chiefly busied himself with matching chorus and aria texts to the *Alceste* numbers, nearly all of which found an eventual place in the work though inevitably losing some of their appositeness in the process. In their earlier context the pieces form an attractively sophisticated frame to a lost picture (the leaden verses of Smollett's only surviving full-length play *The Regicide* scarcely suggest any thrilling possibilities in *Alceste*'s rediscovery) and offer interesting evidence of Handel's abiding strain of musical Gallicism. The spirit which breathes through this music, especially in the handsomely fashioned overture and the two symphonies introducing the final sections of the score, is one which recalls the dances written for Sallé over a decade earlier, reflecting the Frenchified urbanity of the German courts Handel had frequented on his return from Italy.

Its transference to *The Choice of Hercules* is not always happy. Charon's 'Ye fleeting shades, I come', in the earlier work, has an amiably comic touch as a jaunty bass aria, but its mannerisms seem wholly inappropriate to Hercules's 'Lead, goddess, lead the way'. Similarly awkward is 'Go, assert thy heavnly race', in which the divisions originally designed to illustrate the flight of Thetis's messenger are pointlessly applied to Virtue's 'level Pride's high-plumed crest, and bravely succour the distrest'. In its new setting, however, the vocal line of 'Yet can I hear' still seems a perfect illustration of that seductive ease and supple charm with which Handel engaged his singers. Equally good in its buoyant artlessness is Pleasure's gavotte, 'Turn thee, youth'. Best of all, nevertheless, are the newly composed numbers, a thrilling central sequence of a trio, accompanied recitative and air worked out of Virtue's line in the ensemble, and the magnificent 'See the brisk sparkling nectar', modern enough in rhythms and sonorities (with telling use of two horns) to make Pleasure an up-to-date miss in the age of young Haydn and the infant Mozart.

The season closed abruptly on 21 March with 'an Order ... to both Theatres to forbid their Performance on the Account of His Royal Highness the Prince of Wales's Death'. Frederick had died the day before from 'the sudden breaking of a large abscess under the sternum bone, where it had been gathering for two or three years past; having been first occasioned by a fall he rec'd at playing at what they call Prison-Bars'. His deathbed can scarcely have been cheered by the unfeeling reactions of his father and sisters, but Handel must genuinely have lamented the loss of someone whose real love of music he had captured in enduring enthusiasm after an initial muddle of allegiances. Was it wholly without significance that he was not called upon to provide any music for the funeral? The king, constant alike in loyalty and loathing, was not going to have his favourite composer providing threnodies for the son he had so cordially detested.

April saw the customary Foundling Hospital *Messiah* and a performance on the organ Handel had presented to the chapel. He must also have been at the Decayed Musicians' Benefit Concert that month at the Haymarket, which included such well-known numbers as 'Father of Heaven' and 'Return O God of Hosts', but was far more interesting for the reappearance at the King's Theatre, after more than a decade, of a ghost from the Royal Academy days for whom this stage would have held almost intolerably poignant recollections. To the boxes and galleries which once listened enraptured to her Cleopatra and Rodelinda, the ageing and impoverished Francesca Cuzzoni now sang selected numbers from her first major English triumph *Ottone*. The experience of hearing 'Falsa imagine' sung by the spectral remnants of the voice for which it had been composed some 30 years earlier was as memorable in its way as

Giuditta Pasta's comeback in 1850, movingly described by Henry Chorley, or the disastrous Callas–di Stefano tour in 1974. Burney, intrigued by it all, wrote that 'her throat was so nearly ossified by age that all the mellifluous qualities which had made it so enchanting were nearly annihilated'. Handel did not, as is sometimes stated, give her a part in the *Messiah* concerts. As it was, the wretched woman was woefully in debt (on her London visit the previous year her bills had been cleared by the Prince of Wales) and the last we hear of her is at a Hickford's Rooms concert expressly to pay her creditors. She is said to have died in poverty, as a button-moulder, somewhere in Italy. *Sic transit*: 'silly and fantastical' to the last, she could have done with some practical advice from 'brown and sensible' Faustina, now the wife of Johann Adolf Hasse, Europe's most successful opera composer.

That summer Handel set off for Cheltenham again, to try the water cure for a second time. The spa, developed by the Manx merchant Captain Skillicorn, was in its infancy, and though there was a smart little well-house and adjacent assembly rooms and a maltings transformed into a theatre, amusements were still markedly rural, including cudgel-matches, dancing for gowns, bull-baiting and cock-fights. He seems to have lingered there for some time, since on 21 September Miss Viney wrote to Mrs Dewes: 'I hope Mr Handel will not stay all the winter at the Spa, at least hope that he will not neglect Jephtha's Vow.' In fact he had already returned to London, where he was operated upon by Dr Sharp, surgeon to Guy's Hospital, using the technique known as 'couching' which involved knocking the lens of the eye backwards. This was the first of three such attempts to arrest his blindness, all of which were doomed to fail. When Sharp suggested that he might gain assistance from Stanley, Handel, with ghastly humour, retorted: 'Mr Sharp, have you never read the Scriptures? Do you not remember, if the blind lead the blind, they fall into the ditch?' But at any rate he had not forgotten Jephtha's vow, having managed at last to complete the oratorio, which was given its première on the third night of the new season, 26 February 1752.

'My own favourite,' Morell called it in discussing his Handel librettos, and we can easily see why. Undoubtedly his best, it allowed him to develop character in a way which Jennens, far superior as a dramatic poet, would surely not have scorned, besides which the story outline, from the well-known tale in the Book of Judges concerning Jephtha's rash pledge to sacrifice the first living thing he met with after the battle, could easily and convincingly be expanded. Thus the librettist surrounds his protagonist with types who in themselves mirror the unique cultural synthesis which

Handelian oratorio embodies. The hero's wife Storge, for example, does not appear in the biblical source, but her presence in the drama is validated both by such matriarchal ancestors as Erenice in *Sosarme* and Nitocris in *Belshazzar* and by her affinities with grandly agonized characters like Homer's Andromache or Queen Atossa in Aeschylus's *Persae*. An obvious parallel with the Iphigenia story names Jephtha's daughter Iphis, and, as we have already noted, the Asenath – Othniel romance in *Joshua* no doubt laid the ground for her chaste passion for the warrior Hamor, another of Morell's felicitous inventions. They share a world of radiant purity and optimism which Jephtha himself, with the best of intentions, ironically destroys.

We should not be too critical, however, of Morell's decision to alter the ending in the interests of Baroque taste, or assume that Handel had nothing to do with this. The appearance of an Angel, ascribing Jephtha's sacrificial pledge to the Holy Spirit and commuting Iphis's death sentence to a species of nun-like religious virginity in an air of meretriciously spanking newfangledness which already appears in the Foundling Hospital Anthem, is a disappointment only if we expect *Jephtha* to reproduce the authentic gloom of classical tragedy. We should nevertheless recall that none of Handel's music dramas, not even *Tamerlano*, *Saul* or *Hercules*, ends in outright tragedy. Even if the composer himself privately failed to subscribe to the eighteenth-century ethos in this matter (though there is no concrete evidence for this) his audience demanded and nearly always got a happy ending.

Whatever we may think of such a solution, there is no denying the work's superlative aptness as the crown of Handel's unique achievement in music. 'Swansong' is an inappropriate cliché, since he was not to die for another seven years, and we can scarcely believe, in any case, that he must have lacked all hope, as he composed it, of being able subsequently to write another oratorio. Yet the atmosphere of valediction which permeates *Jephtha*'s close has an ideal appropriateness. We are saying farewell not to a worn-out old man, but to a young girl who embodies the vivacity and self-renewal of her creator's genius. Added to this, there is a degree of eclecticism which gives the whole piece an emblematic quality both in a purely Handelian context and in terms of the age in which it was written. For while it is the greatest musico-dramatic work of its decade, it is also fascinating in its mixture of references to what is past and what is to come in European music, especially in the choruses, where the classicism of Handel's style is alloyed by a series of quotations from a work published only five years before *Jephtha* itself.

This was the collection of six masses, entitled *Philomela Pia*, by the Bohemian composer František Habermann, which Handel may have been sent by one of his continental correspondents — Telemann perhaps — and to which he had already alluded in the organ concerto Opus 7 number 3 and in Septimius's air 'From virtue springs' in *Theodora*. Habermann's manner is vigorous, cheerfully melodic and very much *au courant* with the vein of composers like Galuppi and Durante, influential models for younger musicians. We can study Handel's use of this material from his manuscript sketchbooks in the Fitzwilliam Museum and note, as usual, the subtlety with which his style appropriated and transformed the original. In a chorus like 'Cherub and Seraphim', for instance, what seems most authentic is the opening string figure, a series of rising semiquaver patterns over a descending bass, which might easily have come from a page of the *Dixit Dominus*: it is in fact another Habermann quotation, but its Handelian character makes us wonder whether the younger man, who could quite easily have come across the published oratorio scores, had not already absorbed something from the master who now so effectively borrowed from him.

To complicate the issue yet further, what sounds least like Handel is still, so far as we can tell, the genuine article. The Angel's 'Happy Iphis', as has been noted, possesses, in its middle section especially, a kind of lightweight facility in both melodic line and accompaniment which makes it less suitable to English oratorio than to the operas of Hasse or Graun. Perhaps this was indeed what the composer intended, an almost ironical allusion to the world where conventions quash the 'dark decrees' of looming tragedy. Even more interesting in this respect is the duet 'These labours past', in which Iphis and Hamor look forward innocently to a happy future. Combing *Philomela Pia* yields no original source and we are forced to conclude that this thoroughly engaging piece, shot through with features of the latest style, is Handel writing in Habermannesque vein and springing a typical surprise with a sudden change of tempo at 'when gath'ring fruit from conquest's tree' and the eruption of a bizarre little dotted sequence on the strings. It is, in any case, not too far-fetched to see Iphis as an extension, in musical character, of Susanna. The Englishness of the earlier oratorio pervades *Jephtha* as well, and at least one cadence in 'Take the heart you fondly gave' holds within it the unadorned beauty of native folksong.

Structurally, too, *Jephtha* is scarcely conventional. The whole of the first act and half of the second are carefully weighted towards the excitement of the Israelites asserting their freedom against Ammonite tyranny, and towards the happiness of the young lovers. Only Storge, Cassandra-like, marks approaching disaster but is brushed aside, the F minor of her 'Scenes of horror' clashing with the prevailing major tonalities of the surrounding numbers and allayed besides by Iphis's irrepressible gaiety. This mood is successfully carried over into the rejoicings attending the subsequent victory, thereby brilliantly encapsulating, by means of a head-on clash between the two, the conflict of public duty and private passion which lies at the core of all Baroque drama. Iphis's music, to an almost sinister degree, underlines her innocence precisely because we know that the story's central irony lies in her disastrous unawareness of her father's promise to God. As she prepares to 'tune the soft melodious lute', with flute obbligato over *pizzicato* strings, our impulse is to warn her not to.

What follows should be essential study for anyone interested in music as a dramatic medium. When Iphis and her maidens dance inexorably forward to a jolly little gavotte, they and their music seem calculated to determine a chain reaction in which one number magnificently sets up the next. Jephtha's breathless and hauntingly inchoate 'Open thy marble jaws, o tomb' tell us everything about the father's horror at what greets him, as do the close welding of recitative and air (more like arioso) in Storge's appalled remonstrance with her husband and Hamor's 'On me let blind mistaken zeal' which knocks into being the superb, multi-textured quartet 'O spare your daughter'. In this piece music works on manifold levels: an insistently chromatic bass supports a three-part string accompaniment independent of the vocal lines, in which Storge, Hamor and Zebul's pleadings are set in rhythmic and melodic contrast against Jephtha's obstinate constancy to his vow.

What moves him most, however, is the unaffectedly simple resignation of his daughter to her fate. His anguish, a kind of nervous breakdown in music, shows Handel as unequalled in his age for the imaginative exploration of what we are nowadays all too ready to dismiss as the 'dry' or 'static' medium of recitative. 'Deeper and deeper still' carries Jephtha not merely through a wide range of emotions but through such an astonishing variety of keys that the customary tonal flexibility of recitative has seldom been more effectively linked to expressiveness.

The chorus, one of Handel's longest, which concludes the act is a world away from the buoyant aggressiveness flourished by the Israelites in the oratorio's opening section. Neither Habermann nor anybody else could have written an extended choral statement of the drama's essential metaphysical dilemma (well summed up in the opening line, 'How dark,

O Lord, are thy decrees! all hid from mortal sight') which so urges upon us a sense of the limitless perspectives of human moral experience in relation to God. Those who accuse Handel of not being 'profound' in the sense that Bach is apparently so should be made to listen to this chorus and then return, if they can, to so stale a charge. The piece's four sections, beginning with a significant reminiscence of 'The people shall hear' in *Israel in Egypt*, leading to a gloomy canon, followed in turn by a groping chromatic fugue and concluding with a wearily hopeless iteration of Pope's words 'Whatever is is right', are the philosophical essays of an intensely cultivated eighteenth-century mind.

Nowadays among the most highly regarded of all Handel oratorios, *Jephtha* enjoyed a comparative success in its own time. There was, however, only one Covent Garden performance in 1752, with the composer himself directing, as he was to do at the other oratorios and at the Foundling Hospital that year. On 4 November he was couched once more, this time by the Princess of Wales's surgeon William Bromfield, 'when it was thought there was all imaginable Hopes of Success by the Operation, which must give the greatest Pleasure to all Lovers of Musick'. Mrs Delany, nevertheless, recalling *Samson*, thought 'how feelingly he must recollect the "*total eclipse*"' and lamented his 'dark and melancholy circumstances.' On 27 January 1753, after a brief spell of hopes for a positive recovery, one newspaper told its readers that 'Mr Handel has at length, unhappily, quite lost his sight', and the depressing announcement was shortly followed up with an even more dismal rumour that he was now engaged on his own funeral anthem. The Foundling Hospital governors, touchingly concerned and 'expressing their surprize thereat. RESOLVED That the Secretary do acquaint Mr Handel, That the said Paragraph has given this Committee great Concern; they being highly sensible that all Well-Wishers to this Charity must be desirous for the Continuance of his Life, who has been, and is so good and generous a Benefactor thereto.' Is such solicitude, we may wonder, unique in the annals of music history? Were the administrators of the Ospedale della Pietà in Venice similarly anxious for the asthmatic Antonio Vivaldi? Viewed in its most cynical light, the resolution perhaps simply shows that the Foundling governors knew where their advantage lay. The news was, as it turned out, quite baseless.

Alive Handel still was, and though by the beginning of 1754 the eclipse was total he had lost none of his authority in the preparation and direction of the oratorio seasons. The Covent Garden performances, of course, went on attracting a solid following, but more interesting than these in respect of the development of Handel's English reputation are the

Mary Delany in 1782 by John Opie

Facsimile of the first page of the autograph score of *Messiah* records of oratorio in the provinces. By now, owing perhaps to an impetus begun by *Athalia* some 20 years before, Oxford had taken the composer to its heart and his music had found an ardent champion in the Heather Professor William Hayes, who had come out strongly in his favour in a set of published strictures on Charles Avison's *Essay on Musical Expression* (1752) a work designed to establish the primacy of Geminiani's style against the less orthodox but more 'old-fashioned' Handelian manner. In evoking the spirits of Milton, Poussin and Claude in his praises of Handel, Hayes had touched upon the fundamental element which was beginning to gain the composer a following when in certain respects he no longer needed it. We cannot categorize Handel as a 'pre-Romantic', whatever that may be, but neither can we ignore that mid-eighteenth-century sensibility in his work which appealed to the nascent Romanticism of contemporary England and Germany.

The English, in short, were ready for Handel, and Oxford now witnessed regular performances on a par with those in London and featuring such well-known Handelians as Frasi and Beard. At Bath, meanwhile, Thomas Chilcot, one of the most able of younger provincial masters, was dispensing *Judas Maccabaeus* and other pieces to the fashionable 'hot-waterers', while at Bristol the new music room opened in 1756 'with the oratorio of the Messiah'. More significant yet was the annual Music Meeting of the Three Choirs of Worcester, Gloucester and Hereford, the world's oldest surviving musical festival and a positive and vital force in English music. Here, by the mid-1750s, Handel was part of the staple fare: at the Hereford meeting of 1756, for example, *Samson*, *L'Allegro* and the *St Cecilia Ode* were all given, and the following year Gloucester heard *Acis* and *Messiah*, with 'Three Trumpets, a Pair of Kettle-drums, Four Hautboys, Four Bassoons, Two Double basses, Violins, Violincelloes and Chorus Singers in Proportion. The Music to be conducted by Dr Hayes. . . . '

Meanwhile, as London grew, so did its concert life, and town rang with Handel. The increase of the cult of 'feeling' and 'sentiment' had the practical outcome of encouraging the promotion of various hospital schemes, and what Dublin had been doing for well over a decade was now taken up in the City and Westminster, as each new charitable foundation publicized its endeavours with first-rate music. Boyce directed the band at St Margaret's for the Westminster Hospital and Stanley did the same for the Hospital for Smallpox and Inoculation, but who was the '*Widow Gentlewoman* in Great Distress' for whom, presumably with the composer's consent, an *Acis and Galatea* was given at the Great Room in Dean

Street, Soho? We can appreciate the old man's anxiety lest his music fall into improper hands: a letter of Shaftesbury to James Harris, dated 31 December 1757, says: 'I will give directions for sending the score of Joshua to you at Salisbury. But desire when you deliver it that Mr B . . . may be requested to take care not to dirty or hurt the book; and Farther, that on no account he suffer any copy to be taken of the Chorus's etc. lest it should be performed elsewhere. For this, in justice to Mr Handel I ought to insist on.'

Apart from *Messiah*, gaining continuously in popularity throughout the decade, the favourites seem to have been *Acis* (variously described as masque, serenata and oratorio), *Esther*, Samson and *Judas*. *Alexander Balus*, *Susanna* and *Solomon* were each revived for a single season. *Saul* made its way successfully into the provinces and *Deborah*, perhaps for specially local or topical reasons, was always a draw in Ireland. *Athalia* returned to Covent Garden after a 20-year absence and even *Joseph* found a niche in the London programmes. *Semele* alone, of all the eighteen English dramatic works, was never brought back during Handel's lifetime after its six 1744 performances. As for the non-dramatic works to English texts, while the *St Cecilia Ode* and *Alexander's Feast* maintained a more or less constant success rate, the fortunes of *Israel in Egypt* rose as those of *Allegro, Penseroso and Moderato* declined — the blooming landscapes of Gainsborough and *The Seasons* giving way, as it were, to the awful and sublime prospects of Blake and Turner.

At nearly every revival Handel made some sort of adaptation or interpolation, based variously on the quality and nature of the performers or on his sense of what the public desired. For many works there can thus be no standard text because of the essentially elastic aspects of the piece as conceived in a practical sense. A modern conductor or editor will prefer to recommend one version as opposed to another, but can scarcely afford to be dogmatic. In at least one case, that of *Esther*, the composer, as we have already noted, seems never to have been satisfied with leaving the work alone, and its immensely complex textual history (available in full in the relevant chapter of Winton Dean's *Handel's Dramatic Oratorios and Masques*) offers a fascinating indication of his approach to an individual composition. With others, however, we are on safer ground. A revival of the extraordinary 1759 *Solomon*, for example, in which the work's original shape has undergone a truly Procrustean revision (it opens with the judgment scene, excising practically the entire first act) would simply be an exercise in antiquarian perversity, and modern performance has rightly returned us to the 1749 text.

Whatever additions were made cannot, of course, have been Handel's own, though he must certainly have authorized them, and it was in the crucial capacity of intermediary between the blind composer and his audience that the talents of John Christopher Smith came fully into play. The new numbers, including such pieces as 'Wise men flatt'ring', initially designed for a 1758 *Belshazzar* but later coming to rest in *Judas Maccabaeus*, and 'Lost in anguish, quite despairing' for the 1755 *Theodora*, were derived from earlier Handel works on which Smith set his own imprint, that of a musician more closely in touch with newer mannerisms but far more limited in the actual extent of his gifts. It is quite easy, simply by listening to this music, to know that what we are in fact hearing is not quite all by Handel himself, and nothing more blatantly proclaims this than *The Triumph of Time and Truth*, the third and last incarnation of *Il Trionfo del Tempo e della Verità*, produced as a novelty in the Covent Garden season of 1757, and revived the following year.

The Triumph is fascinating for several reasons. On one level it develops the tendency of Smith and Handel in reworking earlier material to concentrate on music from the Italian years which Londoners were unlikely to know. On another, though its ad hoc quality recalls *Deborah* and *The Occasional Oratorio*, it noticeably lacks the sense of homogeneous control which, whatever their faults, permeates those two works. Most important of all, it provides one of the clearest illustrations in all music of the fact that, however powerful the modern arguments in favour of vernacular words for local audiences, the sound and syntax of an original text dictate the composer's disposition of melody, harmony and phrase lengths in communicating his awareness of its meaning to the listener. Handel wrote extensively in two modern languages, and the tones and rhythms of Italian and English ordained distinctive idioms. Except in one or two isolated cases, such as 'La mia sorte fortunata' in *Agrippina*, pressed comfortably into service as 'Freedom now once more possessing' in *Jephtha*, the Italian airs do not easily carry English texts, and the awkwardness of Morell's words in conjunction with the vocal lines of *Il Trionfo* is manifest throughout. Together with Smith's well-grounded but earthbound muse and the additional numbers from the 1707 and 1737 versions, *The Triumph of Time and Truth*, however engaging, represents the *reductio ad absurdum* of the Baroque synthetic principle, a pasticcio in the fullest sense of the word. Mrs Delany, whose instinct was generally right, told her sister 'it did not please me as usual'.

Judas and *Messiah* wound up a successful season, at the end of which

Handel was able to bank the impressive sum of £1,200, evidence that the oratorios were rather belatedly finding their market. Elsewhere in London their commercial bullishness was being exploited: the New Theatre in the Haymarket presented *Acis and Galatea* for the benefit of child prodigy Jonathan Snow, probably the son of Handel's trumpet soloist Valentine, and two months later the evergreen serenata featured again, this time at Ranelagh House, 'for the Benefit of the *Marine Society*, towards cloathing Men and Boys for the Sea to go on Board his Majesty's Ships. . . . Tea, Coffee, &c. included as usual.' The latter performance was conducted by Stanley, also at the keyboard for a *Samson* evening at the Great Room in Dean Street, Soho, for Frasi's benefit. Despite the high fees she commanded (six guineas for a Foundling *Messiah*) the soprano's debts were a continuing problem and ultimately forced her to flee the country.

Throughout most of 1758 Handel's general state of health seems to have been fairly good. We know from an entry in the diary of the barrister John Baker that the tradition of domestic rehearsals at Brook Street continued, and the same source later shows that the composer had not relinquished his summer visits to the spas. On 26 August Baker, newly arrived at Tunbridge Wells, noted: 'Handel and his Dr Murrell, Taylor the oculist. . . . ' Morell was doubtless there as much in the capacity of assistant as friend; Taylor was the quack John 'Chevalier' Taylor, whose attempt at restoring Handel's eyesight, however predictably unsuccessful, was puffed as a triumph in verses in the *London Chronicle* describing the Muses' appeal to Apollo on the blind composer's behalf.

The season of the following year, however, with revivals of *Solomon*, *Susanna* and *Samson*, must have proved especially strenuous and the *Whitehall Evening Post* of 7 April 1759 announced Handel's intention of 'setting out for Bath, to try the Benefit of the Waters'. The journey was never even begun. A *Messiah* on the previous night had taxed him severely: he was 'apparently in great suffering; but when he came to his concerto he rallied, and kindling as he advanced, descanted extemporaneously with his accustomed ability and force; of a most dignified and awe-inspiring port'. Handel went home, took to his bed and never rose from it again. Early in the morning of 14 April, he died at the age of 74.

His last moments are best recalled for us in a touching letter by his friend James Smyth, a perfumier living in nearby Bond Street, who was to have accompanied him to Bath. His account, written to Mrs Delany's brother Bernard Granville, merits quoting in full.

London, April 17th, 1759.

Dear Sir,

According to your request to me when you left London, that I would let you know when our good friend departed this life, *on Saturday last at 8 o'clock in the morn died the great and good Mr Handel.* He was sensible to the last moment; made a codicil to his will on Tuesday, ordered to be buried privately in Westminster Abbey, and a monument not to exceed £600 for him. I had the pleasure to reconcile him to his old friends; he saw them and forgave them, and let all their legacies stand. In the codicil he left many legacies to his friends, and among the rest he left me £500, and has left to you the two pictures *you formerly gave him.* He took leave of all his friends on Friday morning, and desired to see nobody but the Doctor and Apothecary and myself. At 7 o'clock in the evening he took leave of me, and told me we 'should meet again'; as soon as I was gone he told his servant '*not* to let me come to him any more. for that he had *now done with the world.*' He died as he lived, a good *Christian*, with a true sense of his duty to God and man, and in perfect charity with all the world. If there is anything that I can be of further service to you please to let me know. I was to have set out for the Bath tomorrow, but must attend the funeral, and shall then go next week.

>I am, dear Sir,
>Your most obedient humble servant,
>James Smyth.

He has left the Messiah to the Foundling Hospital, and one thousand pounds to the decayed musicians and their children, and the residue of his fortune to his niece and relations in Germany. He has died worth £20,000, and left legacies with his charities to nearly £6000. He has got by his Oratorios this year £1952 12s 8d.

The reference to 'a good Christian, with a true sense of his duty to God and man' reminds us that Handel's religious beliefs had not waned with the years. Some weeks before his death he had been visited by those two evangelical vultures Selina, Lady Huntingdon, and Dr Martin Madan, the former celebrated as 'the Queen of the Methodists', the latter one of those kindly spirits who was subsequently to thicken the spiritual gloom of the poet Cowper, and both of them no doubt hoping for some last-minute tremors of guilty renunciation as Handel prepared to face God. Lady Huntingdon, who had apparently known the composer in her youth, wrote in her diary: 'He is now old, and at the close of his long career; yet he is not dismayed at the prospect before him. Blessed be God for the comforts and consolations which the Gospel affords in every situation, and in every time of our need! Mr Madan has been with him often, and he seems much attached to him.'

He left the world, however, as he had dwelt in it, a Lutheran communicant within the Church of England. The papers were so quick to report his death that they hustled the notice in a day early — 'the great musician' . . . 'the famous musician'. . . . 'greatly regretted' etc. — but, as Smyth noted, he died on Saturday 14th. Though the *London Chronicle* reported that he was to be buried in the Foundling Hospital graveyard, close to Coram himself, Handel had already recorded a wish for a funeral and interment in Westminster Abbey, and on the evening of the 20th the ceremony was carried out. 'On Friday Night the Remains of the late Mr Handel were deposited at the Foot of the Duke of Argyle's Monument in Westminster-Abbey, the Bishop, Prebendaries, and the whole Choir attended to pay the last Honours due to his Memory; and it is computed there were not fewer than 3000 Persons present on this Occasion.' The Bishop was Dr Zachary Pearce of Rochester, who held the Deanery of Westminster *in commendam*: he was a noted preacher, but no funeral address appears to have survived. The Abbey's Clerk of Works observed that the grave lay '8 feet from the Duke of Argyle's Iron Railes. . . . N.B. There may be made very good graves on his Right and Left by Diging up a Foundation of an old Staircase; Room at the feet. . . ' The undertaker was a Mr Gordon, and the spare room at Handel's feet was used over a century later for no less a celebrity than Charles Dickens.

Appropriately he had been placed near Argyle, 'Red John of the Battles', a former governor of the Royal Academy of Music, and, like the duke's, his monument was the work of Roubiliac. The pair make an interesting contrast: it is plain that the sculptor's sympathies were more with the musician than with the warrior. An older Handel than the lyre-player of Vauxhall, but an image no less strikingly intimate and alive. The age's budding romanticism shows in the bardic figure of the cloud-born David, while the trumpet and gamba are throwbacks to rococo decoration, but the essential vitality of the man himself is superbly captured in the *dégagé* yet flamboyant full-length standing effigy, significantly without a wig.

Handel's second name was given on the monument as Frederick, but the codicils of his will indicate that his preferred anglicizing was 'Frideric' and so for us it should ideally remain. The original will, a brief enough document, had been made on 1 June 1750. Handel left all his clothes and

£300 to his manservant Peter Le Blond and a year's wages to the rest of his household. Other bequests were made to German relatives, including his aunt Taust of Giebichenstein and a great-nephew in Copenhagen, with the residue of the estate going to 'my Dear Niece Johanna Friderica Floerken of Gotha in Saxony', the sole executrix. The larger of his two harpsichords, 'my little House Organ' and all his manuscripts went to Johann Christoph Schmidt and the only other English legatee was James Hunter, a scarlet-dyer of Old Ford.

The first of the four codicils, made six years later, shows his finances in better shape, with increased legacies to everyone except Hunter, and the names of Thomas Morell and Newburgh Hamilton included. The Huguenot merchant George Amyand, later M.P. for Barnstaple, now figures as coexecutor, with a £200 bequest. Some nine months later, however, Le Blond died, and Handel transferred his share in the inheritance to his nephew John Duburk. In the same year a third codicil gave the Covent Garden theatre organ to John Rich and a fair copy of *Messiah* score and parts to the Foundling Hospital, in whose possession they still are. Two portrait studies by Balthasar Denner (who had earlier painted Handel himself) were left to Jennens and the landscapes attributed to Rembrandt were presented to Bernard Granville.

It is the last codicil, made on Handel's deathbed and witnessed by Thomas Harris and his fellow lawyer John Hetherington, which best bears witness to the extent of the composer's generosity. His total estate was computed at some £20,000, a handsome reward for all the monetary hiccups of the 1730s and the erratic box-office of the oratorios. The Decayed Musicians' charity, which he had always ardently supported, got £1,000, and the loyal violinist Matthew Dubourg was also remembered. Two widows, Mrs Palmer of Chelsea and Mrs Mayne of Kensington, each received small bequests, and Mrs Delany's friend Anne Donnellan was left 50 guineas. To the Brook Street maidservants Handel left 'each one years wages over and above what shall be due to them at the time of my death', while Mr Cowland, the apothecary of New Bond Street, whose services must have been much in demand during these final years, was recompensed with 50 pounds.

There is absolutely no evidence, either in the will or the codicils, of any intention by Handel to cut out Johann Christoph Schmidt altogether as a beneficiary. It is true that the two had quarrelled while at Tunbridge Wells, but this was probably the result of one of Handel's volcanic explosions of temper. A reconciliation, however, was effected easily enough by John Christopher Smith, by the pardonable use of moral blackmail. 'About three weeks before Handel's death, he desired Smith junior to receive the sacrament with him. Smith asked him how he would communicate, when he was not at peace with all the world, and especially when he was at enmity with his former friend; who, though he might have offended him once, had been faithful and affectionate to him for thirty years. Handel was so much affected by this representation, that he was immediately reconciled. . . . '

The monument was erected, the bequests duly realized (there was a squabble in October 1759 between Amyand and the Tausts as to the size of their legacy) and the mourning muses meanwhile hurried to assume their stations. The *Gazeteer*, the *London Evening Post* and the *Whitehall Evening Post* syndicated their epitaph, by a certain 'H — y' of Lincoln's Inn, with its bathetic concluding couplet:

> 'O for Elijah's car,' great Handel cry'd;
> Messiah heard his voice — and Handel dy'd.

The *Public Advertiser* ventured an acrostic:

> He's gone, the Soul of Harmony is fled!
> And warbling Angels hover round him dead.
> Never, no never, since the Tide of Time,
> Did Music know a Genius so sublime!
> Each mighty Harmonist that's gone before,
> Lessen'd to Mites when we his Works explore.

Worthiest of all poetic tributes was *The Tears of Music* by John Langhorne, issued in 1760 but surely written as a genuinely heartfelt response to the news of the composer's death, and attempting to reproduce the overwhelming effect of the oratorios upon a refined sensibility:

> I feel, I feel the sacred Impulse — hark!
> Wak'd from according Lyres the sweet Strains flow
> In Symphony divine; from Air to Air
> The trembling Numbers fly: swift bursts away
> The Flow of Joy; now swells the Flight of Praise.
> Springs the shrill Trump aloft; the toiling Chords
> Melodious labour thro' the flying Maze;
> And the deep Base his strong Sounds roll away,
> Majestically sweet. . . .

Dead as Handel now was, the bizarre dispositions of Fate had determined that his reputation was to thrive as never before. The oratorio concerts had become an established feature of the London season and John Christopher Smith, keeper, as it were, of the Handelian seal, took over at the Foundling Hospital, assisted at Covent Garden by John Stanley. On his father's death in 1763 he inherited the great collection of autograph manuscripts which, in return for a pension from George III, he left to the Royal Library and which were later transferred to the British Museum.

His audience was a public very different from that which insensate italophilia had driven to scorn and rejection of the composer decades before. London's moral and aesthetic climate had changed in the atmosphere of the shock dealt by the news of the 1755 Lisbon earthquake, assisted by the rise of Methodism and by a sensibility tending away from artifice and decoration towards illusions of spontaneity. Handel now became the favourite of those in search of the natural and the sublime, and a visit to the oratorio was a mark of good taste in polite society. It was during this period that the custom initiated by George II of standing during the Hallelujah Chorus became widespread, and the gradual process began of transforming Handel into something little short of seraphic.

A typical enthusiast was Anna Seward, 'Swan of Lichfield' and friend of Dr Johnson, who wrote of the composer as 'pre-eminent, incomparable, transcendent, unrivalled, unequalled', and observed with some justice that 'in music, when it marries immortal verse, and then only is it truly sublime, Handel stands approachless as Shakespeare himself in grandeur and variety'. She seems to have been undisturbed by what perplexed others, the relationship of oratorio to the eighteenth-century notion of kinds and a prevailing sense of its impropriety if performed in a church, and was moved to describe William Cowper as a 'vapourish egotist' for having presumed to censure such performances in his poem *The Task*.

> Remember Handel? [the offending lines began]
> Who that was not born
> Deaf as the dead to harmony, forgets,
> Or can, the more than Homer of his age?
> Yes — we remember him; and while we praise
> A talent so divine, remember too
> That His most holy book from whom it came
> Was never meant, was never used before,
> To buckram out the memory of man.

'A religious service instituted in honor of a Musician and performed in the house of God,' wrote Cowper to his friend John Newton, 'is a subject that calls loudly for the animadversion of an enlighten'd minister.' Newton, a rabid evangelical with little apparent feeling for the arts, duly responded with a series of 50 sermons on *Messiah*, 'Expository Discourses, on the Series of Scriptural Passages, which form the Subject of the Celebrated Oratorio of Handel', though his admonitions failed to check the work's rising popularity.

Perhaps the most extraordinary manifestation of Handel enthusiasm in the provinces was the series of performances in aid of the charitable foundations set up by the Reverend William Hanbury at Church Langton in Leicestershire. Hanbury's diffuse account of the charity is in fact a slab of autobiography, from which the author emerges as an eccentric, vainglorious bore with a talent for making enemies. While we may sympathize with him for the loss of his pet dogs, one of whom was choked to death with a table-fork by a sadistic gamekeeper belonging to a Mrs Byrd on whose land he had trespassed, we can only gape at his grandiose schemes, which included redecorating the church, installing a new organ, appointing an organist and setting up a school where 36 poor boys were to be taught reading, writing, 'to cast accompts, and sing psalms'. To this were later to be added a printing office, a hospital, a picture gallery, professorships in grammar, botany, music, poetry and antiquity.

Despite increasing quarrelsomeness between Hanbury, the charity trustees and the villagers, the musical events went ahead as planned, and the vicar seems to have been aided in the whole enterprise by the dogged determination which derives from a complete lack of any sense of humour. The performers included some of the best London voices and instrumentalists and Hanbury is deathlessly hyperbolic in his accounts of them — 'Swarms of footmen, horses, coaches, chaises, &c . . . a most brilliant appearance . . . company came pouring in . . . music most affecting . . . tears seen trickling down the faces of many' and so on. The oratorios themselves included *Messiah*, *Judas Maccabaeus* and *Samson*, and though at first given in the parish church were later transferred to a specially constructed concert hall. It need hardly be added that Hanbury's description includes strictures on the tardy arrival of the conductor, no less than Dr William Hayes himself, in whose magisterial riposte, showing up the village Maecenas as ungrateful, litigious and little better than a liar, Hanbury met his match.

The summit of eighteenth-century Handel-worship and an event which set what was ultimately a dire example to succeeding ages of

English Handelians was reached in 1784 with the grand celebration in Westminster Abbey designed to commemorate the supposed centenary of the composer's birth and detailed for us in its various stages by Charles Burney, whose handsome commemorative volume contained illustrations by his sons and a sonorous dedication by Dr Johnson to King George III. There were five concerts in all, spread over a three-week period from the end of May to the beginning of June, the last two being laid on by special command of the music-loving king and queen. The programme for the first was orthodox enough, including the *Dettingen Te Deum* and selections from the Funeral Anthem, but the second, 'judiciously calculated to display his abilities in *Secular* and *Dramatic* Music', may have raised a few eyebrows, for though it took place in the Pantheon, specially decorated and enlarged for the occasion, the items made up a complete Handelian shop-window, placing 'Sorge infausta' from *Orlando* side by side with 'Ye sons of Israel' in *Joshua*, and ending, after favourite numbers from *Rodelinda* and *Alcina*, with the Coronation Anthem *My heart is inditing*. The final concert was a repeat performance of *Messiah*, first given a week earlier, and the whole festival produced the impressive sum of £12,736 12s. 10d., of which over half was presented to the Society for Decayed Musicians and the Westminster Hospital.

For each concert enormous musical forces were mobilized, and though Burney assures us that 'the totality of sound seemed to proceed from one voice, and one instrument', Handel can scarcely have dreamt of hearing his music performed in this steamrolling fashion. There was only one full rehearsal for every programme, and the conductor, Joah Bates, sat at the keyboard behind the choir sopranos, his harpsichord connected to the organ by a chain mechanism originally devised for Handel himself at Covent Garden. The colossal orchestra mustered all the best hands in London, Cramer on the fiddle, Fischer as oboist and Cervetto as principal 'cello, with such vocalists as the favourite Gertrud Elizabeth Mara and the star castrato Gasparo Pacchiarotti. Choral singers came from all over England — Mr Ivitt Loulworth from Cambridge, Mr Salmon from Worcester, Mr Cheese from Manchester, and the counter-tenors featured a certain Lord Dillon, a claimant to the Earldom of Roscommon.

The sheer size of chorus and orchestra made its due impression on foreign visitors. Handel's reputation abroad already stood high, even if, during his lifetime, there were few opportunities outside England for hearing his music. Gluck, as we have already noted, was permanently influenced by Handel in his graver, starker dramatic vein, but it is to Haydn, Mozart and Beethoven that we must turn for evidence of the significant impress made by the composer upon the central traditions of European music.

No one imbued with a full experience of Handel's manner can fail to respond to its presence as an inspiration to the Viennese masters. By a fascinating coincidence all three, though doubtless struck by early encounters with Handel's work, were seriously influenced only when their respective styles had fully matured. In the case of Haydn indeed the full effect was created when the composer was already seen as the doyen of contemporary musicians, and after Mozart had started to reflect that Handelian absorption which runs so powerfully through his later works.

Mozart's case is perhaps the most interesting. We know that his visit to London five years after Handel's death took in such events as a concert at Ranelagh House which featured choruses from *Acis and Galatea* and *Alexander's Feast* and ended with *Zadok the Priest*, and he may have heard *Messiah* given at Mannheim by Georg Joseph Vogler, though his letters suggest otherwise. The real coup was made during the 1780s, at the concerts given in the Vienna house of Baron Gottfried van Swieten, a civil servant and amateur composer with an inordinate Handelian enthusiasm, who had already pioneered a performance by the Tonkünstler Sozietät of *Judas Maccabaeus*. At the baron's, Mozart told his father, 'nothing is played but Handel and Bach', and Swieten's appreciation of the young man's gifts later took the form of entrusting him with providing extra orchestrations for *Acis and Galatea, Messiah, Alexander's Feast* and the *St Cecilia Ode*, all presented in Vienna during 1789–90.

Space does not permit detailed consideration of these Mozartian adornments, but their fascination for us, both as evidence of shifts in eighteenth-century taste and of a direct and painstaking scrutiny by Mozart of some of Handel's finest music, is immense. Their subsequent acceptance in England was to prove crucial to that Victorian overhaul of the Handelian orchestra from which this most refined and discriminating of all Baroque orchestrators has only recently been allowed to recover. Long before these additions, however, Mozart had fallen under Handel's spell. Inevitably the concern was not, as in the case of his interest in Bach, with abstract design, but much more with such issues as treatment of choral texture and with that improvisatory structural freedom with which Handel makes his boldest dramatic strokes. Of this last we can hear a responsive Mozartian echo most powerfully in pieces such as the monumental C minor Adagio and Fugue (K 546), an arrangement for strings of a two-piano fugue with an introduction creating the effect of a French overture, and the two fantasias for mechanical organ K 594 and K

608. In these, as in the Suite K 399, specifically conceived in Handelian style, the appeal to Mozart of that questioning, rhapsodic quality with which Handel invests so many of his overtures is at once clear.

The Handelian stamp in the late choral works needs no further comment. Among its wealth of allusions to the composer the C Minor Mass appears, in the Hosanna, to feature a direct reference to the Concerto Grosso Op. 3 No. 3, and the experience of the oratorios was essential to the achievement represented by the movements of the *Requiem*. A closer study deserves to be made of the operas in this context. Though *Cosi fan tutte*, composed soon after Mozart's *Messiah* reorchestration, is interestingly free of Handel echoes (even if, in numbers such as Fiordiligi's 'Come scoglio', Da Ponte appears to parody the *opera seria* convention reflected in such clichés as Berenice's 'Scoglio d'immota fronte' in *Scipione*) *Don Giovanni*, presented two years earlier, shows them most potently. We cannot listen to Donna Elvira without feeling that she has somehow lost her way en route to a Handelian lyric drama. The world of 'Ah, fuggi il traditor' and 'Ah! chi mi dice mai' is not that of any ordinary late Baroque prima donna but, in orchestration, rhythms and harmonies, that of a Handel heroine in the mould of Dejanira, Athalia or even Alcina. As for *Die Zauberflöte*, whether in its overture, in the final numbers of both acts or in the cantilena of Pamina's 'Ah, ich fühl's' it is enough to echo the judgment of a modern scholar that 'without Handel, especially the Handel of *Messiah*, it is inconceivable'.

The influence upon Haydn and Beethoven was less obvious but no less strong. Well acquainted as he was with Swieten, Haydn made his most important Handelian encounter during his first visit to England in 1791, when that year's Commemoration festival presented *Israel in Egypt, Saul* and *Judas Maccabaeus*. The composer William Shield, for whom Haydn was 'the father of modern harmony', wrote that during a journey from London to Taplow '. . . . I embraced the favourable opportunity of enquiring how he estimated the Chorus in Joshua "The Nations tremble at the dreadful sound." ' The reply: 'He had long been acquainted with the music, but never knew half its powers before he heard it, and he was perfectly certain that only one inspired Author ever did, or ever would pen so sublime a composition. . . . ' Shield later presented Haydn with a score of *Jephtha*, which he hugely admired, and which, with so much else of Handel's, duly contributed to that distinctive vigour and directness of dramatic engagement so typical of his choral style in the last masses, *The Creation* and *The Seasons*.

Altogether similar was the case of Beethoven, who, despite links with

Swieten's circle in his early years, was to be a mature artist by the time Handel's genius made its deepest impression on him. An implied homage to the style of the oratorios hardly needs pointing out in the *Missa Solemnis*, or, more obviously, in the *Weihe des Hauses* overture, an eloquent essay in imitation, and Handelian echoes can be sensed not only in the orchestral works but in *Fidelio* and the later chamber music besides.

The older composer's appeal must in part have lain in that uncompromising treatment of musical form which so often seems to anticipate Beethoven's own approach. He respected the economy of resource in this 'unequalled Master of all Masters'. 'Go to him', he said, 'and learn how, with such modest means, such great effects may be produced.' To the Archduke Rudolph he wrote: 'I beg your Imperial Highness not to forget the works of Handel, since of a certainty they always offer the greatest nourishment to your mature musical spirit and will at the same time lead to admiration for this great man.' An English visitor heard him 'assert very distinctly in German, "Handel is the greatest composer that ever lived." I cannot describe to you with what pathos and I am inclined to say, with what sublimity of language, he spoke of the "Messiah" of this immortal genius. Every one of us was moved when he said, "I would uncover my head and kneel down at his tomb."' During the last weeks of his life Beethoven received the Arnold edition of Handel's works and his pleasure in turning over the scores was that of an enthusiastic pupil. 'Handel is the greatest and most skilful of composers: I can still learn from him,' he acknowledged, though whether his 'There lies the truth' as he contemplated the volumes from his deathbed is apocryphal or not we can hardly be certain.

Samuel Arnold's Handel edition which so excited Beethoven was destined to remain incomplete, and by the time a new edition of the oratorios was set on foot by Novello in the form of the famous vocal scores whose descendants are still in use, the absorption of Handel into the fabric of English musical tradition was complete. Though the process undeniably reflects that quality of universal appeal, the wonderful common touch he shares with Mozart and Verdi, we cannot blind ourselves to its lingering and nearly disastrous effect on his reputation, from which modern performance is only now beginning to rescue him. His overwhelming popularity with the Victorian public not only succeeded in creating him the image of a respectable nineteenth-century bourgeois, but allowed him to fall a victim to that snobbery which continues to hang miasmally over English appreciation of composers who are too tunefully accessible.

We have only to look at the pages of the *Musical Times* to see how greedily they lapped him up. The *ne plus ultra* of orgiastic Handel-worship was reached in the huge Crystal Palace festivals which began in 1857. Among the earliest audience was the invaluable Charles Greville, by now an elderly survivor from a more raffish and romantic age of political gerrymandering and scandals in high life. Despite 'the beauty of the locale, with the vast crowds assembled in it', he found 'the wonderful assembly of 2000 vocal and 500 instrumental performers did not produce musical effects so agreeable and so perfect as the smaller number in the smaller space of Exeter Hall', referring to the concerts given there by the Sacred Harmonic Society. His Regency good taste, however, was not shared by clamorous enthusiasts of the age of the crinoline, the three-decker novel and the Great Western, and big was beautiful at Sydenham, where the triennial festivals thundered onwards into the twentieth century. At the 1862 festival the *Musical Times* praised 'the decorations . . . in excellent taste. The neutral tone of the prevailing colour, relieved by the poly-chromic medallions and arabesques which define the outline; the band that lines the interior, upon which is recorded the works of Handel; the pictorial centrepiece supplied by the stupendous and elaborately-embellished organ, and the thick foreground of plants and flowers make up a tableau of magnificence, the effect of which is astonishing.' As for the public, 'the ladies, without having strictly attended to the direction as to wearing white or light dresses, were sufficiently mindful of effect to produce a goodly display of every colour in the rainbow. Among the audience the white neckcloths of the clergy were most observable, even bishops might have been seen in the crowd. . . .'

Singers were expected to conform to the tone of the occasion. The paper rapped Adelina Patti smartly over the knuckles for performing in the manner of 'one who nightly wins the most enthusiastic demonstrations of approval from the audience at the Royal Italian Opera', but added that 'we have little doubt that she may eventually achieve a name as great in sacred as she has already done in secular music'. By implication Handel thus became the composer for those who either could not afford or else chose to shun the sophistications of aristocratic entertainment. No wonder the reviewer of the 1880 Festival was moved to say: 'As to the good arising from the Handel Festival there can be no doubt. It displays, and also confirms, the public allegiance to a master absolutely blameless in the character and tendency of his works. Simple, massive, strong, and yet tender, Handel stands like some example of pure Doric architecture which, by the force and beauty of its outline, corrects all others.' Ten years

319

later the whole thing had well and truly become 'the great Handelian solemnity'.

In nineteenth-century Germany the composer was the object of an altogether more discriminating interest and the study of his works which had so enriched Beethoven and Schubert in Vienna was equally profitable elsewhere to Liszt, Schumann and Brahms, each of whom acknowledged a sincere admiration. Liszt indeed, in an article in the *Weimarische Zeitung* in 1850, wrote: 'Handel seems to our epigonic generation like one of the giants of the past. In his life he stands out as one of the most energetic and sublime figures known to the history of art, strong, free, unyielding in his pursuit of an exalted goal; even when he seems to be defeated in the struggle against his own epoch, his mighty spirit rises up to gain fresh victories. Such a character inspires his music besides . . . its spontaneity and simplicity is what ensures for Handel's works, especially his oratorios, a permanent and potent influence.'

Wagner, hearing the *Cecilia Ode* in Vienna in 1875, was 'affected to the highest degree by various strokes of genius in the composition itself' and though Cosima later noted of the oratorios: 'astonished at their banality; no depth, no Christianity, a proper Jehovah worship,' her diaries show her husband's none-too-grudging respect for Handel, whose works he would play through enthusiastically at the piano. 'At supper he maintains that Handel must surely have composed *God save the King*: "the fellow was a scoundrel, but a genius as well".'

Germany's ultimate tribute to its vagabond son came in the form of the only complete edition of Handel's works, edited by Friedrich Chrysander, and published in 93 volumes between 1858 and 1902. 'Complete' is of course a relative term: much additional music composed for various operas and oratorios was omitted, certain of the instrumental works were re-ordered in a manner calculated to create lasting confusion, and the significance of Handel's first drafts and experimental sketches, such as those in the Fitzwilliam manuscripts, was apparently ignored. The composer's polyglot indications of tempo, dynamics and instrumentation, in which French, German, Italian, English and Latin figure arbitrarily together, were tidied up, and editorial presumption decreed in several instances that what Handel originally intended should be set aside for what instead appealed to Chrysander's notions of common sense. Worst sin of all was a general disregard of the autograph manuscripts in preference to the albeit valuable evidence of the conducting scores eventually acquired by the Hamburg Staatsbibliothek.

Chrysander can be forgiven, to some extent, when we consider the extraordinary scope of his achievement in the days before microfilm and photocopying. Like many scholars he appears to have been intolerant of his fellow workers in the field, and the vast edition was produced almost single-handed, with the continuing help of his immense dedication to the composer and his music. However faulty his editorial principles, Chrysander had clear-cut ideas about the nature of Handel's art and Baroque music in general which must inevitably have been somewhat in advance of those inspiring the muddy-textured Victorian oratorio concerts. The entire enterprise of the 93 Händel Gesellschaft volumes, constituting one of the noblest monuments of nineteenth-century musicology, has not yet been adequately superseded.

The Frenchman Victor Schoelcher, the saviour of Handel's conducting scores, was a serious biographer in his own right. French interest in the composer was commensurate with the development of those unique characteristics typifying the Parisian musical scene during the last century. We might expect, for example, to find Berlioz showing impatience with 'the heavy, bewigged face of this tun of pork and beer they call Handel', but his comments on *Admeto* in relation to the *Alceste* of Lully and that of his beloved Gluck acquit him if only because of their almost hilarious lack of sympathy with the genre of Baroque *opera seria*. Edouard Lalo's reaction — 'Beautiful, solemn, colossal, but it makes me yawn atrociously, and as I want to keep my jaws on, I'm leaving' — is comparably predictable. But France led the way in presenting *Messiah* and other oratorios in performances more faithful to Handel's intentions than their contemporary equivalents at the Three Choirs or the Crystal Palace, which Paul Dukas scornfully described as 'organ concertos mixed up with acrobatic displays in an agricultural exhibition'. Admiring the directness and simplicity of the man whose manuscripts he had studied in the British Museum, Dukas noted perceptively that 'Handel's music is of a kind in which ingenuity and searches after detail seem superfluous and add nothing to the total impression . . . he reaches a fulness of sonority which a modern orchestra, however well stocked with brass, can never challenge.'

The effect of Lamoureux's respectful and intelligent renditions was to create a minor Handel revival in the exciting context of the metropolitan culture nurturing Proust, Picasso and the Ballets Russes. No wonder a correspondent to the *Musical Times* could write: 'If one wishes to hear Handel it is advisable to settle in Paris,' in 1912, a year when the Sorbonne choral society presented *Messiah*, the Conservatoire offered *Israel in Egypt*, the *Société George Frédéric Handel* did *Alexander's Feast. Saul*, the *St Cecilia Ode* and the *Dettingen Te Deum* were given at Saint Eustache and a Lilli Lehmann recital included airs from *Radamisto*, *Partenope*, *Semele* and *Joshua*. Against such a background Reynaldo Hahn enthusiastically measured Handel with Bach. 'We always feel in Handel,' he wrote, 'the poet and the dramatist imprisoned within the academic musician. Bach, not thus constrained, is at liberty within his bourgeois spirit. But equally he wrote nothing to compare with 'Darius great and good . . . welt'ring in his blood', or with the restlessness of Alexander contemplating his mysterious Thais. Handel's intelligence is always awake and at work. Bach's is drowned in the counterpoint fermenting within his brain and circulating throughout his entire being in a ceaseless mechanical economy. Handel is visionary and objective. Bach is always himself, putting himself before everything else and placing his grandiose personality in front of all the images he seeks to represent'.

Bach's star, however, was now in the ascendant as Handel's was beginning slowly to wane. The jubilant rediscovery, by instrumentalists in the early gramophone years, of the violin partitas, the '48' and the Brandenburg concertos was accompanied by the onset in England of a confused reaction against high Victorian Handelmania. By 1891 George Bernard Shaw, a convinced and ardent admirer of Handel, was writing: 'we know rather less about him in England than they do in the Andaman Islands, since the Andamans are only unconscious of him, whereas we are misconscious. . . . Why, instead of wasting huge sums on the multitudinous dullness of a Handel Festival, does not somebody set up a thoroughly rehearsed and exhaustively studied performance of the *Messiah* in St James's Hall with a chorus of twenty capable artists? Most of us would be glad to hear the work seriously performed once before we die.' Similar irritation elsewhere bred active revolt in such works as Ernest Walker's *Music in England*, heretically questioning Handel's authority, and among the younger composers of a generation eagerly renouncing Leipzig for Paris. The feet of clay were being exposed in the revelations of the master's borrowings — their basis imperfectly grasped — and the sense that the twentieth century was substantially losing touch with him was balefully implied by the headlines of an American newspaper article of 1907 reporting a *Belshazzar* performance, which read: 'Powerful Temperance Lecture Set To Music: Neither the Pomp nor Fervor of the Biblical Occasion in Composer's Work.'

Another disillusioned encounter with *Belshazzar* was that of Igor Stravinsky as an adolescent in St Petersburg at the turn of the century. 'The music relies again and again on the same fugato exposition, the same obvious semicircle of keys, the same small harmonic compass; and when a piece begins with a more interesting chromatic subject, Handel consistently fails to develop and exploit it as soon as all the voices are in, regularity, harmonic and otherwise, rules every episode . . . Handel's inventions are exterior; he can draw from inexhaustible reservoirs of allegros and largos, but he cannot pursue a musical idea through an intensifying degree of development.' Later he was to find *Theodora* 'beautiful and boring. Too many pieces finish too long after the end', and his judgment was ultimately destined to the facile summing-up: 'Handel was the commercial composer of his time, Bach the inward one.'

Such remarks say less about Handel than about the curious limitations of Stravinsky's musical aesthetic. Similar criticism was to be voiced by Schoenberg, who offered the most eloquent evidence of a total failure to appreciate the composer's methods and styles in his grotesque arrangement of the Concerto Grosso Opus 6 No. 7, published in 1933. He told Berg simply that ' . . . it will be a very good piece, and I can say that it is not because of Handel'. No, indeed, simply for the reason that the delicacy and deftness of the original sink beneath the porridge and molasses of a treatment which sounds more like a malicious parody of the Baroque manner than a serious attempt at elaboration. Handel is here transformed into a neurasthenic *schlamper*, and the piece, whatever its intrinsic technical interest, adds little lustre to an already well-established reputation.

The inter-war years witnessed the nadir of Handel's fortunes. During the 1920s Oskar Hagen at Göttingen had undertaken several of the earliest modern revivals of the operas, starting with *Rodelinda*. Fidelity to the text and the cultivation of a suitable performing style were scarcely conceivable during an age in which 'pre-classical' music was being gradually rediscovered with the aid of Wanda Landowska's noble executions of Bach and Nadia Boulanger gallantly proposing Monteverdi with a piano continuo. Yet whereas Landowska and Boulanger treated their material with imaginative respect, Hagen's attitude to Handel was cavalier in the extreme. The operas were not only to be hacked about, but rewritten in such a way as to destroy the fundamental balance of sonorities upon which real enjoyment of them depends. Teutonic imaginations could not embrace the idea of male roles in soprano registers, and since Weimar Germany, whatever its other grotesqueries, was not forthcoming with castrati, down went Giulio Cesare, Bertarido and Serse to the achievement of a wholesome manliness and the effective emasculation of

323

their musical characters. There was no ornament and tempo markings were interpreted in the sluggish ecclesiastical fashion of the day. The English critic who observed of *Giulio Cesare* at Göttingen in 1923 that 'a certain monotony was felt, produced perhaps by the everlasting, never changing beauty of the arias. The soul of man has undergone some changes since the time of Handel,' may indeed be pardoned.

Under the Nazis matters Handelian reached a level of lunacy in obsessive efforts to make the oratorios *judenrein*. It is a scarcely credible fact that *Judas Maccabaeus* was thus transmuted into *Wilhelm von Nassau* and *Israel in Egypt* into *Mongolensturm*: Handel himself, grateful as he always was for Jewish patronage of his performances, must have turned in his grave. German scholars, meanwhile, continued their search for the essentially Germanic in the composer's work, and the egregious Ribbentrop, in an address to the university of Oxford in 1939, depicted Handel in the unmistakeable colours of traditional Socialism.

The speech took place in the Sheldonian theatre: was *Athalia*, with its devout Jewish solemnities, mentioned in this context?

In England attempts to secure the Brook Street house for a Handel museum attracted scant interest and an acrimonious correspondence with Major Benton Fletcher, collector of the antique musical instruments at Fenton House, Hampstead, can have done little credit to Herbert Westerby, secretary to the proposed fund. The *Musical Times* drily commented of the BBC's 1937 Handel revival concert that the hall was scarcely half full and that *Alexander's Feast* had little to say to a generation uninterested in choral singing for its own sake. Conductors continued the heartless process of reorchestration — Henry Wood overhauled *Judas Maccabaeus*, Beecham turned *Solomon* into a mass of lifelessness, and Malcolm Sargent brass-plated *Israel in Egypt* for Huddersfield.

Now and then an ember or two crackled up: staged performances of the oratorios were given by the enterprising Cambridge University Music Society and the Falmouth Opera Singers, and in March, 1933, *Rinaldo* was performed by girl students of the Hammersmith Day Continuation School under the direction of Miss Daunt. 'Such a performance,' wrote a kindly critic, 'is none the worse for being somewhat unsophisticated. One entered into the spirit of the thing, and shared the performers' obvious delight in music and action. In spirit we all "prowlered up and down a bit", and it was a jolly good show.'

The admirable Miss Daunt was a lone pioneer in an English revival of the operas which only really got going in the postwar years. Much is surely owing, in this connexion, to the interest already fostered in Handel as an operatic master by Edward J. Dent, whose scholarly enthusiasm had done so much to broaden awareness not merely of Handel but of the Baroque musical legacy in general. During the 1950s and 60s, for example, the Handel Opera Society showed that his faith had been fully justified, presenting staged performances both of opera and oratorio, notable for their encouragement of promising young singers. Memorably enjoyable during the same period was the series given under the direction of Alan and Frances Kitching at Abingdon and Henley on a heroically limited budget. Appropriate costume and gesture brought the spectator closer to appreciating the essential rhetoric of the works themselves, and the gusto of these performances remains unforgettable. Conviction was, alas, not enough to balance the accounts and in an atmosphere further complicated by acrimony the splendid undertaking folded after the first revival of *Lotario* for over two centuries.

One by one the best of the operas have found their way back into the theatre. If East Germany could still, in 1960, issue a practical edition of *Poro* with the hero unblushingly assigned to the bass register and the names of the two heroines altered with archaeological pedantry from Cleofide and Erissena to Mahamaya and Nimbavati, there was the compensation of performances such as that of *Giulio Cesare* given privately at Birmingham University's Barber Institute in 1977, which gave the work complete and followed the relatively novel practice which restored the overlap of vocal and continuo lines in the closing cadences of the recitative. Singers in their turn began to study a style more suitable to the cantilena of Baroque lyric drama, and the rise of a new breed of countertenor, though it might hardly supply an authentic Senesino or Caffarelli, at any rate offered an adequate solution to the problem of matching roles to voices. As one musicologist remarks, 'there is no humane answer to the castrato problem', but modern compromises have achieved some spectacular results.

The real difficulties facing any opera house eager to bring Handel before a modern audience have seldom been seriously confronted by producers. It is not only a matter of singing the roles at their original pitch but of dealing with what is nowadays considered to be the static nature of Baroque lyric drama itself. While the objection to implausible plots can hardly be sustained by audiences willingly accepting Donizetti, Verdi and Meyerbeer, the principal criticism of the average operagoer seems nowadays to be directed towards the overall lengthiness of the proceedings. The *da capo* form is found to be tedious, directors are charged with not dealing effectively with stage action during the ritornellos and the absence of ensembles, choruses and even ballets is lamented.

Recent revivals have done little to alter this view and the most successful have taken a cavalier attitude towards text and style which has shocked and angered musicologists. Though there is no doubt that the Sutherland-Bonynge *Alcina*, the Beverly Sills *Giulio Cesare* or the more recent production of the same work by the English National Opera made a public nurtured on *Norma*, *Aida* and *Boheme* sit up and take notice, these performances were markedly lacking in respect towards the composer or a feeling for the specialities of the medium, and were ethically less honest in their occasional flourishes of pseudo-authenticity than Beecham and Sargent had been in their reorchestrations.

But Handel has undoubtedly gained from the growth of the recording industry and the serious development of a concern with reproducing the authentic sonorities of early music. The former returned *Messiah*, through the progressive efforts of Colin Davis, Charles Mackerras and Christopher Hogwood, to a condition of almost unrecognizable brilliance and freshness, and reintroduced us to the dramatic oratorios, besides bringing the operas to vivid life in memorable editions of *Admeto* and *Partenope*. John Eliot Gardiner revealed the glories of the Funeral Anthem, *Il Moderato* and *Hercules*, while David Willcocks salutorily reminded us that the inevitable *Zadok* might simply be a thrilling curtain-raiser to three other coronation anthems of outstanding suppleness and strength.

The boom in early music has made it now almost impossible to listen with satisfaction to Handel given in the old manner, with muddy, overloaded string playing, oboes of spinsterly discreetness and ormolu twiddlings from the keyboard. If we can never arrive at a style which pleases all, we are at any rate beginning to do justice to that rhythmic incisiveness, that sense of the spaces between the notes being as important as the notes themselves, which lies at the heart of Handel's music, and the sound of a small, well-drilled band of Baroque strings and winds in a concerto or an overture or carrying along a chorus or an aria communicates an unmatched exhilaration.

What in the end can we take from him? His virtues are hardly modish ones in our own age. His spirituality is essentially human, rooted in an experience of the world and linked with an awareness of individuals in relation to one another. He does not ask us to grovel and cringe, imbued with a sense of our own pettiness, either before his achievements or those of a divine power. Instead he invites us to look at ourselves as we are, noble and preposterous, dignified and vile, to understand the complexities of our nature and what it is truly capable of. The operas and oratorios, thus considered, represent the most comprehensive illustration of human sensibility ever achieved by any composer.

It was Beethoven who described him as contriving great effects by simple means, and this too is an aspect which has puzzled or deterred writers on music in our own day. He is emphatically not a composer for the textbook; the sort of architectonic example so easily culled from the works of Bach is seldom as readily produced by Handel, yet what seems naïve or trifling from merely reading one of his scores will force its originality on us when we actually listen to it. We are still too prone to expect him to fall into the conventional mould of the ideal Baroque composer, inexorably working out the components of a fugue or taking pains to cast his concertos in orthodox forms. The response, on discovering that he does not always choose to fulfil these demands, is all too often an irritated and uncomprehending dismissal of him as an oddity who had the impertinence to live at the same time as Bach, Corelli, Telemann and Scarlatti but is in most other respects alien to their traditions and certainly not 'central' to the development of music along approved historical lines. His unique musical personality, reflected in the long-breathed phrases, the highly personal sense of tonal association, the inimitable grasp of orchestral colour and balance and that sublime command of a vocal line which places singers eternally in his debt, is thus ignored.

We need nevertheless to be reminded that it is not the duty of any artist to satisfy our more banal cravings for order. Undeniably cavalier and elusive, sometimes hurried and haphazard, never afraid to improve upon the designs of others and unfathomably perverse in his treatment of his own works, Handel nevertheless refuses to go away. That loyalty he inspired in his friends, the sheer companionable charm, wit, diversity and intelligence of the man himself return to us again and again irresistibly through his music. To hear 'Wretched lovers' or 'As with rosy steps the morn' or 'Jealousy, infernal pest', 'Falsa imagine' or 'Dopo notte', the D major violin sonata or any of the Opus 6 concertos for the first time is an experience which enriches our inmost resources of wisdom and emotion. If we turn our backs upon Handel the fault is not with him but with us.

Notes

The following notes refer to material not found in Deutsch's documentary biography of the composer.

The numbers on the left refer to text pages.

CHAPTER 1

11 **George Händel medical practitioner**] letter quoted in full in Ernst Friedlaender: 'Einige archivalische Nachrichten über Georg Friedr. Händel und Seine Familie'. *Mitteilungen für die Berlin Mozart-Gemeinde* etc., Vol 2 No. 13, Berlin, 1902.

Rudloff's operation: details and illustrations in Johann Christoph von Dreyhaupt: *Pagus Neletici et Nudzici*, Halle, 1755.

Georg Händel's life history in J. O. Opel: *Mitteilungen zur Geschichte der Familie des Tonkünstlers Händel* &c, from *Neue Mitteilungen aus dem Gebiete historisch-antiquarischer Forschungen*, Halle, 1885.

14 **between the raised roadways**] background details in Günter Thomas: *Friedrich Wilhelm Zachow, Kölner Beiträge zur Musikforschung*. Bd. 38, Regensburg, 1966. See also Dreyhaupt, op. cit.

16 **Friedrich Wilhelm Zachow**] Thomas, op. cit. Also works in *Denkmäler Deutscher Tonkunst*, Folge 21–22.

18 **dedicated to the liberal arts**] Opel, op. cit.

19 **Vintage of ye Rhine**] Letters ed. Graham, Oxford University Press, 1941.

20 **in der Lufft schwebenden Engel**] H. C. Wolff: *Die Barockoper in Hamburg*. 2 vols, Wolfenbuttel, 1957.

21 **in children themselves**] Beekman C. Cannon: *Johann Mattheson, Spectator in Music*, Yale, 1947. See also M.'s *Grundlage einer Ehren-Pforte*, Hamburg, 1740.

22 **was just a mule**] transcribed in *Musical Times* Sept. 1924.

26 **Eclectisch**] reprinted in *Händel Jahrbuch*, Halle, 1977.

CHAPTER 2

28 '**. . . In all the world is dead**'] Mario Fabbri: *Alessandro Scarlatti e il Principe Ferdinando de'Medici*, Florence, Olschki, 1961, pp. 19–21.

31 **. . . one irregular bow**] Charles Burney, *A General History of Music*, modern ed. by Frank Mercer, New York, Dover reprint 1957. Vol 2, p. 443.

32 **would also be given**] James S. Hall: 'Handel among the Carmelites',

Dublin Review, Vol 233, 1959.

33 **Pamphilj**] Lina Montalto: *Un Mecenate in Roma barrocca*, Florence, Sansoni, 1955.

34 **an important patron of Handel**] Ursula Kirkendale: 'The Ruspoli Documents on Handel', *Journal of the American Musicological Society*, Vol XX, No. 2.

37 **is over oneself**] Reinhard Strohm: 'Händel und Seine Italienische Operntexte', *Händel Jahrbuch* 21/22

   J. Merrill Knapp: 'Handel's First Italian Opera' etc. *Music and Letters*, Jan. 1981.

40 **of 1707–8**] Robert Freeman: 'The Travels of *Partenope*' in *Studies in Music History* ed. by Harold S. Powers, Princeton, 1968.

43 **secure employment**] I have relied heavily but not uncritically henceforward on the articles by Reinhard Strohm and Giovanni Morelli in *Händel in Italia*, handbook of the 3rd Vivaldi Festival, Venice 1981.

45 **if you flatter'd me as he did**] Winton Dean: 'Charles Jennens' Marginalia to Mainwaring's *Life of Handel*', *Music and Letters*, 1972.

46 **Mercure Galant**] 1683.

46 **while in Venice**] Venice, *Archivio dello Stato, Giudizi de Petizion, Inventari*, busta 411.

48 **of the bladder**] Marcus Landau: *Rom, Wien, Neapel, während des spanischen Erbfolgekrieges*, Leipzig, 1885, p. 41. An extremely useful source for the period as a whole.

CHAPTER 3

49 **will pass quickly enough**] Mario Fabbri: *L'Attività Fiorentina di Perti, Cristofori e Haendel*, Chigiana XXI, 1964. The *New Grove* work-list considers *Il Pianto di Maria* 'doubtful on stylistic grounds'.

50 **a lifelong enthusiasm**] A balanced modern view is Ragnhild Hatton's in *George I, Elector and King*, London, Thames & Hudson, 1978.

51 **'The greatest Italian master'**] — Alfred Einstein: see also introduction to *Le Rivali Concordi*, ed. H. M. Brown, N.Y. Garland Series, 1977.

53 **in the capital**] *Survey of London*, Vol XXIX Part 1, London, Athlone Press, 1960, pp. 223–250. W. J. Lawrence: 'The Early Years of the First English Opera House', *Musical Quarterly*, Jan. 1921.

54 **artists of the age**] Roger Fiske: *English Theatre Music in the 18th Century*, O.U.P., 1973.

54 **in the expression**] 'Remarks on Several Parts of Italy', in *Misc. Works* ed. A. C. Guthkelch, London, Bell, 1914. Vol II, p. 59.

55 **Popery in wit**] *Epilogue to The Tender Husband*, 1705.

55 **was always going to**] Letter to Philips, 8 March 1709. *Correspondence* ed. Williams, O.U.P., 1963.

55 **Blockhead did Sporus**] 'An essay on the Operas after the Italian

manner', 1706. 'Essay upon the Publick Spirit', 1711.

56 **a full stop**] BM MS Add 38607.

56 **coal and copper mines**] Dorothy Brewster: *Aaron Hill*, New York, Columbia University Press, 1913.

57 **expensive outlay for the period**] BM MS Add 38607.

58 **nakedness so naturally**] Steele, *Tatler*, 113.

60 **in the autumn of 1712**] Robert Elkin: *The Old Concert Rooms of London*, London, Arnold, 1955.

61 **orders on the deep**] attrib. Charles Montagu, Lord Halifax.

62 **as manageable a form as possible**] David Kimbell: 'The Libretto of Handel's *Teseo*', *Music and Letters*, Oct. 1963.

62 **the actress Peg Woffington**] W. J. Lawrence: 'A Famous Wexford Man', *New Ireland Review*, Aug. 1908.

63 **seems never actually to have taken the stage**] J. Merrill Knapp: 'The Libretto of Handel's *Silla*', *Music and Letters*, Jan. 1969.

65 **The work of Nicola Haym**] David Kimbell: 'The Amadis Operas of Destouches & Handel', *Music and Letters*, Oct. 1968.

CHAPTER 4

71 **standing on a joint stool**] Sir John Hawkins: *A General History of the Science and Practice of Music*, London, Novello, 1851. New edn, Vol II, p. 817.

71 **very Handelian impetuosity**] Hawkins, op. cit., p. 852.

72 **actions are divine**] Stoddard Lincoln: 'Handel's Music for Queen Anne', *Musical Quarterly*, 1959.

74 **'my friends beleeve'**] Edward Gregg: *Queen Anne*, London, Routledge and Kegan Paul, 1980. p. 368.

75 **than death was to her**] Ibid, p. 394.

75 **or writing instrumental pieces**] Hatton, op. cit., p. 391.

77 **Lady Ranelagh's villa**] Best account of performance background is in Stanley Sadie: *Handel's Concertos*, London, BBC Publications, 1972.

77 **Energie des Modes**] Crussard: 'Marc-Antoine Charpentier, théoricien', in *Revue de Musicologie*, Paris, XXVII, 1945.

78 **later Duke of Chandos**] C. H. & Muriel Collins Baker: *The Life and Circumstances of James Brydges, First Duke of Chandos*, O.U.P., 1949.

83 **from a Venetian score**] Vitige's *Del mio amor* is the possible source. See Garland Series reprint, N.Y. 1978.

84 **'in London 1718'**] Howard E. Smither: *A History of the Oratorio*, University of North Carolina Press, 1977, Vol 2, p. 189.

CHAPTER 5

86 **the Affairs of the Society**] see, in addition to Deutsch, MS in Public Record Office, L.C. 7/3 15. J. Merrill Knapp: 'Handel, The Royal Academy of Music and its first opera season in London', *Musical Quarterly*,

April 1959.

88   **Antonio Lotti and Santa Stella**] Johannes Gress: 'Händel in Dresden, 1719', *Händel Jahrbuch*, 1963.

90   **sole composition for the Academy**] Burney, op. cit., p. 907.

90   **may be said here about each**] George E. Dorris: *Paolo Rolli and the Italian Circle in London.* The Hague, Mouton, 1967. R. A. Streatfeild: 'Handel, Rolli and the Italian Opera in London in the 18th century', *Musical Quarterly*, July, 1917. No complete modern edition of the poems, but selections in many Italian anthologies.

90   **particularly of ye Foreigners**] BM MS Add 38607.

91   **so long as it's cheap**] Marziale in Albion ed. Tondini, Florence, 1776. Epigram XLVII.

92   **set by Handel as *Berenice***] Original title was *Le Gare di Politica e d'amore*: the words appear in the final *coro*.

93   **'and the ear can hear'**] *Le Rivoluzioni del Teatro Musicale Italiano*, second edn. Venice, 1785. The work deserves to be much better known among those generally interested in the culture of the European Enlightenment.

94   **of fops and triflers**] Burney op. cit., p. 702.

96   **a babe in arms, to poverty**] W. Klenz: *Giovanni Maria Bononcini of Modena: a Chapter in Baroque Instrumental Music*, Durham, N. Carolina, 1962.

100 **'*tempo rubato*'**] Burney, op. cit., p. 736, p. 745.

102 **nightingale in her belly**] Burney, op. cit., p. 721.

103 **of ideas than these passages**] op. cit., p. 722.

105 *Cajo Marzio Coriolano*] *Favourite Songs* published by Walsh, 1723.

105 **King's Theatre productions**] Giulio Bertoni: 'Giuseppe Riva e l'Opera italiana a Londra', *Giornale Storico della Letteratura Italiana*, Vol 89, pp. 317-24.

105 **62 times this last season**] Letters in Vol IV of *Complete Works*, ed. Webb, 1928.

106 **French musical culture**] 'Lowell Lindgren: Parisian Patronage of Performers', *Music and Letters*, Jan. 1977.

CHAPTER 6

111 **entirely in later revivals**] J. Merrill Knapp: 'Handel's *Giulio Cesare in Egitto*, in *Studies in Music History*, op. cit.

113 **from the recitatives than the airs**] Burney, op. cit., p. 729.

113 **Happy soil, adieu, adieu!**] *Minor Poems* ed. Ault & Butt, London, Methuen, 1954, p. 440.

115 **Leave us as we ought to be**] *The Musical Miscellany*, Vol V, 1731.

117 **their opening novelty**] J. Merrill Knapp: 'Handel's *Tamerlano*, The Creation of an Opera', *Musical Quarterly*, July 1970.

120 **for Pollarolo**] Taddeo Wiel: *Catalogo delle Opere in Musica Rappresentate nel Secolo XVIII in Venezia (1701–1750)*, Venice, Visentini, 1892.

331

121   **two years earlier**] Burney, op. cit., p. 731.
122   **for singing and for acting**] Burney, op. cit., p. 745.
123   **Elpidia**] Reinhard Strohm: 'Handel's Pasticci', *Analecta Musicologica 14*, 1974.
123   **a 1723 novelty**] Bodl. MSS. Rawl Letters, 131, dated 5 Nov. 1723.
125   **for near forty years**] Burney, op. cit., p. 734.
125   **annals of musical contests**] Ibid, p. 736.
134   **at the accession of James II in 1685**] Donald Burrows: 'Handel and the 1727 Coronation', *Musical Times*, July 1977.
139   **Every family has its Medarse**] from G. U. Pagani Cesa's *Discorso sopra Il Siroe*, Nice, 1785.

CHAPTER 7

144   **'Now A is trumps, now D'**] see *Boyce's Cathedral Music*, 2nd edn, 1788.
144   **near sixty years of age**] Burney op. cit., p. 765.
145   **the seven pasticcios he presented during the 1730s**] Strohm: 'Handel's Pasticci', op. cit.
145   **on a note of mild optimism**] reconstructed by Strohm: 'Pasticci', op. cit.
147   **'in such foolishness'**] quoted in Angus Heriot: *The Castrati*, London, Calder, pp. 89–90.
154   **since the Italian trip**] Winton Dean: 'Handel's *Sosarme*, a puzzle opera', in *Essays on opera and English music in honour of Sir Jack Westrup*, Oxford, Blackwell, 1975.
156   **Only one Bononcini**] Lowell Lindgren: 'The Three Great Noises Fatal to the Interests of Bononcini', Musical Quarterly, Oct. 1975.
158   **much-needed touch of dignity**] for a balanced view, see Norman Sykes: *Edmund Gibson*, O.U.P., 1926.
159   **ein gar besonders mischmasch!**] Phrase is from Fr. W. Marpurg: *Historisch-Kritische Beyträge zur Aufnahme der Musik IV*. Berlin, 1754.
160   **Dürer and Raphael paintings**] H. C. Wolff: 'Mendelssohn and Handel', *Musical Quarterly*, April 1959.

CHAPTER 8

169   **Nicola Porpora**] Michael F. Robinson: 'Porpora's Operas for London', *Soundings 2*, 1971–2.
170   **'on this great Occasion'**] *The Oxford Act AD 1733*, London, Wilford, 1754.
174   **'in this cursed Place'**] The Oxford Act, a new Ballad Opera, London, 'L. Gulliver', 1733.
175   **'and admirable manner'**] Burney, op. cit., p. 782.
178   **are wholly delightful**] Anthony Hicks: 'Handel and Il Parnasso in Festa', *Musical Times*, April 1971.
179   **as Lord Egmont calls him**] Historical MSS Commission, *Diary of*

Viscount Percival, afterwards First Earl of Egmont, Vol I, 1730–1, 1920.

181 **Marie Sallé**] Emile Dacier: *Mlle Sallé 1707–1756, d'après des documents inédits*, Paris, Plon Nourrit, 1909.

CHAPTER 9

190 **partisanship in the family**] Ruth Loewenthal: 'Newburgh Hamilton', *Musical Times*, Nov. 1971.

190 **Alexander's Feast Concerto**] Basil Lam in Gerald Abraham: *Handel, a Symposium*, O.U.P., 1954. Sadie, op. cit., p. 31.

192 **covering imperfections**] Burney, op. cit., p. 802.

196 **oh affetti, oh morte!**] e.g. Bertarido's Act III invocation in *Rodelinda* to 'Sposa, figlio, sorella, amici'.

196 **'public attention and favour'**] Burney, op. cit., p. 807.

196 **(a similar point in 1744)**] Letter to Edward Holdsworth, 21 Feb. 1744, reproduced in *Autograph Letters of George Frideric Handel and Charles Jennens*. Christie's Sale Catalogue, London, 1973.

201 **astonishingly diverse clientele**] Carl Ludwig von Poellnitz: *The Amusements of Aix-la-Chapelle*, 2 Vols, London, 1748. Anonymous trans.

203 **'where Ceres and Bacchus reside'**] 'The ceremonial Proceeding to a Private Interrment of Her Late Most Excellent Majesty Queen Caroline', London, 1737. British Museum copy (603 k. 28 (I)) attaches the various verses quoted. Morell's address published as a Sermon preached at Kew Chapel.... 'Occasioned by the Death of Our late Gracious Queen', London, 1737. Rolli's ode to Teodoli included in the *Tudertine* published in *Marziale in Albion*, op. cit.

206 **choruses could occupy a major role**] A useful short analysis in intro. to edn by W. Herrmann, N.Y., Schirmer, 1976.

CHAPTER 10

207 **'can never be performed again'**] Sir George Macfarren: 'The Italian Language: its evil influence upon music', *Musical Times*, March 1869.

208 **'the music drama is generally made to consist of'**] Hawkins: op. cit., p. 888.

209 **'clap'd till his arms ak'd'**] Ruth Loewenthal: op. cit.

210 **'1720 by Francesco Gasparini'**] Reinhard Strohm: 'Francesco Gasparini, Le Sue Opere Tarde e Georg Friedrich Handel', in *Quaderni della Rivista Italiana di Musicologia 6, Francesco Gasparini, Atti del Primo Convegno Internazionale*, ed. Della Seta & Piperno, Florence, Olschki, 1981.

211 **Minato for Cavalli in 1645**] Harold S. Powers: 'Il Serse Trasformato', *Musical Quarterly*, Oct. 1961 & Jan. 1962.

211 **'arias fit for musical setting'**] Arteaga, op. cit., vol 2,, p. 67.

213 **'ears of cries in the street'**] noted in J. A. Fuller-Maitland & A. H. Mann: *Catalogue to the Music in the Fitzwilliam Museum*, Cambridge,

London, Clay, 1893, p. 217.

214   **Vauxhall Gardens]** Margaret Whinney: 'Handel & Roubiliac', *Musical Times*, Feb. 1961.

216   **concatenated with stupendous art]** Hawkins op. cit., p. 912.

217   **from Walsh himself]** Hogwood & Luckett, op. cit. Donald Burrows: Walsh's editions of Handel's Opera 1–5, pp. 97–102.

218   **'other impediments out of his way']** John Nichols: *Literary Anecdotes of the 18th century*, London 1812. Vol 3, pp. 120–6.

225   **'both from Scarlatti and Vinci']** Jennens, letter to Holdsworth, 17 Jan 1743.

225   **'musical community during the period']** see, for example, Giorgio Pestelli: 'Un altra elaborazione bachiana' in *Rivista Italiana di Musicologia* Vol XVI, no. 1, 1981; also Norman Carrell: *Bach the Borrower*, Allen & Unwin, 1967.

226   **'Kerll's is surely coincidental']** borrowing suggested by William D. Gudger, *Musical Times*, Dec. 1977.

227   **'the winter dress of that country']** information from *The Political State of Great Britain*, 1739–40 volumes.

228   **'and the Alexander's Feast Concerto']** The poem's original setting, in 1687, was by Giovanni Battista Draghi.

228   **'descended to the lowest']** Avison: *Essay on Musical Expression*, 2nd Ed. London, Davis, 1753, p. 50.

CHAPTER 11

232   **'the Rossini of his day']** Cosima Wagner: *Diaries*, Vol 2.

233   **'here is the truth']** Arthur Hutchings: *The Baroque Concerto*, Faber, 1959, p. 304.

233   **theatres and public gardens]** Burney, op. cit., p. 1004.

234   **'in a roar of laughter']** *Reminiscences*. i. 255, cited in Percy M. Young: *Handel*. New edn, London, Dent, 1975.

234   **'the name of Moderatissimo']** Jennens to Holdsworth, op. cit.

237   **Languid and antique]** Burney, op. cit. *Deidamia* has been occasionally overrated. Dent, in the Abraham *Symposium*, devotes a substantial section of his article on the operas to an analysis of the plot. Dean, reviewing Lang's biographical study in *Musical Times*, June 1967, justly notes that '*Imeneo* is a very moving experience, while *Deidamia* seems the dullest of all the operas.'

238   **'woman in England, his Duchess . . .']** *Memoirs and Portraits*, edited by Matthew Hodgart, London, Batsford, 1963.

239   **'works of public utility']** Stephen Barlow: *History of Ireland*, Vol 1, London, Sherwood etc., 1814.

240   **'not at first sight']** Burney: *An Account of the Musical Performances in Westminster-Abbey and The Pantheon . . . in Commemoration of Handel*,

London, Musical Fund, 1785. His transcription of Handel's English needs to be taken with a pinch of salt.

240 **three sailors and a boy**] Alfred Coward: *Picturesque Cheshire*, London, Sherratt & Hughes, 1903, pp. 232–33.

243 **Susanna was now 28 and Handel was 57**] Article in Highfill, Burnim & Langhans: *A Biographical Dictionary of Actors* etc., S. Illinois University Press, 1975, Vol 3. A modern *biographie romancée* is Mary Nash: *The Provoked Wife*, Hutchinson, 1977.

243 **'The Subject is Messiah'**] 10 July 1741.

244 **the tonal unities governing the piece**] Accounts in Newman Flower: *George Frideric Handel*, London, Cassell, 1923, and elsewhere are, to say the least, fanciful. Most useful works on *Messiah* are: Watkins Shaw: *A Companion to Handel's Messiah*; *The Story of Handel's Messiah, 1741–1784*, Novello, 1963; Jens Peter Larsen: *Handel's* Messiah, *Origin, Composition, Sources*, London, Black, 1957; Robert Manson Myers: *Handel's* Messiah, *A Touchstone of Taste*, N.Y., Macmillan, 1948.

Sir Thomas Armstrong, in an article on 'The Messiah Accompaniments' in *Music and Letters*, Jan. 1928, recommended authentic scoring because it was cheaper to perform!

CHAPTER 12

247 **learned and unlearn'd**] An MS copy by J. C. Smith transcribed in Christie's catalogue, op. cit.

248 **'and Evangelists, and of Jesus Christ'**] letter to Holdsworth, 21 Feb. 1743.

250 **intelligence as an actor**] Burney, p. 1010.

250 **'like a Philistine'**] letter to Holdsworth, 15 Sept. 1743, Holdsworth's reply, 28 Oct. 1743.

253 **'a school dormitory'**] Dean: *Oratorios*.

253 **'bawdy opera'**] in Dean: 'Jennens marginalia', op. cit. Bawdatorio — full reference is in letter to Holdsworth, 16 Oct. 1745: 'Semele was call'd an Oratorio by many; but says the great critick Thomas Rowneius, lege meo periculo Bawdatorio'. I am unable to identify Thomas Rowney.

254 **'rather than too little'**] details in Dean: *Oratorios*.

260 **'madness of Town Diversions'**] letter to Holdsworth, 21 Feb. 1744.

CHAPTER 13

264 **bursting out of a black cloud**] *Commemoration*, p. 27.

264 **and insure esteem**] op. cit., p. 27.

265 **Duke Street Meels**] Fuller-Maitland & Mann, op. cit., p. 194.

265 **your own dirge**] quoted in article by Edward F. Rimbault, *Notes and Queries*, April, 1876. I am indebted to Mrs Laura Hornak for the dictum about the goose, retailed by her father, Lord David Cecil, and probably a

morsel of Handelian oral tradition.

267   **Fisher Littleton's amateur concerts**] Young: *Handel*, op. cit., p. 105.
267   **atmosphere of festive conviviality**] Anthony Hicks: 'Handel's music for *Comus', Musical Times*, Jan. 1976.

Betty Matthews: *Unpublished Letters Concerning Handel, Music and Letters*, 1959.

267   **thought Handel was going mad**] letter to Holdsworth, 16 Oct. 1745.
268   **the National Benefit**] Thurston Dart: 'Maurice Green and the National Anthem', *Music and Letters*, July, 1959. Dart also offers the riposte theory.
268   **were chiefly Roman Catholics**] Burney: *Gen. Hist.*, p. 844.
269   **and acknowledge him as such**] Young, op. cit., p. 176. Gluck to Kelly: ibid.
271   **he is delighted**] quoted in Betty Matthews: 'Handel — More Unpublished Letters', *Musical Quarterly*, April 1961.
272   **for a considerable time afterwards**] *Gen. Hist.*, p. 841.
273   **a total stranger to economy**] Anecdotes, op. cit., pp. 651–6.
274   **decline into claptrap**] Young, endorsed by Dean: *Oratorios*.
275   **learned by his ear**] Burney: *Gen. Hist.*, p. 1010.
275   **What may we not expect**] Burney: *Commemoration*, p. 26.
276   **and irreverence of the age**] *Epistles for the Ladies*, Vol. 1, Ep. xix.

CHAPTER 14

280   **'that he was out of humour'**] Burney: *Handel Commem.*, op. cit., p. 23.
282   **rebuked emperors and duchesses**] Kurt Hueber: 'Gli Ultimi Anni di Giovanni Bononcini' in *Accademia di Scienze, Lettere e Arti di Modena*, Serie 5, Vol XII, 1954.
287   **on the 27 April 1749**] for fuller details see *A Description of the Machine for the Fireworks etc.*, (anonymous), London, W. Bowyer, 1749.
290   **on the fringes of Bloomsbury**] A good modern account in Ruth McClure: *Coram's Children*, 1979.
291   **'. . . full of spirits'**] Betty Matthews: 'Handel — More Unpublished Letters', op. cit. Letter dated 3 Jan. 1748/9.
292   **'. . . think as I do'**] Ibid. Letter dated 24 March 1749/50.

CHAPTER 15

297   **has help'd his contribution vastly**] Matthews, op. cit. letter dated 16 Feb. 1750/1.
302   **'From virtue springs' in *Theodora***] 'From virtue springs' is based on the *Domine Deus* of the first mass, *S. Wenceslai M.* in *Philomela Pia*.
306   **'I ought to insist on'**] Matthews, op. cit. letter dated 31 Dec. 1757.
306   **returned to the 1749 text**] see in this connexion Anthony Hicks: 'The late additions to Handel oratorios and the role of the younger Smith' in *Music in Eighteenth-Century England, Essays in memory of Charles*

Cudworth, ed. Hogwood & Luckett, C.U.P., 1983.

312 **he was immediately reconciled**] William Coxe: *Anecdotes of George Frederick Handel and John Christopher Smith*, London, Bulmer, 1799, pp. 48–9.

313 **in his poem *The Task***] quoted variously in Robert Manson Myers: *Early Moral Criticism of Handelian Oratorio*, Williamsburg, Virginia, 1947, and *Handel's Messiah, A Touchstone of Taste*, New York, Macmillan, 1948.

314 **'of an enlighten'd minister'**] letter dated 21 June 1784, in *The Letters and Prose Writings of William Cowper*, Vol 2, ed. King & Ryskamp, O.U.P. Clarendon Press, 1981.

314 **Hanbury met his match**] see William Hanbury: *The History of the Rise and Progress of the Charitable Foundations at Church Langton*, London, 1767, and William Hayes: *Anecdotes of the Five Music Meetings on Account of the Charitable Foundations at Church Langton*, Oxford, Jackson, 1768.

315 **a claimant to the Earldom of Roscommon**] standard account is Burney: *Commemoration*, op. cit.

317 **it is inconceivable**] see in this connexion Walther Siegmund-Schulze: 'Georg Friedrich Händel als ein Wegbereiter der Wiener Klassik', *H.J.* 1981. Also letter to Leopold Mozart on visits to Swieten, 10 April 1782, in *Mozart, Briefe und Aufzeichnungen III*, ed. Bauer & Deutsch, Bärenreiter, 1963.

317 ***The Creation* and *The Seasons***] quoted in H. C. Robbins Landon: *Haydn in England, 1791–5*, London, Thames & Hudson, 1976.

318 **we can hardly be certain**] for various references, see Donald MacArdle: 'Beethoven and Handel', *Music and Letters*, 1960.

319 **Adelina Patti**] *Musical Times*, July 1865.

320 **the great Handelian solemnity**] *Musical Times*, 1 July 1862.

320 **'As to the good. . . . '**] *Musical Times*, July 1880.

321 **can never challenge**] *A Travers Chants*, Paris, Michel Lévy Frères, 1862, pp. 130–98.

321 **Lalo yawning**] Myers *Messiah* p. 266. No source given.

321 **Dukas notes**] ed. G. Samazeuilh: *Les Ecrits de Paul Dukas sur la Musique*, Société d'Editions Françaises et Internationales, Paris, 1948.

322 **the images he seeks to represent**] quoted in Emile Damais: *Haendel*, Paris, Hachette 1970. No source given.

322 **once before we die**] article in *The World*, 21 Jan. 1891, quoted in Myers: *Messiah*, p. 245.

322 **'Bach the inward one'**] see Stravinsky & Craft: *Expositions and Developments*, Faber, 1962. Also Craft: *Stravinsky, Chronicle of a Friendship, 1948–71*, Gollancz, 1972.

323 **an already well-established reputation**] General remarks on Handel in 'New Music, Outmoded Music, Style and Idea' (1946) in *Style and Idea, Selected Writings of Arnold Schoenberg*, ed. Stein, London, Faber, 1975.

324 **may indeed be pardoned]** *Musical Times*, Sept. 1923.

324 **secretary to the proposed fund]** Westerby–Benton Fletcher correspondence in *Musical Times*, 1937–9.

324 **and it was a jolly good show]** *Musical Times*, March 1933.

325 **Mahamaya and Nimbarati]** The edition in question is that of the 'Deutscher Verlag für Musik', ed. by Heinz Ruckert in a *Freie Nachrichtung und Buhnenfassung*.

325 **humane answer to the castrato problem]** Brian Trowell: 'Handel as a Man of the Theatre' in R.M.A. *Proceedings*, Vol 88, 1961–2.

338

Bibliography

The following brief bibliography is intended to supplement the references to individual articles made by the notes to each chapter. It should be stressed that the handful of works listed here represents a mere fraction of a vast Handel literature.

Abraham, Gerald ed.: *Handel: a Symposium* (1954)
Burney, Charles: *An Account of the Musical Performances. . . . 1784: in Commemoration of Handel* (1785)
Dean, Winton: *Handel's Dramatic Oratorios and Masques* (1959)
  Handel and the Opera Seria (1969)
Dent, Edward J.: *Handel* (1934)
Deutsch, Otto Erich: *Handel: a Documentary Biography* (1955)
Eisenschmidt, J.: *Die szenische Darstellung der Opern Händels auf der Londoner Bühne seiner Zeit* (1940–1)
Hogwood, Christopher & Luckett, Richard: *Music in Eighteenth-Century England: Essays in memory of Charles Cudworth* (1983)
Larsen, J. P.: *Handel's* Messiah: *Origins, Composition, Sources* (1957)
Mainwaring, J.: *Memoirs of the Life of the Late George Frederic Handel* (1760)
Myers, Robert Manson: *Handel's* Messiah: *a Touchstone of Taste* (1948)
New Grove Handel, The: article by Winton Dean, work list by Anthony Hicks (1980, reprinted separately 1982)
Rolland, Romain: *Haendel* (1910, English trans. 1916)
Sadie, Stanley: *Handel* (1962)
Shaw, Watkins: *The Story of Handel's* Messiah (1963)
  A Textual and Historical Companion to Handel's Messiah (1965)
Smither, Howard: *A History of the Oratorio* (1977)
Streatfeild, R. A.: *Handel* (1909)

General Index

Aachen (Aix-la-Chapelle) H. at, 201–2
Abingdon, Unicorn Theatre, 325
Accademia Arcadiana, 34
Addison, Joseph, 19, 54, 58, 60
Adelaide (Orlandini), 146
Adlington Hall, Cheshire, 239
Adriano in Siria (Veracini), 187
Aix-la-Chapelle, Peace of, 287
Albinoni, Tommaso, 40, 46
Alessandro in Persia (Lampugnani), 238
Amelia, Princess, 131, 194
Amyand, George, 311–2
Anne, Queen, 52, 74–5
Anne, Princess Royal, 131, 194
Annibali, Domenico, 146, 194–5, 200
Arbuthnot, John, 64, 75, 79–80, 86, 89
Arne, Thomas, 159
Arne, Thomas Augustine, 13, 233, 242
Arsinoe (Stanzani), 54
Artaserse (Ariosti), 119
Arteaga, Stefano, 92, 211
Astianatte (Bononcini), 132
Avison, Charles, 76, 116, 228, 305
Avoglio, Cristina Maria, 242, 248, 253

Babell, William, 59
Bach, J. S., 36, 67–8, 88, 97, 99, 147, 223, 225, 298, 327
Baker, John, 308
Baldassari, Benedetto, 95
Banister, John, 70
Bates, Joah, 315
Beard, John, 190, 228, 250, 253, 255, 272, 275, 282
Beethoven, Ludwig van, 259, 317–9
Beggar's Opera, The (Gay), 137, 140
Beregan, Nicola, 197
Berenstadt, Gaetano, 113, 115
Bernacchi, Antonio, 117, 146, 147–8
Berlioz, Hector, 321
Bertolli, Francesca, 149, 158
Blathwayt, Col. John, 89
Bononcini, Giovanni, 30, 78, Ch. 5 passim, 115–6, 130, 132, 137, 148, 155–6, 211, 255, 282
Bonynge, Richard, 185
Borosini, Francesco, 116, 123

Borrowing, H.'s recourse to, 224–6
Boschi, Giuseppe Maria, 46, 57, 95, 113, 115
Boyle, Robert, 292–3
Bramston, James, 158, 222
Briani, Francesco, 136
Bristol, Countess of, 131
Britton, Thomas, 70–1
Bromfield, William, 304
Brook Street, H. at, 107–8
Broughton, Thomas, 258
Brown, Lady, 256–7, 271
Burlington, Countess of, 131
Burlington, Earl of, 64–5, 78, 86, 96, 167
Burney, Charles, 59, 75, 90, 94, 100, 103, 121, 136, 167, 175, 196, 233, 239–40, 243, 256, 264, 266, 271, 275, 280–1, 295, 300, 314
Buxtehude, Dietrich, 21–2
Byrom, John, 114, 288

Caduta dei Giganti, La (Gluck), 268
Cajo Marzio Coriolano (Ariosti), 105
Camilla (Bononcini), 55, 127
Caffarelli (Gaetano Majorani), 209
Cannons, H. at, 78–85
Capece, Carlo Sigismondo, 41–2, 140, 161
Caporale, Andrea, 189
Carbonelli, Stefano, 119
Carestini, Giovanni, 146, 175, 185, 194
Carey, Henry, 139, 159
Carissimi, Giacomo, 42
Carnarvon, Earl of, 78–85, 87, 204
Caroline, Queen (wife of George II), 50–1, 67, 177–8, 202–6
Carter, Elizabeth, 261, 275
Castrucci, Pietro, 31, 126, 189, 230
Castrucci, Prospero, 126, 189
Catone in Utica (Leo), 146, 160, 165
Chandos, Duke of, see Carnarvon, Earl of
Charpentier, Marc Antoine, 77
Cheltenham, H. at, 300
Chester, H. at, 239
Chilcot, Thomas, 305
Church Langton Handel Festival, 314
Chrysander, Friedrich, 320
Cibber, Colley, 53, 138

Cibber, Susannah, 22, 155, 242–3, 248–9
Clari, Giovanni Maria, 226
Clayton, Thomas, 54
Clement XI, Pope, 29, 41, 43, 222
Clive, Kitty, 22, 248–9
Cluer, John, 109, 119, 179
Colman, Francis, 61, 65, 102, 129, 152
Collingwood, Catherine, 237
Concert Clubs, London, 70–1
Congreve, William, 251–3
Conti, Gioacchino (Gizziello), 192–3, 195, 200
Coram, Capt. Thos., 290
Corelli, Arcangelo, 31, 34, 41, 76, 230
Covent Garden Theatre, 181, 227–8, 256, Chs.
    13–15 passim
Cowper, Countess, 94, 131
Cowper, William, 313–4
Craftsman, The, 167–8
Crispo (Bononcini), 104
Croft, William, 69, 80, 116, 129
Crystal Palace Festivals, 319–20
Cumberland, Duke of, 269–71
Cuzzoni, Francesca, 37, Chs. 5, 6, 7 passim, 169,
    299–300

Dampier, Thomas, 238
Daunt, Miss, 324
Dean, Winton, 221, 253, 306
Decayed Musicians, Society for, 214, 299, 315
Delany, Mary, 95, 108, 121, 127, 137, 147–9, 179,
    184, 195, 197, 237, 239, 253, 255, 256, 265, 292, 295,
    304, 307
Delany, Dr Patrick, 240, 243
Delawarr, Earl of, 166
Denner, Balthasar, 215
Dennis, John, 55
Dent, Edward J., 325
Dettingen, Battle of, 251
Devonshire, Duke of, 238–9
Donnellan, Anne, 179, 311
Dotti, Anna, 116, 119
Dryden, John, 188–90
Dublin, H. at, 240–6
Dubourg, Matthew, 71, 126, 194, 240, 243, 248,
    266, 281, 311
Duck, Stephen, 202
Dukas, Paul, 321
Durante, Francesco, 51, 225
Durastanti, Margherita, 22, 37, 41, 46, Ch. 5
    passim, 113, 155, 175, 222

Eccles, John, 69–70, 71, 251
Egmont, Earl of, 145, 159, 168, 191, 213, 238, 239
Elpidia (pasticcio), 123
Euripides, 128, 219
Exton Hall, Rutland, H. at, 267

Fabbri, Annibale, 147–9

Fabrice, M. de, 98
Farinelli (Carlo Broschi), 145, 169–70, 192, 200
Faustina (Bordoni Hasse), 37, 117, Ch. 6 passim,
    145–6
Festa d' Imeneo, La (Porpora), 200
Festing, Michael, 156, 214, 230
Fetonte (Paradies), 271
Feustking, Friedrich Christian, 24–6
Fielding, Henry, 186, 234
Finger, Gottfried (Godfrey), 70
Flemming, Jacob Heinrich, 89, 99, 111, 259
Florence, H. at, 27, 37–40, 46
Flower, Sir Newman, 23
'Forty-Five' Rebellion, 267–71
Foundling Hospital, 290, 299, 304
Fougeroux, Pierre Jacques, 141
Francesina (Elisabeth Duparc), 209, 228,
    236
Frasi, Giulia, 208, 275, 294, 308
Frederick, Charles, 287–8
Froberger, Johann, 17
Fuhrmann, Martin, 17

Galli, Caterina, 272, 294
Gambarini, Elisabetta de', 272
Gainsborough, Earl of, 267
Gardiner, John Eliot, 326
Garrick, David, 243, 294
Garth, Samuel, 54
Gasparini, Francesco, 40, 46, 210
Gates, Bernard, 72, 157–9
Gay, John, 64, 81–5, 98, 102, 137, 181
Geminiani, Francesco, 75–6, 126, 130, 230, 240
George I, 50, 74–8, 105, 133
George II, 50, 177–8, 181, 191, 251, 287, 313
George III, 22, 50, 133
Gibson, Edmund, Bp of London, 157–8, 170, 196
Gismondi, Celeste, 161
Gluck, Christoph Willibald von, 136, 138, 268–71,
    315
Gordon, Alexander, 95
Goupy, Joseph, 265
Granville, Bernard, 179, 266, 291, 311
Gravelot, Hubert, 215
Gray, Thomas, 193–4
Green Park Fireworks, 286–8
Greene, Maurice, 116, 156, 168, 179, 268, 298
Greville, Charles, 319
Grimani, Vincenzo, 43, 46–8
Griselda (Bononcini), 104
Guadagni, Gaetano, 246, 272, 294–5

Habermann, Frantisex, 226, 302–3
Hagen, Oskar, 323–4
Hahn, Reynaldo, 320
Hamburg, H. at, 19–26, opera in, 19–20
Hamilton, Newburgh, 189, 209, 213, 248, 269–70,
    283

Hanbury, William, 314
Handel family, 12
Handel, Dorothea (mother), 12–13, 52
Handel, Dorothea (sister), 13, 87
Handel, Georg (father), 11–13, 15–16, 18
Handel Commemoration, 314–15
Handel Opera Society, 325
Handl, Jacob, 205
Hanover, H. at, 50–2, 59
Harms, Johann Oswald, 20
Harris, James, 197, 200, 267, 271
Harris, William, 267, 269, 272
Harty, Sir Hamilton, 77
Hasse, Johann Adolf, 23
Haydn, Josef, 277, 317
Hawkins, Sir John, 26, 144, 176, 208, 264, 266
Hayes, William, 235, 305, 314
Haym, Nicola, 31, 60–1, 65, 78, 90, 106, 111, 116, 117, 120, 132, 139, 147
Hearne, Thomas, 158, 170, 172
Heidegger, Johann Jacob, 56, 89, Chs. 5–10 passim, 265, 290–1
Hervey, Viscount, 149, 160–1, 177, 187–8
Heywood, Eliza, 276
Hill, Aaron, 56–7
Hogarth, William, 214–5, 259, 290
Holdsworth, Edward, 210, 218, 225, 234, 243–4, 247, 250, 259, 267
Hudson, Thomas, 215, 295
Hughes, John, 59–60, 71
Humphreys, Samuel, 157, 168, 173
Huntingdon, Selina, Countess of, 309–10
Hutchings, Arthur, 232–3

Idaspe fedele, L' (Mancini), 58
Iphigénie en Tauride (Gluck), 136
Ireland, H.'s journey to, 238–40
Irwin, Lady Anne, 168

Jenkins's Ear, War of, 229
Jennens, Charles, 45, 72, 210, 217–9, 225, 234, 241, 243–4, 247–8, 250, 253, 259–62, 267, 273, 311
Johann Wilhelm, Elector Palatine, 52–3, 59

Keiser, Reinhard, 20, 23–6
Kelway, Joseph, 292
Kelly, Michael, 234, 271
Kerll, Johann Caspar, 17, 226
Kielmansegg, Baron, 50, 76, 78
King's Theatre, Haymarket, Chs. 3–12 passim
Krieger, Johann Goothilf, 15, 17
Krieger, Johann Philipp, 16, 205, 226
Kusser (Cousser), Johann Sigismund, 240
Kytsch, Johann Christian, 214

Lalli, Domenico, 93
Langhorne, John, 312

Legh, Charles, 239
Legrenzi, Giovanni, 20, 83, 197–8
Leo, Leonardo, 49, 144, 165, 176
L'Epine, Margherita, 61
Leporin, Johann Christoph, 18
Lincoln's Inn Fields Theatre, 176–7, 227–8
Liszt, Franz, 320
Littleton, Fisher, 267
Lotti, Antonio, 40, 88, 156
Lowe, Thomas, 246, 271, 275
Lowth, Dr Robert, 298
Lübeck, H.'s journey to, 21–2
Lucio Papirio (Giacomelli), 147
Lucio Vero (Ariosti), 127
Lustig, Jacob Wilhelm, 132
Luxborough, Lady, 213, 275

Macfarren, Sir George, 207
Maclaine, Mrs, 242
Madan, Dr Martin, 309–10
Mainwaring, John, 13, 27, 39, 47, 50, 79, 167, 250
Manchester, Duke of, 52
Marcello, Alessandro, 40, 122
Marcello, Benedetto, 40, 122
Marchesini, Maria Antonia, 209
Marlborough, Henrietta, Duchess of, 115, 132, 155
Marpurg, Friedrich, 159
Mattheson, Johann, 15, 21–6, 87, 225, 235
Mattei, Pippo (Filippo Amadei), 31, 96–7
Mauro, Ortensio, 51, 124–5, 127
Meares, Richard, 71, 95
Medici, Ferdinando de', 27, 28, 39, 49, 53
Mendelssohn Bartholdy, Felix, 160
Mercier, Philip, 167, 215
Merighi, Anna, 146, 148–9, 165, 202, 208
Metastasio, Pietro, 138, 150, 152, 175, 236
Michaelsen, Michael Dietrich, 87, 147, 194
Middlesex, Earl of, 238, 251, 271
Milton, John, 233–5, 248–9
Miller, Joseph, 254–5
Minato, Niccolo, 211
Montagnana, Antonio, 152–3, 158, 169, 202, 208
Montagu, Lady Mary Wortley, 58
Montague, Duke of, 89, 254, 287–8
Monza, Maria, 237
Morell, Thomas, 203, 272–4, 278, 291–3, 298, 300–1, 308
Mozart, Wolfgang Amadeus, 128, 138, 196, 259, 316–7
Musique de Table (Telemann), 226, 259, 270, 289

Naples, H. at, 42–4
National Anthem, H. and, 268
Neuburg, Prince Carl von, 50–1
Newcastle, Duke of, 87, 106
Newcomb, Thomas, 222
Nicolini (Niccolo Grimaldi), 57

Noris, Matteo, 20, 106
Numitore (Porta), 90

Opera of the Nobility, 166–7, 169, 176, 208
Opera seria, 91–3
Oreste (pasticcio), 182
Orfeo ed Euridice (Gluck), 138, 189, 272, 295
Orlandini, Giuseppe Maria, 123, 165
Ottoboni, Cardinal Pietro, 30, 34
Oxford, H. at, 170–5

Pacini, Andrea, 117, 123
Pamphilj, Cardinal Benedetto, 33, 34, 43, 45
Pariati, Paolo, 156, 176, 197
Patti, Adelina, 319
Pellegrini, Valeriano, 46, 61
Pembroke, Countess of, 131
Pepusch, Johann Christoph, 61, 79, 115, 116, 130, 159
Percival, Lord see Egmont, Earl of
Pergolesi, Giovanni, 144
Peterborough, Earl of, 104
Philips, Ambrose, 72, 115
Philomela Pia (Habermann), 226, 302
Piave, Francesco Maria, 273, 278
Pifferari, 28, 245
Pilotti, Elisabetta, 57
Piovene, Agostino, 117, 119
Poellnitz, Count Carl Ludwig von, 201–2
Pollarolo, Francesco, 30, 209
Pope, Alexander, 64, 84–5, 89, 113, 181
Porpora, Nicola, 169, 200, 235
Porta, Giovanni, 144
Pradon, Jacques Nicholas, 117–8
Prévost, Abbé, 174, 181–2, 185
Purcell, Henry, 53, 69, 73, 281

Quantz, Johann Joachim, 100, 122
Quin, James, 242
Quinault, 61

Racine, Jean, 84, 173, 219
Reinhold, Henry Theodore, 248, 253, 272, 279, 294
Rich, John, 127, 227, 181
Richmond, Duke of, 166
Riemschneider, Johann Gottfried, 148
Robinson, Anastasia, 73, 100, 104, 115
Rocchetti, Filippo, 170
Rolli, Paolo Antonio, 22, 31, Chs. 5, 6 passim, 145–6, 147–9, 168, 175, 203, 236
Rome, H. at, 28–37, 41–6
Rossi, Giacomo, 57, 147
Roubiliac, Louis François, 215
Royal Academy of Music, Chs. 5, 6 passim
Rudeluff, Andreas, 11–12
Ruspoli, Francesco Maria, 34–5, 37, 41–2, 45, 222
Rutland, Duke of, 119, 166

Sallé, Marie, 181–5
Salvi, Antonio, 38, 92, 117, 119–20, 147, 154, 183, 195, 199, 311–3
Sammartini, Giuseppe, 189, 196, 200
San Giovanni Grisostomo Theatre, 46, 136
Scalzi, Carlo, 175
Scandalizade, The, 265
Scarabelli, Diamate Maria, 46
Scarlatti, Alessandro, 30–1, 34, 39–40, 225
Scarlatti, Domenico, 140
Scheibe, Johann Adolf, 225
Schmidt, Johann Christoph, 38, 297, 311–2
Schoenberg, Arnold, 323
Schulenburg, Melusine von der, 76, 89
Semele (Congreve), 70
Senesino (Francesco Bernardi), 22, 88, Chs. 5–8 passim
Servandoni, Giovanni Nicola, 287–8, 291
Seward, Anna, 313
Shaftesbury, Countess of, 282
Shaftesbury, Earl of, 167, 200, 221, 253, 261, 271, 291–2, 297, 306
Sharp, Dr, 300
Shaw, George Bernard, 322
Shield, William, 277
Silvani, Francesco, 99
Smith, John Christopher, 38, 297, 307
Smith, Joseph, 146
Smollett, Tobias, 291, 297–8
Smyth, James, 208–9
Snow, Valentine, 189
Song of Deborah and Barak, The (Greene), 168
Sophia, Electress of Hanover, 50, 59
Spanish Succession War, 28–9, 42–3
Stampiglia, Silvio, 149, 211, 235
Stanley, John, 297–8, 300, 313
Steele, Richard, 55, 57, 60
Steevens, George, 218
Steffani, Agostino, 51–2, 125
Strada, Anna, 22, 146, Chs. 7–9 passim
Stradella, Alessandro, 32, 42, 226, 269
Stravinsky, Igor, 322–3
Streatfeild, R. A., 221
Sullivan, Daniel, 255
Sundon, Lady, 131, 157
Sutherland, Joan, 185
Swieten, Baron van, 316
Swift, Jonathan, 55, 73, 75, 203, 241
Swiney (MacSwiney), Owen, 56, 146
Synge, Dr Edward, Bp. of Elphin, 247

Tarquini, Vittoria, 22, 40
Tate, Nahum, 72
Taylor, John, 308
Telemann, Georg Philipp, 15, 19, 151, 153, 295–6
Teofane (Lotti), 99, 103
Terradellas, Domenico, 271
Teuzzone (Ariosti), 135

Three Choirs Festival, 305
Turner, Sir Edward, 283, 296
Tyers, Jonathan, 214, 288

Urio, Francesco, 251
Utrecht, Treaty of, 73–4

Valeriani, Belisario, 193
Valesio, Francesco, 28
Vanbrugh, Sir John, 53, 56, 105
Vauxhall Gardens, 214–6
Venice, H. at, 40–1, 145–6
Veracini, Francesco Maria, 75–6
Verdi, Giuseppe, 273, 278
Vespasiano (Ariosti), 123
Vignanello, H. at, 37
Vincent, Richard, 214
Vinci, Leonardo, 123, 225

Wagner, Richard, 232, 320
Wake, Archbishop, 134
Wales, Augusta, Princess of, 191, 196, 214, 266
Wales, Frederick, Prince of, 167, 177, 191, 196–7,
 214–5, 256, 299

Walpole, Horace, 100, 229, 238, 248, 250–1, 275
Walpole, Lady, 132
Walpole, Sir Robert, 106, 157–8
Willcocks, Sir David, 326
Waltz, Gustavus, 170
Warton, Joseph, 235
West, Richard, 229
Weidemann, Carl Friedrich, 214
Weissenfels, H. at, 15–16
Wentworth, Lady Lucy, 168, 209
Wentworth, Lord, 221
Westminster Abbey, 134, 310
Wheeley, Samuel, 71
Willes, Edward, 204

York Buildings, 60, 157
Young, Cecilia, 161, 282
Young, Esther, 253, 282

Zachow, Friedrich Wilhelm, 16–17, 52
Zambeccari, Francesco, 88, 146
Zamboni, Matteo, 116, 117
Zauberflöte, Die (Mozart), 162, 317
Zeno, Apostolo, 122, 123, 209

Index of Handel's Works

STAGE WORKS:

Admeto, 127–9, 134, 139, 233, 321
Agrippina, 23, 25, 38, 40, 46–8, 57, 83, 93, 107, 118
Alcina, 36, 184–5, 258
Alessandro, 23, 125–7, 128, 145, 220, 251, 275
Alessandro Severo (pasticcio), 213
Almira, 24–5, 38, 213
Amadigi, 65–6, 125
Arianna, 146, 176–7
Ariodante, 182–4, 233
Arminio, 195–6, 230
Atalanta, 191–4, 213
Berenice, 92, 198–200
Deidamia, 23, 236–7
Ezio, 28, 152–4
Faramondo, 41, 146, 209–11
Flavio, 106–7, 121
Floridante, 98–9, 176
Florindo, 26
Giove in Argo, (pasticcio), 226
Giulio Cesare, 111–13, 144, 325
Giustino, 146, 197–8, 230
Imeneo, 226, 235–6, 241
Lotario, 144, 147–9
Lucio Vero, (pasticcio), 275
Muzio Scevola, 23, 97–8
Nero, 25–6
Orlando, 143, 161–3
Ottone, 101–4, 125, 144
Partenope, 36, 40, 144, 149–50
Pastor Fido, Il, 60–1, 93, 144, 181–2
Poro, 150–2, 177, 195, 325
Radamisto, 93–4
Riccardo Primo, 135–7, 139
Rinaldo, 57–9, 75, 125, 198, 324
Rodelinda, 120–1, 125
Rodrigo, 37–40
Scipione, 124–5
Serse, 211–13, 233
Silla, 64
Siroe, 91, 138–40
Sosarme, 154–5, 177
Tamerlano, 41, 91, 117–19, 258
Teseo, 61–3
Tolomeo, 140–1

ORATORIOS, ODES, MASQUES &
INCIDENTAL MUSIC

Aci, Galatea e Polifemo, 43–4
Acis and Galatea, 44, 60, 81–5, 149, 158–9, 233
Alceste, 291, 297–8
Alexander Balus, 278–9
Alexander's Feast, 188–91, 324
Allegro, Il Penseroso ed Il Moderato, L', 130, 143, 197, 233–5, 240, 283
Athalia, 144, 172–4, 178, 188, 219
Belshazzar, 260–3, 280, 322–3
Choice of Hercules, The, 198, 297–9
Comus, 267
Deborah, 167–9, 174, 178, 270
Esther, 84–5, 156–9, 170, 306
Hercules, 118, 160, 256–60, 263, 280
Israel in Egypt, 28, 32, 143, 160, 219, 221–4, 249, 304
Jephtha, 118, 143, 276, 296–7, 300–4
Joseph, 251, 253–5
Joshua, 17, 23, 224, 275–7
Judas Maccabaeus, 160, 272–5, 280–1
Messiah, 15, 28, 242–6, 247–8, 286, 290, 321, 326
Occasional Oratorio, The, 224, 269–71, 273
Ode for the Birthday of Queen Anne, 71–3
Ode for St Cecilia's Day, 228, 231, 320
Parnasso in Festa, Il, 178
Resurrezione, La, 41, 118
Samson, 90, 247–50
Saul, 82, 143, 218–21, 250, 259
Semele, 143, 149, 160, 232, 251–4, 257–8, 263
Solomon, 90, 144, 244, 281, 285–6, 306
Susanna, 15, 130, 280, 282–6
Theodora, 15, 143, 244, 270, 280, 291–4, 323
Trionfo del Tempo e del Disinganno, Il (Triumph of Time and Truth), 23, 33–4, 221, 297, 307

SACRED CHORAL WORKS

Anthems, Chandos, 67, 80–1, 217
    Coronation, 134–5, 172
    Foundling Hospital, 290
    Funeral (*The Ways of Zion Do Mourn*), 204–6, 222
Brockes Passion, 67–8, 83, 118, 286
Coelestis dum spirat aura, 37
Dettingen Te Deum, 251

Laudate Pueri, 1st setting, 17
Laudate Pueri, 2nd setting, 32
Nisi Dominus, 32–3
Pianto della Vergine Maria, 49
Utrecht Te Deum & Jubilate, 73–4, 80, 172

SECULAR VOCAL WORKS

Cantatas, Italian, 35–7
Cecilia, volgi uno sguardo, 190
'From scourging rebellion', 271
'Stand round, my brave boys', 268
Venus and Adonis, 60

INSTRUMENTAL WORKS

Concerti a due Cori, 289
Concerti Grossi Op. 3, 180–1
Concerti Grossi Op. 6, 230–3
Music for the Royal Fireworks, 286–9, 290
Organ Concertos Op. 4, 216–7
Organ Concertos Op. 7, 289–90
Suites de Pièces pour le Clavecin, 109–10
Terpsichore, 182
Trio Sonatas Op. 2, 179–80
Trio Sonatas Op. 5, 217
Water Music, The, 76–8